Lecture Notes in Computer Science 7620

Commenced Publication in 1973
Founding and Former Series Editors:
Gerhard Goos, Juris Hartmanis, and Jan van Leeuwen

Jerome R. Busemeyer   François Dubois
Ariane Lambert-Mogiliansky
Massimo Melucci (Eds.)

Quantum Interaction

6th International Symposium, QI 2012
Paris, France, June 27-29, 2012
Revised Selected Papers

 Springer

Volume Editors

Jerome R. Busemeyer
Indiana University, Bloomington, IN 47405, USA
E-mail: jbusemey@indiana.edu

François Dubois
Conservatoire National des Arts et Métiers, 75003 Paris, France
E-mail: francois.dubois@cnam.fr

Ariane Lambert-Mogiliansky
Paris School of Economics, 75014 Paris, France
E-mail: alambert@pse.ens.fr

Massimo Melucci
University of Padua, 35131 Padua, Italy
E-mail: melo@dei.unipd.it

ISSN 0302-9743   e-ISSN 1611-3349
ISBN 978-3-642-35658-2   e-ISBN 978-3-642-35659-9
DOI 10.1007/978-3-642-35659-9
Springer Heidelberg Dordrecht London New York

Library of Congress Control Number: 2012953929

CR Subject Classification (1998): F.1.1-3, F.2.1-2, I.6.3-5, I.2.4, I.2.8, F.4.1, J.2

LNCS Sublibrary: SL 1 – Theoretical Computer Science and General Issues

Typesetting: Camera-ready by author, data conversion by Scientific Publishing Services, Chennai, India

Printed on acid-free paper

Springer is part of Springer Science+Business Media (www.springer.com)

Preface

Quantum interaction (QI) is an emerging field which applies quantum theory (QT) to domains such as economics, organizations and social interaction, psychology, artificial intelligence, human language, cognition, information retrieval, biology, and political science. The application areas addressed typically operate at a macroscopic scale and could not be considered quantum in a quantum mechanical sense, they may share many key properties with quantum systems including: non-commutativity of measurement, indeterminacy, non-separability, contextuality, and harmonic oscillations.

After highly successful previous meetings (QI 2007 at Stanford, QI 2008 at Oxford, QI 2009 in Saarbruecken, QI 2010 in Washington DC, and QI 2011 in Aberdeen), the 6th International Symposium on Quantum Interaction took place during June 27–29, 2012, in Paris, France.

QI 2012 received 32 submissions. All contributions were reviewed by at least two reviewers. In total, 23 papers were accepted for presentation at the conference. Two keynote speakers were featured. Michel Bitbol (Department of Epistemology, École Polytechnique Paris) gave a presentation on "Quantum Theory in the Light of a Relational Conception of Knowledge." Philippe Grangier (Department of Physics, École Polytechnique Paris) gave a talk on "Quantum Information: From Fundamental Ideas to Experimental Implementations." The symposium hosted three tutorials: "Conceptual Spaces" given by Peter Bruza, "Quantum Indeterminacy in Social Sciences: From a Theory of Knowledge to a Theory of Decision-Making and Behavior" given by Ariane Lambert-Mogiliansky, and "Quantum Search" given by Dominic Widdows.

These proceedings include the 21 accepted papers that were presented and revised based on the reviewers' comments and the discussion at the symposium.

We would like to take the opportunity to thank everybody who made this symposium possible: the Steering Committee, the Program Committee members for their reviewing job, the Proceedings and the Publicity Chairs, those responsible for the website design and management, and all the conference participants and presenters. We are grateful for the support given by the Paris School of Economics and the Conservatoire National des Arts et Métiers.

September 2012

Jerome R. Busemeyer
François Dubois
Ariane Lambert-Mogiliansky
Massimo Melucci[1]

[1] The work of Massimo Melucci in these proceedings has received funding from the EU Seventh Framework Programme (FP7/2007-2013) under grant agreement n° 247590.

Organization

Steering Committee

Peter Bruza   Queensland University of Technology, Australia
William F. Lawless   Paine College, USA
Donald A. Sofge   Naval Research Laboratory, USA
Keith van Rijsbergen   University of Glasgow, UK
Dominic Widdows   Microsoft Bing, USA

General Chairs

François Dubois   Conservatoire National des Arts et Métiers, France
Ariane Lambert-Mogiliansky   Paris School of Economics, France

Program Committee Chairs

Jerome R. Busemeyer   Indiana University, USA
Massimo Melucci   University of Padua, Italy

Program Committee

Diederik Aerts   Free University of Brussels, Belgium
Sven Aerts   Free University of Brussels, Belgium
Sachi Arafat   University of Glasgow, UK
Harald Atmanspacher   Institute for Frontier Areas of Psychology and Mental Health (IGPP), Germany
Peter Bruza   Queensland University of Technology, Australia
Jerome R. Busemeyer   Indiana University, USA
Bob Coecke   Oxford University, UK
Trevor Cohen   University of Texas, USA
Riccardo Franco   Politecnico di Torino, Italy
Emmanuel Haven   University of Leicester, UK
Andrei Khrennikov   Linnaeus University, Sweden
Kirsty Kitto   Queensland University of Technology, Australia
Ariane Lambert-Mogiliansky   Paris School of Economics, France
William F. Lawless   Paine College, USA
Massimo Melucci   University of Padua, Italy
Jian-Yun Nie   Université de Montréal, Canada
Dusko Pavlovic   Royal Holloway, University of London, UK

Emmanuel M. Pothos   Swansea University, UK
Donald A. Sofge   Naval Research Laboratory, USA
Dawei Song   The Open University, UK
Keith van Rijsbergen   University of Glasgow, UK
Salvador E. Venegas-Andraca Tecnológico de Monterrey, Mexico
Giuseppe Vitiello   University of Salerno, Italy
Dominic Widdows   Microsoft Bing, USA
Vyacheslav Yukalov   Joint Institute for Nuclear Research, Russia

Publicity Chair

Giorgio Maria Di Nunzio   University of Padua, Italy

Proceedings Chair

Emanuele Di Buccio   University of Padua, Italy

Website

Aneesha Bakharia   Queensland University of Technology, Australia

Table of Contents

The Quantum Inspired Modelling of Changing Attitudes and Self-organising Societies

Kirsty Kitto[1], Fabio Boschetti[2,3], and Peter Bruza[1]

[1] Information Systems School, Queensland University of Technology
{kirsty.kitto,p.bruza}@qut.edu.au
[2] Marine Research, Commonwealth Scientific and Industrial Research Organisation
[3] School of Earth and Geographical Sciences, The University of Western Australia
fabio.boschetti@csiro.au

Abstract. We utilise the quantum decision models, now well-developed in the QI community, to create a higher order social decision making model. A simple Agent Based Model (ABM) of a society of agents with changing attitudes towards a social issue is presented, where the private attitudes of individuals in the system are represented using a geometric structure inspired by quantum theory. We track the changing attitudes of the members of that society, and their resulting propensities to act, or not, in a given social context. A number of new issues surrounding this "scaling up" of quantum decision theories are discussed, as well as new directions and opportunities.

Keywords: Attitudes, Quantum Decision Theory, Context, Information Minimisation, Self-organisation.

1 Introduction

The quantum inspired modelling of human decision making has become quite advanced in recent years [1,2,3,4], and could now be regarded as a relatively mature field in the Quantum Interaction (QI) community. In this paper we propose that these theories can be 'scaled up' into the realm of social modelling. In particular, we will show that the notion of an *attitude* as it arises in Social Psychology [5] provides a natural candidate for a quantum state, and introduce a simple extension to the quantum approach which considers the manner in which the attitudes of a society of decision making agents will be influenced by two broad factors: each agent's natural internal disposition; and the social context in which they are embedded (i.e. the other agents in the system).

When considering social systems, the notion of an *attitude* is a key, indispensable concept [6]. Attitudes drive an individual's overall evaluation of people (including themselves), objects and issues [7], and so play a critical role in the

> choices people make regarding their own health and security as well as those of their families, friends, and nations. From purchase decisions provoked by liking for a product to wars spurned by ethnic prejudices,

J.R. Busemeyer et al. (Eds.): QI 2012, LNCS 7620, pp. 1–12, 2012.

attitudes help to determine a wide variety of potentially consequential outcomes. [7]

However, this very potentiality of attitudes makes them extremely difficult to model. How will a given person think about 'global warming' vs 'climate change'? What if their daughter has just had her house flooded? Or if they are about to make a very large tax payment that includes a carbon component? People's attitudes are not static immutable objects, but change in response to persuasion [8], and the demands of cognitive consistency [9]. We often express different attitudes and opinions in accordance with the social scenario we find ourselves in [10,11], and it is frequently the case that an explicitly expressed attitude is quite different from an internally held one [12].

Two models of attitude change arose in the 1970's; the Elaboration Likelihood Model (ELM) [13]; and the Heuristic-Systematic Model (HSM) [14]. Both utilise a dual-process approach that takes a form of mental effort as its key switching variable. Where individuals are motivated to pay attention to a message, or have the cognitive capacities to consider it carefully, an attitude change requires relatively high amounts of mental effort. In these *high elaboration* processes, people's attitudes will be determined by an effortful examination of all relevant information, and so changing them will expend high amounts of cognitive energy. In contrast, other processes of persuasion require relatively little mental effort on the part of the persuadee, resulting in attitudes that are determined by factors like emotions, 'gut feeling', liking, and reference to authority. Similar amounts of attitude change can be produced via either process, however, the changes induced by the high mental effort processes are postulated to be more persistent, resistant to counter-persuasion, and predictive of behaviour, than low effort attitude changes. The difference between these two processes has a number of implications for public policy. In an era of high-frequency press reporting periods (i.e. the 24 hour news cycle) we have entered a climate where low effort attitudes appear to predominate [15,16], and the transitional nature of this process could be seen to result in the apparent increase in undecided or swinging voters in the modern age. However, few mathematically oriented or computationally implementable models of these low effort processes exist, and those that do tend to make unrealistic commitments to the ontological status of attitudes, implying that these are held in some objective sense and always have a well defined value [17]. We consider this unlikely to be the case; people tend to form their low effort attitudes 'on the fly', frequently changing them in response to the social context in which they are currently embedded.

We have recently proposed [18] that the very contextuality of the low effort processes makes them prime candidates for a quantum inspired model. This paper will summarise that model in section 2 before moving onto a consideration in section 3 of the implications that this model has for the QI community. We will emphasise our model's divergence from the more direct application of the quantum formalism that tends to be utilised by QI members, drawing attention to it's novel time evolution paradigm.

2   A Geometric Model of Attitude Change

The social model that we shall present here is a large scale agent based model (ABM), roughly based upon the quantum decision theory (QDT) reviewed by Busemeyer et. al [2]. In this section we shall briefly introduce the notion of an agent, A, making a decision to act that is affected by their attitude within a particular social context. Thus, our agent might be answering a question, they might be voting for a particular politician, perhaps they need to work out if they should immunise their child, or drive to work. In order to maintain generality in the model that follows we shall term all of these different decisions as *actions*, and treat them equivalently. We note here that this is not a particularly realistic scenario, and that different actions will have a very different meaning in different contexts. We shall return to this point in the conclusions, but for now shall continue with the presentation of our model.

Importantly, our agent has not yet made a decision, and how they eventually do choose to act will depend upon both their own attitudes (implicit and explicit), and on the attitudes of those that surround them (i.e. their social context). Note that an agent with the same initial cognitive state may choose a different course of action if they find themselves in a different context, and this uncertainty should lie in the mind of the agent. Seating uncertainty in the mind of the agent further implies that even if the same agent is presented with the same context then they might choose something different, a situation that we feel reflects the true uncertainty of human decision making (and its modelling). Finally, we draw attention to the recursive nature of attitudes within a system of this form; the actions of our agent will likely affect the social context of other agents in the system, so changing their attitudes and hence their decisions.

2.1   A Quantum-Like Decision

We shall represent the cognitive state of our agent as $|A\rangle$, which A may not have direct access to (i.e. A may not be aware of this state for reasons of context to be explained below). If A has decided to act then we shall denote this state of action using the symbol $|1\rangle$, to represent a situation where it is *true* that they have *chosen to act* (in contrast to a state of inaction which we denote as $|0\rangle$). However, a decision to act (or not) depends on the context in which it is made; we are immediately faced with the dilemma that our social agent cannot be described as making a decision without reference to a context. Thus, we must specify that *within a given context*, say p, our agent will have a certain probability of acting, and note that a change in context might change this probability.

In what follows, we shall represent both the current state of an agent, and that of their context explicitly. This is done by expanding the notion of a state from that of a point in a space, to that of a vector in a Hilbert space, which is a real or complex inner product space that is also a complete metric space with respect to the distance function induced by the inner product [19]. At this point we can start to ask what the state of our undecided agent might be. Requiring that they have a probability of acting in any way whatsoever that is equal to 1

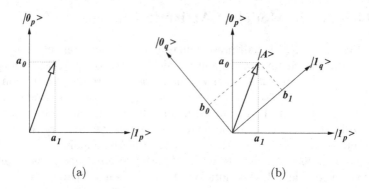

Fig. 1. An agent attempts to decide whether or not to act. (a) Their probability of action is proportional to the length squared of the projection of their state onto the axes labelled $|0_p\rangle$ (no action) and $|1_p\rangle$ (action); (b) The changing context of a decision. The probability of the agent acting changes between the two contexts p and q.

(as is standard), then there is one obvious choice for the representation of the current state of our agent, $|A\rangle$, in some context p:

$$|A\rangle = a_0|0_p\rangle + a_1|1_p\rangle, \text{ where } |a_0|^2 + |a_1|^2 = 1, \tag{1}$$

a situation that is illustrated in Figure 1(a). Here, $\{|0_p\rangle, |1_p\rangle\}$ are taken to define an orthonormal basis, the inner product (denoted in the quantum formalism as $\langle .|. \rangle$) of which returns 0 or 1: $\langle 0_p|0_p\rangle = \langle 1_p|1_p\rangle = 1$ and $\langle 1_p|0_p\rangle = \langle 0_p|1_p\rangle = 0$. Thus, we have used the orthonormal basis $\{|0_p\rangle, |1_p\rangle\}$ to represent the set of 'not act' or 'act' decisions to be made by our agent in the context p. We note that in this case orthogonality is entirely appropriate as an agent cannot do both, however, before they make their decision, the agent can be genuinely undecided; in a different context their probability of choosing an action may change quite significantly. QDT extracts this probability from the cognitive state of an agent using a notion of measurement, and we take the position that the same can be done for social scenarios. Thus, when a person responds to a survey they could be said to be undergoing a social measurement of their attitudes, and the same can be said of all actions as they were defined above. The decision to act (or not) entails the measurement of a state of an agent, but this very act of measurement may itself affect the decision to act. For example, consider push polling [20], or the manner in which the framing of a question in a positive or negative light can lead to risk averse or risk taking behaviour [21]. Such results suggest that the act of measurement can itself influence the outcomes that are obtained, but the geometric formulation of decisions that is used by QDT can easily incorporate such effects [2].

Measurement of the state (1) is defined in this approach with respect to a projection operator V, where

$$V = |0_p\rangle\langle 0_p| + |1_p\rangle\langle 1_p| = V_0 + V_1. \tag{2}$$

Thus, the basis vectors $\{|0_p\rangle, |1_p\rangle\}$ *define the current context* p of our agent, which in turn affects their decisions about whether or not to perform an action during the process of measurement. This effect is reflected in the probability of our agent acting in a given context p, which is given by

$$P = \langle A|V_1|A\rangle \tag{3}$$
$$= \langle A|1_p\rangle\langle 1_p|A\rangle \tag{4}$$
$$= \left(a_0^*\langle 0_p|1_p\rangle + a_1^*\langle 1_p|1_p\rangle\right) \times \left(a_0\langle 1_p|0_p\rangle + a_1\langle 1_p|1_p\rangle\right) \tag{5}$$
$$= |a_1|^2. \tag{6}$$

Similarly, their probability of inaction in the context p is given by $|a_0|^2$.

Perhaps the most important feature of this new model arises from a consideration of context itself; it is not just a label. We can immediately develop a far richer notion of context by asking: what would happen if the social context of our agent A changed? QT provides us with a particularly elegant mechanism for dealing with this scenario via a change of basis. Consider figure 1(b), which is an elaboration of figure 1(a), and represents the changing probabilities of action that arise in the case of two different contexts, p and q. With reference to figure 1(b) we can quickly see that while our agent is highly likely to act in context q, this is not the case in context p, where A is much less likely to act (since by examination of the figure we can see that while $|a_0| > |a_1|$ in context p, $|b_1| > |b_0|$ in context q).

2.2 Social Agents Minimise Cognitive Loads

We shall now extend the framework of QDT with a consideration of the *uncertainty* that an agent experiences. An agent who has decided to act has reduced their uncertainty about a situation, as has one who has decided not to act. In contrast, an agent who is most undecided (i.e. has a current state that forms a $45°$ angle between choosing to act and choosing not to act in the context p) is highly uncertain about their future action in that context, and we consider this a state that people tend not to enjoy finding themselves in. Certainly, they tend not even to make decisions (i.e. to 'act' or 'not act') when they find themselves in such situations of uncertainty [22,3].

This leads us to introduce a minimisation principle which takes as its basis the desire of people to be 'decided'. That is, we assume that people tend not to enjoy living in states of uncertainty, and that they will preferentially seek a state in which they can maximise their chances of being decided about an action. In order to model this behaviour we require a way in which to quantify the uncertainty that an agent experiences in their current context, and *binary entropy* provides a suitable measure of this notion. Defined as the entropy of a Bernoulli trial (e.g. a two-outcome random variable such as a coin toss), with a probability of success given by P, it is specified as:

$$H_b(P) \equiv -P\log_2 P - (1 - P)\log_2(1 - P), \tag{7}$$

which is a concave function taking its minimum values at $P = 0$ and $P = 1$, and its maximum at $P = 1/2$.

Our agent, who is uncomfortable with uncertainty, will seek to minimise the binary entropy associated with their current attitude through time, by aligning their state with the context in which they are currently making a decision to act. Thus, we require that agents seek to minimise the binary entropy associated with their current state or attitude, in whatever frame is currently relevant to the agent. This means that the time evolution of $|A\rangle$ will reduce $H_b(P)$ for the context p by moving towards one of the basis states $\{|0_p\rangle, |1_p\rangle\}$. Referring to figure 1(a), we can rewrite the binary entropy (7) for our agent within the context p as

$$H_b(P) = -|a_1|^2 \log_2(|a_1|^2) - |a_0|^2 \log_2(|a_0|^2) \tag{8}$$

$$= -cos^2\theta . \log_2(cos^2\theta) - sin^2\theta . \log_2(sin^2\theta) \tag{9}$$

where θ is the angle between the $|1_p\rangle$ basis state and the state of the agent $|A\rangle$. Rewriting (7) in this manner draws attention to the way in which the entropy of the agent will change if either (a) the agent undergoes a change in state, or (b) finds themselves in a changed context. However, we are yet to propose the manner in which the social context of our agent might emerge.

2.3   The Local and Global Framing of an Issue

A final extension of QDT is required; we shall assume that multiple frames (i.e. contexts) can be used by a society to understand an issue, and that these can work at two different scales. Thus, agents in a society will make decisions to act in both *local* and *global* contexts, representing their individual and private understanding's of an issue, as well as a collective and global understanding of that same issue.

For example, each member of a society will have an attitude towards a public issue (e.g. the need to combat climate change, or the 'pro-life' lobby) but this will quite often remain local and un-shared. When an agent is exposed to an argument about that issue, they will frequently form an opinion, or choose to act, according to that argument but we will consider such decisions to be local and broadly unshared with the other agents in the society. A local context might depend upon a wide range of both external and internal factors, such as the agent's socioeconomic status, educational background, race etc. and so is a highly complex, and multidependent variable, although the implementation in this paper takes a simple two dimensional form.

In addition to these local and private decisions, sometimes agents interact, leading them to make decisions of a more global form (e.g. they might be asked to vote in an election, or be polled). In this situation, issues are considered in a frame that is somehow aggregated from the attitudes of each member in the society (such as the spin of a major political party, or a voting card that represents all of the candidates in an election and their policies). We note here that a society frequently understands an issue from a small number of broadly definable perspectives (e.g. capitalism vs socialism, or pro-green vs pro-development etc.), and so it seems likely that more than one global frame may exist in a society at any one time (and these will not necessarily be orthogonal). This leads us to surmise that for every issue confronting a society, a set of global frames will gradually emerge. Agents would then align their understanding of an issue with a particular global frame, and make their choices on this basis. However, these actions can in turn influence the society's understanding of that issue; the global frame might itself evolve.

The model presented below considers the orientation of each agent's local frame as resulting from an attempt to navigate two different drives for cognitive consistency:

1. A desire for internal cognitive consistency. This results in a drive to minimise the binary entropy that applies to their decisions through a choice of local frame that results in their current state being maximally decided.
2. A desire to 'fit in' with the society and its current norms. This desire is expressed by a pull of their local frame towards the current global frame to which they belong.

These two drives may prove to compete with one another in the mind of the agent, and indeed, they might have a different pull for agents of different personality types (e.g. a 'conformist' agent vs a highly 'individualistic' one). In what follows, we shall define Θ as the angle between the agent's current state $|A\rangle$, and the $|1\rangle$ axis, in the global context to which they currently belong, and take θ to perform a similar function in their local frame. This allows us to define an individual entropy measure for each agent

$$H(|A\rangle, \theta) = w_i(A)H_b(p(\theta)) + w_s(A)H_b(p(\Theta)) \tag{10}$$

where the weights $w_i(A)$ and $w_s(A)$ refer to agent A's need for internal consistency and social conformity respectively. These weights can range over a population of agents, giving a rough parameterisation of a society's social make-up.

2.4   Updating the State and the Local Frame

A previously undecided agent who has chosen to act in a certain context will experience some *cognitive dissonance*, meaning that this decision will not reflect the agent's perceived internal state, and this will result in psychological discomfort [9]. This gives people a drive to either alter their existing cognitions, or to reframe their interpretation of a situation, through a re-orientation of their local frame. We note that since an agent has no direct control over the global frame they may not always be able to minimise their uncertainty as represented by (10), however, depending upon their personality type, they may be able to reduce it over time if the global frame remains relatively stable.

Rather than positing a collapse of the agent's cognitive state to whichever axis represents their decision, this model updates $|A\rangle$ after a decision by shifting it towards the axis representing the decision by a certain amount. The size of this shift will depend upon the agent's personality variables (w_i and w_s), and upon the angle θ between the state at time t, $|A_t\rangle$, and the frame in which the decision is being made (as represented by context p, $\{|0_p\rangle, |1_p\rangle\}$). Writing θ_0 for the angle between the agent's state and the $|0_p\rangle$ axis, and θ_1 for the angle between their state and the $|1_p\rangle$ axis, the new angle between the agent's state and the relevant frame is defined to become:

$$\text{if } A \text{ decides} \begin{cases} \text{to act: } \theta_1(|A\rangle_{t+1}, w(A)) = \theta_1(|A_t\rangle) \times (1 + w(A)) \\ \text{not to act: } \theta_0(|A\rangle_{t+1}, w(A)) = \theta_0(|A_t\rangle) \times (1 - w(A)) \end{cases} \quad (11)$$

where $w(A)$ depends upon the comfort of A with holding two dissonant attitudes; if A's decision is being made in a global frame then $w(A) = w_s(A)$, whereas if it is being made in their local frame then $w(A) = w_i(A)$. Thus, the state of agents who decide to act will rotate by a certain distance towards the relevant $|1\rangle$ axis, and the state of agents who decide not to act will exhibit a rotation in the opposite direction. This means that agents who are comfortable with dissonance will likely be able to maintain attitudes that do not conform to their actions, while those who prefer a consistent cognitive state will experience significant swings in attitude as a result of actions that they choose to take.

Over time, we expect the agents to self-organize towards a scenario where they are highly aligned within groups who all hold similar ideologies (or global frames). This process will be measured by the total entropy of the system, given by a summation of each agent's individual entropy

$$H = \sum_{i=1}^{N} H(|i\rangle, \theta_i). \quad (12)$$

The next section will briefly discuss a computational implementation of this social model of low effort attitude change, the interested reader can find far more details in the longer paper [18].

2.5 Computational Implementation

A computational implementation of this model has been performed using MAT-LAB, where attitudes and frames evolve in a simple two dimensional space. This model is currently only at the proof of concept stage, and will be further developed in a more realistic higher dimensional space in future work. At present, simulations can be run with a varying collection of agents, with varying weightings of personality variables, and different numbers of global frames. Clustering was utilised to find a specified number of global frames in this implementation. In this case the vertex substitution heuristic (VSH) algorithm was used [23]. It is also important to note that the current model is obviously symmetric, and agents who are at precisely 180° to one another will exhibit the same probabilities of action in the one global frame. This should be remembered when considering the figures below.

In figures 2 and 3 we see a society of 100 agents, with their current states represented by long black lines, the global frames in the system by large red

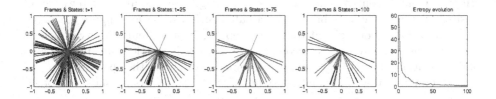

Fig. 2. The time-wise behaviour of a typical run with only one global frame

dots, and the local frames of each agent by the short red lines. These are seen to evolve over 100 timesteps, and even with this particularly simple implementation we can illustrate two key effects that are of interest to social modelling.

Firstly, the vast majority of runs have demonstrated the anticipated timewise minimisation of the total entropy of the system. Thus, over time the value of equation (12) decreases, which represents a lessening of the uncertainty of most agents in the system about their actions. In figure 2 we see a typical system run with one global frame specified, and consistency and conformity randomly assigned according to a normal distribution. This run starts from a random distribution of states, but quickly settles into a scenario where clusters of agents are centred around the global frame, with a couple of other groupings also in existence. The total entropy of this system is seen to quickly settle down to a low value, but we note that some runs have seen well defined spikes arise in this measure of system uncertainty, denoting a scenario where an unstable global frame undergoes a marked shift, which requires the agents to re-evaluate their current attitudes.

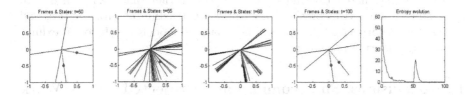

Fig. 3. Guided Self-Organisation example. Time evolution patterns for a system of 100 agents all characterised by the same personality values (consistency and conformity =.5). After 50 iterations the system reaches a stable state with 2 global frames and all agents aligned to their local frames as well as to one of the global frame. At iteration 51 an external perturbation rotates one of the global frames 30° clockwise. At iteration 55 and 60 we see the system re-organising. After 100 iterations the system reaches a new, different stable state. The rightmost panel shows the time evolution of the total entropy measure, clearly displaying the effect of the intervention at iteration 51.

This shift in global frames suggests that it may be possible for a policy maker or interested party to identify places where they could potentially interfere in a system of this form. Indeed, entropy measures might be utilised to identify 'tipping points' from which a social system might be manipulated towards a desired outcome. We have briefly investigated such a scenario in figure 3, where a perturbation of one global frame at step 51, in a system with two global frames, causes the system to reconfigure an eventually settle down into a new stable position. The entropy mapped in figure 3(e) shows the spike in entropy that results from this manipulation, so linking the entropy to such shifts in global frame.

3   New Time Evolution Paradigms

At this point it is worth taking a step back from the model itself and considering its implications for the broader QI paradigm. This is because while the model is quantum inspired, it has characteristics that do not satisfy a standard quantum model. Specifically, no continuous time evolution satisfying the Schrödinger equation takes place, and while agents change their state in response to measurement they do not exhibit complete collapse.

We note that the evolution operator given in equation (11) can be defined in such a manner that it is invertible by setting $\theta_1^{-1} = \theta_0$ and vice versa. This has the result of implying that the time evolution in this system is unitary [19]:

$$U_\theta U_\theta^\dagger = 1. \tag{13}$$

However, this time evolution equation is different from the time evolution of standard quantum mechanics, and so provides us with a genuinely new form of probability conserving time evolution. We anticipate that many other forms of evolution exist, and propose that the QI community should strive to identify them and classify their behaviour.

We have designated this model as geometric rather than quantum due to its reliance upon Pythagoras' theorem in the extraction of probabilities, and suggest that it forms part of a class of non-classical models which do not exhibit completely quantum behaviour.

4   Conclusions, Shortcomings and Projected Future Work

The model presented in section 2 is obviously very simplistic, and has many deficiencies. For example, a genuine model of attitude change must be implemented in more than a two dimensional plane. A current project involves trying to identify a suitable set of relevant variables from social psychology that could take the role of basis states. This higher dimensional setting would entail significant new complexities. Measurement in particular would require the specification of some sort of plane or cut through the higher dimensional space before a frame could be suitably defined. However this extra complexity would serve to further clarify the notion of an action. For example, we anticipate that the designation of relevant dimensions from social psychology would restrict the notion of an action to the system of interest. Thus, a model that was designed to explore political ideologies, and their influence upon environmental decisions would perhaps not include a dimension that could be used to explore an attitude towards immunisation, or a propensity to donate to charity, and so the decisions that were modelled would be of a similar type. The different psychological effort involved in carrying out some actions compared to others is also a factor that needs to be explored, and future work will investigate the possibility of incorporating this model as a module into an existing ELM-style model (e.g. [17]).

We note that this model has not been designed to exhibit either interference, or non-separability effects at this stage, although this is not in principle ruled out. The design of the model is such that interference effects between competing decisions to be made by an individual should be evident, with choices made in one frame affecting choices in another etc., as has already been discussed in a number of QDT's (e.g. [2,3]). A more novel phenomenon would centre around interference effects between different agents in a society. Indeed, depending upon how a global frame is defined, we could anticipate scenarios where the decisions of one agent might have pronounced effects upon other agents in the system. For example, it would not be difficult to define a 'presidential' agent, whose decisions shape a specific global frame in the system, and so interfere with the decisions of all other agents. We might then ask what would be signified by the emergence of a new global frame — perhaps the emergence of a new set of political ideologies?

More broadly, the ability to represent and computationally model effects such as cognitive dissonance and low elaboration attitude change is undoubtedly useful for broader social analysis, which is frequently dominated by either computational models that are overly simplified and physically motivated, or social models that are too qualitative to be of use in predicting large scale behaviour. Much has been learned from this new model, even at this preliminary stage. We believe that the geometric representation employed in this paper allows natural scientists and engineers to model, and thus more easily accept, a set of models that social scientists hold particularly dear. Similarly, the adoption of our proposed framework may in some cases provide social scientists with some confidence that important aspects of social theory can be considered within quantitative models, so making them to relevant to the real world problems that they are seeking to address. For the QI community, we see a new way forwards, towards a class of quasi-quantum systems displaying contextualised probabilistic behaviour, but within a new set of measurement paradigms. This further opens up the field towards a new broader class of formalisms able to treat context in a sophisticated manner, of which quantum mechanics is only one example.

Acknowledgements. Supported by the Australian Research Council Discovery grant DP1094974.

References

1. Khrennikov, A.Y.: Ubiquitous Quantum Structure: From Psychology to Finance. Springer (2010)

2. Busemeyer, J.R., Pothos, E., Franco, R., Trueblood, J.: A Quantum Theoretical Explanation for Probability Judgment Errors. Psychological Review 118(2), 193–218 (2011)
3. Yukalov, V.I., Sornette, D.: Decision theory with prospect interference and entanglement. Theory and Decision, 1–46 (2010)
4. Busemeyer, J., Bruza, P.: Quantum Models of Cognition and Decision. Cambridge University Press (2012)
5. Augoustinos, M., Walker, I., Donaghue, N.: Social Cognition, 2nd edn. Sage, London (2006)
6. Allport, G.W.: Attitudes. In: Murchison, C. (ed.) Handbook of Social Psychology, pp. 798–884. Clark University Press, Worcester (1935)
7. Petty, R.E., Wegener, D.T.: Attitude change: Multiple roles for persuasion variables. In: Gilbert, D., Fiske, S., Lindzey, G. (eds.) The Handbook of Social Psychology, pp. 323–390. McGraw-Hill (1998)
8. Seiter, R.H., Gass, J.S.: Persuasion, social influence, and compliance gaining, 4th edn. Allyn & Bacon, Boston (2010)
9. Cooper, J.: Cognitive dissonance: 50 years of a classic theory. Sage (2007)
10. Asch, S.E.: Studies of independence and conformity: A minority of one against a unanimous majority. Psychological Monographs 70(9), 1–70 (1956)
11. Bond, R., Smith, P.B.: Culture and Conformity. Psychological Bulletin 119, 111–137 (1996)
12. Greenwald, A.G., Banaji, M.R.: Implicit social cognition: Attitudes, self-esteem, and stereotypes. Psychological Review 102, 4–27 (1995)
13. Petty, R.E., Cacioppo, J.T.: Communication and Persuasion: Central and Peripheral Routes to Attitude Change. Springer, New York (1986)
14. Chaiken, S.M.: The heuristic model of persuasion. In: Zanna, P., Olson, J.M., Herman, C.P. (eds.) Social Influence: The Ontario Symposium, vol. 5, pp. 3–39. Erlbaum, Hillsdale (1987)
15. Rosenberg, H., Feldman, C.S.: No Time To Think: The Menace of Media Speed and the 24-hour News Cycle. Continuum, London (2008)
16. Tanner, L.: Sideshow: Dumbing Down Democracy. Scribe, Australia (2011)
17. Mosler, H.J., Schwarz, K., Ammann, F., Gutscher, H.: Computer Simulation as a Method of Further Developing a Theory: Simulating the Elaboration Likelihood Model. Personality and Social Psychology Review 5, 201–215 (2001)
18. Kitto, K., Boschetti, F.: Attitudes, ideologies and self-organisation: Information load minimisation in multi-agent decision making (under review, 2012)
19. Isham, C.J.: Lectures on Quantum Theory. Imperial College Press, London (1995)
20. Fox, J.S.: Push Polling. Florida Law Review 49, 563 (1997)
21. Tversky, A., Kahneman, D.: The framing of decisions and the psychology of choice. Science 211(4481), 453–458 (1981)
22. Shafir, E., Tversky, A.: Thinking through uncertainty: Nonconsequential reasoning and choice. Cognitive Psychology 24, 449–474 (1992)
23. Teitz, M., Bart, P.: Heuristic methods for estimating the generalized vertex median of a weighted graph. Operations Research 16, 955–961 (1968)

On Least Action Principles
for Discrete Quantum Scales

François Dubois[1], Isabelle Greff[2], and Thomas Hélie[3]

[1] Conservatoire National des Arts et Métiers, Paris, France
[2] Department of Mathematics, University of Pau, France
[3] IRCAM, Paris, France
francois.dubois@cnam.fr, isabelle.greff@univ-pau.fr,
thomas.helie@ircam.fr

Abstract. We consider variational problems where the velocity depends on a scale. After recalling the fundamental principles that lead to classical and quantum mechanics, we study the dynamics obtained by replacing the velocity by some physical observable at a given scale into the expression of the Lagrangian function. Then, discrete Euler-Lagrange and Hamilton-Jacobi equations are derived for a continuous model that incorporates a real-valued discrete velocity. We also examine the paradigm for complex-valued discrete velocity, inspired by the scale relativity of Nottale. We present also rigorous definitions and preliminary results in this direction.

Keywords: quantum operators, scale relativity.

1 Some Philosophical Principles for Physics

In this contribution, we first introduce some general philosophical hypotheses that are also widely discussed by several authors (see *e.g.* Bitbol [1], d'Espagnat [4], Filk and von Müller [5] among others). We set three hypotheses. The two first ones are of ontological type and the third one is concerned with experiments.

(H1)-Principle of Reality. It exists a reality which is independent of any observer.

(H2)-Continuous Space-time. The space-time is a continuous manifold on which the movement of particles can be described by continuous trajectories.

(H3)-Measurement and Scale. The measurement of a physical quantity (time, space, velocity, energy, *etc*) involves a notion of scale.

In classical physics, hypothesis (H2) is more constrained: trajectories are supposed to be differentiable or more regular. In this case, the particle velocity is uniquely defined by $v = \frac{dq}{dt}$ which is independent of the scale. Observe that if the trajectory is not regular (continuous but nowhere differentiable) or if some general hypothesis of continuous but non-differentiable space-time is done (as in scale relativity [12]), hypothesis (H3) remains true but the previous velocity has no meaning. On the contrary, a discrete velocity associated with a given scale can still be well-defined.

J.R. Busemeyer et al. (Eds.): QI 2012, LNCS 7620, pp. 13–23, 2012.

This framework leads to a first paradigm (labelled by the letter "a" in table 1) of continuous classical physics. We recall in section 2 the main point about Euler-Lagrange and Hamilton-Jacobi equations. As noticed by Gondran [7], a complexification of the Hamilton-Jacobi framework provides a natural introduction to the Schrödinger equation. This second paradigm (letter "b" in table 1) is shortly displayed in section 3. As a consequence the differentiability of the trajectories is lost and they can be interpreted in terms of Brownian motion (see *e.g.* Nelson [11]).

In this contribution, we develop a scale point of view based on the analysis of reality associated with observations at a given discrete scale. We develop in section 4 a paradigm (labeled with the letter "c" in table 1) based on the knowledge of real-valued discrete velocities. In other words, the velocity at a given scale remains a real number. The idea of introducing discrete operators as fundamental principles of mechanics and quantum mechanics has been proposed by several authors as Greenspan [8], Friedberg and Lee [6] and recently by Khrennikov *et al.* [9,10] as well as Odake and Sasaki [13]. Nevertheless, our approach does not follow the paradigms suggested by the above references. Our objective is to develop our understanding of the ideas of Nottale [12] who introduced a set of discrete complex velocities (see the label "d" in table 1). We propose some preliminary remarks in this direction in section 5.

Table 1. Proposition of four paradigms

	Continuous Geometry	Given Scale Geometry
Classical Physics	ⓐ Hamilton-Jacobi	ⓒ Real-valued velocity
Quantum Physics	ⓑ Schrödinger	ⓓ Complex-valued velocity

2 Some Classical Results on Hamilton-Jacobi Equations

In order to reduce the notations, a Lagrangian function $L(x, v)$ independent of the time is given. To fix the ideas, this Lagrangian can be chosen as

$$L(x, v) = \frac{1}{2} m v^2 - \varphi(x). \tag{1}$$

The potential energy $\varphi(x)$ structures the space-time with objects governed by physical laws (H1), whereas the kinetic energy $K(v) \equiv \frac{mv^2}{2}$ catches the dynamics through the velocity. Consider a regular trajectory $\theta \longmapsto X(\theta)$ for $0 \leq \theta \leq t$ and the associated action

$$A(t, X(\bullet)) = \int_0^t L\left(X(\theta), \frac{\mathrm{d}}{\mathrm{d}\theta} X(\theta)\right) \mathrm{d}\theta.$$

For an arbitrary variation δt and for all C^1-functions X and associated variations δX, we introduce the variation δA of the action. It is given by:

$$\delta A\big(t, X(\bullet)\big) = L\Big(X(t), \frac{\mathrm{d}}{\mathrm{d}\theta}X(t)\Big)\,\delta t$$
$$+ \int_0^t \Big[\partial_x L\Big(X(\theta), \frac{\mathrm{d}}{\mathrm{d}\theta}X(\theta)\Big)\,\delta X(\theta) + \partial_v L\Big(X(\theta), \frac{\mathrm{d}}{\mathrm{d}\theta}X(\theta)\Big)\frac{\mathrm{d}}{\mathrm{d}\theta}\delta X(\theta)\Big]\,\mathrm{d}\theta$$

and after integrating by parts:

$$\delta A = L\Big(X(t), \frac{\mathrm{d}}{\mathrm{d}\theta}X(t)\Big)\delta t + \int_0^t \frac{\mathrm{d}}{\mathrm{d}\theta}\Big[\partial_v L\Big(X(\theta), \frac{\mathrm{d}}{\mathrm{d}\theta}X(\theta)\Big)\delta X(\theta)\Big]\,\mathrm{d}\theta$$
$$+ \int_0^t \Big(\partial_x L\Big(X(\theta), \frac{\mathrm{d}}{\mathrm{d}\theta}X(\theta)\Big) - \frac{\mathrm{d}}{\mathrm{d}\theta}\Big[\partial_v L\Big(X(\theta), \frac{\mathrm{d}}{\mathrm{d}\theta}X(\theta)\Big)\Big]\Big)\,\delta X(\theta)\,\mathrm{d}\theta\,. \tag{2}$$

Let q_0 be fixed and consider the class of functions $\mathcal{C}^1_{q_0}(0,t) = \{X \in \mathcal{C}^1(0,t)$ such that $X(0) = q_0\}$. Notice that the difference between two functions of $\mathcal{C}^1_{q_0}(0,t)$ belongs to $\mathcal{C}^1_0(0,t)$. Thus, if $\delta X \in \mathcal{C}^1_0(0,t)$, then $\delta X(0) = 0$. Vanishing the first variations of the action leads to the well-known Euler-Lagrange equation given by

$$\partial_x L\Big(X(\theta), \frac{\mathrm{d}}{\mathrm{d}\theta}X(\theta)\Big) - \frac{\mathrm{d}}{\mathrm{d}\theta}\Big[\partial_v L\Big(X(\theta), \frac{\mathrm{d}}{\mathrm{d}\theta}X(\theta)\Big)\Big] = 0\,, \tag{3}$$
$$\text{with } X(0) = q_0\,,\ X(t) = q\,.$$

Moreover, for any arbitrary time $t > 0$ and any arbitrary state q, let $X^{\mathrm{opt}}(\bullet; t, q)$ be the solution $X(\bullet)$ in $\mathcal{C}^1_{q_0}(0,t)$ of the Dirichlet boundary problem given by the Euler-Lagrange equation (3). Observe that $X^{\mathrm{opt}}(\bullet; t, q)$ is parameterized by the time of arrival t and the value q, as precised in (3). At fixed time t and position q, the optimal trajectory $X^{\mathrm{opt}}(\bullet; t, q)$ is supposed to exist and to be unique. We have the initial condition $X^{\mathrm{opt}}(0; t, q) = q_0$ and the final condition $X^{\mathrm{opt}}(t; t, q) = q$. Moreover the trajectory $\theta \longmapsto X^{\mathrm{opt}}(\theta; t, q)$ has a velocity at time t and position q equal to $\partial_\theta X^{\mathrm{opt}}(\theta; t, q)\big|_{\theta=t}$ that can also be considered as a "natural" velocity $\frac{\mathrm{d}q}{\mathrm{d}t}(t) = \partial_\theta X^{\mathrm{opt}}(\theta; t, q)\big|_{\theta=t}$.
Let the momentum $p(t, q)$ be defined by

$$p(t, q) = \partial_v L\big(q, \partial_\theta X^{\mathrm{opt}}(t; t, q)\big) \tag{4}$$

and the optimal action $S(t, q)$ as the action along the optimal trajectory :

$$S(t, q) = A\big(t, X^{\mathrm{opt}}(\bullet; t, q)\big)\,. \tag{5}$$

At fixed time t, due to the Euler-Lagrange equation (3), we deduce from (2) that $\delta A\big(t, X^{\mathrm{opt}}(\bullet)\big) = \partial_v L\big(q\,\partial_\theta X^{\mathrm{opt}}(t; t, q)\big) = p(t, q)$. In other words, the first variation of the optimal action with respect to the final state is the momentum, namely

$$\partial_q S(t, q) = p(t, q)\,. \tag{6}$$

If time t is varying and considering the optimal trajectory $\theta \longmapsto X^{\mathrm{opt}}(\theta; t, q)$, we have $\partial_t A\big(t, X^{\mathrm{opt}}(\bullet)\big) = L\big(q, \partial_\theta X^{\mathrm{opt}}(t; t, q)\big)$. Writing that this quantity is the time variation of the optimal action (5) and taking into account the velocity of the optimal trajectory at the location q, we deduce

$$\partial_t S + \partial_q S \bullet \partial_\theta X^{\mathrm{opt}}(t; t, q) = \partial_t A\big(t, X^{\mathrm{opt}}(\bullet)\big) = L\big(q, \partial_\theta X^{\mathrm{opt}}(t; t, q)\big)\,. \tag{7}$$

Introduce now the Legendre transform of the Lagrangian L relatively to the second variable v. Suppose that the function $v \longmapsto y = \partial_v L(x, v)$ is invertible and denote by $V(x, y)$ its inverse. The Hamiltonian $H(y, x)$ is classically defined by

$$H(y, x) = y \bullet V(x, y) - L\big(x, V(x, y)\big).$$

Observe that if (4) holds then $\partial_\theta X^{\mathrm{opt}}(t; t, q) = V(q, p)$ and $H(p, q) = p \bullet V(q, p)$ $-L(q, V(q, p))$. We deduce from (7),

$$\begin{aligned} L\big(q, \partial_\theta X^{\mathrm{opt}}(t; t, q)\big) &= \partial_t S + \big(\partial_q S\big) \bullet \partial_\theta X^{\mathrm{opt}}(t; t, q) \\ &= \partial_t S + p(t, q) \bullet V\big(q, p(t, q)\big). \end{aligned}$$

This leads to the well-known Hamilton-Jacobi equation

$$\partial_t S + H\big(\partial_q S, q\big) = 0. \tag{8}$$

3   How to Derive the Schrödinger Equation ?

The "break through" from classical Hamilton-Jacobi equations to quantum dynamics is due to Schrödinger [14]. Introduce the wave function ψ according to

$$\psi = \exp\left(i \frac{S}{\hbar}\right) \tag{9}$$

and inject this relation into (4) and (8). We get $\frac{i}{\hbar}\, \mathrm{d}S = \frac{1}{\psi}\, \mathrm{d}\psi$ and due to (6), we have $p = \frac{\hbar}{i} \frac{1}{\psi} \partial_q \psi$. Then Schrödinger transforms the momentum p into the so-called momentum operator P defined by $P \bullet \psi = -i\hbar\, \partial_q \psi$. Observe that the momentum P becomes now a complex derivative operator. Starting from the usual Lagrangian, we observe that the good generalisation of quantum mechanic of v^2 is not $|v|^2$ (or PP^*) but vv (or PP in the classical formalism). Then the Hamiltonian H takes the expression $H = \frac{1}{2m} P^2 + \varphi(q) = -\frac{\hbar^2}{2m} \Delta + \varphi(q)$ and the Schrödinger equation

$$i\hbar\, \partial_t \psi = -\frac{\hbar^2}{2m} \Delta \psi + \varphi(q)\, \psi \tag{10}$$

is a direct consequence of the Hamilton-Jacobi equation (8).

An other way to derive the Schrödinger equation has been proposed by Nottale [12]. The idea consists in replacing the classical trajectory derivative $\frac{\mathrm{d}}{\mathrm{d}t} \equiv \partial_t + v \bullet \partial_q$ by the complex Dynkin operator $\frac{\mathrm{d}}{\mathrm{d}t} \equiv \partial_t + v \bullet \partial_q - i \frac{\hbar}{2m} \Delta$. Then, equation (7) takes the form: $L = \partial_t S + v \bullet \big(\partial_q S\big) - i \frac{\hbar}{2m} \Delta S$ and $\partial_t S + \frac{1}{m} \big(\partial_q S\big)^2 - i \frac{\hbar}{2m} \Delta S + \varphi(q) - \frac{m}{2} \big(\frac{1}{m} \partial_q S\big)^2 = 0$. Following Gondran [7], one can derive a complex Hamilton-Jacobi equation

$$\partial_t S + \frac{1}{2m} (\partial_q S)^2 + \varphi(q) - i \frac{\hbar}{2m} \Delta S = 0. \tag{11}$$

If we decompose the complex optimal action S into its real and imaginary parts, *id est* $S = \Sigma - i\hbar \log R$, an elementary calculus allows to transform the complex Hamilton-Jacobi equation (11) into the form proposed by Bohm and Hiley [2]:

$$\partial_t \Sigma + \frac{1}{2m}(\partial_q \Sigma)^2 + \varphi(q) - \frac{\hbar}{2m}\frac{\partial_q R}{R} = 0, \quad \partial_t R^2 + \mathrm{div}\left(\frac{R^2}{m}\partial_q \Sigma\right) = 0. \quad (12)$$

The quantum potential $Q \equiv -\frac{\hbar}{2m}\frac{\partial_q R}{R}$ is the quantity that has to be added to transform the classical Hamilton-Jacobi equation (8) into the real part of the complex Hamilton-Jacobi equation (11).

Introduce now the change of variables (9) into the complex Hamilton-Jacobi equation (11). If we derive once again the relation $\frac{i}{\hbar}\partial_q S = \frac{1}{\psi}\partial_q \psi$ towards the space variable q, we get $\frac{i}{\hbar}\partial_q^2 S = -\frac{1}{\psi^2}(\partial_q \psi)^2 + \frac{1}{\psi}\partial_q^2 \psi$. The left hand side of the complex Hamilton-Jacobi equation (11) is now equal to

$$\frac{1}{\psi}\left[\frac{\hbar}{i}\partial_t \psi + \frac{1}{2m\psi}\left(\frac{\hbar}{i}\partial_q \psi\right)^2 + \varphi(q)\,\psi - i\frac{\hbar}{2m}\frac{\hbar}{i}\left(-\frac{1}{\psi}(\partial_q \psi)^2 + \partial_q^2 \psi\right)\right]$$

and the Schrödinger equation (10) is established.

4   Real-Valued Discrete-Measured Velocity at a Given Scale

We consider now that the classical velocity is not a relevant observable. We introduce a given strictly positive scale parameter ε, a "fat" initial condition $q_0 \in \mathcal{C}([-\varepsilon, 0])$ as a continuous function and the classical discrete so-called finite difference operators

$$(d_\varepsilon^- q)(\theta) \equiv \frac{1}{\varepsilon}(q(\theta) - q(\theta - \varepsilon)), \quad (d_\varepsilon^+ q)(\theta) \equiv \frac{1}{\varepsilon}(q(\theta + \varepsilon) - q(\theta)). \quad (13)$$

Let us notice that the velocity $v_\varepsilon^\pm = d_\varepsilon^\pm q$ is now measured at the given scale ε by two possible schemes (13), as a consequence of the hypothesis (H3). We consider a given (final) time t strictly positive and a continuous trajectory $([-\varepsilon, t] \ni \theta \longmapsto q(\theta)) \in \mathcal{C}([-\varepsilon, t])$ with the initial condition q_0. This initial condition is not classical, q_0 is not anymore given at a time $t = 0$, but on a small interval depending on the scale ε. It has to be considered in the following sense: restricted to the interval $[-\varepsilon, 0]$, function q is equal to the given function q_0. As in the classical case described in section 2, we introduce an action A based on a regular Lagrangian $L(x, v)$ which is similar to that introduced at the relation (1):

$$A(t, q) \equiv \int_0^t L(q(\theta), d_\varepsilon^- q(\theta))\, d\theta. \quad (14)$$

In the following, we examine the choice of $d_\varepsilon^- q$ as the observed velocity. Thus the paradigm based on this choice and (14) is studied. We have just formally replaced velocity v in the second argument of the Lagrangian (1) by the discrete velocity $v_\varepsilon = d_\varepsilon^- q$. We have the following result.

Proposition 1. Variation of the discrete action
The variation δA of the action A defined in (14) when trajectory q is varying by an increment δq and time by an increment δt is given by

$$
\begin{aligned}
\delta A = L\,\delta t - \frac{1}{\varepsilon}\int_{-\varepsilon}^{0} \partial_v L(\theta+\varepsilon)\,\delta q(\theta)\,\mathrm{d}\theta \\
+ \int_{t-\varepsilon}^{t}\left[\partial_x L + \frac{1}{\varepsilon}\partial_v L\right](\theta)\,\delta q(\theta)\,\mathrm{d}\theta \\
+ \int_{0}^{t-\varepsilon}\left[\partial_x L - d_\varepsilon^+\left(\partial_v L\right)\right](\theta)\,\delta q(\theta)\,\mathrm{d}\theta\,.
\end{aligned}
\tag{15}
$$

The first integral in (15) is null *a priori* since initial condition q_0 is supposed to be fixed between $-\varepsilon$ and 0.

Proof of Proposition 1.
Since Lagrangian L in (1) is a regular function, differentiating (14) yields

$$
\delta A = L\,\delta t + \int_0^t \left(\partial_x L\right)\delta q(\theta)\,\mathrm{d}\theta + \int_0^t \left(\partial_v L\right)\frac{1}{\varepsilon}\left(\delta q(\theta) - \delta q(\theta-\varepsilon)\right)\mathrm{d}\theta
$$

$$
= L\,\delta t + \int_0^t \left(\partial_x L\right)\delta q(\theta)\,\mathrm{d}\theta + \frac{1}{\varepsilon}\int_0^t \left(\partial_v L\right)\delta q(\theta)\,\mathrm{d}\theta - \frac{1}{\varepsilon}\int_{-\varepsilon}^{t-\varepsilon}\left(\partial_v L\right)(\theta+\varepsilon)\,\delta q(\theta)\,\mathrm{d}\theta
$$

$$
= L\,\delta t - \frac{1}{\varepsilon}\int_{-\varepsilon}^{0}\left(\partial_v L\right)(\theta+\varepsilon)\,\delta q(\theta)\,\mathrm{d}\theta
$$

$$
+ \int_0^{t-\varepsilon}\left(\partial_x L - \frac{1}{\varepsilon}\left[(\partial_v L)(\theta+\varepsilon) - (\partial_v L)(\theta)\right]\right)\delta q(\theta)\,\mathrm{d}\theta
$$

$$
+ \int_{t-\varepsilon}^{t}\left[\partial_x L + \frac{1}{\varepsilon}\partial_v L\right](\theta)\,\delta q(\theta)\,\mathrm{d}\theta\,,
$$

so that (15) is a consequence of the definition of the operator d_ε^+ given by (13). $\square$

We deduce from relation (15) that an optimal trajectory satisfies the discrete version of the Euler-Lagrange equation, that is

$$
\partial_x L\big(q(\theta), d_\varepsilon^- q\big) - d_\varepsilon^+\left[\partial_v L\big(q(\theta), d_\varepsilon^- q\big)\right] = 0\,, \qquad 0 \le \theta \le t - \varepsilon\,.
\tag{16}
$$

This discrete-time dynamics is formally very similar to the classical Euler-Lagrange dynamics (3). Remark that it is nothing but an implicit finite difference scheme:

$$
\begin{aligned}
\partial_x L\left(q(\theta), \frac{1}{\varepsilon}\big(q(\theta) - q(\theta-\varepsilon)\big)\right) - \frac{1}{\varepsilon}\partial_v L\left(q(\theta+\varepsilon), \frac{1}{\varepsilon}\big(q(\theta+\varepsilon) - q(\theta)\big)\right) \\
+ \frac{1}{\varepsilon}\partial_v L\left(q(\theta), \frac{1}{\varepsilon}\big(q(\theta) - q(\theta-\varepsilon)\big)\right) = 0\,.
\end{aligned}
\tag{17}
$$

From (17), it is clear that the dynamics of the optimal trajectory is that of a delay system, and more precisely,

$$q(\theta) \text{ is a function of } \theta, q\left(\theta - \varepsilon\right), q(\theta - 2\varepsilon). \tag{18}$$

Function q is the solution of the two-step finite-difference scheme (17). Because $q_0(\theta)$ is known for $-\varepsilon \leq \theta \leq 0$, the knowledge of $q(\theta)$ for $0 \leq \theta \leq \varepsilon$ is generically sufficient for solving the scheme (17) under the form (18). The knowledge of q_0 on $[-\varepsilon, \varepsilon]$ is equivalent to the knowledge of the discrete derivative $d_\varepsilon^+ q(\theta)$ for $-\varepsilon \leq \theta \leq 0$. Let us define this initial variation $(d_\varepsilon^+ q)_0$ as

$$\left(d_\varepsilon^+ q\right)_0 (\theta) = \frac{1}{\varepsilon}\left(q(\theta + \varepsilon) - q(\theta)\right), \quad -\varepsilon \leq \theta \leq 0. \tag{19}$$

From the knowledge of $q_0(\theta)$ and $(d_\varepsilon^+ q)_0$ we construct *a priori* without major difficulty the continuous trajectory q solution of (17) of the type (18) for $0 \leq \theta \leq t$. We obtain in this way a "final state" q^f which is now a piece of trajectory q:

$$q^f(\theta) = q(t + \theta), \quad -\varepsilon \leq \theta \leq 0.$$

This leads to the functional $Q_t : (d_\varepsilon^- q)_0 \longmapsto q^f = Q_t\left((d_\varepsilon^+ q)_0\right)$ defined from $\mathcal{C}([-\varepsilon, 0])$ to $\mathcal{C}([-\varepsilon, 0])$, for q_0 fixed. We suppose this functional to be one to one. In consequence, we can suppose the optimal trajectory parameterized by the final state $q^f \in \mathcal{C}([-\varepsilon, 0])$. We denote by $S(t, q^f)$ the corresponding optimal action. We observe that at fixed q_0, it depends only on the final time t and the final state q^f whereas the action A is a functional of all the states along the whole trajectory.

Proposition 2. Derivative of the optimal action
Under a variation δq^f of the final state, the optimal action admits a variation $\delta S(t, q^f)$ given by

$$\delta S(t, q^f) \equiv \frac{\partial S}{\partial q^f} \bullet \delta q^f = \int_{t-\varepsilon}^{t} \left[\partial_x L + \frac{1}{\varepsilon} \partial_v L\right]\left(q(\theta), (d_\varepsilon^- q)(\theta)\right) \delta q(\theta)\, d\theta. \tag{20}$$

Proof of Proposition 2.
Due to the discrete Euler-Lagrange equations (16), the optimal trajectory vanishes the third term of the right hand side of the relation (15). The first one is identically null because the initial condition q_0 remains fixed. The result is then a simple consequence of the relation (15) when time t is fixed.   □

In the right hand side of relation (20) the final state is not explicit. In order to exhibit the variation δq^f we introduce

$$\Gamma(t, q^f)(\theta) \equiv \left(\partial_v L + \varepsilon\, \partial_x L\right)\left(q(t + \theta), (d_\varepsilon^- q)(t + \theta)\right), \quad -\varepsilon \leq \theta \leq 0. \tag{21}$$

Then, $\Gamma(t, q^f) \in \mathcal{C}([-\varepsilon, 0])$ and relation (20) can be also written as

$$\frac{\partial S}{\partial q^f} \bullet \delta q^f = \frac{1}{\varepsilon} \int_{-\varepsilon}^{0} \Gamma(t, q^f)(\theta)\, \delta q^f(\theta)\, d\theta. \tag{22}$$

Let us observe that expression $\Gamma(t, q^f)$ is a good candidate for a momentum variable analogous to the one that satisfies the relation (6) in differentiable mechanics.

The natural question is now to determinate the "total variation" with time of the optimal action, *id est* the discrete analogous of the expression (7). This is not possible if we restrict to solely continuous trajectories. Nevertheless we propose a result for a discrete variation in time of amplitude exactly equal to ε. We denote by $\widetilde{q}^f$ the trajectory obtained from the final state q^f after a time extension of amplitude ε: $\widetilde{q}^f(\theta) \equiv q(t + \varepsilon + \theta)$ for $-\varepsilon \leq \theta \leq 0$. Then we have a simple expression for the difference $S(t + \varepsilon, \widetilde{q}^f) - S(t, q^f)$ because the two integrals in (14) operates on the same optimal trajectory:

$$S(t + \varepsilon, \widetilde{q}^f) - S(t, q^f) = \int_t^{t+\varepsilon} L\Big(q(\theta), \big(\mathrm{d}_\varepsilon^- q\big)(\theta)\Big) \, \mathrm{d}\theta. \tag{23}$$

Proposition 3. Discrete variation of the optimal action
Let ξ be a continuous function in the space $\mathcal{C}([-\varepsilon, 0])$. We have

$$S(t, q^f + \xi) - S(t, q^f) = \frac{1}{\varepsilon} \int_{-\varepsilon}^0 \left[\int_0^1 \Gamma(t, q^f + \eta\,\xi)(\theta) \, \mathrm{d}\eta \right] \xi(\theta) \, \mathrm{d}\theta. \tag{24}$$

Proof of Proposition 3.
We introduce $\Phi(\eta) \equiv S(t, q^f + \eta\,\xi)$ for $0 \leq \eta \leq 1$. It is a derivable function of the real variable η and we have

$$\frac{\mathrm{d}\Phi}{\mathrm{d}\eta} = \frac{\partial S}{\partial q^f}(t, q^f + \eta\,\xi) \bullet \frac{\mathrm{d}}{\mathrm{d}\eta}(q^f + \eta\,\xi) = \frac{\partial S}{\partial q^f}(t, q^f + \eta\,\xi) \bullet \xi$$

$$= \frac{1}{\varepsilon} \int_{-\varepsilon}^0 \Gamma(t, q^f + \eta\,\xi)(\theta) \, \xi(\theta) \, \mathrm{d}\theta.$$

Then the relation (24) is obtained by integration relative to $\eta \in [0, 1]$ and using Fubini theorem. $\qquad \square$

Then, we present here the main result of this contribution.

Proposition 4. Discrete temporal variation of the optimal action
Let $\Gamma_\varepsilon(t, q^f)$ be a mean value at final time t of the momentum introduced in (21):

$$\Gamma_\varepsilon(t, q^f)(\theta) \equiv \int_0^1 \Gamma\big(t+\varepsilon,\, q^f + \varepsilon\,\eta\,(\mathrm{d}_\varepsilon^- q)(t+\varepsilon+\theta)\big)(\theta) \, \mathrm{d}\eta, \qquad -\varepsilon \leq \theta \leq 0. \tag{25}$$

The following discrete Hamilton-Jacobi type equation holds

$$\mathrm{d}_\varepsilon^+ S + \frac{1}{\varepsilon} \int_{-\varepsilon}^0 \Gamma_\varepsilon(t, q^f)(\theta) \, (\mathrm{d}_\varepsilon^- q)(t + \varepsilon + \theta)) \, \mathrm{d}\theta$$

$$- \frac{1}{\varepsilon} \int_t^{t+\varepsilon} L\Big(q(\tau), (\mathrm{d}_\varepsilon^- q)(\tau)\Big) \, \mathrm{d}\tau = 0. \tag{26}$$

Proof of Proposition 4.

We recall that $\mathrm{d}_\varepsilon^+ S \equiv \dfrac{1}{\varepsilon}\left(S(t+\varepsilon,\, q^{\mathrm f})-S(t,\, q^{\mathrm f})\right)$. Then we have the decomposition

$$\varepsilon\,\mathrm{d}_\varepsilon^+ S = -\left(S(t+\varepsilon,\, \widehat{q}^{\,\mathrm f}) - S(t+\varepsilon,\, q^{\mathrm f})\right) + \left(S(t+\varepsilon,\, \widehat{q}^{\,\mathrm f}) - S(t,\, q^{\mathrm f})\right).$$

We remark also that $\widehat{q}^{\,\mathrm f}(\theta)-q^{\mathrm f}(\theta) = q(t+\varepsilon+\theta)-q(t+\theta) = \varepsilon\left(\mathrm{d}_\varepsilon^- q\right)(t+\varepsilon+\theta)$. Then we have from (24) with $\xi = \epsilon\left(\mathrm{d}_\varepsilon^- q\right)(t+\varepsilon+\theta)$:

$$S(t+\varepsilon,\, \widehat{q}^{\,\mathrm f}) - S(t+\varepsilon,\, q^{\mathrm f}) =$$

$$= \frac{1}{\varepsilon}\int_{-\varepsilon}^0 \left[\int_0^1 \Gamma\left(t+\varepsilon,\, q^{\mathrm f}+\varepsilon\,\eta\left(\mathrm{d}_\varepsilon^- q\right)(t+\varepsilon+\theta)\right)(\theta)\,\mathrm{d}\eta\right]\left(\widehat{q}^{\,\mathrm f}(\theta)-q^{\mathrm f}(\theta)\right)\mathrm{d}\theta$$

$$= \frac{1}{\varepsilon}\int_{-\varepsilon}^0 \left[\int_0^1 \Gamma\left(t+\varepsilon,\, q^{\mathrm f}+\varepsilon\,\eta\left(\mathrm{d}_\varepsilon^- q\right)(t+\varepsilon+\theta)\right)(\theta)\,\mathrm{d}\eta\right]\varepsilon\left(\mathrm{d}_\varepsilon^- q\right)(t+\varepsilon+\theta)\,\mathrm{d}\theta$$

and the second term of the left hand side of the relation (26) is clear. The end of the proof is a consequence of the decomposition of $\varepsilon\,\mathrm{d}_\varepsilon^+ S$ and relation (23). □

The analogy between the classical Hamilton-Jacobi equation (8) and the discrete version (26) is clear. We observe that the Lagrangian is replaced by its mean value on an interval of size ε. Moreover the natural associated momentum $\Gamma_\varepsilon(t,\, q^{\mathrm f})(\theta)$ defined at relation (25) is not *a priori* strictly equal to the momentum $\Gamma(t,\, q^{\mathrm f})(\theta)$ introduced at relation (21). This splitting at the discrete scale of the moment p satisfying both relations (4) and (6) is a real difficulty that we will consider in a future contribution.

5 Towards Complex-Valued Discrete-Measured Velocity

The discrete scaled velocity $v_\varepsilon = \mathrm{d}_\varepsilon^- q$ introduced in section 4 is purely real. We consider now a complex discrete velocity v_ε. Following an idea proposed by Nottale [12], we introduce a discrete complex derivation operator $\square_\varepsilon$ according to

$$\left(\square_\varepsilon q\right)(\theta) \equiv \frac{1}{2\,\varepsilon}\left(q(\theta+\varepsilon)-q(\theta-\varepsilon)\right) + \frac{i\,\mu}{2\,\varepsilon}\left(q(\theta+\varepsilon)-2\,q(\theta)+q(\theta-\varepsilon)\right), \quad (27)$$

with $\mu^2 = 1$. We decompose the discrete operator $\square_\varepsilon q$ under the form $\square_\varepsilon q \equiv \square_\varepsilon^{\mathrm r} q + i\,\mu\,\square_\varepsilon^{\mathrm i} q$. We have

$$\left(\square_\varepsilon^{\mathrm r} q\right)(\theta) \equiv \frac{1}{2\,\varepsilon}\left(q(\theta+\varepsilon)-q(\theta-\varepsilon)\right) = \frac{1}{2}\left(\mathrm{d}_\varepsilon^+ q(\theta)+\mathrm{d}_\varepsilon^- q(\theta)\right)$$

$$\left(\square_\varepsilon^{\mathrm i} q\right)(\theta) \equiv \frac{1}{2\,\varepsilon}\left(q(\theta+\varepsilon)-2\,q(\theta)+q(\theta-\varepsilon)\right) = \frac{1}{2}\left(\mathrm{d}_\varepsilon^+ q(\theta)-\mathrm{d}_\varepsilon^- q(\theta)\right). \tag{28}$$

The real part $\square_\varepsilon^{\mathrm r} q$ is the standard time derivative for regular trajectories when ε goes to 0. The imaginary part $\square_\varepsilon^{\mathrm i} q$ is asymptotically null for a regular function and accounts for the slope jump at a given time. This framework has been proven to be well-posed by Cresson and Greff [3] introducing a limit when ε goes to zero in a well-defined projection functional space.

As remarked previously, the appropriate generalization of the kinetic energy $\frac{m}{2} v^2$ is obtained by taking the (complex) square of the momentum operator. So in the expression of the Lagrangian we have to replace v^2 by $(\Box_\varepsilon q)^2$. We set

$$K_\varepsilon \equiv \frac{m}{2} (\Box_\varepsilon q)^2 = \frac{m}{2} \left[(\Box_\varepsilon^r q)^2 - (\Box_\varepsilon^i q)^2 + 2 i \mu (\Box_\varepsilon^r q)(\Box_\varepsilon^i q) \right]. \tag{29}$$

If K_ε is real, i.e. $\operatorname{Im} K_\varepsilon = 0$, the product $(\Box_\varepsilon^r q)(\Box_\varepsilon^i q)$ is null and two cases occur.

(i)   If $K_\varepsilon \geq 0$, then $\Box_\varepsilon^i q = 0$ and we have a natural reference to a regular trajectory.

(ii)   If $K_\varepsilon < 0$, then then $\Box_\varepsilon^r q = 0$. The position $q(\theta)$ is essentially unchanged during one ε-step but the jump is not null and the direction of the trajectory has changed abruptly.

If the kinetic energy is imaginary, $\operatorname{Re} K_\varepsilon = 0$ and we have $(\Box_\varepsilon^r q)^2 = (\Box_\varepsilon^i q)^2$ that implies $d_\varepsilon^+ q(\theta) = 0$ or $d_\varepsilon^- q(\theta) = 0$. The particle has not moved just before time t or just after!

We consider now the iterate of the operator $\Box_\varepsilon$ with itself. This type of algebraic formula is natural for the extension of $\frac{d}{dt}\left(m \frac{d}{dt}\right)$ in the Euler-Lagrange equation. We emphasise the role of $\mu^2 = 1$ when we consider the composed operator. We have

$$\begin{cases} \operatorname{Re}\left((\Box_\varepsilon \circ \Box_\varepsilon)q\right) = (1 - \mu^2)\left(\Box_\varepsilon^r \circ \Box_\varepsilon^r\right)q + \mu^2 \left(\Box_{\frac{\varepsilon}{2}}^r \circ \Box_{\frac{\varepsilon}{2}}^r\right)q \\ \operatorname{Im}\left((\Box_\varepsilon \circ \Box_\varepsilon)q\right) = 2\mu \left(\Box_\varepsilon^r \circ \Box_\varepsilon^i\right)q. \end{cases}$$

Roughly speaking the product "jump by jump" allows to recover some regularity at a smaller scale $\varepsilon/2$.

We propose to introduce the following complex action for $q \in \mathcal{C}([-\varepsilon, t + \varepsilon])$:

$$A_\varepsilon(t, q) \equiv \int_0^t L\big(q(\theta), (\Box_\varepsilon q)(\theta)\big)\, d\theta = \int_0^t \left[\frac{m}{2} (\Box_\varepsilon q)^2 - \varphi(q(\theta)) \right] d\theta.$$

Our working plan follows the ideas presented in sections 2 and 3. In an analogous way as the one proposed in section 3, we will consider the Euler-Lagrange optimality condition, introduce the optimal trajectories, derive a Hamilton-Jacobi like equation for the optimal value of the action. Then make the change of variable (9) to transform the evolution equation (26) into a Schrödinger type equation.

References

1. Bitbol, M.: Mécanique quantique, une introduction philosophique. Champs-Flammarion, Paris (1997)

2. Bohm, D., Hiley, B.J.: The Undivided Universe: An Ontological Interpretation of Quantum Theory. Routledge, New York (1993)
3. Cresson, J., Greff, I.: Non-differentiable embedding of Lagrangian systems and partial differential equations. Journal of Mathematical Analysis and Applications 384(2), 626–646 (2011)
4. d'Espagnat, B.: Le réel voilé; Analyse des concepts quantiques. Fayard, Paris (1994)
5. Filk, T., von Müller, A.: Quantum physics and consciousness: The quest for a common conceptual foundation. Mind and Matter 7, 59–79 (2009)
6. Friedberg, R., Lee, T.D.: Discrete Quantum Mechanics. Nuclear Physics B 225(1), 1–52 (1983)
7. Gondran, M.: Complex calculus of variations and explicit solutions for complex Hamilton-Jacobi equations. C. R. Acad. Sci. Paris 332(1), 677–680 (2001); Complex analytical mechanics, complex nonstandard stochastic process and quantum mechanics. C. R. Acad. Sci. Paris 333(1), 593–598 (2001)
8. Greenspan, D.: A new explicit discrete mechanics with applications. J. Franklin Institute 294, 231–240 (1972)
9. Khrennikov, A., Volovich, J.I.: Discrete time dynamical models and their quantumlike context-dependent properties. J. Modern Optics 51(6/7), 113–114 (2004)
10. Khrennikov, A.: Discrete time dynamics. In: Contextual Approach to Quantum Formalism, ch. 12, Springer, Heidelberg (2009)
11. Nelson, E.: Derivation of the Schrödinger Equation from Newtonian Mechanics. Physical Review 150, 1079–1085 (1966)
12. Nottale, L.: Fractal space-time and microphysics: towards a theory of scale relativity, p. 333. World Scientific (1993)
13. Odake, S., Sasaki, R.: Discrete Quantum Mechanics. Journal of Physics A: Mathematical and Theoretical 44(35), 353001 (2011)
14. Schrödinger, E.: Quantizierung als Eigenwertproblem (Erste Mitteilung). Annalen der Physik 79, 361–376; Über das Verhältnis der Heisenberg Born Jordanischen Quantenmechanik zu der meinen. Annalen der Physik 79, 734–756 (1926)

Real, Complex, and Binary Semantic Vectors

Dominic Widdows[1] and Trevor Cohen[2]

[1] Microsoft Bing
[2] University of Texas School of Biomedical Informatics at Houston

Abstract. This paper presents a combined structure for using real, complex, and binary valued vectors for semantic representation. The theory, implementation, and application of this structure are all significant.

For the theory underlying quantum interaction, it is important to develop a core set of mathematical operators that describe systems of information, just as core mathematical operators in quantum mechanics are used to describe the behavior of physical systems. The system described in this paper enables us to compare more traditional quantum mechanical models (which use complex state vectors), alongside more generalized quantum models that use real and binary vectors.

The implementation of such a system presents fundamental computational challenges. For large and sometimes sparse datasets, the demands on time and space are different for real, complex, and binary vectors. To accommodate these demands, the Semantic Vectors package has been carefully adapted and can now switch between different number types comparatively seamlessly.

This paper describes the key abstract operations in our semantic vector models, and describes the implementations for real, complex, and binary vectors. We also discuss some of the key questions that arise in the field of quantum interaction and informatics, explaining how the wide availability of modelling options for different number fields will help to investigate some of these questions.

1   Introduction

The contribution described in this paper is a learning and representation system that enables vector models to be built easily using real, complex, or binary numbers as coordinates for semantic vectors.

Quantum mechanics, statistical machine learning, and hyperdimensional computing have used some notion of state-vector or feature-vector for decades. While these and many other fields use common mathematical vector-space theories, in practice they often differ in their choice of a ground-field, or basic number type. That is, if a vector is a list of coordinates, what sort of numbers should the coordinates be?

In quantum mechanics, and other areas of physics including electromagnetism, complex numbers are indispensable. The Schrödinger equations and Pauli matrices involve complex numbers explicitly, complex numbers are part of the relationship between positions and momenta, and complex Hilbert spaces are

J.R. Busemeyer et al. (Eds.): QI 2012, LNCS 7620, pp. 24–35, 2012.

so normal that the logic of projections in Hilbert space is sometimes called a Standard Logic [1, Ch 1].

Logical semantics and computer science, on the other hand, use mainly binary and set theoretic representations, stemming from George Boole's innovation of describing an Aristotelian predicate as a mapping from a set of objects to the binary numbers [2]. Representations in information theory and modern computing assume an underlying quantized bit-vector, and in software engineering, a 'real number' is really a string of bits mediated by IEEE standards. Standard logic in these fields is Boolean logic.

The growing community of practice in statistical machine learning uses real vectors for most representations. Feature vectors are used to describe items to be classified or ranked, and the features are most often measurable quantities (such as the redness of a pixel in an image, or the weight of a particular term in a given document). This makes idea of using real numbers as features intuitively practical, and standard statistical distributions and techniques are so readily available that the use of 'real' mathematics leaves little to be desired in many successful applications to date [3].

Today, the sciences of intelligence are part of this arena as well. Artificial intelligence and computational linguistics have grown, and partly shifted from an emphasis on binary and logical representations to real and statistical ones. Psychological and cognitive applications of real vectors and their similarities include Prototype Theory [4], Pathfinder Networks [5], and the Conceptual Spaces of Gardenförs [6]. Kanerva's hyperdimensional computing [7] (and of course, Boole's Laws of Thought [8]) use binary representations to model cognitive processes of learning, remembering, and reasoning. The use of complex numbers to model cognitive processes is still apparently in its infancy (see for example [9,10]), but we might well expect this area to grow as well.

Another rapidly growing area is the application of more sophisticated product operations in semantic vector space models. For many decades, the main operations used in vector space models were just vector addition for composition and the cosine or related measures for judging similarity. Though many other operations are well-known in the theoretical literature (for summaries, see e.g., [11,12]), practical implementations have lagged behind, partly for computational reasons. This has changed dramatically over the past few years: several operators have been used successfully in practice to model word-order dependencies [13,14] and operations such as verb-argument binding [15,16], adjective-noun modification [17], and formal ontological relationships [18]. The old notion that distributional semantics is a 'bag-of-words' methodology has been comprehensively superseded, at least in the research literature.

The accelerated development of so many sciences and technologies has naturally left many possible combinations of empirical challenge and mathematical representation unexplored. That is (for example), there are many cognitive models or machine learning tasks to which complex or binary vector representations have not been applied. Of course, if complex numbers, including their so-called 'imaginary' parts, turned out to be a key to modelling mental processes, we might be surprised and skeptical: but perhaps no more surprised than we should already be at the usefulness of imaginary numbers in electrical engineering.

Some strides have already been made in statistical learning using complex numbers [10] (with theory based on [9]), and with binary numbers [19] (with theory based on [7]). The project undertaken by the authors, and reported in this paper, is to unify these mathematical options in a system that makes it possible to easily experiment with all three (and potentially more) standard ground fields for vector representations. The system is implemented and released in the Semantic Vectors package [20], an open-source package that can be freely downloaded from `semanticvectors.googlecode.com`. For real, binary, and complex vectors, the package now supports training of term and document based semantic models, and makes available a range of product operators for learning similarity, directional, and logical relationships.

This paper is organized as follows. Section 2 describes the mathematical abstractions supported in all representations. Sections 3, 4, and 5 describe the specific operators and implementation decisions for real, complex, and binary vectors respectively. Section 6 discusses the relationship with quantum interaction in more detail. The models used in practice have some significant similarities and differences with the 'classical' quantum mechanical model of complex Hilbert space, and this can be used to shed fresh insight on the important question of what generalizations are appropriate in generalized quantum structures. While this section draws some points in conclusion, readers whose primary interest is in quantum interaction and generalized quantum structures may consider reading Section 6 first. Section 7 briefly refers to experiments conducted using the system. These experiments are described in full in a separate paper.

2   Common Mathematical Operators

This section owes much to the theoretical framework of Kanerva's hyperdimensional computing [7], and the experimental implementation and notation used in [19]. Some of the core concepts are from the literature on Vector Symbolic Architectures (see [9,12,11] and others). Please refer to these papers for detailed motivation: due to space constraints, many of the more subtle points are not discussed in this section.

The goal (as with much of abstract mathematics) is to define a core set of operations that all semantic vector models should support, and rules surrounding these operations. The most basic rules are listed in Table 2. To date, it is better to think of these as rules of thumb, rather than formal axioms that described an algebraic structure such as a group or lattice: such a hardened theory may arise from this work in the future, but it is not yet here.

There are many key discussion points that make these vector systems functionally appealing. In high dimensions, they are easy to build. Randomly allocated elemental vectors are overwhelmingly likely to be unrelated (e.g., pseudo-orthogonal), and large numbers of these elemental vectors can be created before there is any appreciable danger of confusing two vectors. It follows from this that

Table 1. The core mathematical operations performed on representation vectors

- **Generate Random Vector**. Creates a random vector that can be used to represent an elemental concept.
- **Measure Overlap**. Measures the similarity between two vectors A and B: a real number, $A \cdot B$, typically between 0 (no similarity) and 1 (exact match). Negative values are possible. The overlap between two randomly generated elemental vectors should be near to zero (or some other value that means 'no significant overlap').
- **Superpose**. Takes two vectors A and B and generates a third vector $A + B$, such that $A \cdot (A + B)$ and $B \cdot (A + B)$ are relatively large. Superposition is sometimes called *bundling* in the literature.
  - Superpositions can be weighted by any real (in practice, double-precision floating point) number.
  - This, and the presence of a zero vector, gives us the practical ability to perform regular 'scalar multiplication', at least with real number scaling factors.
- **Normalize** Takes a vector A and rescales it to a vector $\hat{A}$ such that $\hat{A} \cdot \hat{A} = 1$.
- **Bind**. Takes two vectors A and B and generates a third vector $A \otimes B$, such that $A \cdot (A \otimes B)$ and $B \cdot (A \otimes B)$ are usually near to zero.
- **Release**. Inverse of bind, written as $A \oslash B$. Should behave in such a way that $(A \oslash (A \otimes B)) \cdot B \approx 1$.

Operator precedence when written is as expected: $+$ comes before $\otimes$ which comes before $\oslash$ which comes before $\cdot$.

superposition is normally quite easy and natural to define (natural in the mathematical sense, that a choice of overlap measure makes some particular choice of superposition operator appealing).

Binding is different: given a choice of overlap measure, there are usually many options for defining an appropriate binding operation. This leaves much freedom for choosing options that are computationally appealing: as we will see in the implementation sections, this is important for building tractable systems. Since many binding operations are available, hybrid systems that use more than one binding operation to represent different semantic combination operations are quite likely to emerge.

Training a model — that is, the process of deriving semantically significant representation vectors from elemental vectors and a training corpus — can then be performed in linear time by taking linear combinations of elemental vectors. Many details of available training processes are available in our earlier works, e.g., [20]. There are several more algorithmically sophisticated training techniques available, including singular value decomposition (see [21] and related literature).

In practice, these core vector operations are declared by a `Vector` interface and implemented by all vector types. Note that the use of an interface (as opposed an abstract base class containing some shared implementation) means that we are making no presuppositions about the physical representation of vectors: in particular, we do not explicitly assume that vectors are lists of coordinates. The implementations so far released in Semantic Vectors are indeed coordinate-based, but coordinate-free representations are not unthinkable.

Other mathematical operations including orthogonalization are supported as utility functions derived from the primitive operations. This allows representations to make use of quantum-logical connectives for search (see [22, Ch 8]). Optimized linear-time search and k-nearest-neighbour ranking are implemented. Each vector implementation is also required to implement common serialization operations, for e.g., writing to long-term storage hardware. In practice, each vector implementation comes with lightweight (often sparse) representations to support large numbers of elemental vectors, and more costly representations for dense semantic vectors.

This concludes our summary of the operations common to all vectors. We will now proceed to describe the three implementations available so far, for vectors using real, complex, and binary numbers as coordinates.

3   Real Vectors

The use of real vectors for representation in empirical learning is by far the most common choice of ground-field to date. In the Semantic Vectors package, real vectors are implemented using single-precision, 4-byte floating point numbers. Randomly-generated elemental vectors are sparse ternary vectors: ternary, meaning that they use only values from the set $\{-1, 0, 1\}$, and sparse, meaning that most values are left as zero. Superposition is implemented using standard component-wise vector addition, and overlap is measured using cosine similarity [22, Ch 5].

For binding, options in the literature include:

- Superposition after permutation of coordinates (introduced by [14]). That is, $A \otimes B$ is implemented by permuting the coordinates of B and then superposing with A. Since there are $n!$ possible permutations, there are $n!$ possible binding operations. The availability of so many options has been used to give different permutations based on the number of words between two terms [14], and to represent different semantic relationships from a knowledge base [19].
- Convolution of vectors, as described in [9]. This was used to model word-order relationships by [13].

Due to computational considerations, the operation used for binding real vectors in the Semantic Vectors package is permutation of coordinates, though an implementation of circular convolution using fast Fourier transforms is available in codebase.

We note in passing that traditional LSA (that is, the creation of a reduced term-document matrix using singular value decomposition) is only available for real vectors.

4   Complex Vectors

The use of complex numbers for semantic representation is discussed in [9] and was first introduced to the Semantic Vectors package in [10]. The extra richness over real representations comes largely from complex multiplication, which has a an angular or 'turning' effect. This has powerful consequences. For example, since complex multiplication can effectively turn a vector through a right angle, multiplication can turn a cosine similarity of 1 to a cosine similarity of 0. This makes multiplication an effective candidate for the bind operation. The variety of effective options available has encouraged us to implement two different modes for complex vectors: a Cartesian mode where rectilinear options are used by default, and a polar mode where circular operations are used. In more detail, the operations for complex numbers implemented in Semantic Vectors are as follows.

Random elemental vectors have coordinates that are either zero, or elements of the unit circle group $U(1)$ of complex numbers whose modulus is 1. This is an apt generalization of elemental real ternary vectors, since the set $\{-1, 1\}$ is the intersection of the circle group $U(1)$ and the real line. Both sparse vectors (mainly zeros) and dense vectors (all coordinates members of $U(1)$) have been used in practice, and changing this is an easy command-line configuration. As an optimization, a lookup table for sines and cosines of angles is created, and many of the procedures involving complex number multiplication are implemented using addition of keys in this table. Such a key is often called a *phase angle*.

In polar mode, entries remain confined to the unit circle, and normalization is implemented by projecting each complex coordinate (that is, each pair of real coordinates) to the corresponding angle on the unit circle. Of course, this projection is undefined for zero entries. For this reason, we have introduced a zero element in the angle lookup table, with expected the rule that the zero element maps any other value to zero under multiplication.

The main operations in each mode are as follows:

- **Measure Overlap**
  - In polar mode, normalized sum of differences between each pair of corresponding phase angles.
  - In Cartesian mode, the cosine similarity of the corresponding real vectors: in other words, the real part of the standard Hermitian scalar product.
- **Superposition**
  - In polar mode, the weighted average of the corresponding phase angles. This operation is not associative: angles added later in the process have more significance.
  - In Cartesian mode, standard complex vector addition.
- **Normalization**
  - In polar mode, mapping each complex number to the corresponding phase angle.
  - In Cartesian mode, scaling each coordinate so that the sum of the squares is equal to 1.
- **Binding**
  - In polar mode, circular convolution. The key observation here is that, because the representation is already in a phase angle form, it is in the

'frequency domain' and no Fourier transform is necessary for optimization. Thus, circular convolution is simply the addition of phase angles [9,10].

- In Cartesian form, no such optimization is so naturally available, and permutation of coordinates is used instead.

– **Release** naturally used the inverse of the corresponding bind operations.

Thus the system for complex semantic vectors has the option of treating a complex number as essentially a rectilinear construct, or as essentially a circular construct. These could be combined further by introducing a modulus representation as well as the phase angle representation. We have not done this yet, partly for computational performance reasons, and partly because the virtues of the two representations are still actively under investigation, and we feel that conflating them may be premature.

5 Binary Vectors

The binary vector representation utilized in Semantic Vectors follows the approach originated by Pentti Kanerva, known as the Binary Spatter Code (BSC) [23]. The BSC depends upon hyperdimensional (d on the order of 10,000) binary vectors. As in our other representations, these can be categorized as elemental vectors and semantic vectors, where elemental vectors are randomly constructed so as to be approximately orthogonal to one another, and semantic vectors are generated by superposition of elemental vectors during the training process. However, there are a number of important differences between this and the other representations we have discussed up to this point.

Firstly, distance in the binary space is measured using the Hamming Distance (HD), a count of the number of bits that differ between two vectors (for example, $HD(1001, 0111) = 3$). Orthogonality is defined as a HD of half the dimensionality of the space [24] — a normalized HD of 0.5. This is in keeping with the construction of elemental vectors, which are constructed by distributing an equal number of 1's and 0's at random across the dimensionality of the space. While these vectors are therefore not sparse in the sense of having mostly zero values, the *space* is sparsely occupied in the sense that elemental vectors tend to be far apart from one another. A set of elemental vectors constructed in this manner will have a mean pairwise HD of $\frac{d}{2}$, with a standard deviation of $\frac{\sqrt{d}}{2}$ As the pairwise distances are normally distributed, this implies that in a 10,000 dimensional space, we'd anticipate approximately 99.7 percent of elemental vectors having a HD from one another of between 4700 and 5300. This sparseness of the space confers a level of robustness to the model, as an elemental vector can be distorted considerably while remaining closer to its original self than to any other elemental vector in the space.

Superposition of binary vectors occurs by summing up the number of 1's and 0's in each dimension across all of the binary vectors added. If there are more 1's than 0's in a dimension, the superposition is assigned the value 1. If there are more 0's, a zero is assigned, and ties are broken at random (this can only occur when an even number of vectors are superposed). So the superposition of 01 and 00 could be either 00 or 01, each with a probability of 0.5. The need to keep track of the votes in each dimension raises an interesting implementation issue, as the memory requirements of retaining an exhaustive voting record for a set of 10,000 dimensional vectors prohibit assigning a floating point number to each dimension, and Semantic Vectors often retains a store of term or document vectors in memory during the superposition process.

Consequently, we have opted for a space-optimized implementation of the voting record, comprising of an ordered array of binary vectors, implemented using Lucene's OpenBitSet class. This implementation also allows for superposition to occur using efficient bitwise operators, without the need for iteration across the $O(10,000)$ dimensions individually, as illustrated in Table 2. This is accomplished by maintaining a temporary 'cursor' vector, of the same dimensionality as the rows, and performing a series of sequential bitwise XOR and NOT operations. The superposition can be weighted by initiating the process at an appropriate level of the voting record, and the size of the voting record can be constrained by maintaining a global minimum value and ensuring that only values beyond this are stored in the record.

Table 2. Space Optimized Superposition. VR = Voting Record. CV = Cursor Vector (initially, the vector to be superposed). $\hat{VR}$ = altered Voting Record (VR XOR CV). $\hat{CV}$ = altered Cursor Vector (CV NOT $\hat{VR}$).

Row	VR	CV	$\hat{VR}$	$\hat{CV}$
1	1 0 1	1 0 1	0 0 0	1 0 1
2	0 1 1	1 0 1	1 1 0	0 0 1
3	0 0 0	0 0 1	0 0 1	0 0 0
Value	1 2 3		2 2 4	

Once the voting is complete, the value in each dimension is calculated. If this is more than a half of the number of votes in total, a one is assigned to the superposition product in this dimension. If it is less than half, a zero is assigned, and ties are broken at random. The binary vector implementation also facilitates binding, which is an invertible multiplication-like operator that is used to combine vectors with one another. In the BSC [23], elementwise exclusive OR (XOR) is used to accomplish binding. As this operator is its own inverse, is also used to reverse the binding process. It is also possible to accomplish reversible transformation using a permutation, by shifting or swapping the bits of a vector. As elementwise operations on hyperdimensional binary vectors are computationally inconvenient, Semantic Vectors implements permutation 64 bits at a time, by shifting or swapping the elements of the array of *long* integers that underlie Lucene's binary vector (OpenBitSet) implementation.

In addition to the fundamental Vector Symbolic operations of superposition (or bundling) and binding [12], we have implemented binary approximations of orthogonalization, and quantum disjunction [25]. Orthogonality in binary vector space is defined by a HD of a half of the dimensionality of the space. Give two similar vectors, A and B, A can be rendered almost-orthogonal to B by introducing random noise in dimensions that these vectors have in common. Conversely, two vectors with a HD of more than half the dimensionality can be rendered orthogonal by randomly selecting dimensions in which these vectors differ, and changing them accordingly. The binary approximation of orthogonalization facilitates a binary approximation of quantum disjunction. This operator involves transforming the component vectors for disjunction into a subspace made up of mutually orthogonal vectors using the Gram-Schmidt procedure, so that no information is redundantly represented. Subsequently, a vector C can be compared to this subspace by measuring the length of C's projection in the subspace, $\hat{C}$, and comparing this to the length of C ($\frac{\|\hat{C}\|}{\|C\|}$ is the cosine of the angle between C and the subspace). In binary space, we approximate this projection by adding together the normalized HD - 0.5 between the vector C and each of the components of the subspace, to provide a measure of the extent to which the cumulative similarity between the vector C and all of the components of the subspace is greater than what one would anticipate by chance.

6   Typed Vectors and Quantum Interaction

This section examines the mathematical structures we have developed from the point of view of quantum interaction and informatics. Our hope here is that comparing the behaviour of real, binary, and complex vectors will help to answer one of the most pertinent questions in Quantum Interaction: what makes a system "quantum" at all?

Some strong candidate answers to this question have been proposed. Some have suggested that Born's rule for probabilities is key, Aerts *et al.* have concentrated on the Bell inequalities [26], Bruza and Kitto on entanglement [27]. In information retrieval, quantum formalisms are central to the geometric models described by [28] and [22], the former focussing particularly on representing conditionals, and the latter on representing logical connectives.

There is an accompanying debate on how central the quantum properties should be: for example, is it proper to talk more about quantum-like or Generalized Quantum Systems following Khrennikov [29]. The situation is complicated by history: several properties of vector spaces (especially the logic of projection onto subspaces) were explored in the service of quantum mechanics, and even with hindsight it is not always easy to say which parts of the theory are necessarily quantum, and which would be better described as properties of all vector space models.

One property common to all our high-dimensional models is the sparseness of point distribution. Semantic vectors are not all sparse in the sense of having most coordinates equal to zero, but they are sparse in the sense of being very spread out in their spaces: there are very few actual elemental or semantic vectors compared with the number of points available. Thus, even those spaces that are continuous in theory (such as those based on real and complex numbers) are sparse and thus highly "quantized" in practice.

Thus, many of the quantized properties of semantic vector models arise generally, and not because of any special parallel with the quantum *mechanical* model of complex Hilbert space. For example, there is no preference yet discovered for self-adjoint operators in semantic vector models.

Here, our work has a particular contribution to make. We can now do many experiments in textual informatics while comparing complex, real, and binary vector space models. If a strong correspondence with quantum mechanics itself actually exists, we would expect to see complex Hilbert space representations to be distinctly superior for at least some modelling operations.

If, on the other hand, real or binary representations work best, we may come to the more guarded conclusion that our semantic models are (obviously) vector models, as are quantum Hilbert space models, but the similarity between semantic models and quantum mechanics goes no further. Such findings would even further motivate the question "What characterizes quantum systems?", rather than especially quantum *mechanical* systems. Consider the way the voting record for binary vectors is maintained during learning and quantized to binary values during normalization: the practical benefits of quantization itself are clearer in the binary representation than in either the real or complex representation. Many 'quantum' properties (such as entanglement and non-commutativity of observables) may be formulated with vectors and matrices over any ground field.

We note also that there our particular use of Vector Symbolic Architectures, which owes much to [9] and [7], is a specific class of vector models in which product operations yield other vectors. The mathematical options are of course much richer and sometimes demand more computational resources: for recent and empirically successful examples, see the use of tensor products [16] and matrices by [17].

7   Experiments and Evaluation

Using the system described in this paper, detailed experiments (using especially complex and binary vectors) have already been conducted on using multiple cues for analogical reasoning. These experiments use quantum disjunction to model the many possible relationships that could be used as premises to deduce new semantic relationships. Due to space constraints, these experiments are not described here but in a separate paper [30]. These experiments also introduce an innovative notion of 'binary quantum disjuction', which is altered from the standard real or complex version, partly because the average similarity between unrelated binary vectors is the normalized Hamming distance of 0.5. Of course, these are (we hope) the first of many experiments that will compare and adapt real, complex and binary techniques.

What we do present in the current paper is an appropriate computational framework (if you will, a laboratory) in which such experiments will be conducted.

We sincerely hope that comparisons between different ground fields for semantic representation will become the norm rather than the exception. If so, this will catalyze technological progress and lead to core scientific insight.

Acknowledgments. This research was supported in part by the US National Library of Medicine grant R21LM010826.

References

1. Varadarajan, V.S.: Geometry of Quantum Theory. Springer (1985)
2. Boole, G.: The Mathematical Analysis of Logic. Macmillan (1847) (republished by St Augustine's Press, 1998, introduction by John Slater)
3. Hastie, T., Tibshirani, R., Friedman, J.H.: The Elements of Statistical Learning. Springer Series in Statistics (2001)
4. Rosch, E.: Principles of categorization. In: Collins, A., Smith, E.E. (eds.) Readings in Cognitive Science: A Perspective from Psychology and Artificial Intelligence, Kaufmann, San Mateo, CA, pp. 312–322 (1988)
5. Schvaneveldt, R.W.: Pathfinder Associative Networks: Studies in Knowledge Organization. Intellect Books (1990)
6. Gärdenfors, P.: Conceptual Spaces: The Geometry of Thought. Bradford Books MIT Press (2000)
7. Kanerva, P.: Hyperdimensional computing: An introduction to computing in distributed representation with high-dimensional random vectors. Cognitive Computation 1(2), 139–159 (2009)
8. Boole, G.: An Investigation of the Laws of Thought. Macmillan (1854) Dover edition (1958)
9. Plate, T.: Holographic Reduced Representations: Distributed Representation for Cognitive Structures. CSLI Publications (2003)
10. de Vine, L., Bruza, P.: Semantic oscillations: Encoding context and structure in complex valued holographic vectors. In: Proceedings of the AAAI Fall Symposium on Quantum Informatics for Cognitive, Social, and Semantic Processes, QI 2010 (2010)
11. Aerts, D., Czachor, M., De Moor, B.: Geometric analogue of holographic reduced representation. Journal of Mathematical Psychology 53(5), 389–398 (2007)
12. Gayler, R.W.: Vector symbolic architectures answer Jackendoff's challenges for cognitive neuroscience. In: Slezak, P. (ed.) ICCS/ASCS International Conference on Cognitive Science, pp. 133–138. University of New South Wales, Sydney (2004)
13. Jones, M.N., Mewhort, D.J.K.: Representing word meaning and order information in a composite holographic lexicon, vol. 114, pp. 1–37 (2007)
14. Sahlgren, M., Holst, A., Kanerva, P.: Permutations as a means to encode order in word space. In: Proceedings of the 30th Annual Meeting of the Cognitive Science Society (CogSci 2008), Washington D.C., USA, July 23-26 (2008)
15. Widdows, D.: Semantic vector products: Some initial investigations. In: Proceedings of the Second International Symposium on Quantum Interaction (2008)
16. Grefenstette, E., Sadrzadeh, M.: Experimental support for a categorical compositional distributional model of meaning. In: Proceedings of the 2011 Conference on Empirical Methods in Natural Language Processing, EMNLP (2011)

17. Baroni, M., Zamparelli, R.: Nouns are vectors, adjectives are matrices: Representing adjective-noun constructions in semantic space. In: Proceedings of the 2011 Conference on Empirical Methods in Natural Language Processing, EMNLP (2010)
18. Cohen, T., Widdows, D., Schvaneveldt, R., Rindflesch, T.: Logical leaps and quantum connectives: Forging paths through predication space. In: Proceedings of the AAAI Fall Symposium on Quantum Informatics for Cognitive, Social, and Semantic Processes, QI 2010 (2010)
19. Cohen, T., Widdows, D., Schvaneveldt, R., Rindflesch, T.: Finding Schizophrenia's Prozac Emergent Relational Similarity in Predication Space. In: Song, D., Melucci, M., Frommholz, I., Zhang, P., Wang, L., Arafat, S. (eds.) QI 2011. LNCS, vol. 7052, pp. 48–59. Springer, Heidelberg (2011)
20. Widdows, D., Cohen, T.: The semantic vectors package: New algorithms and public tools for distributional semantics. In: Fourth IEEE International Conference on Semantic Computing, ICSC (2010)
21. Landauer, T., Dumais, S.: A solution to plato's problem: The latent semantic analysis theory of acquisition. Psychological Review 104(2), 211–240 (1997)
22. Widdows, D.: Geometry and Meaning. CSLI Publications (2004)
23. Kanerva, P.: Binary spatter-coding of ordered k-tuples. In: Artificial Neural Networks, ICANN 1996, pp. 869–873 (1996)
24. Kanerva, P.: Sparse distributed memory. The MIT Press, Cambridge (1988)
25. Widdows, D., Peters, S.: Word vectors and quantum logic. In: Proceedings of the Eighth Mathematics of Language Conference, Bloomington, Indiana (2003)
26. Aerts, D., Aerts, S., Broekaert, J., Gabora, L.: The violation of bell inequalities in the macroworld. Foundations of Physics 30, 1387–1414 (2000)
27. Galea, D., Bruza, P., Kitto, K., Nelson, D., McEvoy, C.: Modelling the Acitivation of Words in Human Memory: The Spreading Activation, Spooky-activation-at-a-distance and the Entanglement Models Compared. In: Song, D., Melucci, M., Frommholz, I., Zhang, P., Wang, L., Arafat, S. (eds.) QI 2011. LNCS, vol. 7052, pp. 149–160. Springer, Heidelberg (2011)
28. van Rijsbergen, K.: The Geometry of Information Retrieval. Cambridge University Press (2004)
29. Khrennikov, A.: Ubiquitous Quantum Structure: From Psychology to Finance. Springer (2010)
30. Cohen, T., Widdows, D., De Vine, L., Schvaneveldt, R., Rindflesch, T.C.: Many Paths Lead to Discovery: Analogical Retrieval of Cancer Therapies. In: Busemeyer, J.R., Dubois, F., Lambert-Mogiliansky, A. (eds.) QI 2012. LNCS, vol. 7620, pp. 90–101. Springer, Heidelberg (2012)

The Guppy Effect as Interference

Diederik Aerts[1], Jan Broekaert[1], Liane Gabora[2], and Tomas Veloz[2]

[1] Center Leo Apostel (Clea) and Department of Mathematics,
Brussels Free University (VUB), Pleinlaan 2, 1050 Brussel, Belgium
{diraerts,jbroekae}@vub.ac.be
[2] Department of Psychology and Mathematics,
University of British Columbia, Kelowna, British Columbia, Canada
{liane.gabora,tomas.veloz}@ubc.ca

Abstract. People use conjunctions and disjunctions of concepts in ways that violate the rules of classical logic, such as the law of compositionality. Specifically, they overextend conjunctions of concepts, a phenomenon referred to as the Guppy Effect. We build on previous efforts to develop a quantum model [1,2,3], that explains the Guppy Effect in terms of interference. Using a well-studied data set with 16 exemplars that exhibit the Guppy Effect, we developed a 17-dimensional complex Hilbert space $\mathcal{H}$ that models the data and demonstrates the relationship between overextension and interference. We view the interference effect as, not a logical fallacy on the conjunction, but a signal that out of the two constituent concepts, a *new* concept has emerged.

Keywords: theory of concepts, quantum cognition, Guppy effect, concept combination, interference.

1 The Guppy Effect – Introduction

A concrete formal understanding of how concepts combine is vital to significant progress in many fields including psychology, linguistics, and cognitive science. However, concepts have been resistant to mathematical description because people use conjunctions and disjunctions of concepts in ways that violate the rules of classical logic; i.e., concepts interact in ways that are non-compositional [4]. This is true also with respect to properties (e.g., although people do not rate *talks* as a characteristic property of *Pet* or *Bird*, they rate it as characteristic of *Pet Bird*) and exemplar typicalities (e.g., although people do not rate *Guppy* as a typical *Pet*, nor a typical *Fish*, they rate it as a highly typical *Pet Fish* [5]). This has come to be known as the Pet Fish Problem, and the general phenomenon wherein the typicality of an exemplar for a conjunctively combined concept is greater than that for either of the constituent concepts has come to be called the Guppy Effect, although further investigation revealed that the Pet Fish Problem is not a particularly good example of the Guppy Effect, and that other concept combinations exhibit this effect more strongly [6].

One can refer to the situation wherein people estimate the typicality of an exemplar of the concept combination as more extreme than it is for one of the constituent concepts in a conjunctive combination as *overextension*. One can

J.R. Busemeyer et al. (Eds.): QI 2012, LNCS 7620, pp. 36–47, 2012.
© Springer-Verlag Berlin Heidelberg 2012

refer to the situation wherein people estimate the typicality of the exemplar for the concept conjunction as higher than that of *both* constituent concepts as *double overextension*. We posit that overextension is not a violation of the classical logic of conjunction, but that it signals the emergence of a whole new concept. The aim of this paper is to model the Guppy Effect as an interference effect using a mathematical representation in a complex Hilbert space and the formalism of quantum theory to represent states and calculate probabilities. This builds on previous work that shows that Bell Inequalities are violated by concepts [7,8] and in particular by concept combinations that exhibit the Guppy Effect [1,2,3,9,10], and add to the investigation of other approaches using interference effects in cognition [11,12,13].

Our approach is best explained with an example. Consider the data in Tab. 1. It is based on data obtained by asking participants to estimate how typical various exemplars are of the concepts *Furniture*, *Household Appliances*, and *Furniture and Household Appliances* [14].

Table 1. Interference data for concepts A=*Furniture* and B=*Household Appliances*. The probability of a participant choosing exemplar k as an example of *Furniture* or *Household Appliances* is given by $\mu(A)_k$ or $(\mu(B)_k$, respectively. The probability of a participant choosing a particular exemplar k as an example of *Furniture and Household Appliances* is $\mu(A$ and $B)_k$. The classical probability would be $\frac{\mu(A)_k+\mu(B)_k}{2}$. The quantum phase angle θ_k introduces a quantum interference effect. Values are approximated to their third decimal, and angles to their second decimal.

		$\mu(A)_k$	$\mu(B)_k$	$\mu(A$ and $B)_k$	$\frac{\mu(A)_k+\mu(B)_k}{2}$	θ_k	λ_k	β_k
A=*Furniture*, B=*Household Appliances*								
1	*Filing Cabinet*	0.079	0.040	0.062	0.059	87.61	-0.056	-87.61
2	*Clothes Washer*	0.026	0,118	0.078	0.072	84.01	0.055	84.01
3	*Vacuum Cleaner*	0.017	0,118	0.051	0.068	112.21	-0.042	-112.21
4	*Hifi*	0.056	0.079	0.090	0.067	70.58	0.063	70.58
5	*Heated Waterbed*	0.089	0.050	0.082	0.070	79.28	-0.066	-79.28
6	*Sewing Chest*	0.075	0.058	0.061	0.067	94.74	0.066	94.74
7	*Floor Mat*	0.052	0.023	0.031	0.037	100.87	-0.034	-100.87
8	*Coffee Table*	0,100	0.025	0.050	0.062	104.78	0.048	104.78
9	*Piano*	0.084	0.020	0.043	0.052	101.67	0.040	101.67
10	*Rug*	0.056	0.019	0.028	0.037	106.58	0.031	106.58
11	*Painting*	0.057	0.014	0.021	0.035	120.16	-0.024	-120.16
12	*Chair*	0.099	0.030	0.047	0.065	109.41	-0.052	-109.41
13	*Fridge*	0.042	0,117	0.085	0.079	85.23	0.070	85.23
14	*Desk Lamp*	0.066	0.079	0.085	0.072	79.85	-0.071	-79.85
15	*Cooking Stove*	0.037	0,118	0.088	0.078	81.57	-0.066	-81.57
16	*TV*	0.065	0.092	0.099	0.078	61.89	0.075	61.89

Although Hampton's original data was in the form of typicality estimates, for the quantum model that we built it is more appropriate for data to be in the form of 'good examples'. Thus we calculated from Hampton's typicality data estimates for the following experimental situation. Participants are given the list of exemplars in Tab. 1 and asked to answer the following questions. *Question A* is 'Choose one exemplar that you consider a good example of *Furniture*'. *Question B* is 'Choose one exemplar that you consider a good example of *Household Appliances*'. Finally, *Question A and B* is 'Choose one exemplar that you consider a good example of *Furniture and Household Appliances*'. Hence, concretely, the data in Tab. 1 were not collected by asking the three 'good example'-questions but calculated from Hampton's data, derived from an experiment in which participants were asked to give typicality estimates. This transformation of Hampton's data retains the basic pattern of results because estimated typicality of an exemplar is strongly correlated with the frequency with which it is chosen as a good example [15].

2   A Quantum Model

In this section we build a quantum model of the Guppy Effect by modeling Hampton's data in complex Hilbert space for the pair of concepts *Furniture* and *Household Appliances*, and their conjunction *Furniture and Household Appliances*. The way in which we calculated the 'good example' data from Hampton's 'typicality' data is by normalizing for each exemplar the typicality estimates of each participant giving rise to an estimate of the extent to which this exemplar constitutes a 'good exemplar'. We then average on all the participants obtaining $\mu(A)_k$, $\mu(B)_k$ and $\mu(A \text{ and } B)_k$ (see Tab. 1). We interpret the resulting values as estimates of the probability that exemplar k is chosen as an answer for *Questions A, B*, and '*A and B*', respectively. Tab. 1 gives the probabilities of responses. Hampton's original typicality data, which ranged between -3 and +3, were rescaled to a $[0, 6]$ Likert scale to avoid negative values, and then afterwards normalized and averaged for each of the three concepts (A, B and, 'A and B') (see Tab.1).

The 'good example' measurement has 16 possible outcomes, namely each of the considered exemplars, and hence is represented in quantum theory by means of a self-adjoint operator with spectral decomposition $\{M_k \mid k = 1, \ldots, 16\}$ where each M_k is an orthogonal projection of the Hilbert space $\mathcal{H}$ corresponding to exemplar k from the list in Tab. 1. The concepts *Furniture* and *Household Appliances* are represented by orthogonal unit vectors $|A\rangle$ and $|B\rangle$ of the Hilbert space $\mathcal{H}$, and the combination *Furniture and Household Appliances* is represented by $\frac{1}{\sqrt{2}}(|A\rangle + |B\rangle)$, which is the normalized superposition of $|A\rangle$ and $|B\rangle$. It is by means of this superposition that the quantum framework can describe how a new concept 'A and B', emerges out of A and B. In the following, the standard rules of quantum mechanics are applied to calculate the probabilities, $\mu(A)_k$, $\mu(B)_k$ and $\mu(A \text{ and } B)_k$

$$\mu(A)_k = \langle A|M_k|A\rangle \quad \mu(B)_k = \langle B|M_k|B\rangle \tag{1}$$

$$\mu(A \text{ and } B)_k = \tfrac{1}{2}(\langle A| + \langle B|)M_k(|A\rangle + |B\rangle)$$
$$= \tfrac{1}{2}(\langle A|M_k|A\rangle + \langle B|M_k|B\rangle + \langle A|M_k|B\rangle + \langle B|M_k|A\rangle)$$
$$= \tfrac{1}{2}(\mu(A)_k + \mu(B)_k) + \Re\langle A|M_k|B\rangle \tag{2}$$

where $\Re\langle A|M_k|B\rangle$ is the interference term. Let us introduce $|e_k\rangle$ the unit vector on $M_k|A\rangle$ and $|f_k\rangle$ the unit vector on $M_k|B\rangle$, and put $\langle e_k|f_l\rangle = \delta_{kl}c_k e^{i\gamma_k}$. Then we have $|A\rangle = \sum_{k=1}^{16} a_k e^{i\alpha_k}|e_k\rangle$ and $|B\rangle = \sum_{k=1}^{16} b_k e^{i\beta_k}|f_k\rangle$, and with $\phi_k = \beta_k - \alpha_k + \gamma_k$, this gives

$$\langle A|B\rangle = (\sum_{k=1}^{16} a_k e^{-i\alpha_k}\langle e_k|)(\sum_{l=1}^{16} b_l e^{i\beta_l}|f_l\rangle) = \sum_{k=1}^{16} a_k b_k c_k e^{i(\beta_k - \alpha_k + \gamma_k)}$$
$$= \sum_{k=1}^{16} a_k b_k c_k e^{i\phi_k} \tag{3}$$

$$\mu(A)_k = (\sum_{l=1}^{16} a_l e^{-i\alpha_l}\langle e_l|)(a_k e^{i\alpha_k}|e_k\rangle) = a_k^2 \tag{4}$$

$$\mu(B)_k = (\sum_{l=1}^{16} b_l e^{-i\beta_l}\langle f_l|)(b_k e^{i\beta_k}|f_k\rangle) = b_k^2 \tag{5}$$

$$\langle A|M_k|B\rangle = (\sum_{l=1}^{16} a_l e^{-i\alpha_l}\langle e_l|)M_k|(\sum_{m=1}^{16} b_m e^{i\beta_m}|f_m\rangle)$$
$$= a_k b_k e^{i(\beta_k - \alpha_k)}\langle e_k|f_k\rangle = a_k b_k c_k e^{i\phi_k} \tag{6}$$

which, making use of (2), gives

$$\mu(A \text{ and } B)_k = \frac{1}{2}(\mu(A)_k + \mu(B)_k) + c_k\sqrt{\mu(A)_k\mu(B)_k}\cos\phi_k \tag{7}$$

We choose ϕ_k such that

$$\cos\phi_k = \frac{2\mu(A \text{ and } B)_k - \mu(A)_k - \mu(B)_k}{2c_k\sqrt{\mu(A)_k\mu(B)_k}} \tag{8}$$

and hence (7) is satisfied. We now have to determine c_k in such a way that $\langle A|B\rangle = 0$. Note that from $\sum_{k=1}^{16}\mu(A \text{ and } B)_k = 1$ and (7), and with the choice of $\cos\phi_k$ made in (8), it follows that $\sum_{k=1}^{16} c_k\sqrt{\mu(A)_k\mu(B)_k}\cos\phi_k = 0$. Taking into account (3), which gives $\langle A|B\rangle = \sum_{k=1}^{16} a_k b_k c_k(\cos\phi_k + i\sin\phi_k)$, and making use of $\sin\phi_k = \pm\sqrt{1 - \cos^2\phi_k}$, we have

$$\langle A|B\rangle = 0 \Leftrightarrow \sum_{k=1}^{16} c_k\sqrt{\mu(A)_k\mu(B)_k}(\cos\phi_k + i\sin\phi_k) = 0 \tag{9}$$

$$\Leftrightarrow \sum_{k=1}^{16} c_k\sqrt{\mu(A)_k\mu(B)_k}\sin\phi_k = 0 \tag{10}$$

$$\Leftrightarrow \sum_{k=1}^{16} \pm\sqrt{c_k^2\mu(A)_k\mu(B)_k - (\mu(A \text{ and } B)_k - \frac{\mu(A)_k + \mu(B)_k}{2})^2} = 0 \tag{11}$$

We introduce the following quantities

$$\lambda_k = \pm\sqrt{\mu(A)_k\mu(B)_k - \left(\mu(A \text{ and } B)_k - \frac{\mu(A)_k + \mu(B)_k}{2}\right)^2} \tag{12}$$

and choose m the index for which $|\lambda_m|$ is the biggest of the $|\lambda_k|$'s. Then we take $c_k = 1$ for $k \neq m$. We now explain the algorithm used to choose a plus or minus sign for λ_k as defined in (12), with the aim of being able to determine c_m such that (11) is satisfied.

We start by choosing a plus sign for λ_m. Then we choose a minus sign in (12) for the λ_k for which $|\lambda_k|$ is the second biggest; let us call the index of this term m_2. This means that $0 \leq \lambda_m + \lambda_{m_2}$. For the λ_k for which $|\lambda_k|$ is the third biggest – let us call the index of this term m_3 – we choose a minus sign if $0 \leq \lambda_m + \lambda_{m_2} - |\lambda_{m_3}|$, and otherwise we choose a plus sign, and in the present case we have $0 > \lambda_m + \lambda_{m_2} - |\lambda_{m_3}|$. We continue this way of choosing, always considering the next biggest $|\lambda_k|$, and hence arrive at a global choice of signs for all of the λ_k, such that $0 \leq \lambda_m + \sum_{k \neq m} \lambda_k$. Then we determine c_m such that (11) is satisfied, or more specifically such that

$$c_m = \sqrt{\frac{(-\sum_{k \neq m} \lambda_k)^2 + (\mu(A \text{ and } B)_m - \frac{\mu(A)_m + \mu(B)_m}{2})^2}{\mu(A)_m \mu(B)_m}} \tag{13}$$

We choose the sign for ϕ_k as defined in (8) equal to the sign of λ_k. The result of the specific solution thus constructed is that we can take $M_k(\mathcal{H})$ to be rays of dimension 1 for $k \neq m$, and $M_m(\mathcal{H})$ to be a plane. This means that we can make our solution still more explicit. Indeed, we take $\mathcal{H} = \mathbb{C}^{17}$, the canonical 17-dimensional complex Hilbert space, and make the following choices

$$|A\rangle = \left(\sqrt{\mu(A)_1}, \ldots, \sqrt{\mu(A)_m}, \ldots, \sqrt{\mu(A)_{16}}, 0\right) \tag{14}$$

$$|B\rangle = \left(e^{i\beta_1}\sqrt{\mu(B)_1}, \cdots, c_m e^{i\beta_m}\sqrt{\mu(B)_m}, \cdots, \right.$$
$$\left. e^{i\beta_{16}}\sqrt{\mu(B)_{16}}, \sqrt{\mu(B)_m(1 - c_m^2)}\right) \tag{15}$$

$$\beta_m = \arccos\left(\frac{2\mu(A \text{ and } B)_m - \mu(A)_m - \mu(B)_m}{2c_m\sqrt{\mu(A)_m \mu(B)_m}}\right) \tag{16}$$

$$\beta_k = \pm \arccos\left(\frac{2\mu(A \text{ and } B)_k - \mu(A)_k - \mu(B)_k}{2\sqrt{\mu(A)_k \mu(B)_k}}\right) \tag{17}$$

where the plus or minus sign in (17) is chosen following the algorithm introduced for choosing the plus and minus sign for λ_k in (12). Let us construct this quantum model for the data in Tab. 1. The exemplar that gives the biggest value of $|\lambda_k|$ is TV, and hence we choose a plus sign and get $\lambda_{16} = 0.0745$. The exemplar that gives the second biggest value of λ_k is $Desk~Lamp$, and hence we choose a minus sign, and get $\lambda_{14} = -0.0710$. Next comes $Fridge$ having $|\lambda_{13}| = 0.0698$, and since $\lambda_{16} + \lambda_{14} < 0$, we choose a plus sign for λ_{13}. We determine in a recursive way the signs for the remaining exemplars. Tab. 1 gives the values of λ_k calculated following this algorithm. From (13) it follows that $c_{16} = 0.564$.

Making use of (14), (15), (17) and (16), and the values of the angles given in Tab. 1, we put forward the following explicit representation of the vectors $|A\rangle$ and $|B\rangle$ in $\mathbb{C}^{17}$ representing concepts $Furniture$ and $Household~appliances$.

$$|A\rangle = (0.280, 0.161, 0.131, 0.236, 0.299, 0.274, 0.229, 0.316, 0.289, 0.236, 0.238,$$
$$0.315, 0.205, 0.257, 0.193, 0.255, 0) \tag{18}$$
$$|B\rangle = (0.200e^{-i87.61°}, 0.343e^{i84.01°}, 0.343e^{-i112.20°}, 0.281e^{i70.58°}, 0.225e^{-i79.28°},$$
$$0.242e^{i94.73°}, 0.151e^{-i100.87°}, 0.157e^{i104.78°}, 0.140e^{i101.67°}, 0.137e^{i106.58°},$$
$$0.119e^{-i120.16°}, 0.174e^{-i109.41°}, 0.342e^{i85.23°}, 0.280e^{-i79.85°},$$
$$0.344e^{-i81.57°}, 0.171e^{i61.89°}, 0.250). \tag{19}$$

This proves it is possible to make a quantum model of the [14] data such that the values of $\mu(A \text{ and } B)_k$ are determined from the values of $\mu(A)_k$ and $\mu(B)_k$

as a consequence of quantum interference effects. For each exemplar k, the value of θ_k in Tab. 1 gives the quantum interference phase.

3   Visualization of Interference Probabilities

A previous paper provided a quantum representation of the concepts *Fruits* and *Vegetables* and their disjunction *Fruits or Vegetables*, and gave a way to graphically represent possible quantum interference patterns that result when concepts combine [10]. Here we follow this procedure to generate a graphical representation for the concepts *Furniture*, *Household Appliances*, and their conjunction *Furniture and Household Appliances*. Each concept is represented by complex valued wave functions of two real variables $\psi_A(x,y)$, $\psi_B(x,y)$ and $\psi_{A\text{and}B}(x,y)$. We choose $\psi_A(x,y)$ and $\psi_B(x,y)$ such that the square of the absolute value of both wave functions is a Gaussian in two dimensions, which is always possible since we only have to fit 16 values, namely those of $|\psi_A|^2$ and $|\psi_B|^2$ for each of the exemplars of Tab. 1. These Gaussians are graphically represented in Figs. 1 a) and 1 b), and the exemplars of Tab. 1 are located in spots such that the Gaussian distributions $|\psi_A(x,y)|^2$ and $|\psi_B(x,y)|^2$ properly model the probabilities $\mu(A)_k$ and $\mu(B)_k$ in Tab. 1 for each of the exemplars.

For example, for *Furniture* (Fig. 1 a)), *Coffee Table* is located in the centre of the Gaussian because it was most frequently chosen in response to *Question A*. *Chair* was the second most frequently chosen, hence it is closest to the top of the Gaussian. Note that in Fig. 1 b) there is one point labelled by X, which is the maximum of the Gaussian representing $\mu(B)$. We preferred not to locate the highest value of typicality by the maximum of the Gaussian, because doing so did not lead to an easy fit of both Gaussians. For *Household Appliances*, represented in Fig. 1 b), X is located in the maximum of the Gaussian, and since *Clothes Washer* and *Vacuum Cleaner* are the most frequently chosen (with exactly the same frequency) they are located closest to X at an equal distance radius. *Cooking Stove* was the third most frequently chosen, then *Fridge* and so on, with *Painting* as the least chosen 'good examples' of *Household Appliances*. Metaphorically, we could regard the graphical representations of Figs. 2 a), 2 b) as the projections of a light source shining through two holes such that a screen captures it and the holes make the intensity follow a Gaussian distribution when projected on the screen. The centre of the first hole, corresponding to *Furniture*, is located where exemplar *Coffee Table* is at point $(0,0)$, indicated by 8 in both figures. The centre of the second hole, corresponding to *Household Appliances*, is located where point X is at $(10,4)$, indicated by 17 in both figures. In Fig. 1 c) the data for *Furniture and Household Appliances* are graphically represented. This is not 'just' a normalized sum of the two Gaussians of Figs. 2 a) and b), since it is the probability distribution corresponding to $\frac{1}{\sqrt{2}}(\psi_A(x,y)+\psi_B(x,y))$, which is the normalized superposition of the wave functions in Figs. 2 a) and b). The numbers are placed at the locations of the different exemplars, according to the labels of Tab. 1, with respect to the probability distribution $\frac{1}{2}|\psi_A(x,y)+\psi_B(x,y)|^2 = \frac{1}{2}(|\psi_A(x,y)|^2+|\psi_B(x,y)|^2)+|\psi_A(x,y)\psi_B(x,y)|\cos\theta(x,y)$, where

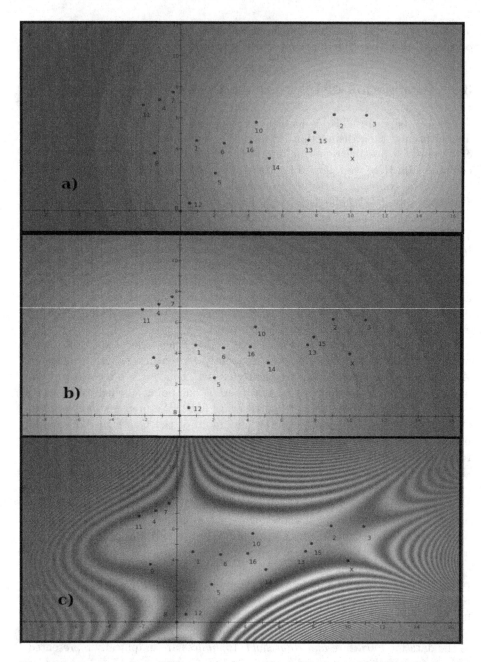

Fig. 1. A representation of our quantum model of *Furniture, Household Appliance* and *Furniture and Household Appliance* by a double slit interference situation. The brightness of the light source in a region corresponds to the probability that an exemplar in this region is chosen as a 'good example' of the concept *Furniture* in figure a), *Household Appliance* in figure b), and *Furniture and Household Appliance* in figure c). Numbers indicate the exemplars as numbered in Table 1.

$|\psi_A(x,y)\psi_B(x,y)|\cos\theta(x,y)$ is the interference term and $\theta(x,y)$ the quantum phase difference at (x,y). The values of $\theta(x,y)$ are given in Tab. 1 for the locations of the different exemplars. The interference pattern in Fig. 1 c) is very similar to well-known interference patterns of light passing through an elastic material under stress. In our case, it is the interference pattern corresponding to *Furniture and Household Appliances*. Bearing in mind the analogy with the light source and holes for Figs. 1 a) and b), in Fig. 1 c) we can see the interference pattern produced when both holes are open. (For the mathematical details – the exact form of the wave functions and the calculation of possible interference patterns – and other examples of conceptual interference, see [10].)

4 Interpretation of Interference in Cognitive Space

If we consider equations (2) and (7), the fundamental interference equations used in this quantum model, we see that $\mu(A \text{ and } B)$ becomes equal to the average $\frac{1}{2}(\mu(A)+\mu(B))$ in case of no interference, i.e., if the interference terms are zero. Thus the description of the conjunction as a no interference situation does not coincide with what is obtained using the minimum rule from fuzzy set theory. Note that in the double slit situation, a classical particle passing through with both slits open gives rise to a probability distribution on the screen which is equal to $\frac{1}{2}(\mu(A)+\mu(B))$, i.e. the average of the probabilities with only one of the

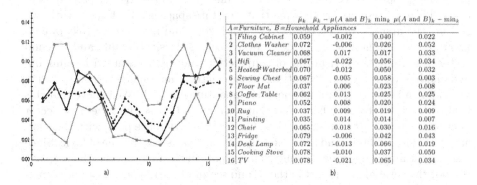

		$\bar{\mu}_k$	$\bar{\mu}_k - \mu(A \text{ and } B)_k$	$\min_k$	$\mu(A \text{ and } B)_k - \min_k$
A=Furniture, B=Household Appliances					
1	Filing Cabinet	0.059	-0.002	0.040	0.022
2	Clothes Washer	0.072	-0.006	0.026	0.052
3	Vacuum Cleaner	0.068	0.017	0.017	0.033
4	Hifi	0.067	-0.022	0.056	0.034
5	Heated Waterbed	0.070	-0.012	0.050	0.032
6	Sewing Chest	0.067	0.005	0.058	0.003
7	Floor Mat	0.037	0.006	0.023	0.008
8	Coffee Table	0.062	0.013	0.025	0.025
9	Piano	0.052	0.008	0.020	0.024
10	Rug	0.037	0.009	0.019	0.009
11	Painting	0.035	0.014	0.014	0.007
12	Chair	0.065	0.018	0.030	0.016
13	Fridge	0.079	-0.006	0.042	0.043
14	Desk Lamp	0.072	-0.013	0.066	0.019
15	Cooking Stove	0.078	-0.010	0.037	0.050
16	TV	0.078	-0.021	0.065	0.034

Fig. 2. a) Estimations of concept combination probabilities. The horizontal axis corresponds to the exemplar label denoted by k in Tab.1 and the vertical axis measures estimated probability. The two grey curves represent the minimum and maximum for each k of the probabilities $\mu(A)_k$ and $\mu(B)_k$. The black curve represents the probability $\mu(A \text{ and } B)_k$ obtained from the data, and the dashed curve represents the average between $\mu(A)_k$ and $\mu(B)_k$. b) Comparison between the concept conjunction probability, and the classical average and minimum probabilities of the concepts A and B. $\bar{\mu}_k = \frac{\mu(A)_k+\mu(B)_k}{2}$ is the the classical average probability (third column) and $\min_k = \min\{\mu(A)_k, \mu(B)_k\}$ is the minimum probability (fifth column). The fourth (sixth) column shows the deviation of the average (the minimum) with respect to the concept combination probability. The probability $\mu(A \text{ and } B)_k$ deviates 0.011 from the average $\bar{\mu}_k$, but 0.026 from the minimum.

two slits open. Hence, in both the interference quantum model and its double slit representation, the average plays the role of the classical default, not the minimum, as one would expect to be the case if the conjunction were modeled using fuzzy set theory.

This aspect of our model needs further explanation. First, as in an earlier interference based model of disjunction [10], for the conjunction, the average is the classical default, not the maximum, as would follow from a fuzzy set theory model. Second, if we consider Hampton's data, the average $1/2(\mu(A) + \mu(B))$ is effectively closer to the frequency of the combined concept $\mu(A \text{ and } B)$ than the fuzzy set minimum value. More concretely, on average, the probability for the combined concept differs 0.011 from the classical average, but 0.026 from the fuzzy set minimum measure (Fig.-Tab. 2). Also, calculation of the correlation between the probability for the combined concept and the average and the minimum, yields 0.899 and 0.795 respectively, which indicates that experimentally the average is a better estimate than the minimum.

The findings that (1) the average is the classical default in our quantum model, and in the double slit representation of it, and (2) the average is also a better experimental approximation than the minimum, indicate that the connective 'and' in a conjunction of concepts does not play the role that we imagine it to play intuitively and from our experience with logic. Similarly, the connective 'or' in a disjunction of concepts does not play the role we imagine it to play [10]. A similar phenomenon was identified for Hampton's data on membership weights of exemplars with respect to conjunctive and disjunctive combinations of pairs of concepts. This was resolved by showing that the state space is a Fock space with two sectors, the first sector describing this 'non logical and interference role' of conjunction and disjunction, with indeed the average as classical default, and a second sector describing the logical role of conjunction and disjunction, with minimum and maximum as classical defaults in the case of conjunction and respectively disjunction, and quantum entanglement as a quantum effect [3]. We believe that this is also the state of affairs here, and that we have only described the 'first sector Fock space' part in the present article, hence the interference part, with the average as classical default, and a role of conjunction that is not the one of logic. Since the present model describes the interference part in the first sector of Fock space, but not the entanglement part in the second sector of Fock space, it can be seen as complementary to an entanglement quantum model that was worked out for the Pet-Fish concept combination in a tensor product Hilbert space [1].

An more intuitive way of looking at this is that when it comes to first sector of Fock space effects, hence interference effects, participants mainly consider '*Furniture and Household Appliances*' in its root combination '*Furniture–Household Appliances*', without taking into account the 'and' as a logical connective. The 'and' merely introduces an extra context on this root combination, which, for example, will be different from the extra context introduced by the 'or' on the root combination.

At first sight it may seem that our interference quantum model does not incorporate order effects, which are known to exist experimentally. More concretely, experiments on the combination 'A and B' will often lead to different data than experiments on the combination 'B and A'. However, order effect can be modeled without problems in our interference approach, because in the first sector of Fock space, although 'A and B' and 'B and A' are described by the same superposition state, the phase of this state is different, leading to different interference angles, and hence different values for the collapse probabilities. This is how the first sector of a Fock space interference model copes in a natural way with order effects.

The double slit representation also helps clarify aspects of the situation and thus provides new insight into concept combination. The role of the two slits is played by *Furniture* and *Household Appliances*, and the role of the specific positions on the detection screen where the interference pattern is formed are played by the measuring locations for the exemplars. We can see clearly that the mind is not working with these concepts in a classical manner. If this were the case, each individual would simply substitute the combined concept *Furniture and Household Appliances* by one of the two constituent concepts – in a manner similar to how the classical particle passes through one of the two slits. This would result in a perfect average, and hence no interference. However, on many occasions individual judgements of typicality for the conjunction deviate from the average, in a manner similar to how the statistical average of typicality deviates from the average. This means that interference is operating, similar to the interference pattern observed in quantum mechanics even with single quantum 'particles' in a double slit set-up [16]. Physicists introduced the term 'self-interference' to indicate this behavior. The above suggests that the individual ponders each of the constituents of a combined concept and this process takes place 'in superposition' when referring to the individual constituents of the combination. This is the expression of the emergence of a new concept for this combination. Other aspects of the origin of conceptual interference effects, and their implications for cognition and creativity, are analyzed and discussed elsewhere [2,3,9,17,18].

Let us finish this section by returning to the issue of overextension of the conjunction. Since from our analysis it follows that the average, a first order classical default (namely the default of the first sector of Fock space), is stronger than the minimum, the classical default (of the second sector of Fock space), the notion of 'overextension' no longer covers correctly the 'deviation from classicality'. However, an interesting relation with interference can be found. Overextension takes place when

$$\mu(A \text{ and } B)_k - \min\{\mu(A)_k, \mu(B)_k\} > 0 \qquad (20)$$

which is equivalent to

$$\max\{\mu(A)_k, \mu(B)_k\} > \frac{\mu(A)_k + \mu(B)_k}{2} - \Re\langle A|M_k|B\rangle \qquad (21)$$

Overextension occurs when the average modulated by the interference term cannot equal the largest of the constituent typicalities. This is consistent with the contention that 'Conjunctions tend to be overextended to include exemplars that are good members of one class, but are marginal to the other' [14]. Only for double overextension is interference necessary. On the other hand, situations where one concept in the conjunction is very atypical, while the other is highly typical, a situation traditionally considered unproblematic, could require a large interference deviation from the classical average.

5 Conclusions

We presented a quantum model that demonstrates how the Guppy Effect can be modeled as interference. A data set for two concepts and their conjunction – with an ontology of 16 exemplars – was modeled in a 17-dimensional Hilbert space $\mathcal{H}$. The non-compositionality of the conjunction of concepts was identified by its close convergence to the classical average of probabilities, while the quantum interference appears as a modulation to fit the effect of the logical connectives. Our core finding is that this effect produces a quantifiable deviation from classical analyses, signalling the emergence of a new concept. One implication is that in some situations, particularly when new content emerges, cognitive processes cannot be described using classical logic.

References

1. Aerts, D., Gabora, L.: A Theory of Concepts and Their Combinations I&II. Kybernetes 34, 167–191, 192–221 (2005)
2. Aerts, D.: Quantum Interference and Superposition in Cognition: Development of a Theory for the Disjunction of Concepts. In: Aerts, D., Broekaert, J., D'Hooghe, B., Note, N. (eds.) Worldviews, Science and Us: Bridging Knowledge and Its Implications for Our Perspectives of the World. World Scientific, Singapore (2011)
3. Aerts, D.: Quantum Structure in Cognition. Journal of Mathematical Psychology 53, 314–348 (2009)
4. Hampton, J.: Inheritance of Attributes in Natural Concept Conjunctions. Memory & Cognition 15, 55–71 (1987)
5. Osherson, D., Smith, E.: On the Adequacy of Prototype Theory as a Theory of Concepts. Cognition 9, 35–58 (1981)
6. Storms, G., De Boeck, P., Van Mechelen, I., Ruts, W.: Not guppies, Nor Goldfish, But Tumble Dryers, Noriega, Jesse Jackson, Panties, Car Crashes, Bird Books, and Stevie Wonder. Memory & Cognition 26, 143–145 (1998)
7. Aerts, D., Aerts, S., Broekaert, J., Gabora, L.: The Violation of Bell Inequalities in the Macroworld. Foundations of Physics 30, 1387–1414 (2000)
8. Gabora, L., Aerts, D.: Contextualizing Concepts Using a Mathematical Generalization of the Quantum Formalism. Journal of Experimental and Theoretical Artificial Intelligence 14, 327–358 (2002)
9. Aerts, D.: General Quantum Modeling of Combining Concepts: A Quantum Field Model in Fock space (2007) Archive reference and link, http://uk.arxiv.org/abs/0705.1740
10. Aerts, D.: Quantum Particles as Conceptual Entities: A Possible Explanatory Framework for Quantum Theory. Foundations of Science 14, 361–411 (2009)

11. Franco, R.: The Conjunction Fallacy and Interference Effects. Journal of Mathematical Psychology 53, 415–422 (2009)
12. Franco, R., Zuccon, G.: Social Tagging, Guppy Effect and Interference Effects. In: CNS-ECCS 2010 (2010)
13. Lambert Mogiliansky, A., Zamir, S., Zwirn, H.: Type Indeterminacy: A Model of the KT(Kahneman-Tversky)-Man. Journal of Mathematical Psychology 53, 349–361 (2009)
14. Hampton, J.A.: Overextension of Conjunctive Concepts: Evidence for a Unitary Model for Concept Typicality and Class Inclusion. Journal of Experimental Psychology: Learning, Memory, and Cognition 14, 12–32 (1988)
15. Hampton, J.A.: Typicality, Graded Membership and Vagueness. Cognitive Science 31, 355–383 (2007)
16. Donati, O., Missiroli, G.F., Pozzi, G.: An Experiment on Electron Interference. American Journal of Physics 41, 639–644 (1973)
17. Aerts, D., D'Hooghe, B.: Classical Logical Versus Quantum Conceptual Thought: Examples in Economics, Decision Theory and Concept Theory. In: Bruza, P., Sofge, D., Lawless, W., van Rijsbergen, K., Klusch, M. (eds.) QI 2009. LNCS (LNAI), vol. 5494, pp. 128–142. Springer, Heidelberg (2009)
18. Veloz, T., Gabora, L., Eyjolfson, M., Aerts, D.: Toward a Formal Model of the Shifting Relationship between Concepts and Contexts during Associative Thought. In: Song, D., Melucci, M., Frommholz, I., Zhang, P., Wang, L., Arafat, S. (eds.) QI 2011. LNCS, vol. 7052, pp. 25–34. Springer, Heidelberg (2011)
19. Gabora, L., Aerts, D.: A Model of the Emergence and Evolution of Integrated Worldview. Journal of Mathematical Psychology 53, 434–451 (2009)

A Quantum Model for the Ellsberg and Machina Paradoxes

Diederik Aerts[1], Sandro Sozzo[1], and Jocelyn Tapia[2]

[1] Center Leo Apostel (CLEA),
Vrije Universiteit Brussel (VUB), Pleinlaan 2, 1050 Brussel, Belgium
{diraerts,ssozzo}@vub.ac.be
[2] Pontificia Universidad Católica de Chile,
Avda. Libertador Bernardo OHiggins 340, Santiago, Chile
jntapia@uc.cl

Abstract. The *Ellsberg* and *Machina paradoxes* reveal that *expected utility theory* is problematical when real subjects take decisions under uncertainty. Suitable generalizations of expected utility exist which attempt to solve the Ellsberg paradox, but none of them provides a satisfactory solution of the Machina paradox. In this paper we elaborate a quantum model in Hilbert space describing the Ellsberg situation and also the Machina situation, and show that we can model the specific aspect of the Machina situation that is unable to be modeled within the existing generalizations of expected utility.

Keywords: Ellsberg paradox, Machina paradox, ambiguity aversion, quantum modeling.

1 Introduction

In economics, the predominant model of decision making is the *Expected Utility Theory* (EUT) [1,2]. Notwithstanding its simplicity, mathematical tractability and predictive success, the empirical validity of EUT at the individual level is questionable. Indeed, examples exist in the literature which show an inconsistency between real preferences and the predictions of EUT. These deviations were put forward by considering specific situations of uncertainty often commonly referred to now as paradoxes [3,4].

EUT was formally developed by von Neumann and Morgenstern [1]. They presented a set of axioms that allow to represent decision–maker preferences over the set of *acts* (functions from the set of states of the world into the set of consequences) by the functional $E_p u(.)$, for some real–valued Bernoulli utility function u on the set of consequences and an objective probability measure p on the set of states of the nature. An important aspect of EUT concerns the treatment of uncertainty. Knight had highlighted the difference between *risk* and *uncertainty* reserving the term *risk* for ventures that can be described by known (or physical) probabilities, and the term *uncertainty* to refer to situations in which agents did not know the probabilities associated with each of the possible outcomes of an

J.R. Busemeyer et al. (Eds.): QI 2012, LNCS 7620, pp. 48–59, 2012.

Table 1. The payoff matrix for the Ellsberg paradox situation

Act	red	yellow	black
f_1	12\$	0\$	0\$
f_2	0\$	0\$	12\$
f_3	12\$	12\$	0\$
f_4	0\$	12\$	12\$

act [5]. However, probabilities in the von Neumann and Morgenstern modeling are *objectively* or, physically, given. Later, Savage extended EUT allowing agents to construct their own subjective probabilities when physical probabilities are not available [2]. Then according to Savage's model, the distinction put forward by Knight seems to be irrelevant. Ellsberg's experiments instead showed that Knightian's distinction is empirically meaningful [3]. In particular, he presented the following experiment. Consider one urn with thirty red balls and sixty balls that are either yellow or black, the latter in unknown proportion. One ball will be drawn from the urn. Then, free of charge, a person is asked to bet on one of the acts f_1, f_2, f_3 and f_4 defined in Table 1.

When asked to rank these gambles most of the persons choose to bet on f_1 over f_2 and f_4 over f_3. This empirical result cannot be explained by EUT. In fact, we can see that individuals' ranking of the sub–acts [12 on *red*; 0 on *black*] versus [0 on *red*; 12 on *black*] depends upon whether the event *yellow* yields a payoff of 0 or 12, contrary to what is suggested by the Sure–Thing principle, an important axiom of Savage's model. Nevertheless, these choices have a direct intuition: f_1 offers the 12 prize with an *objective probability* of 1/3, and f_2 offers the same prize but in an element of the *subjective partition* $\{black, yellow\}$. In the same way, f_4 offers the prize with an objective probability of 2/3, whereas f_3 offers the same payoff on the union of the unambiguous event *red* and the ambiguous event *yellow*. Thus, in both cases the unambiguous bet is preferred to its ambiguous counterpart, a phenomenon called by Ellsberg *ambiguity aversion*.

After the work of Ellsberg many extensions of EUT have been developed to represent this kind of preferences, all replacing the Sure–Thing Principle by weaker axioms. The first extension is *Choquet Expected Utility*, also known as expected utility with *non–additive* probabilities [6]. This model considered a subjective non–additive probability *(capacity)* over the states of nature instead of a subjective probability. Thus, decision–makers could underestimate or over-estimate probabilities in the Ellsberg experiment and the ambiguity aversion is equivalent to the convexity of the capacity (pessimistic beliefs). A second approach is the *Max − Min Expected Utility*, or expected utility with multi–prior [7]. In this case the lack of knowledge about the states of nature of the decision–maker cannot be represented by a unique probability measure, instead he or she thinks are relevant a set of probability measures, then an act f is preferred to g if $\min_{p \in P} E_p u(f) > \min_{p \in P} E_p u(f)$, where P is a convex and closed set of additive probability measures. The ambiguity aversion is represented by the pessimistic beliefs of the agent which takes decisions considering the worst

Table 2. The payoff matrix for the Machina paradox situation

Act	E_1	E_2	E_3	E_4
f_1	202	202	101	101
f_2	202	101	202	101
f_3	303	202	101	0
f_4	303	101	202	0

probabilistic scenario. The third model is *Variational Preferences* [8], and it is a dynamic generalization of the Max-Min expected utility. In this case agents rank acts according to the criterion: $\inf_{p \in \triangle}\{E_p u(f) + c(p)\}$, where $c(p)$ is a closed and convex penalty function associated with the probability election. Finally, the *Second Order Probabilities* approach [9] proposes a model of preferences over acts such that the decision–maker prefers an act f to an act g if and only if $E_\mu \phi(E_p u(f)) \geq E_\mu \phi(E_p u(g))$, where E is the expectation operator, u is a von Neumann–Morgenstern utility function, ϕ is an increasing transformation, and μ is a subjective probability over the set of probability measures p that the decision–maker thinks are feasible. In this kind of model the ambiguity aversion is represented by the concavity of the transformation ϕ.

Notwithstanding the models above have been widely used in economics and finance, they are not absent of critics (see, e.g., [4,10]). In the same spirit as Ellsberg, Machina proposed an example introducing a trade off between ambiguity aversion and Bayesian advantages that cannot be represented by the Choquet expected utility model [4]. Recently it has been proved that no one of the mentioned extensions of EUT can represent the behavior described by the Machina paradox [11]. For the Machina paradox an experiment is considered consisting of an urn with four kind of different balls identified with a number between 1 and 4. The amount of balls with the number 1 plus the amount of balls with the number 2 is fifty and the amount of balls with the number 3 plus the amount of balls with the number 4 is fifty–one. Agents are asked to rank the set of acts in Table 2.

The event E_j indicates that a ball with a number j has been drawn from the urn, the act f_1 has been defined as contingent payoff in each event, so that in E_1, f_1 pays 202, in E_2, f_1 pays 202, and so on. Equally are defined f_2, f_3 and f_4. Then, free of charge a person is asked to bet on f_1 or to bet on f_2, if he or she are sufficiently uncertainty averse then will prefer f_1 instead f_2, because f_1 has not ambiguity in its payoffs although f_2 presents a slight Bayesian advantage due to the 51 balls may yield 202. The person is also asked to bet on f_3 or f_4. In this case, both acts present ambiguity in their payoffs, there is not an informational advantage between them. Thus a decision–maker who values unambiguous information would be indifferent between f_3 and f_4. On the other hand f_4 benefits from the 51 balls, hence in this case the Bayesian advantage implies that $f_4 \succ f_3$. The paradox appears because none of the reviewed models can represent this dual behavior. As a consequence, the Machina paradox, as well as the construction of a unified framework explaining both the Ellsberg and Machina paradoxes, are still open problems in decision making.

Ambiguity in economics is typically considered as a situation without a unique probability model describing it as opposed to *risk*, which is defined as a situation with such a probability model describing it. It is however presupposed usually that a classical probability model is considered, defined on a σ–algebra of events. In the above approaches generalizing EUT [6,7,8,9], more general structures are considered than that of a single classical probability model on a σ–algebra. Having looked in detail at the above mentioned structural generalizations, it can be noticed however that they all envisage generalizations of some specific aspects of the traditional situation of one classical probability model on one σ–algebra. Recently we have also proposed an approach to this problem, introducing the notion of *contextual risk*, inspired by the probability structure of quantum mechanics, which is intrinsically different from a classical probability on a σ-algebra, the set of events is indeed *not* a Boolean algebra [12,13,14,15].

In the present article we work out a direct mathematical representation of the Ellsberg and Machina paradox situations, in the standard formalism of quantum mechanics, hence by using a complex Hilbert space, and representing the probability measures by projection valued measures on this complex Hilbert space. As we will see when we explain the details of the Hilbert space representation of Ellsberg and Machina, it is not only the structure of the probability models which is essentially different from the known approaches – projection valued measures instead of σ–algebra valued measures – but also the way in which states are represented in quantum mechanics, i.e. by unit vectors of the Hilbert space, brings in an essential different aspect, coping both mathematically and intuitively, with the notion of ambiguity as introduced in economics.

2   A Quantum Model for the Ellsberg Paradox

To work out a quantum model for the Ellsberg paradox situation we consider the example resumed in Tab. 1, Sec. 1. We will realize the quantum model in the three dimensional complex Hilbert space $\mathbb{C}^3$. Let us denote its canonical basis by the vectors $\{|1,0,0\rangle, |0,1,0\rangle, |0,0,1\rangle\}$.

For the sake of clarity, we introduce the model in different steps. First, we define the part of the model, which we will refer to as the conceptual Ellsberg entity, as it consists of the Ellsberg situation without considering the different actions and also without considering the person and the bet to be taken. Hence it is the situation of the urn with 30 red balls and 60 black and yellow balls in unknown proportion. In the next steps we will add the remaining elements.

Already in the first part the presence of the ambiguity can be taken into account mathematically in a specific way by the quantum mechanical formalism. To this aim we introduce a quantum mechanical context e, represented by means of the spectral family $\{P_r, P_{yb}\}$, where P_r is the one dimensional orthogonal projection operator on the subspace generated by the vector $|1,0,0\rangle$, and P_{yb} is the two dimensional orthogonal projection operator on the subspace generated by the vectors $|0,1,0\rangle$ and $|0,0,1\rangle$, $\{P_r, P_{yb}\}$ is indeed a spectral family, since $P_r \perp P_{yb}$ and $P_r + P_{yb} = \mathbb{1}$. Contexts, or more specifically measurement contexts, are indeed represented by spectral families of orthogonal projection operators, or by a self–adjoint operator determined by such a family. A state in quantum mechanics is represented by a unit vector of the complex Hilbert space. For example, the vector

$$|v_{ry}\rangle = |1/\sqrt{3} \cdot e^{i\theta_r}, \sqrt{2/3} \cdot e^{i\theta_y}, 0\rangle \tag{1}$$

can be used to represent a state describing the Ellsberg situation $\mathbb{C}^3$. Indeed, we have

$$|\langle 1,0,0|v_{ry}\rangle|^2 = \langle v_{ry}|1,0,0\rangle\langle 1,0,0|v_{ry}\rangle = \parallel P_r|v_{ry}\rangle \parallel^2 = 1/3 \tag{2}$$

which shows that the probability for 'red' in the state represented by $|v_{ry}\rangle$ equals $1/3$. On the other hand, we have

$$\parallel P_{yb}|v_{ry}\rangle\parallel^2 = \langle 0, \sqrt{2/3} \cdot e^{i\theta_y}, 0|0, \sqrt{2/3} \cdot e^{i\theta_y}, 0\rangle = 2/3 \tag{3}$$

which shows that the probability for 'yellow or black' in the state represented by $|v_{ry}\rangle$ is $2/3$. But this is not the only state describing the Ellsberg situation, the set of all such states (*Ellsberg state set*) is

$$\Sigma_{Ells} = \{p_v : |v\rangle = |1/\sqrt{3} \cdot e^{i\theta_r}, \rho_y e^{i\theta_y}, \rho_b e^{i\theta_b}\rangle \mid 0 \le \rho_y, \rho_b, \ \rho_y^2 + \rho_b^2 = 2/3\} \tag{4}$$

which is a subset of $\mathbb{C}^3$. A state contained in Σ_{Ells}, together with the context e represented by the spectral family $\{P_r, P_{yb}\}$, delivers a quantum description of the Ellsberg situation.

We come now to the second step, namely the introduction of a description of the different actions f_1, f_2, f_3 and f_4. Here a second measurement context is introduced which we denote by g. It describes the ball taken out of the urn, and its color verified, red, yellow or black. Also g is represented by a spectral family of orthogonal projection operators $\{P_r, P_y, P_b\}$, where P_r is already defined, while P_y is the orthogonal projection operator on $|0,1,0\rangle$ and P_b is the orthogonal projection operator on $|0,0,1\rangle$. This means that the probabilities, given a state p_v represented by the vector $|v\rangle = |\rho_r e^{i\theta_r}, \rho_y e^{i\theta_y}, \rho_b e^{i\theta_b}\rangle$, are

$$\mu_r(g, p_v) = \parallel P_r|v\rangle \parallel^2 = \langle v|P_r|v\rangle = \rho_r^2 \tag{5}$$
$$\mu_y(g, p_v) = \parallel P_y|v\rangle \parallel^2 = \langle v|P_y|v\rangle = \rho_y^2 \tag{6}$$
$$\mu_b(g, p_v) = \parallel P_b|v\rangle \parallel^2 = \langle v|P_b|v\rangle = \rho_b^2 \tag{7}$$

where $\mu_r(g, p_v)$, $\mu_y(g, p_v)$ and $\mu_b(g, p_v)$ are the probabilities to draw a red ball, a yellow ball and a black ball, respectively, in the state p_v. Of course, if $p_v \in \Sigma_{Ells}$ we require that $\rho_r^2 = 1/3$ and $\rho_y^2 + \rho_b^2 = 2/3$.

The different actions f_1, f_2, f_3 and f_4 are observables, and hence represented by self-adjoint operators, built all on the spectral decomposition $\{P_r, P_y, P_b\}$.

$$\hat{f}_1 = 12\$P_r \quad \hat{f}_2 = 12\$P_b \quad \hat{f}_3 = 12\$P_r + 12\$P_y \quad \hat{f}_4 = 12\$P_y + 12\$P_b = 12\$P_{yb} \tag{8}$$

Let us analyze now the expected payoffs connected with the different acts, or the utility. Let us remark here that for reasons of simplicity, we identify the utility with the expected payoff, although of course in general the utility is a much more general variable. This implies that we are considering a risk neutral agent. Hence, consider an arbitrary state $p_v \in \Sigma_{Ells}$ and the acts f_1 and f_4. We have

$$U(f_1, g, p_v) = \langle v|\hat{f}_1|v \rangle = 12\$\langle v|P_r|v \rangle = 12\$ \cdot 1/3 = 4\$ \tag{9}$$

$$U(f_4, g, p_v) = \langle v|\hat{f}_4|v \rangle = 12\$\langle v|P_{yb}|v \rangle = 12\$ \cdot 2/3 = 8\$ \tag{10}$$

which shows that both these utilities are completely *independent* of the considered state of Σ_{Ells}. They are *ambiguity free*. Consider now the acts f_2 and f_3, and again an arbitrary state $p_v \in \Sigma_{Ells}$. We have

$$U(f_2, g, p_v) = \langle v|\hat{f}_2|v \rangle = 12\$\langle v|P_b|v \rangle = 12\$\mu_b(g, p_v) \tag{11}$$

$$U(f_3, g, p_v) = \langle v|\hat{f}_3|v \rangle = 12\$\langle v|(P_r + P_y)|v \rangle = 12\$(\mu_r(g, p_v) + \mu_y(g, p_v)) \tag{12}$$

which shows that both utilities depend heavily on the state p_v, due to the ambiguity where the two acts are confronted with.

Let us now take into account some extreme cases to see explicitly the dependence on the state. Consider, e.g., the states $p_{v_{r_y}}$, introduced in (1), and $p_{v_{r_b}}$ represented by the vector $|v_{rb} \rangle = |1/\sqrt{3} \cdot e^{i\phi_r}, 0, \sqrt{2/3} \cdot e^{i\theta_b} \rangle$. These states give rise for the act f_2 to utilities

$$U(f_2, g, p_{v_{r_y}}) = 12\$\mu_b(g, p_{v_{r_y}}) = 12\$ \cdot 0 = 0\$ \tag{13}$$

$$U(f_2, g, p_{v_{r_b}}) = 12\$\mu_b(g, p_{v_{r_b}}) = 12\$ \cdot 2/3 = 8\$. \tag{14}$$

This shows that a state $p_{v_{r_b}}$ exists within the realm of ambiguity, where the utility of act f_2 is greater than the utility of act f_1, and also a state $p_{v_{r_y}}$ exists within the realm of ambiguity, where the utility of act f_2 is smaller than the utility of act f_1. If we look at act f_3, we find for the two considered extreme states the following utilities

$$U(f_3, g, p_{v_{r_y}}) = 12\$(\mu_r(g, p_{v_{r_y}}) + \mu_y(g, p_{v_{r_y}})) = 12\$(1/3 + 2/3) = 12\$ \tag{15}$$

$$U(f_3, g, p_{v_{r_b}}) = 12\$(\mu_r(g, p_{v_{r_b}}) + \mu_y(g, p_{v_{r_b}})) = 12\$(1/3 + 0) = 4\$. \tag{16}$$

We are in a very similar situation, namely one of the states gives rise to a greater utility, while the other gives rise to a smaller utility than the independent one obtained in act f_4.

We come finally to the third step, and take into account the presence of the ambiguity in a proper way. Relying on quantum mechanical modeling of situations that violate the Sure–Thing Principle, such as the Hawaii situation [17], we put forward the hypothesis that the two extreme states $p_{v_{r_y}}$ and $p_{v_{r_b}}$ play a role in the mind of the person that is asked to bet. Hence, it is a superposition state of these two states that will guide the decision of the person to bet. Let us construct a general superposition state p_{v_s} of these two states. Hence the vector $|v_s \rangle$ representing p_{v_s} can be written as follows

$$|v_s \rangle = ae^{i\alpha}|v_{rb} \rangle + be^{i\beta}|v_{ry} \rangle \tag{17}$$

where a, b, α and β are chosen in such a way that $\langle v_s|v_s\rangle = 1$, which means that $1 = (ae^{-i\alpha}\langle v_{rb}| + be^{-i\beta}\langle v_{ry}|)(ae^{i\alpha}|v_{rb}\rangle + be^{i\beta}|v_{ry}\rangle) = a^2 + b^2 + 2ab/3 \cdot \cos(\beta - \alpha + \theta_r - \phi_r)$, whence

$$\cos(\beta - \alpha + \theta_r - \phi_r) = 3(1 - a^2 - b^2)/2ab \tag{18}$$

Straightforward calculations show that the transition probabilities in the superposition state p_{v_s} are given by

$$|\langle 1, 0, 0|v_s\rangle|^2 = 1/3 \cdot (3 - 2a^2 - 2b^2) = \mu_r(g, p_{v_s}) \tag{19}$$
$$|\langle 0, 1, 0|v_s\rangle|^2 = 2/3 \cdot b^2 = \mu_y(g, p_{v_s}) \tag{20}$$
$$|\langle 0, 0, 1|v_s\rangle|^2 = 2/3 \cdot a^2 = \mu_b(g, p_{v_s}) \tag{21}$$

and that we can represent a general superposition state as

$$|v_s\rangle = 1/\sqrt{3} \cdot |ae^{i(\alpha+\phi_r)} + be^{i(\beta+\theta_r)}, \sqrt{2}be^{i(\beta+\theta_y)}, \sqrt{2}ae^{i(\alpha+\theta_b)}\rangle \tag{22}$$

and that the utilities corresponding to the observables of the different actions are given by

$$U(f_1, g, p_{v_s}) = \langle v_s|\hat{f}_1|v_s\rangle = 12\$ \cdot 1/3 \cdot (3 - 2a^2 - 2b^2) = 4\$ \cdot (3 - 2a^2 - 2b^2) \tag{23}$$
$$U(f_2, g, p_{v_s}) = \langle v_s|\hat{f}_2|v_s\rangle = 12\$ \cdot 2/3 \cdot a^2 = 4\$ \cdot 2a^2 \tag{24}$$
$$U(f_3, g, p_{v_s}) = \langle v_s|\hat{f}_3|v_s\rangle = 12\$ \cdot 1/3 \cdot (3 - 2a^2 - 2b^2) + 12\$ \cdot 2/3 \cdot b^2 = 4\$ \cdot (3 - 2a^2) \tag{25}$$
$$U(f_4, g, p_{v_s}) = \langle v_s|\hat{f}_4|v_s\rangle = 12\$ \cdot 2/3 \cdot b^2 + 12\$ \cdot 2/3 \cdot a^2 = 4\$(2a^2 + 2b^2) \tag{26}$$

We can see that it is not necessarily the case that $\mu_r(g, p_{v_s}) = 1/3$, which means that choices of a and b can be made such that the superposition state p_{v_s} is not a state contained in Σ_{Ells}. The reason is that Σ_{Ells} is not a linearly closed subset of $\mathbb{C}^3$. A conservative choice within our quantum modeling is that we require the superposition state to be an element of Σ_{Ells} – we plan in future work to explore situations where this is not the case, e.g. situations of interference with respect to Ellsberg-type examples – and this leads to

$$1/3 = \mu_r(g, p_{v_s}) = 1/3 \cdot (3 - 2a^2 - 2b^2) \Leftrightarrow a^2 + b^2 = 1 \tag{27}$$

which implies that $\cos(\beta - \alpha + \theta_r - \phi_r) = 0$ and hence $\beta = \pi/2 + \alpha - \theta_r + \phi_r$. Let us construct now two examples of superposition states that conserve the $1/3$ probability for drawing a red ball, and hence are conservative superpositions, and express the ambiguity as is thought to be the case in the Ellsberg paradox situation. The first state refers to the comparison for a bet between f_1 and f_2. The ambiguity of not knowing the number of yellow and black balls in the urn, only their sum to be 60, as compared to knowing the number of red balls in the urn to be 30, gives rise to the thought that 'eventually there are perhaps almost no black balls and hence an abundance of yellow balls'. Jointly, and in superposition, the thought also comes that 'it is of course also possible that there are more black balls than yellow balls'. These two thoughts in superposition, are mathematically represented by a state p_{v_s}. The state p_{v_s} will be closer to $p_{v_{ry}}$, the extreme state with no black balls, if the person has a lot of ambiguity aversion, while it will be closer to $p_{v_{rb}}$, the extreme state with no yellow balls, if the person is attracted by the ambiguity. Hence, these two tendencies are expressed by the values of a and b in the superposition state. If we consider again the utilities, this time with $a^2 + b^2 = 1$, we have

$$U(f_1, g, p_{v_s}) = 4\$ \qquad\qquad U(f_2, g, p_{v_s}) = 4\$ \cdot 2a^2 \qquad (28)$$
$$U(f_3, g, p_{v_s}) = 4\$ \cdot (3 - 2a^2) \quad U(f_4, g, p_{v_s}) = 8\$ \qquad (29)$$

So, for $a^2 < 1/2$, which exactly means that the superposition state p_{v_s} is closer to the state $p_{v_{ry}}$ than to the state $p_{v_{rb}}$, we have that $U(f_2, g, p_{v_s}) < U(f_1, g, p_{v_s})$, and hence a person with strong ambiguity aversion in the situation of the first bet, will then prefer to bet on f_1 and not on f_2. Let us choose a concrete state for the bet between f_1 and f_2, and call it $p_{v^{12}}$, and denote its superposition state by $|v_s^{12}\rangle$. Hence, for $|v_s^{12}\rangle$ we take $a = 1/2$ and $b = \sqrt{3}/2$ and hence $a^2 = 1/4$ and $b^2 = 3/4$. For the angles we must have $\beta - \alpha + \theta_r - \phi_r = \pi/2$, hence let us choose $\theta_r = \phi_r = 0$, $\alpha = 0$, and $\beta = \pi/2$. This gives us

$$|v_s^{12}\rangle = 1/2\sqrt{3} \cdot |1 + \sqrt{3}e^{i\pi/2}, \sqrt{2}\sqrt{3}e^{i\pi/2}, \sqrt{2}\rangle = 1/2\sqrt{3} \cdot |1 + i\sqrt{3}, i\sqrt{6}, \sqrt{2}\rangle \quad (30)$$

On the other hand, for $1/2 < a^2$, which means that the superposition state is closer to the state $p_{v_{rb}}$ than to the state $p_{v_{ry}}$, we have that $U(f_3, g, p_{v_s}) < U(f_4, g, p_{v_s})$, and hence a person with strong ambiguity aversion in the situation of the second bet, will then prefer to bet on f_4 and not on f_3. Also for this case we construct an explicit state, let us call it $p_{v^{34}}$, and denote it by the vector $|v_s^{34}\rangle$. Hence, for $|v_s^{34}\rangle$ we take $a = \sqrt{3}/2$ and $b = 1/2$ and hence $a^2 = 3/4$ and $b^2 = 1/4$. For the angles we must have $\beta - \alpha + \theta_r - \phi_r = \pi/2$, hence let us choose $\theta_r = \phi_r = 0$, $\alpha = 0$, and $\beta = \pi/2$. This gives us

$$|v_s^{34}\rangle = 1/2\sqrt{3} \cdot |\sqrt{3} + e^{i\pi/2}, \sqrt{2}e^{i\pi/2}, \sqrt{2}\sqrt{3}\rangle = 1/2\sqrt{3} \cdot |\sqrt{3} + i, i\sqrt{2}, \sqrt{6}\rangle \quad (31)$$

3   A Quantum Model for the Machina Paradox

In this section we elaborate a quantum model for the Machina paradox which is similar to the model constructed for the Ellsberg paradox. To this aim let us consider again the payoff matrix for the Machina situation in Tab. 2, Sec. 1.

We consider the four dimensional complex Hilbert space $\mathbb{C}^4$ endowed with the canonical basis $\{|1, 0, 0, 0\rangle, |0, 1, 0, 0\rangle, |0, 0, 1, 0\rangle, |0, 0, 0, 1\rangle\}$. First, we describe the conceptual Machina entity, consisting of the Machina situation without the different actions and also without the person and the bet to be taken. Hence it is the situation of the urn with 50 balls of type 1 or type 2 and 51 balls of type 3 or type 4. This is described by the context e represented by the spectral family $\{P_{12}, P_{34}\}$, where P_{12} is the two dimensional orthogonal projection operator on the subspace generated by $\{|1, 0, 0, 0\rangle, |0, 1, 0, 0\rangle\}$, and P_{34} is the two dimensional orthogonal projection operator on the subspace generated by $\{|0, 0, 1, 0\rangle, |0, 0, 0, 1\rangle\}$.

Then, as in Sec. 2, let us define the set of states of the Machina situation which we call the *Machina state set*

$$\Sigma_{Mach} = \{p_v : |v\rangle = |v_1, v_2, v_3, v_4\rangle \mid |v_1|^2 + |v_2|^2 = 50/101, |v_3|^2 + |v_4|^2 = 51/101\}. \tag{32}$$

A state contained in Σ_{Mach} delivers a quantum description of the Machina situation, together with the measurement e represented by the spectral family $\{P_{12}, P_{34}\}$ in $\mathbb{C}^4$.

We come now to the second step, we provide a description of the different actions f_1, f_2, f_3 and f_4, by means of the introduction of a second measurement context which we denote by g, and which describes how a ball is taken from the urn, and it is verified whether it is of type 1, 2, 3 or 4. Hence g is represented by the spectral family $\{P_1, P_2, P_3, P_4\}$, where P_1, P_2, P_3 and P_4 are the orthogonal projection operators on the subspaces generated by $|1, 0, 0, 0\rangle$, $|0, 1, 0, 0\rangle$, $|0, 0, 1, 0\rangle$ and $|0, 0, 0, 1\rangle$, respectively. Thus, the probability $\mu_j(g, p_v)$ to draw a ball of type j, $j = 1, 2, 3, 4$, in the state p_v represented by the vector $|v\rangle = |v_1, v_2, v_3, v_4\rangle$, is given by

$$\mu_1(g, p_v) = \langle v|P_1|v\rangle = |v_1|^2, \quad \mu_2(g, p_v) = \langle v|P_2|v\rangle = |v_2|^2, \tag{33}$$

$$\mu_3(g, p_v) = \langle v|P_3|v\rangle = |v_3|^2, \quad \mu_4(g, p_v) = \langle v|P_4|v\rangle = |v_4|^2, \tag{34}$$

Let us then calculate the expected utilities associated with each of the feasible acts, proceeding as in the Ellsberg case. The acts f_1 to f_4 are observables, we represent them by self-adjoint operators built on the spectral family $\{P_1, P_2, P_3, P_4\}$ in the following way: $\hat{f}_1 = \$202P_1 + \$202P_2 + \$101P_3 + \$101P_4$, $\hat{f}_2 = \$202P_1 + \$101P_2 + \$202P_3 + \$101P_4$, $\hat{f}_3 = \$303P_1 + \$202P_2 + \$101P_3 + \$0P_4$ and $\hat{f}_4 = \$303P_1 + \$101P_2 + \$202P_3 + \$0P_4$. Then we find

$$U(f_1, p_v) = 202 \cdot |v_1|^2 + 202 \cdot |v_2|^2 + 101 \cdot |v_3|^2 + 101 \cdot |v_4|^2 = 151 \tag{35}$$

$$U(f_2, p_v) = 202|v_1|^2 + 101|v_2|^2 + 202|v_3|^2 + 101|v_4|^2 \tag{36}$$

$$U(f_3, p_v) = 303|v_1|^2 + 202|v_2|^2 + 101|v_3|^2 \tag{37}$$

$$U(f_4, p_v) = 303|v_1|^2 + 101|v_2|^2 + 202|v_3|^2 \tag{38}$$

and see that only $U(f_1, p_v)$ is independent of p_v. Finally, as we did in the case of Ellsberg, let us calculate the utility for the three acts f_2, f_3 and f_4 for the Machina entity being in the extreme states $p_{v_{13}}$ and $p_{v_{24}}$ represented by the vectors

$$|v_{13}\rangle = |\sqrt{50/101} \cdot e^{i\theta_1}, 0, \sqrt{51/101} \cdot e^{i\theta_3}, 0\rangle \tag{39}$$

$$|v_{24}\rangle = |0, \sqrt{50/101} \cdot e^{i\theta_2}, 0, \sqrt{51/101} \cdot e^{i\theta_4}\rangle \tag{40}$$

We have $U(f_2, p_{v_{13}}) = 202$, $U(f_3, p_{v_{13}}) = 201$, $U(f_4, p_{v_{13}}) = 252$, $U(f_2, p_{v_{24}}) = 101$, $U(f_3, p_{v_{24}}) = 100$ and $U(f_4, p_{v_{24}}) = 50$, which shows that for the state $p_{v_{13}}$ the utilities of all three acts f_2, f_3 and f_4 are maximal, and much bigger than the utility of f_1 as state independent act without ambiguity. On the contrary, for the state $p_{v_{24}}$, we are in the inverse situation, for all three acts f_2, f_3 and

f_4 the utilities are minimal, and much smaller than the utility of act f_1. Let us consider a superposition state $|v_s\rangle$ of these two extreme states

$$|v_s\rangle = ae^{i\alpha}|v_{13}\rangle + be^{i\beta}|v_{24}\rangle \tag{41}$$

where a, b are such that $a^2 + b^2 = 1$, and α and β are arbitrary, because indeed this makes $\langle v_s|v_s\rangle = 1$, since $|v_{13}\rangle$ and $|v_{24}\rangle$ are orthogonal. We have

$$\langle 1,0,0,0|v_s\rangle = ae^{i\alpha}\langle 1,0,0,0|v_{13}\rangle + be^{i\beta}\langle 1,0,0,0|v_{24}\rangle = a\sqrt{50/101}e^{i(\alpha+\theta_1)} \tag{42}$$

$$\langle 0,1,0,0|v_s\rangle = ae^{i\alpha}\langle 0,1,0,0|v_{13}\rangle + be^{i\beta}\langle 0,1,0,0|v_{24}\rangle = b\sqrt{50/101}e^{i(\beta+\theta_2)} \tag{43}$$

$$\langle 0,0,1,0|v_s\rangle = ae^{i\alpha}\langle 0,0,1,0|v_{13}\rangle + be^{i\beta}\langle 0,0,1,0|v_{24}\rangle = a\sqrt{51/101}e^{i(\alpha+\theta_3)} \tag{44}$$

$$\langle 0,0,0,1|v_s\rangle = ae^{i\alpha}\langle 0,0,0,1|v_{13}\rangle + be^{i\beta}\langle 0,0,0,1|v_{24}\rangle = b\sqrt{51/101}e^{i(\beta+\theta_4)} \tag{45}$$

which shows that

$$|\langle 1,0,0,0|v_s\rangle|^2 = 50a^2/101 = \mu_1(g,p_{v_s}) \tag{46}$$
$$|\langle 0,1,0,0|v_s\rangle|^2 = 50b^2/101 = \mu_2(g,p_{v_s}) \tag{47}$$
$$|\langle 0,0,1,0|v_s\rangle|^2 = 51a^2/101 = \mu_3(g,p_{v_s}) \tag{48}$$
$$|\langle 0,0,0,1|v_s\rangle|^2 = 51b^2/101 = \mu_4(g,p_{v_s}) \tag{49}$$

This means that for the utilities in the superposition state p_{v_s} we find

$$\begin{aligned} U(f_1,p_{v_s}) &= 202\cdot 50a^2/101 + 202\cdot 50b^2/101 + 101\cdot 51a^2/101 + 101\cdot 51b^2/101 \\ &= 2\cdot 50(a^2+b^2) + 51(a^2+b^2) = 151 \end{aligned} \tag{50}$$

$$\begin{aligned} U(f_2,p_{v_s}) &= 202\cdot 50a^2/101 + 101\cdot 50b^2/101 + 202\cdot 51a^2/101 + 101\cdot 51b^2/101 \\ &= 2\cdot 50a^2 + 50b^2 + 2\cdot 51a^2 + 51b^2 = 202a^2 + 101b^2 \end{aligned} \tag{51}$$

$$\begin{aligned} U(f_3,p_{v_s}) &= 303\cdot 50a^2/101 + 202\cdot 50b^2/101 + 101\cdot 51a^2/101 \\ &= 3\cdot 50a^2 + 2\cdot 50b^2 + 51a^2 = 201a^2 + 100b^2 \end{aligned} \tag{52}$$

$$\begin{aligned} U(f_4,p_{v_s}) &= 303\cdot 50a^2/101 + 101\cdot 50b^2/101 + 202\cdot 51a^2/101 \\ &= 3\cdot 50a^2 + 50b^2 + 2\cdot 51a^2 = 252a^2 + 50b^2 \end{aligned} \tag{53}$$

Before we further our quantum description, we stress that there is ample and convincing experimental evidence showing that ambiguity aversion is not related to the size of the payoffs involved [16]. This means that if we want to model the effect of ambiguity, we should identify it mainly on the level of the states of the Ellsberg and Machina situations, and only on the level of the utilities as far as we take into account that it should not be linked to the size of the payoffs. This is exactly what we have done in our quantum model in the case of the Ellsberg paradox situation. Indeed, in (17), we have considered a superposition state of the two extreme ambiguity states, and put forward the hypothesis that depending on the ambiguity aversion of a person, he or she will consider the Ellsberg conceptual entity in a state closer to one, or to the other, of the extreme states. Let us analyze the Machina situation in an analogous way now.

Consider first the situation of a bet on f_1 or f_2. There is no ambiguity on f_1, since all states give rise to the same payoff, whereas there is a lot of ambiguity on f_2. A person with strong ambiguity aversion will consider the Machina conceptual entity to be in a superposition state close to the extreme state $p_{v_{24}}$, hence the value of a will be small, and the value of b large. Let us introduce the following values as an example to make a quantitative calculation possible, we take $a = 1/\sqrt{10}$ and $b = 3/\sqrt{10}$. Then we have $U(f_1, p_v) = 151$, and $U(f_2, p_v) = 202/10 + 101 \cdot 9/10 = 20.2 + 90.9 = 111.1$. Hence, $U(f_2, p_v) < U(f_1, p_v)$, and this person will bet on f_1 and not on f_2. Consider now the situation of a bet on f_3 or f_4. In this case, for both actions there is an equal amount of ambiguity. This means that in principle no preference is present on the level of the 'ambiguity choice' with respect to the superposition state that a person will consider the Machina conceptual entity to be in. Statistically this amounts to the superposition state being with equal values of a and b and hence we have $a = b = 1/\sqrt{2}$. Let us calculate for these values of a and b the utilities corresponding to these actions. We have $U(f_3, p_v) = 201/2 + 100/2 = 150.5$ and $U(f_4, p_v) = 252/2 + 50/2 = 151$. This means that $U(f_3, p_v) < U(f_4, p_v)$ and hence the person will bet on f_4 and not on f_3.

We conclude with some remarks on the novelties of our quantum modeling.

(i) We incorporate the subjective preference, hence the subjective probabilities, of traditional economics approaches in the quantum state, which represents the conceptual entity of the Ellsberg and Machina paradox situations. The quantum state is indeed introduced as describing the 'conceptual entity', and not the 'physical entity'. At variance with existing proposals, the subjective preference can be in our case different for each one of the acts f_j, since it is not derived from the mathematical structure of the state space of the Machina situation modeling. In the other approaches such a mathematical rule exists, which renders the Machina situation with f_1 preferred to f_2 and f_4 preferred to f_3 impossible. We have just seen that this is not impossible in our modeling scheme.

(ii) Since in our approach there is no mathematical rule for the subjective probability measure that arises from the interaction of the person with the Machina conceptual entity, hence, from the interaction between the conceptual landscape carried by the person and the Machina conceptual entity, there is no problem to construct the exact probability measure, i.e. superposition, that will model the eventually collected experimental data for the Machina example.

(iii) All existing proposals mathematically lead to a subjective probability, hence in our quantum model, to a specific superposition state, 'as if this subjective probability i.e. superposition state, could be determined from a theoretical perspective'. We believe that the specific structure of this probability depends instead on the interaction of the betting person with the Ellsberg or Machina situation, and its values should be determined experimentally.

We have not yet introduced the quantum model of the bet itself. This is indeed another aspect of the quantum formalism where an essential deviation from the existing approaches occurs. Indeed, the bet itself, as a decision process, can be modeled in the same quantum formalism, by means of a spectral family of projection operators. We have already done this for the Ellsberg situation, and were able to model the experimental data on the Ellsberg paradox we collected in [13]. We leave this part of the quantum model of Ellsberg and Machina for a forthcoming publication. In future work we also plan to investigate the relation to the already existing and fruitful approaches of introducing quantum structures in situations of decision under uncertainty in economics and decision theory [18].

References

1. von Neumann, J., Morgenstern, O.: Theory of Games and Economic Behavior. Princeton University Press, Princeton (1944)
2. Savage, L.J.: The Foundations of Statistics. Wiley, New York (1954)
3. Ellsberg, D.: Risk, Ambiguity, and the Savage Axioms. Quart. J. Econ. 75(4), 643–669 (1961)
4. Machina, M.J.: Risk, Ambiguity, and the Dark–dependence Axioms. Am. Econ. Rev. 99(1), 385–392 (2009)
5. Knight, F.H.: Risk, Uncertainty and Profit. Houghton Mifflin, Boston (1921)
6. Gilboa, I.: Expected Utility with Purely Subjective Non-additive Probabilities. J. Math. Econ. 16, 65–88 (1987)
7. Gilboa, I., Schmeidler, D.: Maxmin Expected Utility With Non–unique Prior. J. Math. Econ. 18, 141–153 (1989)
8. Maccheroni, F., Marinacci, M., Rustichini, A.: Dynamical Variational Preferences. The Carlo Alberto Notebooks 1, 37 (2006)
9. Klibanoff, P., Marinacci, M., Mukerji, S.: A smooth model of decision making under ambiguity. Econometrica 73(6), 1849–1892 (2005)
10. Epstein, L.G.: A Definition of Uncertainty Aversion. Rev. Econ. Stud. 66, 579–608 (1999)
11. Baillon, A., L'Haridon, O., Placido, L.: Ambiguity Models and the Machina Paradoxes. Am. Econ. rev. 101(4), 1547–1560 (2011)
12. Aerts, D., Broekaert, J., Czachor, M., D'Hooghe, B.: A Quantum-Conceptual Explanation of Violations of Expected Utility in Economics. In: Song, D., Melucci, M., Frommholz, I., Zhang, P., Wang, L., Arafat, S. (eds.) QI 2011. LNCS, vol. 7052, pp. 192–198. Springer, Heidelberg (2011)
13. Aerts, D., D'Hooghe, B., Sozzo, S.: A Quantum Cognition Analysis of the Ellsberg Paradox. In: Song, D., Melucci, M., Frommholz, I., Zhang, P., Wang, L., Arafat, S. (eds.) QI 2011. LNCS, vol. 7052, pp. 95–104. Springer, Heidelberg (2011)
14. Aerts, D., Sozzo, S.: Quantum Structure in Economics: The Ellsberg Paradox. In: D'Ariano, M., et al. (eds.) Quantum Theory: Reconsideration of Foundations, vol. 6, pp. 487–494. AIP, Melville (2012)
15. Aerts, D., Sozzo, S.: Contextual Risk and Its Relevance in Economics; A Contextual Risk Model for the Ellsberg Paradox. J. Eng. Sci. Tech. Rev. 4, 241–245, 246–250 (2012)
16. Camerer, C.F.: Ambiguity Aversion and Non–additive Probability: Experimental Evidence, Models and Applications. In: Luini, L. (ed.) Uncertain Decisions: Bridging Theory and Experiments, pp. 53–80. Kluwer Acad. Pub., Dordrecht (1999)
17. Aerts, D.: Quantum Structure in Cognition. J. Math. Psych. 53, 314–348 (2009)
18. Busemeyer, J.R., Lambert-Mogiliansky, A.: An Exploration of Type Indeterminacy in Strategic Decision-Making. In: Bruza, P., Sofge, D., Lawless, W., van Rijsbergen, K., Klusch, M. (eds.) QI 2009. LNCS, vol. 5494, pp. 113–127. Springer, Heidelberg (2009)

A Quantum-Like Model of *Escherichia coli*'s Metabolism Based on Adaptive Dynamics

Masanari Asano[1], Irina Basieva[2], Andrei Khrennikov[2], Masanori Ohya[1], Yoshiharu Tanaka[1], and Ichiro Yamato[3]

[1] Department of Information Sciences, Tokyo University of Science,
Yamasaki 2641, Noda-shi, Chiba, 278-8510 Japan
[2] International Center for Mathematical Modeling in Physics and Cognitive Sciences,
Linnaeus University, S-35195, Växjö, Sweden
[3] Department of Biological Science and Technology, Tokyo University of Science
Yamasaki 2641, Noda-shi, Chiba, 278-8510 Japan

Abstract. Recently it is pointed out that there exists the experimental data in *Escherichia coli*'s metabolism which violate the law of total probability in classical probability. In this report, we propose a model which describes such phenomenon based on adaptive dynamics.

Keywords: *Escherichia coli*, quantum-like model, adaptive dynamics, lifting.

1 Introduction

Recently, it was pointed out [1] that a complex microscopic biological dynamics of metabolism violates one of basic laws of classical probability theory – the law of total probability, which is crucial in Bayesian analysis.

In biology, the gene regulation of *glucose/lactose metabolism* has been studied well with a bacterium, *Escherichia coli* (*E.coli*). The energy for *E.coli*'s activity is produced by metabolizing sugar such as glucose, lactose, etc. Many microbiological studies demonstrated that *E.coli* has a preference for carbon resources, that is, *E.coli* likes glucose better than lactose. When *E.coli* is incubated in a test tube containing both glucose and lactose, *E.coli* will digest glucose first and lactose second. In this phenomenon, the functioning unit of genes which is called *lactose operon* plays an important role. Since the operon theory was proposed in 1956–1961 [2], the regulatory system of lactose operon has been extensively studied and its molecular mechanism were mostly figured out. Here it is important to notice that *E. coli*'s metabolism is context dependent; *E. coli* is adaptive to the context of the surroundings (lactose/glucose concentrations). In such system, the conditional probability can not be defined well within usual mathematical framework: classical probability theory. The formula of total probability is based on the classical definition of conditional probability (Bayes rule). We show that this formula is violated by experimental statistical data for *E. coli*'s methabolism. Hence, we do not proceed with the classical definition of conditional probability.

J.R. Busemeyer et al. (Eds.): QI 2012, LNCS 7620, pp. 60–67, 2012.

In this report based on the paper [3], we describe the *E. coli*'s metabolism system as a model based on non-Kolmogorovian probability inspired by the quantum phenomena. We call it *quantum-like* models [4]. We define a new conditional probabilities by the idea of *adaptive dynamics* [4,5], we express the adaptive dynamics of the gene regulation in cells by operators on complex Hilbert spaces, quantum channel and lifting map. We analyze statistical data obtained from biological experiments [7], and we compute the degree of *E.coli*'s preference in adaptive dynamics. We do not need difficult simulation of complex biochemical systems. We use only simple calculation based on adaptive dynamics and its operational representation.

2 New Mathematical Law Computing the Probability in Adaptive Dynamics for Glucose Effect of *E.coli*

Let us introduce a state vector $|x_0\rangle$ which is written by

$$|x_0\rangle = \frac{1}{\sqrt{2}}|e_1\rangle + \frac{1}{\sqrt{2}}|e_2\rangle = \frac{1}{\sqrt{2}}\begin{pmatrix}1\\1\end{pmatrix}$$

with $\{|e_1\rangle = (0,1)^t, |e_2\rangle = (1,0)^t\}$. Before the detection of lactose or glucose, the initial state of *E. coli* is given by

$$\rho_0 = |x_0\rangle\langle x_0| = \frac{1}{2}\begin{pmatrix}1 & 1\\1 & 1\end{pmatrix}$$

on Hilbert space $\mathbb{C}^2$. The basis $\{|e_1\rangle, |e_2\rangle\}$ denotes the detection of lactose (or glucose) by *E. coli*, and we express these events as L (or G). When the *E. coli* recognizes these molecules, the following state change occurs;

$$\rho_0 \to \rho_D \equiv \frac{D\rho_0 D^*}{\mathrm{tr}\left(|D|^2 \rho_0\right)} = \begin{pmatrix}|\alpha|^2 & \alpha\beta^*\\\alpha^*\beta & |\beta|^2\end{pmatrix},$$

where D is an operator given by a complex diagonal matrix

$$D = \begin{pmatrix}\alpha & 0\\0 & \beta\end{pmatrix}$$

with $|\alpha|^2 + |\beta|^2 = 1$. The operator D represents *E. coli*'s adaptive effect for surroundings (concentration of lactose or glucose), and it is called *detection operator*. Note that $|\alpha|^2$ and $|\beta|^2$ imply the probabilities for the events L and G, that is, $P_D(L)$ and $P_D(G)$. The state $\sigma_D \equiv DD^*$ means the distribution of $P(L)$ and $P(G)$. In this sense, the state σ_D is derived from the solution concentrations of lactose and glucose. The state determining the activation of the operon in *E. coli* depends on the detection state ρ_D. We can give such state by the following state change

$$\rho_D \rightarrow \rho_{\text{op}} \equiv \frac{Q\rho_0 Q^*}{\text{tr}\left(|Q|^2 \rho_0\right)} = \frac{1}{|a\alpha + b\beta|^2 + |c\alpha + d\beta|^2}$$

$$\times \begin{pmatrix} |a\alpha + b\beta|^2 & (a\alpha + b\beta)(c\alpha + d\beta)^* \\ (a\alpha + b\beta)^*(c\alpha + d\beta) & |c\alpha + d\beta|^2 \end{pmatrix},$$

where

$$Q = \begin{pmatrix} a & b \\ c & d \end{pmatrix} \qquad a, b, c, d \in \mathbb{C}$$

is an operator representing the state change of lactose operon and we call it *activation operator*. The correlation between the activity of lactose operon and concentrations of lactose and glucose is described as the lifting (map)

$$\mathcal{E}_{D,Q}^*(\rho) = \Lambda_Q^* \Lambda_D^* \rho \otimes \Lambda_D^* \rho,$$

with a chanel (map) $\Lambda_X^* \rho \equiv X\rho X^* / \text{tr} |X|^2 \rho$. With this lifting $\mathcal{E}_{D,Q}^*$, one can define the joint probabilities as

$$P_D(+, L) \equiv \text{tr}(E_1 \otimes E_1)\mathcal{E}_{D,Q}^*(\rho_0),$$
$$P_D(-, L) \equiv \text{tr}(E_2 \otimes E_1)\mathcal{E}_{D,Q}^*(\rho_0),$$
$$P_D(+, G) \equiv \text{tr}(E_1 \otimes E_2)\mathcal{E}_{D,Q}^*(\rho_0),$$
$$P_D(-, G) \equiv \text{tr}(E_2 \otimes E_2)\mathcal{E}_{D,Q}^*(\rho_0),$$

where E_1 and E_2 are projection operator given by

$$E_1 = |e_1\rangle\langle e_1| = \begin{pmatrix} 1 & 0 \\ 0 & 0 \end{pmatrix}, \quad E_2 = |e_2\rangle\langle e_2| = \begin{pmatrix} 0 & 0 \\ 0 & 1 \end{pmatrix}.$$

Also one can define conditional probability as

$$P_D(+|L) \equiv \text{tr}(E_1 \otimes I)\mathcal{E}_{D,Q}^*(E_1) = \frac{|a|^2}{|a|^2 + |b|^2}, \tag{1}$$

$$P_D(+|G) \equiv \text{tr}(E_1 \otimes I)\mathcal{E}_{D,Q}^*(E_2) = \frac{|b|^2}{|a|^2 + |b|^2}, \tag{2}$$

$$P_D(-|L) \equiv \text{tr}(E_2 \otimes I)\mathcal{E}_{D,Q}^*(E_1) = \frac{|c|^2}{|c|^2 + |d|^2}, \tag{3}$$

$$P_D(-|G) \equiv \text{tr}(E_2 \otimes I)\mathcal{E}_{D,Q}^*(E_2) = \frac{|d|^2}{|c|^2 + |d|^2} \tag{4}$$

and

$$P_D(+|L \cup G) \equiv \mathrm{tr}(E_1 \otimes I)\mathcal{E}^*_{D,Q}(\rho_0)$$

$$= \frac{|a\alpha + b\beta|^2}{|a\alpha + b\beta|^2 + |c\alpha + d\beta|^2},$$

$$P_D(-|L \cup G) \equiv \mathrm{tr}(E_2 \otimes I)\mathcal{E}^*_{D,Q}(\rho_0)$$

$$= \frac{|c\alpha + d\beta|^2}{|a\alpha + b\beta|^2 + |c\alpha + d\beta|^2}.$$

The above definition of the conditional probability is different from classical one. We remark the following property;

$$P_D(\pm|L) \neq \frac{P_D(\pm \cap L)}{P_D(L)} \text{ and } P_D(\pm|L) \neq \frac{P_D(\pm \cap G)}{P_D(G)}$$

From Eqs.(1) - (4), we can decompose the activation operator as

$$Q = \begin{pmatrix} \sqrt{P_{E_1}(+|L)} & \sqrt{P_{E_2}(+|G)} \\ \sqrt{P_{E_1}(-|L)} & \sqrt{P_{E_2}(-|G)} \end{pmatrix} \begin{pmatrix} k_L & 0 \\ 0 & k_G e^{i\theta} \end{pmatrix} \tag{5}$$

with some real numbers k_L, k_G and θ. Then we can express the conditional probabilities $P_D(+|L \cup G)$ as

$$P_D(+|L \cup G) = \frac{P_{E_1}(+|L)P(L)\sqrt{\frac{k_L}{k_G}} + P_{E_2}(+|G)P(G)\sqrt{\frac{k_G}{k_L}} + 2\delta\cos\theta}{P(L)\sqrt{\frac{k_L}{k_G}} + P(G)\sqrt{\frac{k_G}{k_L}} + 2\tilde{\delta}\cos\theta} \tag{6}$$

with

$$\delta = \sqrt{P_{E_1}(+|L)P_{E_2}(+|G)P(L)P(G)},$$

$$\tilde{\delta} = \sqrt{P(L)P(G)}\left[\sqrt{P_{E_1}(+|L)P_{E_2}(+|G)} + \sqrt{P_{E_1}(-|L)P_{E_2}(-|G)}\right].$$

Note that, iff $k_L/k_G = 1$ and $\theta = \pi/2$, the total probability law (TPL) is hold;

$$P_D(\pm|L \cup G) = P_{E_1}(\pm|L)P_D(L) + P_{E_2}(\pm|G)P_D(G).$$

However, for general k_L, k_G and θ , TPL is violated;

$$P_D(\pm|L \cup G) \neq P_{E_1}(\pm|L)P_D(L) + P_{E_2}(\pm|G)P_D(G).$$

The violation of TPL means that *E. coli* prefers glucose (of lactose*)*, and

$\{k_L/k_G, \theta\}$ specify these preference.

Remark 1. (Comparison with classical probabilistic transformations) In classical probability theory, transition probability matrix is used in the following way;

$$\begin{pmatrix} P(+) \\ P(-) \end{pmatrix} = \begin{pmatrix} P(+|L) & P(+|G) \\ P(-|L) & P(-|G) \end{pmatrix} \begin{pmatrix} P(L) \\ P(G) \end{pmatrix}. \tag{7}$$

This is nothing else than encoding of the law of total probability. As we have seen, the experimental data on activation of *lac* operon violates the formula of total probability.

Table 1. Results of beta-galactosidase assay. (The symbol '+' or '-' means the genotype of each strain. The values with † are cited from the paper (Inada et al. 1996) and the values with ‡ are cited from the online page http://ro119.com/archive/nagoya.cool.ne.jp/planta/bio/lac_operon.htm

data	A	B	C	D	E
strain	W3110	W3110	ML30	ML308	ML308-2
lacI	+	+	+	-	-
lacY	+	+	+	+	-
preculturing	LB	Gly	LB	LB	LB
MU(1)	2920†	957	1763	2563	6140
MU(2)	33†	5	14	1592	3062
MU(3)	3000†,2200‡	1059	3133	2438	5326
MU(4)	43†	486	184	2074	2668
MU(5)	64‡	421	78	2050	862

3   Comparison of Preferences among Several Types of *E.coli*

In this section, we show the *E. coli*'s preferece $\{k_L/k_G, \theta\}$ calculated from experimental data. This calculation is based on the idea of new probabilities explained in the previous section.

3.1   *E.coli*'s Preference for Lactose or Glucose

By the method of beta-galactosidase assay (Miller 1972), we measured the values of Miller unit (MU) in five different situations: *E. coli* grown in the media containing (1) 0.4% lactose; (2) 0.4% glucose; (3) 0.2 mM IPTG; (4) 0.1% glucose and 0.4% lactose; (5) 0.4% glucose and 0.4% lactose. In this experiment, we used four types of *E.coli* (Bechwith and Zipser 1970); W3110, ML30, ML308 (*lacI⁻*), ML308-2 (*lacI⁻*, *lacY⁻*). We also used two types of preculture condition; grown in minimal medium with 0.4% glycerol(Gly) or in Luria broth(LB). The Table 1 shows the results of our experiment.

In data A and C, we can see that both MU(4) and MU(5) are similarly small values as MU(2). The strains of W3110 and ML30 are wild type *E. coli*, and these show stronger preference for glucose than for lactose. On the other hand, as seen in data D, the strain ML308 has weak preference for glucose since MU(4) and MU(5) are as small as MU(2). ML308 is a mutant of repressor minus (*lacI⁻*), so that the beta-galactosidase is produced in the cell even in the presence of high concentration of glucose. As seen in data E, ML308-2 shows different behaviour from other strains; MU(4) and (5) is smaller than MU(1) in data E. ML308-2 is a mutant which is not only repressor minus but also lactose transport system minus ($lacY^-$), so that, data E is different from data D. The Table 1 also shows the result for two different preculture conditions as seen in data A and B. We clearly see that the value of MU(4) and MU(5) in data B is very high in comparison to those in data A. This result shows that *E. coli*'s preference are affected by the preculture condition.

From the added concentration of lactose and glucose, we can calculate the probabilities $P_D(L)$ and $P_D(G)$. For example, the probabilities in the case of (4) is calculated as

$$P_D(L) = \frac{0.4\%}{0.4\% + 0.1\%} = 0.8, P_D(G) = \frac{0.1\%}{0.4\% + 0.1\%} = 0.2,$$

and the detection operator is determined as

$$D = \begin{pmatrix} \sqrt{0.8} & 0 \\ 0 & \sqrt{0.2} \end{pmatrix}.$$

Similarly, the probabilities in the case of (5) is calculated as

$$P_{D'}(L) = 0.5, P_{D'}(G) = 0.5,$$

and the detection operator is determined as

$$D' = \begin{pmatrix} \sqrt{0.5} & 0 \\ 0 & \sqrt{0.5} \end{pmatrix}.$$

Also we can calculate the conditional probabilities $\{P_{E_1}(\pm|L), \ P_{E_2}(\pm|G), \ P_D(+|L \cup G), \ P_{D'}(+|L \cup G)\}$ from the obtained MU values. For example, we can calculate them with MU(3)-(5) of data C as follows.

$$P_{E_1}(+|L) = \frac{1763}{3133}, P_{E_2}(+|G) = \frac{14}{3133},$$
$$P_D(+|L \cup G) = \frac{184}{3133}, P_{D'}(+|L \cup G) = \frac{78}{3133}.$$

The probabilities for each data (A)-(E) are shown in Table 2.

One can confirm that the probabilities in data A and C do not satisfy TPL;

$$P_D(+|L \cup G)$$

is not equal to

$$P_{E_1}(+|L)P_D(L) + P_{E_2}(+|G)P_D(G).$$

On the other hand, one can see that the probabilities in data (D) satisfy TPL approximately. The strain of ML308 is a mutant which can not produce the repressor protein. Therefore, beta-galactosidase is always produced in the cell of ML308. ML308-2 is not only $lacI^-$ but also $lacY^-$, so that the lactose transporting system of ML308-2 is defective and different from that of other strains. Hence, the violation of TPL is also seen in data (E).

Table 2. Calculated probabilities for data A,B,C,D and E

	A	B	C	D	E
$P_D(L)$	0.8	0.8	0.8	0.8	0.8
$P_{D'}(L)$	0.5	0.5	0.5	0.5	0.5
$P_{E_1}(+|L)$	0.973	0.904	0.563	1.000	1.000
$P_{E_2}(+|G)$	0.011	0.005	0.005	0.653	0.575
$P_D(+|L \cup G)$	0.014	0.459	0.059	0.851	0.501
$P_{D'}(+|L \cup G)$	0.029	0.398	0.025	0.841	0.462
$P_{E_1}(+|L)P_D(L) + P_{E_2}(+|G)P_D(G)$	0.780	0.723	0.117	0.722	0.660
$P_{E_1}(+|L)P_{D'}(L) + P_{E_2}(+|G)P_{D'}(G)$	0.492	0.455	0.284	0.827	0.788

Table 3. *E. coli*'s preferences calculated from each data

	A	B	C	D	E
$\sqrt{k_L/k_G}$	0.066	0.406	0.190	0.838	0.697
$\cos\theta$	−0.842	1.000	−0.461	0.251	−0.733

Here, let us remember the Eq.(6) in order to calculate lactose/glucose preferences $\{k_L, k_G, \theta\}$. By assigning these values of probabilities $\{P_D(L), P_{E_1}(+|L), P_{E_2}(+|G), P_D(+|L \cup G)\}$ and $\{P_{D'}(L), P_{E_1}(+|L), P_{E_2}(+|G), P_{D'}(+|L \cup G)\}$ to Eq.(6), we have two equations:

$$P_{E_1}(+|L)\{P_{D'}(L)\Delta - P_D(L)\Delta'\} \frac{k_L}{k_G}$$
$$+ \{P_D(+|L \cup G)\Delta' - P_{D'}(+|L \cup G)\Delta\} \sqrt{\frac{k_L}{k_G}}$$
$$+ P_{E_2}(+|G)\{P_{D'}(G)\Delta - P_D(G)\Delta'\} = 0, \tag{8}$$

$$\cos\theta = \frac{P_D(+|L \cup G) - \left\{P_{E_1}(+|L)P(L)\sqrt{\frac{k_L}{k_G}} + P_{E_2}(+|G)P(G)\sqrt{\frac{k_G}{k_L}}\right\}}{2\Delta}, \tag{9}$$

where

$$\Delta = P_D(-|L \cup G)\sqrt{P_{E_1}(+|L)P_{E_2}(+|G)P_D(L)P_D(G)}$$
$$+ P_D(+|L \cup G)\sqrt{P_{E_1}(-|L)P_{E_2}(-|G)P_D(L)P_D(G)},$$
$$\Delta' = P_{D'}(-|L \cup G)\sqrt{P_{E_1}(+|L)P_{E_2}(+|G)P_{D'}(L)P_{D'}(G)}$$
$$+ P_{D'}(+|L \cup G)\sqrt{P_{E_1}(-|L)P_{E_2}(-|G)P_{D'}(L)P_{D'}(G)}.$$

From Eqs.(8) and (9), we can obtain $\sqrt{k_L/k_G}$ and $\cos\theta$, and Table 3 shows these values for each data.

We remark that the values of $\left(\sqrt{k_L/k_G}, \cos\theta\right)$ in data A is different from those in data B. This result means that the preculture condition affects on *E.*

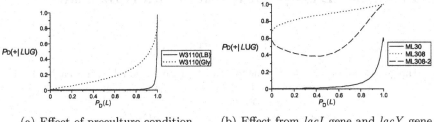

(a) Effect of preculture condition   (b) Effect from *lacI* gene and *lacY* gene

Fig. 5. Computed values of $P_D(+|L \cup G)$ with respect to $P_D(L)$

coli's preference. With those values, we can compute $P_D(+|L \cup G)$ with respect to $P_D(L)$ by assigning the preferences $\left(\sqrt{k_L/k_G}, \theta\right)$ to Eq. (6). For each data, we plot the values of $P_D(+|L \cup G)$ with respect to $P_D(L)$ in Fig. 5. The Figure 5(a) shows how much the preculture condition affects the behaviour of lactose operon. The $P_D(+|L \cup G)$ of W3110(Gly) in Fig. 5(a) is increasing rather linearly than that of W3110(LB). Therefore, the violation of TPL for W3110 precultured on glycerol is smaller than that for W3110 precultured in LB. The Figure 5(b) shows how much *lacI* gene or *lacY* gene affects the behaviour of lactose operon. The $P_D(+|L \cup G)$ of ML308 in Fig. 5(b) is linearly-increasing with respect to $P_D(L)$, so that the computed result shows that TPL is not violated so much in case of ML308.

References

1. Basieva, I., Khrennikov, A., Ohya, M., Yamato, I.: Quantum-like interference effect in gene expression glucose-lactose destructive interference. Syst. and Synth. Biol. 5(1-2), 59–68 (2010)
2. Jacob, F., Monod, J.: Genetic regulatory mechanism in the synthesis of proteins. J. Mol. Biol. 3, 318–356 (1961)
3. Asano, M., Basieva, I., Khrennikov, A., Ohya, M., Tanaka, Y., Yamato, I.: Quantum-like model for the adaptive dynamics of the genetic regulation of *E. coli*'s metabolism of glucose/lactose. Syst. Synth. Biol. (2012), doi:10.1007/s11693-012-9091-1
4. Khrennikov, A.: Ubiquitous quantum structure: from psychology to finance. Springer, Heidelberg (2010)
5. Ohya, M.: Adaptive dynamics and its applications to chaos and NPC problem. QP-PQ: Quantum Prob. White Noise Anal. 21, 186–216 (2008)
6. Asano, M., Ohya, M., Togawa, Y., Khrennikov, A., Basieva, I.: Dynamics of entropy in quantum-like model of decision making. J. Theor. Biology 281, 56–64 (2011)
7. Inada, T., Kimata, K., Aiba, H.: Mechanism responsible for glucose-lactose diauxie in Escherichia coli challenge to the cAMP model. Genes and Cells 1, 293–301 (1996)

Fractals, Dissipation and Coherent States

Giuseppe Vitiello

Dipartimento di Fisica "E. R. Caianiello" and Istituto Nazionale di Fisica Nucleare
Universitá di Salerno, I-84084 Fisciano (Salerno), Italy
vitiello@sa.infn.it
www.sa.infn.it/giuseppe.vitiello/

Abstract. Self-similarity properties of fractal structures, including the logarithmic spiral, are related to quantum dissipative dynamics, generalized squeezed coherent states and noncommutative geometry in the plane. The rôle played by the fractal Hamiltonian which actually turns out to be the fractal free energy is discussed. Time evolution characterized by the breakdown of time-reversal symmetry is controlled by the entropy. Coherent boson condensation induced by the generators of the coherent states is shown to control the formation of fractals. Viceversa, coherent generalized states are recognized to possess self-similar fractal structure. The global nature of fractals appears to emerge from irreversible coherent local deformation processes.

Keywords: fractals, logarithmic spiral, dissipation, squeezed coherent states, noncommutative geometry.

1 Introduction

In Refs. [1,2] it has been shown that the self-similarity property of deterministic fractals can be studied in the framework of the theory of entire analytical functions, which are the mathematical tool adopted in the construction of coherent states in the Fock–Bargmann representation [3]. There it has been discussed also the functional realization of fractals in terms of the q-deformed algebra of squeezed coherent states. In the present paper I further pursue these studies considering the relation between scale free (fractal) structures and quantum dissipation. I consider in particular the case of the logarithmic spiral, also related, in the specific case of the golden spiral, to the Fibonacci progression, which provides a most interesting example of self-similarity. My discussion also applies to other examples of fractals and in general to deterministic fractals. The conclusions of Refs. [1,2] are confirmed with the additional result that a relation emerges between fractals, quantum dissipation and noncommutative geometry. The plan of the paper is the following. The geometrical properties of the logarithmic spiral necessary to our discussion are summarized in Section 2. Self-similarity and dissipative time evolution are discussed in Section 3. In Section 4 is presented the formalism of quantum dissipation, and are discussed thermal properties and the fractal fee energy. Dissipation is finally related to noncommutative geometry in Section 5. Section 6 is devoted to conclusions.

J.R. Busemeyer et al. (Eds.): QI 2012, LNCS 7620, pp. 68–79, 2012.
© Springer-Verlag Berlin Heidelberg 2012

2   Geometrical Properties of the Logarithmic Spiral

The defining equation for the logarithmic spiral in polar coordinates (r, θ) is [4]

$$r = r_0 \, e^{d\theta} \, , \tag{1}$$

with r_0 and d arbitrary real constants and $r_0 > 0$. The anti-clockwise versus (left-handed or *direct*) spiral has the factor $q \equiv e^{d\theta} > 1$; the clockwise versus (right-handed or *indirect*) spiral has $q < 1$ (see Fig. 1). When θ is shifted by a given quantity, say $\theta \to \theta + 2\pi$, the radius vector of the curve scales in geometric progression with the ratio $e^{2\pi d}$:

$$r_1 = r_0 \, e^{d\theta} e^{d 2\pi} = r \, e^{2\pi d}, \quad r_2 = r \, (e^{2\pi d})^2, \quad ..., \quad r_m = r \, (e^{2\pi d})^m, \tag{2}$$

for $\theta \to \theta + 2m\pi$, $m = 1, 2, ...$ The rate of variation of the radius as θ changes, i.e. the logarithmic derivative of r with respect to θ, is:

$$\frac{1}{r} \frac{dr}{d\theta} = d \, . \tag{3}$$

d thus provides a measure of how "tight" is the spiral. Eq. (1) can be represented by the straight line of slope d in a log-log plot with abscissa $\theta = \ln e^\theta$:

$$d\theta = \ln \frac{r}{r_0} \, , \tag{4}$$

and we see that Eq. (3), which also holds for r_m for any m, is nothing but the derivative of such a straight line $f(\theta) = \ln r(\theta)$ in the log-log plot $(\ln r, \, \theta = \ln e^\theta)$. Eq. (4) is invariant under θ-scaling, i.e. rescaling of θ by the scale factor n, i.e. $\theta \to n\theta$, affects the ratio r/r_0 by the power $(r/r_0)^n$ since $d\,n\,\theta = n \ln(r/r_0))$. We thus have a power law; in geometrical terms, the self-similarity property of the logarithmic spiral is expressed by the constancy of the angular coefficient $\tan^{-1} d$ of the straight line in the log-log plot, which reflects in the constancy, at any of the points of the spiral curve, of the angle δ between the tangent line and the radius at that point: $\cot \delta = d$. This shows that the spiral degenerates into the circle of radius r_0 in the limit $d \to 0$ (i.e., $\delta \to \pi/2$). For $d \to \infty$ it approaches *asymptotically* to a straight half-line ($\delta \to 0$). The curvature $\chi(\theta) \equiv 1/\rho(\theta)$, with $\rho(\theta)$ the curvature radius at θ, is given by $\chi(\theta) = \sin \delta / r(\theta) = e^{-d\theta} \sin \delta / r_0$. Thus the "zero curvature" is obtained only *asymptotically*, either in the case $d \to \infty$, consistently with the fact that in such a limit it approaches (asymptotically) to a straight half-line, or, for finite non-vanishing d, after an infinite number of 2π rotations, $\theta \to 2\pi m$, with $m \to \infty$. For finite non-vanishing (positive) d, the infinite curvature is obtained and the origin O is *asymptotically* reached by "undoing" an infinite number of 2π rotations, $\theta \to \theta - 2\pi m$, $m \to \infty$. So the curve has a singularity at the "origin" O. This singularity at the origin should be excluded since starting from there no point on the curve can be reached with a finite number of 2π rotations for finite non-vanishing d. On the other hand, the length of the arc l_P of the curve at a certain θ_P, defined to be the measure from the (singular) origin O to the point P of the curve, is $l_P = r_P/\cos\delta$, with $r_P \equiv r(\theta_P)$. The length of the arc l_{PQ} between any two points P and Q of the curve, thus excluding the singularity at the origin, is $l_{PQ} = (r_Q - r_P)/\cos\delta$.

The logarithmic spiral is called the *golden spiral* [4] when at $\theta = \pi/2$ in Eq. (1) one has $r/r_0 = e^{d\,(\pi/2)} = \phi$, with ϕ denoting the golden ratio, $\phi = (1 + \sqrt{5})/2$. In such a case, we may put $d_g \equiv (\ln\phi)/(\pi/2)$, where the subscript g stays for *golden* and the polar equation for the golden spiral is $r_g(\theta) = r_0\, e^{d_g\,\theta}$.

The radius of the golden spiral grows in geometrical progression of ratio ϕ as θ grows of $\pi/2$: $r_g(\theta + n\,\pi/2) = r_0\, e^{d_g\,(\theta + n\,\pi/2)} = r_0\, e^{d_g\,\theta}\,\phi^n$ and $r_{g,n} \equiv r_g(\theta = n\,\pi/2) = r_0\,\phi^n$, $n = 0, 1, 2, 3, \ldots$. A good "approximate" construction of the golden spiral is obtained by using the so called Fibonacci tiling, obtained by drawing in a proper way [4] squares whose sides are in the Fibonacci progression $\{F_n\}$: $1, 1, 2, 3, 5, 8, 13, \ldots$. The Fibonacci spiral is then made from quarter-circles tangent to the interior of each square and it does not perfectly overlap with the golden spiral. The reason is that the ratio $F_n/F_{n-1} \to \phi$ in the $n \to \infty$ limit, but is *not equal* to ϕ for given finite n and $n - 1$. I recall that the generic number in the Fibonacci progression is defined by $F_n = F_{n-1} + F_{n-2}$, with $F_0 = 0$; $F_1 = 1$ and, in terms of the golden ratio ϕ and its "conjugate" $\psi = 1 - \phi = -1/\phi = (1 - \sqrt{5})/2$, F_n is given by the Binet-de Moivre formula $F_n = (\phi^n - \psi^n)/(\phi - \psi)$.

The results obtained in this paper apply also to the *golden spiral*. The logarithmic spiral and the golden spiral and the relation to the Fibonacci progression is of great interest since these spirals and the Fibonacci progression appear in many phenomena, ranging from solid state physics to cosmology, from botany to physiological and functional properties in living systems. In Ref. [5] their role has been analyzed also in an evolutionary context in connection with morphogenesis problems (e.g., how to explain the appearance and the apparent optimization of *forms*). Even in linguistics, the Fibonacci progression is known to play a relevant rôle [5,6]. Analyzing these phenomena is not the aim of this report. However, since many of these phenomena are dissipative ones, I am led to consider, in the following Section, the dissipative properties of the logarithmic spiral and of fractals in general.

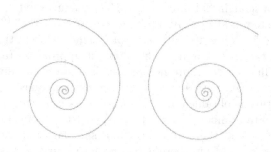

Fig. 1. The anti-clockwise and the clockwise logarithmic spiral

3 Self-similarity and Dissipative Time Evolution

Before considering dissipation in fractal dynamics, let me summarize the relation between self-similarity properties of Koch curve (and other fractals such as the Sierpinski gasket and carpet, the Cantor set, etc.) and q-deformed coherent states. As usual [1,2,7,8], let the n-th step or stage of the Koch curve construction be denoted by $u_{n,q}(\alpha)$, with $\alpha = 4$ and $q = 1/3^d$. Setting the starting stage $u_0 = 1$, one has [1,2]

$$u_{n,q}(\alpha) = (q\,\alpha)^n = 1, \qquad \text{for any } n, \tag{5}$$

from which the fractal dimension or self-similarity dimension [4] $d = \ln 4/\ln 3 \approx 1.2619$ is obtained. Notice that self-similarity is properly defined only in the $n \to \infty$ limit. Note also that use of $q = e^{-d\theta}$, with d the fractal dimension, allows us to write the self-similarity equation $q\,\alpha = 1$ in polar coordinates as $u = u_0\,\alpha\,e^{d\theta}$, which is similar to Eq. (1). By considering in full generality the complex α-plane, and putting $q = e^{-d\theta}$, Eq. (5) is written as $d\theta = \ln\alpha$ and the functions $u_{n,q}(\alpha)$ are, apart the normalization factor $1/\sqrt{n!}$, nothing but the restriction to real $q\,\alpha$ of the functions

$$u_{n,q}(\alpha) = \frac{(q\,\alpha)^n}{\sqrt{n!}}\,, \qquad n \in \mathcal{N}_+\,, \quad q\,\alpha \in \mathbb{C}\,, \tag{6}$$

which form a basis in the space $\mathcal{F}$ of the entire analytic functions. Thus, the study of the fractal properties is carried on in $\mathcal{F}$, by restricting, at the end, the conclusions to real $q\,\alpha$, $q\,\alpha \to Re(q\,\alpha)$ [1,2]. The connection between fractal self-similarity properties and coherent states is then readily established since one realizes that $\mathcal{F}$ is the vector space providing the so-called Fock-Bargmann representation of the Weyl–Heisenberg algebra [3] and the frame where the (Glauber) coherent states are described. By setting $q = e^{\zeta}$, $\zeta \in \mathbb{C}$, the q-deformed algebraic structure is obtained by introducing the finite difference operator $\mathcal{D}_q$. The n-th iteration stage of the fractal is "seen" by applying $(a)^n$ to $|q\alpha\rangle$ and restricting to real $q\alpha$

$$\langle q\alpha|(a)^n|q\alpha\rangle = (q\alpha)^n = u_{n,q}(\alpha), \qquad q\alpha \to Re(q\alpha). \tag{7}$$

The operator $(a)^n$ thus acts as a "magnifying" lens [1,2,7]. Thus the fractal n-th stage of iteration, with $n = 0, 1, 2, .., \infty$, is represented, in a one-to-one correspondence, by the n-th term in the coherent state series. $|q\alpha\rangle$ is actually a squeezed coherent state[19], $\zeta = \ln q$ is the squeezing parameter.

By proceeding for the logarithmic spiral in a similar fashion, its relation with squeezed coherent states may be shown and thus the logarithmic spiral also appears to be a *macroscopic quantum system* arising from the q-deformed (squeezed) coherent states through coherent boson condensation processes. Such a conclusion is obtained also by a closer analysis of the parametric equations of the logarithmic spiral [9]:

$$x = r(\theta)\cos\theta = r_0\,e^{d\theta}\cos\theta\,, \tag{8a}$$
$$y = r(\theta)\sin\theta = r_0\,e^{d\theta}\sin\theta\,. \tag{8b}$$

The point on the curve in the complex z-plane is given by $z = x + i\,y = r_0\,e^{d\theta}\,e^{i\theta}$, and it is fully specified only when the sign of $d\theta$ is assigned, thus specifying one of the two components of the (hyperbolic) basis $\{e^{-d\theta}, e^{+d\theta}\}$. Actually, the completeness of the basis $\{e^{-d\theta}, e^{+d\theta}\}$ requires that both the factors $e^{\pm d\theta}$ must be considered. On the other hand, this is suggested also by the fact that in many instances in nature, as e.g. in phyllotaxis studies, the direct $(q > 1)$ and the indirect $(q < 1)$ spirals are both realized in the same system.

Thus, I consider z_1 and z_2 given by:

$$z_1 = r_0\,e^{-d\theta}\,e^{-i\theta}\,, \qquad z_2 = r_0\,e^{+d\theta}\,e^{+i\theta}\,, \tag{9}$$

where opposite signs for the imaginary exponent $i\theta$ have been chosen for convenience. By introducing the parameter t, $\theta = \theta(t)$, one realizes that z_1 and z_2 solve the equations

$$m\,\ddot{z}_1 + \gamma\,\dot{z}_1 + \kappa\,z_1 = 0\,, \tag{10a}$$

$$m\,\ddot{z}_2 - \gamma\,\dot{z}_2 + \kappa\,z_2 = 0\,, \tag{10b}$$

respectively, provided the relation

$$\theta(t) = \frac{\gamma}{2\,m\,d}\,t = \frac{\Gamma}{d}\,t \tag{11}$$

holds (up to an arbitrary additive constant c, here set equal to zero for simplicity). As usual, "dot" denotes derivative with respect to t; m, γ and κ are positive real constants. The notations $\Gamma \equiv \frac{\gamma}{2m}$, $\Omega^2 = (1/m)(\kappa - \gamma^2/4m) = \Gamma^2/d^2$ and $\kappa > \gamma^2/4m$ also will be used. At $T = 2\,\pi\,d/\Gamma$ it is $\theta(T) = 2\,\pi$.

Thus, the solutions of Eqs. (10a) and (10b), $z_1(t) = r_0\,e^{-i\Omega t}\,e^{-\Gamma t}$ and $z_2(t) = r_0\,e^{+i\Omega t}\,e^{+\Gamma t}$, are the parametric expressions for the logarithmic spiral. At $t = m\,T$, $z_1 = r_0\,(e^{-2\pi d})^m$, $z_2 = r_0\,(e^{2\pi d})^m$, with the integer $m = 1, 2, 3...$

The above discussion suggests to us that the parameter t can be interpreted as the time parameter. Then, Eqs. (10a) and (10b) for the damped and amplified harmonic oscillator describe the time-evolution of the system of direct and indirect spirals. The spiral "angular velocity" is given by $|\,d\theta/dt\,| = |\,\Gamma/d\,|$.

I remark that the oscillator z_1 is an *open* non-hamiltonian system and we are able to set up the canonical formalism only provided that we consider the *closed* system (z_1, z_2), made by z_1 and its time-reversed image z_2 [10]. The closed system Lagrangian, from which Eqs. (10a) and (10b) are both derived, is

$$L = m\dot{z}_1\dot{z}_2 + \frac{1}{2}\gamma(z_1\dot{z}_2 - \dot{z}_1 z_2) - \kappa z_1 z_2\,. \tag{12}$$

The canonical momenta are:

$$p_{z_1} = \frac{\partial L}{\partial \dot{z}_1} = m\dot{z}_2 - \frac{1}{2}\gamma z_2\,, \qquad p_{z_2} = \frac{\partial L}{\partial \dot{z}_2} = m\dot{z}_1 + \frac{1}{2}\gamma z_1\,. \tag{13}$$

This brings us to the following crucial remark in our analysis. The "two copies" (z_1, z_2) of the z-coordinate (the logarithmic spiral and its time-reversed copy) can be viewed as describing the forward in time path and the backward in time path in the phase space $\{z, p_z\}$, respectively, and is well known that as far as $z_1(t) \neq z_2(t)$ the system exhibits quantum behavior and quantum interference takes place [11,12,13,14]. This can be explicitly proven, for example by following Schwinger [15], by considering the double slit experiment in quantum mechanics [11,12,13,14]. Also in the quantum mechanical formalism of the Wigner function and density matrix it is required, in order to have quantum interference, that the forward in time action $A(z - z_1, t)$ must be different from the backward in time action $A(z - z_2, t)$ [11,12]. The classical behavior of the system is obtained only when $z_1(t) \approx z_2(t) \approx z_{classical}(t)$. When, on the contrary, $z_1(t) \neq z_2(t)$ at the same time t, then the system behaves in a quantum mechanical fashion. Of course, when z is actually measured there is only one classical $z_{classical}$. This scenario also agrees with 't Hooft conjecture, which states that provided some specific energy conditions are met and some constraints are imposed, classical, deterministic systems presenting loss of information (dissipation) might behave according to a quantum evolution [16,17]. Thus, the logarithmic spiral and its time-reversed double manifest themselves as *macroscopic quantum systems*, in agreement with the conclusion already reached above. It is evident that our conclusions for the logarithmic spiral can be immediately extended to other fractals by considering also for them their parametric equations in the z plane starting from their self-similarity equation $u = u_0 \, \alpha \, e^{d\theta}$ mentioned above. I will present some details of the quantum formalism in the following Section.

4 Free Energy and Coherent States

For brevity I only summarize few features of the quantum formalism since it is available in the quoted references. The canonical commutators are $[z_1, p_{z_1}] = i\hbar = [z_2, p_{z_2}]$, $[z_1, z_2] = 0 = [p_{z_1}, p_{z_2}]$. As customary, the annihilation and creation operators are then introduced:

$$a \equiv \left(\frac{1}{2\hbar\Omega}\right)^{\frac{1}{2}} \left(\frac{p_{z_1}}{\sqrt{m}} - i\sqrt{m}\Omega z_1\right), \quad b \equiv \left(\frac{1}{2\hbar\Omega}\right)^{\frac{1}{2}} \left(\frac{p_{z_2}}{\sqrt{m}} - i\sqrt{m}\Omega z_2\right), \quad (14)$$

and their hermitian conjugate $a^\dagger$ and $b^\dagger$, with $[a, a^\dagger] = 1 = [b, b^\dagger]$, $[a, b] = 0 = [a, b^\dagger]$. Use of the linear canonical transformation $A \equiv \frac{1}{\sqrt{2}}(a+b)$, $B \equiv \frac{1}{\sqrt{2}}(a-b)$, with commutation relations $[A, A^\dagger] = 1 = [B, B^\dagger]$, $[A, B] = 0 = [A, B^\dagger]$, allows us to obtain the quantum Hamiltonian [10] for the closed system described by the Lagrangian Eq. (12): $\mathcal{H} = \mathcal{H}_0 + \mathcal{H}_I$, with

$$\mathcal{H}_0 = \hbar\Omega(A^\dagger A - B^\dagger B), \qquad \mathcal{H}_I = i\hbar\Gamma(A^\dagger B^\dagger - AB), \qquad (15a)$$

which I will call the *fractal Hamiltonian*. Its group structure is that of $SU(1,1)$:

$$J_+ = A^\dagger B^\dagger, \quad J_- = J_+^\dagger = AB, \quad J_3 = \frac{1}{2}(A^\dagger A + B^\dagger B + 1), \qquad (16)$$

generate the $su(1,1)$ algebra: $[J_+, J_-] = -2J_3$, $[J_3, J_\pm] = \pm J_\pm$, with the Casimir operator $\mathcal{C}$: $\mathcal{C}^2 \equiv \frac{1}{4} + J_3^2 - \frac{1}{2}(J_+J_- + J_-J_+) = \frac{1}{4}(A^\dagger A - B^\dagger B)^2$. The Hamiltonian (15) then can be written as

$$\mathcal{H}_0 = 2\hbar\Omega\mathcal{C} \ , \quad \mathcal{H}_I = i\hbar\Gamma(J_+ - J_-) \equiv -2\hbar\Gamma J_2 \ , \tag{17}$$

with $[\mathcal{H}_0, \mathcal{H}_I] = 0$.

Let $\{|n_A, n_B\rangle\}$ denote the set of simultaneous eigenvectors of $A^\dagger A$ and $B^\dagger B$, with n_A, n_B non-negative integers. The eigenvalue of $\mathcal{H}_0$ is the constant (conserved) quantity $\hbar\Omega(n_A - n_B)$. For the ground state (the vacuum) $|0\rangle \equiv |n_A = 0, n_B = 0\rangle$, $A|0\rangle = 0 = B|0\rangle$, we have $\mathcal{H}_0|0\rangle = 0$. Its time evolution is given by

$$|0(t)\rangle = \frac{1}{\cosh(\Gamma t)} \exp\left(\tanh(\Gamma t)J_+\right)|0\rangle \ , \tag{18}$$

namely an $su(1,1)$ generalized coherent state, produced by condensation of couples of (entangled) A and B modes: $(AB)^n$, $n = 0, 1, 2....\infty$ [3,10]. The single mode Glauber coherent state obtained for the logarithmic spiral and the Koch curve is now upgraded to the coherent state of two entangled modes (Eq. (18)) upon closing the system z with its time-reversed copy. For any t, $\langle 0(t)|0(t)\rangle = 1$. As $t \to \infty$ we have

$$\lim_{t\to\infty} \langle 0(t)|0\rangle = \lim_{t\to\infty} \exp\left(-\ln\cosh(\Gamma t)\right) \to 0 \ , \tag{19}$$

which expresses the decay (dissipation) of the vacuum under the time evolution operator $\mathcal{U}(t) \equiv \exp\left(-it\mathcal{H}_I/\hbar\right)$. This equation gives the ratio $r_0/r(t)$ (cf. Eqs. (4) and (11)) and the limit consistently expresses the (unbounded) growth of $r(t)$. The action of the operator $\mathcal{U}$ induces the Bogoliubov transformations:

$$A \to A(t) = e^{-i\frac{t}{\hbar}\mathcal{H}_I} A e^{i\frac{t}{\hbar}\mathcal{H}_I} = A\cosh(\Gamma t) - B^\dagger \sinh(\Gamma t) \ , \tag{20a}$$

$$B \to B(t) = e^{-i\frac{t}{\hbar}\mathcal{H}_I} B e^{i\frac{t}{\hbar}\mathcal{H}_I} = -A^\dagger \sinh(\Gamma t) + B\cosh(\Gamma t) \ . \tag{20b}$$

The $su(1,1)$ generalized coherent state $|0(t)\rangle$ is known to be a thermal state [10] and the time evolution induced by $\mathcal{H}_I$ may be written as [10,14]:

$$|0(t)\rangle = \exp\left(-it\frac{\mathcal{H}_I}{\hbar}\right)|0\rangle = \exp\left(-\frac{1}{2}\mathcal{S}_A(t)\right)\exp\left(A^\dagger B^\dagger\right)|0\rangle \ , \tag{21}$$

where

$$\mathcal{S}_A(t) \equiv -\left\{A^\dagger A \ln\sinh^2(\Gamma t) - AA^\dagger \ln\cosh^2(\Gamma t)\right\} \ , \tag{22}$$

and similar expression for $|0(t)\rangle$ can be obtained with $\mathcal{S}_A(t)$ replaced by $\mathcal{S}_B(t)$ where B and $B^\dagger$ replace A and $A^\dagger$, respectively. Thus, one simply writes $\mathcal{S}$ for either $\mathcal{S}_A$ or $\mathcal{S}_B$. $\mathcal{S}$ in Eq. (22) is recognized to be the entropy for the dissipative system [10] (see also [14,18]).

The fractal Hamiltonian $\mathcal{H}$ then turns out to be the fractal free energy for the coherent boson condensation process out of which the fractal is formed. We can identify $\mathcal{H}_0/\hbar = 2\,\Omega\mathcal{C}$ with the "internal energy" U and $2\,J_2/\hbar$ with the entropy

S. Putting $k_B = 1$, the defining equation for the temperature T, $\partial S/\partial U = 1/T$ gives $T = \hbar\,\Gamma$. The heat contribution in $\mathcal{F} = U - TS$ is given by $2\,\Gamma\,J_2$. We also have $(\partial\mathcal{F}/\partial T)|_\Omega = -2\,J_2/\hbar$. It is remarkable that the temperature $T = \hbar\,\Gamma$ is proportional to the background zero point energy: $\hbar\,\Gamma \propto \hbar\,\Omega/2$ [13,14,17]. Finally, the Planck distribution for the A and B modes is obtained by extremizing the free energy functional [10,13,14,18].

I remark that the fact that it is the entropy S that actually controls the time evolution signals the breakdown of time-reversal symmetry, i.e. the *time arrow* in the fractal formation process; in the case of the logarithmic spiral the breakdown of time-reversal symmetry manifests itself in the chirality of the spiral: the indirect (right-handed) spiral is the time-reversed image of the direct (left-handed) spiral and they are *separate* from each other by a chirality transformation (Fig. 1).

Let me now comment on the fact that $|0(t)\rangle$ is a squeezed state. I only observe that the operator $\mathcal{U}(t)$ written as [14,19]

$$\mathcal{U}(t) = \exp\left(-\frac{\Gamma t}{2}\left(\left(a^2 - a^{\dagger 2}\right) - \left(b^2 - b^{\dagger 2}\right)\right)\right), \qquad (23)$$

appears to be the two mode squeezing generator with squeezing parameter $\zeta = -\Gamma t$ [9,14,19]. A similar observation, which here I omit for brevity, can be made for the case of the Koch curve and other fractals (see [9]).

Finally, I remark that so far for simplicity my discussion has been framed in the context of quantum mechanics. However, it is important to stress that the correct mathematical framework to study quantum dissipation is the quantum field theory (QFT) framework [10,14], where one considers an infinite number of degrees of freedom. This is also physically more realistic, because the realizations of the logarithmic spiral and in general of fractal structures in the many cases they are observed in nature involve an infinite number of elementary degrees of freedom, as it always happens in solid state and many-body physics. The interested reader may find details of the QFT formalism necessary to study the quantum dissipation process presented above in Refs. [9,10,14]. I also remark that the whole construction here presented may be "reversed", in the sense that the statement that the squeezed coherent state $|0(t)\rangle$ possesses self-similarity fractal properties or fractal geometry also holds.

In conclusion, the logarithmic spiral and other fractals, in their many realizations in nature, appear as a global system emerging from local microscopic quantum condensation process. The quantum dynamical scheme here depicted seems to underly the *morphogenesis* processes which manifest themselves in the global, macroscopic appearances (*forms*) of the fractals. Vice-versa, one may also conclude that coherent generalized states possess self-similar fractal structure.

5   Dissipation and Noncommutative Geometry

In this Section I show that in the case of the two mode description of the logarithmic spiral and other fractals, dissipation, which is related to the squeezing parameter (cf. Eq. (23)), induces noncommutative geometry in the plane.

In Refs. [1,2], in the case of the Koch curve represented by a single mode q-deformed (squeezed) coherent state, it has been shown that noncommutative geometry in the (x_1, x_2) plane is induced by the q-deformation (squeezing). The q-deformation parameter plays indeed the rôle of the noncommutative geometric length L:

$$[x_1, x_2] = iL^2. \tag{24}$$

Then the quantum interference phase ϑ (of the Aharanov-Bohm type) between two alternative paths $\mathcal{P}_1$ and $\mathcal{P}_2$ in the plane [13,14,20] is determined by the noncommutative deformation parameter q and the enclosed area $\mathcal{A}$: $\vartheta = \mathcal{A}/q^2$. The deformation parameter also controls the zero point uncertainty relation (we are using $\hbar = 1$) $\Delta x_1 \Delta x_2 \geq (q^2/2)$.

Let me consider now the case of the two mode description of the logarithmic spiral and other fractals discussed in previous Sections. In the (z_1, z_2) plane, introducing for simplicity the index notation $+ \equiv 1$ and $- \equiv 2$ and using Eq. (13) for the momenta $p_{z_{\pm}}$, the components of forward in time and backward in time velocity $v_{\pm} = \dot{z}_{\pm}$ are given by

$$v_{\pm} = \frac{1}{m}\left(p_{z_{\mp}} \mp \frac{1}{2}\gamma z_{\pm}\right) \tag{25}$$

and they do not commute

$$[v_+, v_-] = -i\,\frac{\gamma}{m^2}. \tag{26}$$

A canonical set of conjugate position coordinates (ξ_+, ξ_-) may be defined by putting $\xi_{\pm} = \mp(m/\gamma)v_{\pm}$, so that

$$[\xi_+, \xi_-] = i\,\frac{1}{\gamma}. \tag{27}$$

Equation (27) characterizes the noncommutative geometry in the plane (z_+, z_-). Since in the present case $L^2 = 1/\gamma$, the quantum dissipative interference phase ϑ associated with the two paths $\mathcal{P}_1$ and $\mathcal{P}_2$ in the noncommutative plane is $\vartheta = \mathcal{A}/L^2 = \mathcal{A}\gamma$, provided $z_+ \neq z_-$.

Thus, in the case of the two mode description of the logarithmic spiral and other fractals the interference phase appears as a "dissipative interference phase" [11,20], which provides a relation between dissipation and noncommutative geometry in the plane of the doubled coordinates.

In order to sheds some light on the physical meaning of the relation between dissipation (which is at the origin of q-deformation), noncommutative geometry and the non-trivial topology of paths in the phase space [22,23] (see also [24]), I observe that in the formalism of the algebra doubling the noncommutative q-deformed Hopf algebra plays a relevant rôle [13,14,22]. The map $\mathcal{A} \to \mathcal{A}_1 \otimes \mathcal{A}_2$ which duplicates the algebra is the Hopf coproduct map $\mathcal{A} \to \mathcal{A} \otimes 1 + 1 \otimes \mathcal{A}$. The Bogoliubov transformations of "angle" Γt (cf. Eqs. (20)) are obtained by convenient combinations of the deformed coproduct $\Delta a_q^{\dagger} = a_q^{\dagger} \otimes q^{1/2} + q^{-1/2} \otimes a_q^{\dagger}$, where $a_q^{\dagger}$ are the creation operators in the q-deformed Hopf algebra [22]. These deformed coproduct maps are noncommutative and the q-deformation parameter is related to the coherent condensate content of the state $|0(t)\rangle$.

6   Conclusions

In this paper I have discussed the realization of the logarithmic spiral and other self-similar fractal structures in terms of $SU(1,1)$ generalized coherent states, which are squeezed thermal states [10]. The dynamics underlying the formation of the fractals and the logarithmic spiral appears to be the one of boson condensation processes in quantum field theory and therefore fractals appear to emerge as the macroscopic result of microscopic coherent quantum dynamics: they are examples of *macroscopic quantum systems*, in the specific sense that their macroscopic properties cannot be derived without recurring to the underlying quantum dynamics. This has been shown to be controlled by the *fractal free energy* and the rôle played by the entropy in the system time-evolution thus has been recognized. Quantum dissipation characterizes the fractal dynamics, and is related with quantum deformation and squeezing of the coherent state fractal representation [1,2]. Dissipation is therefore at the root of the fractal self-similarity properties observed at a macroscopic level. This is also in agreement with the observation [25] that in a crystal submitted to deforming stress actions the so produced crystal lattice defects (dislocations) form, at low temperature, self-similar fractal patterns. These are the result of non-homogeneous coherent phonon (boson) condensation [18,14] and provide an example of "emergence of fractal dislocation structures" [25] in nonequilibrium (dissipative) systems.

It is remarkable that the entropy controls the system time-evolution. This is consistent with the breakdown of time-reversal symmetry characteristic of dissipative systems and the *arrow of time* is clearly manifest in the observed formation processes of fractals; it is for example related to the chirality in the logarithmic spiral where the indirect (right-handed) spiral is the time-reversed, but *distinct*, image of the direct (left-handed) spiral (or vice-versa). These features of the fractal formation, or *growth*, suggest that the quantum dynamics here analyzed is actually at basis of the *morphogenesis* processes responsible of the fractal macroscopic appearance. An interesting question is the one of the relation of the quantum coherent dynamical processes controlled by the entropy operator as described above and the so called *laws of the form* in biology (see, e.g. Ref. [5] and references there quoted).

The noncommutative geometry has been shown to be implicit in the fractal squeezed coherent state and the dissipative quantum interference phase between two alternative paths in the plane is determined by the enclosed area between the paths and the noncommutative length scale, which is related to the squeezing parameter and to the zero point fluctuations in the coordinates. For practical applications, the link between fractals and noncommutative geometry may open interesting perspectives in condensed matter physics, in quantum optics and in quantum computing and in many applications where quantum dissipation cannot be actually neglected. The results here presented provide a powerful predictive tool, since experimental measurements representable by a straight line with given non-vanishing slope in a log-log plot may signal that a specific coherent state dynamics underlies the phenomenon under study. Such a kind of *theorem* has been positively confirmed in some applications in neuroscience [2,21] and more applications will be studied in the future.

Also interesting for applications is the fact that the proof that fractals properties may be described in terms of coherent states may be reversed in the statement that coherent states have fractal properties, namely there is a "geometry" characterizing coherent states which may exhibit fractal properties. This may have practical consequences in view of the important rôle played by coherent states in many applications, ranging from condensed matter physics to quantum optics and molecular biology, elementary particle physics and cosmology. The general emerging perspective is the one of an *integrated ecological vision* which appears "fractal modulated" by coherence, rather than "hierarchically layered" in isolated compartments as it would appear in the nave multi-coded collections of isolated systems (solid state matter, living matter, sea phenomena, earth phenomena, atmospheric phenomena, etc.). Many different coherent domains may coexist, although always among them entangled. Fractal modulation points to a unique, although complex, *code* incorporating the whole set of deformation parameters of the basic coherent state of Nature.

Acknowledgments. Financial support from INFN and Miur is acknowledged. Useful discussions with Antonio Capolupo are also acknowledged.

References

1. Vitiello, G.: Fractals and the Fock-Bargmann Representation of Coherent States. In: Bruza, P., Sofge, D., Lawless, W., van Rijsbergen, K., Klusch, M., et al. (eds.) QI 2009. LNCS, vol. 5494, pp. 6–16. Springer, Heidelberg (2009)
2. Vitiello, G.: Coherent states, fractals and brain waves. New Mathematics and Natural Computation 5, 245–264 (2009); Vitiello, G.: Topological defects, fractals and the structure of quantum field theory. In: Licata, I., Sakaji, A.J. (eds.) Vision of Oneness, pp. 155–180. Aracne Edizioni, Roma (2011)
3. Perelomov, A.: Generalized Coherent States and Their Applications. Springer, Heidelberg (1986)
4. Peitgen, H.O., Jürgens, H., Saupe, D.: Chaos and Fractals. New Frontiers of Science. Springer, Heidelberg (1986)
5. Fodor, J., Piattelli-Palmarini, M.: What Darwin got wrong. Farrar Straus and Giroux, New York (2010)
6. Piattelli-Palmarini, M., Uriagereka, J.: Still a bridge too far? Biolinguistic questions for grounding language on brains. Physics of Life Reviews 5, 207–224 (2008)
7. Bunde, A., Havlin, S. (eds.): Fractals in Science. Springer, Heidelberg (1995)
8. Bak, P., Creutz, M.: Fractals and self-organized criticality. In: Bunde, A., Havlin, S. (eds.) Fractals in Science, pp. 1–25. Springer, Heidelberg (1995)
9. Vitiello, G.: Fractals, coherent states and self-similarity induced noncommutative geometry. Phys. Lett. A 376, 2527–2532 (2012)
10. Celeghini, E., Rasetti, M., Vitiello, G.: Quantum dissipation. Annals Phys. 215, 156–170 (1992)

11. Blasone, M., Srivastava, Y.N., Vitiello, G., Widom, A.: Phase coherence and quantum Brownian motion. Annals Phys. 267, 61–74 (1998); Graziano, E., Pashaev, O.K., Vitiello, G.: Dissipation and topologically massive gauge theories in pseudoeuclidean plane. Annals Phys. 252, 115–132 (1996)

12. Srivastava, Y.N., Vitiello, G., Widom, A.: Quantum dissipation and quantum noise. Annals Phys. 238, 200–207 (1995)

13. Vitiello, G.: Links. Relating different physical systems through the common QFT algebraic structure. In: Unruh, W.G., Schuetzhold, R. (eds.) Quantum Analogues: From Phase Transitions to Black Holes and Cosmology. Lectures Notes in Physics, vol. 718, pp. 165–205. Springer, Heidelberg (2007); hep-th/0610094

14. Blasone, M., Jizba, P., Vitiello, G.: Quantum Field Theory and its macroscopic manifestations. Imperial College Press, London (2011)

15. Schwinger, J.: Brownian Motion of a Quantum Oscillator. J. Math. Phys. 2, 407–433 (1961)

16. 't Hooft, G.: Quantum Gravity as a Dissipative Deterministic System. Class. Quant. Grav. 16, 3263–3279 (1999);
    't Hooft, G.: In: Basics and Highlights of Fundamental Physics. Erice (1999) [arXiv:hep-th/0003005]
    't Hooft, G.: A mathematical theory for deterministic quantum mechanics. J. Phys.: Conf. Series 67, 012015 (2007)

17. Blasone, M., Jizba, P., Vitiello, G.: Dissipation and quantization. Phys. Lett. A 287, 205–210 (2001); Blasone, M., Celeghini, E., Jizba, P., Vitiello, G.: Quantization, group contraction and zero point energy. Phys. Lett. A 310, 393–399 (2003); Blasone, M., Jizba, P., Scardigli, F., Vitiello, G.: Dissipation and quantization in composite systems. Phys. Lett. A 373, 4106–4112 (2009)

18. Umezawa, H., Matsumoto, H., Tachiki, M.: Thermo Field Dynamics and Condensed States. North-Holland, Amsterdam (1982)

19. Celeghini, E., De Martino, S., De Siena, S., Rasetti, M., Vitiello, G.: Quantum groups, coherent states, squeezing and lattice quantum mechanics. Annals Phys. 241, 50–67 (1995); Celeghini, E., Rasetti, M., Tarlini, M., Vitiello, G.: $SU(1,1)$ Squeezed States as Damped Oscillators. Mod. Phys. Lett. B 3, 1213–1220 (1989); Celeghini, E., Rasetti, M., Vitiello, G.: On squeezing and quantum groups. Phys. Rev. Lett. 66, 2056–2059 (1991)

20. Sivasubramanian, S., Srivastava, Y.N., Vitiello, G., Widom, A.: Quantum dissipation induced noncommutative geometry. Phys. Lett. A 311, 97–105 (2003)

21. Freeman, W.J., Livi, R., Obinata, M., Vitiello, G.: Cortical phase transitions, nonequilibrium thermodynamics and the time-dependent Ginzburg-Landau equation. Int. J. Mod. Phys. B 26, 1250035 (2012) arXiv:1110.3677v1 [physics.bio-ph]

22. Celeghini, E., De Martino, S., De Siena, S., Iorio, A., Rasetti, M., Vitiello, G.: Thermo field dynamics and quantum algebras. Phys. Lett. A 244, 455–461 (1998)

23. Iorio, A., Vitiello, G.: Quantum groups and Von Neumann theorem. Mod. Phys. Lett. B 8, 269–276 (1994)

24. Banerjee, R.: Dissipation and noncommutativity in planar quantum mechanics. Mod. Phys. Lett. A 17, 631–645 (2002); Banerjee, R., Mukherjee, P.: A Canonical approach to dissipation. J. Phys. A: Math. Gen. 35, 5591–5598 (2002)

25. Chen, Y.S., Choi, W., Papanikolaou, S., Sethna, J.P.: Bending Crystals: Emergence of fractal dislocation structures. Phys. Rev. Lett. 105, 105501 (2010)

Hierarchical Bayesian Estimation of Quantum Decision Model Parameters

Jerome R. Busemeyer[1], Zheng Wang[2], and Jennifer S. Trueblood[3]

[1] Indiana University, Bloomington, USA
[2] Ohio State University, Columbus, USA
[3] University of California, Irvine, USA

Abstract. Quantum decision models have been recently proposed to account for findings that have resisted explanation by traditional decision theories. This paper compares quantum versus Markov models of decision making for explaining a puzzling empirical finding from human decision making called dynamic inconsistency – that is the failure of decision makers to carry out their planned decisions. A large data set that empirically investigated dynamic inconsistency was used to quantitatively evaluate the quantum and Markov models. In this application, the quantum model reduces to the Markov model when one of the parameters is set to zero. The parameters of the quantum model were estimated using Hierarchical Bayesian estimation. The distribution of the key quantum parameter was clearly located in the quantum regime and far below zero as predicted by the Markov model. These results provide further support for quantum models as compared to the traditional models of decision making.

1 Introduction

Several new quantum models of decision making have been introduced to account for decision making paradoxes that have resisted explanations by "classical" type of decision theories (Busemeyer, Wang, Lambert-Mogiliansky [3]; Lambert-Mogiliansky, Zamir, Zwirn [5]; Khrennikov and Haven [4]; Pothos & Busemeyer [6]; Yukalov & Sornette [8]). Perhaps quantum models succeed where classic models fail simply because quantum models are more complex and have greater model fitting flexibility (after all they are based on complex numbers). The purpose of this paper is to examine this issue by comparing a classic type of Markov model with a quantum model using Hierarchical Bayesian parameter estimation methods [2]. The model comparison is based on a large experiment designed to examine dynamic inconsistency in choices among two stage gambles [1]. Dynamic consistency is a principle of decision making required for backward induction when applied to decision trees. Dynamic consistency requires that a planned course of action for a future decision is implemented as planned when that decision is finally realized. Barkan and Busemeyer [1] observed systematic violations of dynamic consistency, and they used a random utility version of prospect theory to account for these findings. But more recently, Yukalov and

J.R. Busemeyer et al. (Eds.): QI 2012, LNCS 7620, pp. 80–89, 2012.

Sornette argued that quantum theory can also account for these findings [9]. Therefore, in this paper, two different types of models are proposed to explain these findings: a Markov model and a quantum decision model [6].

The paper is organized as follows. First we review the Barkan and Busemeyer [1] experimental methods and results. Second, we describe the two models that are being compared. Third, we present fits to the mean data for each model to get a rough idea about how well each model accounts for the findings (but this is not our main concern). Fourth, we present the results of the Hierarchical Bayesian parameter (which is our main concern). Finally, we draw some preliminary conclusions from this model comparison analysis.

2   Barkan and Busemeyer (2003)

A two stage gambling paradigm was used to study dynamic consistency, which was a modification of the paradigm used by Tversky and Shafir [7] to study the disjunction effect. A total of 100 people participated and each person played the 17 gambles involving real money shown in Table 1 twice except for the first one. Each gamble had an equal chance of producing a win or a loss. The columns labeled 'win' and 'loss' indicate the money that could be won or lost for each gamble (one unit was worth one cent). For each gamble in Table 1, the person was forced to play the first round, and then contingent on the outcome of the first round, they were given a choice whether or not to play the second round with the same gamble. On each trial the person was first asked to make a plan for the second play contingent on each possible outcome of the first play. In other words, during the planning stage they were asked two questions: "if you win the first play, do you plan to play the second gamble? and "if you lose the first play, do you plan to play the second gamble?" Following the plan, the outcome of the first gamble was revealed, and then the person was given a final choice: decide again whether or not to play the second gamble after observing the first play outcome. To incentivize both plan and final choices, the computer randomly selected either the planned choice or the final choice to determine the real monetary payoff for each trial. The final payment for the trial was then shown to the person at the end of each trial. Participants were paid by randomly selecting four problems from the entire set, randomly selecting either their plan or final choice, and randomly selecting an outcome for each gamble to determine the actual payment.

Table 1 displays the results obtained after averaging across the two replications for each person, and after averaging across all 100 participants. The probability of planning to take the gamble is shown under the column labeled "Plan." There was little or no difference between the probabilities of taking the gamble, contingent on each planned outcome of the first gamble, and so the results shown here are averaged across the two hypothetical outcomes during the plan. See Barkan and Busemeyer [1] for the complete results listed separately for each contingent outcome. The probability of taking the gamble during the final stage is shown under the column labeled "Final." The columns under the label "Gamble" display the amount to win and lose for each gamble. Changes in probabilities down the rows of the Table show the effect of the gamble payoffs on the probability of taking the gamble. The difference between the planned and final columns indicates a dynamic inconsistency effect. Notice that following a win (the first 4 columns), the probability of taking the gamble at the final stage was always smaller than the probability of taking the gamble at the planning stage. In other words, participants changed their minds and became more risk averse after experiencing a win as compared to planning for a win. Notice that following a loss (the last 4 columns), the probability of taking the gamble at the final stage was always greater than the probability of taking the gamble at the planning stage. In other words, participants changed their minds and became more risk seeking after experiencing a loss as compared to planning for a loss.

Table 1. Barkan and Busemeyer (2003) Experiment

Gamble		Win First Play		Gamble		Lose First Play	
Win	Loss	Plan	Final	Win	Loss	Plan	Final
200	220	0.46	0.34	80	100	0.36	0.44
180	200	0.45	0.35	100	120	0.47	0.63
200	200	0.59	0.51	100	100	0.63	0.64
120	100	0.70	0.62	200	180	0.57	0.69
140	100	0.62	0.54	160	140	0.68	0.69
200	140	0.63	0.53	200	160	0.67	0.72
200	120	0.74	0.68	160	100	0.65	0.73
200	100	0.79	0.70	180	100	0.68	0.80
				200	100	.85	.82

3   Decision Models

3.1   Quantum Decision Model

The quantum model used to account for the dynamic inconsistency effect is the same model that was previously developed by Pothos and Busemeyer [6] to account for the disjunction effect. The essential idea is that the decision maker uses a consistent utility function for plans and final decisions and always incorporates the outcomes from the first stage into the decision for the second stage. The planned decision differs from the final decision, because the plan is based on a superposition over possible first stage outcomes that will be faced during the final stage.

The two stage game involves a set of four mutually exclusive and exhaustive outcomes $\{WT, WR, LT, LR\}$ where for example WT symbolizes the event 'win the first stage' and 'take the second stage gamble,' and LR represents the event 'lose the first stage' and 'reject the second stage gamble.' These four events correspond to four mutually exclusive and exhaustive basis states

$\{|WT\rangle, |WR\rangle, |LT\rangle, |LR\rangle\}$. The four basis states are represented in the quantum model as four orthonormal basis vectors that span a four dimensional vector space. The state of the decision maker is a superposition over these four orthonormal basis states.

$$|\psi\rangle = \psi_{WT} \cdot |WT\rangle + \psi_{WR} \cdot |WR\rangle + \psi_{LT} \cdot |LT\rangle + \psi_{LR} \cdot |LR\rangle, \qquad (1)$$
$$\| |\psi\rangle \|^2 = 1.$$

The initial state is represented by a 4×1 matrix ψ_I containing elements ψ_{ij} $i = W, L$ and $j = T, R$ which is the amplitude distribution over the four basis states. Initially, during the planning stage, an equal distribution is assumed so that ψ_I has elements $\psi_{ij} = 1/2$ for all four entries. The state following experience of a win is updated to ψ_W which has $1/\sqrt{2}$ in the first two entries and zeros in the second two. The state following experience of a loss is updated to ψ_L which has $1/\sqrt{2}$ in the last two entries and zeros in the first two entries. Note that $\left(\psi_W^\dagger \cdot \psi_L\right) = 0$, and also we can write $\psi_I = \frac{1}{\sqrt{2}}\psi_W + \frac{1}{\sqrt{2}}\psi_L$.

Evaluation of the payoffs causes the initial state ψ_I to be "rotated" by a unitary operator U into the final states used to make a choice about taking or rejecting the second stage gamble:

$$\psi_F = U \cdot \psi_I \qquad (2)$$
$$U = \exp\left(-i \cdot \frac{\pi}{2} \cdot (H_1 + H_2)\right)$$

where

$$H_1 = \begin{bmatrix} \frac{h_W}{\sqrt{1+h_W^2}} & \frac{1}{\sqrt{1+h_W^2}} & 0 & 0 \\ \frac{1}{\sqrt{1+h_W^2}} & \frac{-h_W}{\sqrt{1+h_W^2}} & 0 & 0 \\ 0 & 0 & \frac{h_L}{\sqrt{1+h_L^2}} & \frac{1}{\sqrt{1+h_L^2}} \\ 0 & 0 & \frac{1}{\sqrt{1+h_L^2}} & \frac{-h_L}{\sqrt{1+h_L^2}} \end{bmatrix}, \quad H_2 = \frac{-\gamma}{\sqrt{2}}\begin{bmatrix} 1 & 0 & 1 & 0 \\ 0 & -1 & 0 & 1 \\ 1 & 0 & -1 & 0 \\ 0 & 1 & 0 & 1 \end{bmatrix}. \qquad (3)$$

The upper left corner of H_1 is defined by the payoffs given a win; and the bottom right corner of H_1 is defined by the payoffs given a loss (this is described in more detail below). The matrix H_2 aligns beliefs and actions by amplifying the potentials for states WT, LR and and attenuating potentials for states WR, LT. The parameter γ is a free parameter that allows changes in beliefs during the decision process.

The utilities for taking the gamble or not are mapped into the parameters h_W and h_L in H_1, and the latter must be scaled between -1 to $+1$. To accomplish this, the parameter h_W used to define H_1 is defined as

$$h_W = \frac{2}{1 + e^{-D_W}} - 1, \qquad (4)$$
$$D_W = u(G|Win) - x_W^a,$$
$$u(G|Win) = (.50) \cdot (x_W + x_W)^a + (.50) \cdot (x_W - x_L)^a, \text{if } (x_W - x_L) > 0$$
$$u(G|Win) = (.50) \cdot (x_W + x_W)^a - (.50) \cdot b \cdot |(x_W - x_L)|^a, \text{if } (x_W - x_L) < 0$$

where x_W represents the amount won on gamble G. The parameter h_L used to define H_1 is defined as

$$h_L = \frac{2}{1 + e^{-D_L}} - 1 \tag{5}$$

$$D_L = u(G|Loss) - (-b \cdot x_L^a)$$

$$u(G|Loss) = (.50) \cdot (x_W - x_L)^a - (.50) \cdot b \cdot (x_L + x_L)^a, \text{if } (x_W - x_L) > 0$$

$$u(G|Loss) = -(.50) \cdot b \cdot |(x_W - x_L)|^a - (.50) \cdot b \cdot (x_L + x_L)^a, \text{if } (x_W - x_L) < 0$$

where x_L represents the amount lost on gamble G. Parameters a and b are risk aversion and loss aversion parameters respectively. The projection matrix

$$M = \begin{bmatrix} T & 0 \\ 0 & T \end{bmatrix}, \quad T = \begin{bmatrix} 1 & 0 \\ 0 & 0 \end{bmatrix}. \tag{6}$$

is used to map states into the response for taking the gamble on the second stage. The probability of planning to take the second stage gamble equals

$$p(T|Plan) = ||M \cdot U \cdot \psi_I||^2. \tag{7}$$

The probability of taking the second stage game following the experience of a win equals

$$p(T|Win) = ||M \cdot U \cdot \psi_W||^2. \tag{8}$$

The probability of taking the second stage game following the experience of a loss equals

$$p(T|Loss) = ||M \cdot U \cdot \psi_L||^2. \tag{9}$$

If $\gamma \neq 0$ then we find that the quantum model produces interference that helps account for the observed dynamic inconsistency effects:

$$||M \cdot U \cdot \psi_I||^2 = \frac{1}{2} \cdot ||M \cdot U \cdot (\psi_W + \psi_L)||^2 \tag{10}$$

$$= \frac{1}{2} \cdot ||M \cdot U \cdot \psi_W + M \cdot U \cdot \psi_L||^2$$

$$= \frac{1}{2} \cdot ||M \cdot U \cdot \psi_W||^2 + \frac{1}{2} \cdot ||M \cdot U \cdot \psi_L||^2$$

$$+ \frac{1}{2} \cdot (\psi_W^\dagger \cdot U \cdot M) \cdot (M \cdot U \cdot \psi_L)$$

$$+ \frac{1}{2} \cdot (\psi_L^\dagger \cdot U \cdot M) \cdot (M \cdot U \cdot \psi_W).$$

In sum, this quantum model has only three parameters: a and b are used to determine the utilities; the third is the parameter γ for changing beliefs to align with actions. These three parameters were fit to the 33 data points in Table 1 (each gamble played twice expect for the first), and the best fitting parameters (minimizing sum of squared error) are $a = .7101$, $b = 2.5424$, and $\gamma = -4.4034$. The risk aversion parameter is a bit below one as expected, and the loss parameter b exceeds one, as it should be. The model produced an $R^2 = .8234$ and an *adjusted* $R^2 = .8120$ (the adjusted R-square includes a penalty that depends on the number of model parameters fit to the data).

3.2   Markov Decision Model

The Markov model is a special case of the quantum model when the key parameter, γ, is set to zero. In this case ($\gamma = 0$) there are no interference effects:

$$U = \exp\left(-i \cdot \frac{\pi}{2} \cdot H_1\right) = \begin{bmatrix} U_1 & 0 \\ 0 & U_2 \end{bmatrix}, \qquad (11)$$

$$M \cdot U \cdot \psi_W = \frac{1}{\sqrt{2}} \begin{bmatrix} T \cdot U_1 \\ 0 \end{bmatrix},$$

$$M \cdot U \cdot \psi_L = \frac{1}{\sqrt{2}} \begin{bmatrix} 0 \\ T \cdot U_2 \end{bmatrix},$$

$$(\psi_W^\dagger \cdot U \cdot M) \cdot (M \cdot U \cdot \psi_L) = 0.$$

So if we force $\gamma = 0$, then the quantum model no longer produces 'quantum like' interference effects. Instead, the choice probability for the plan is an equal weight average of the two choice probabilities produced after either winning or losing the first stage: $p(T|plan) = (.50) \cdot p(T|Win) + (.50) \cdot p(T|loss)$, where $p(T|Win)$ is defined by Equation 8 with $\gamma = 0$ and $p(T|loss)$ is defined by Equation 9 with $\gamma = 0$. This model was fit to the results in Table 1 by using only two parameters a and b for the quantum model (with $\gamma = 0$), and it produced an $R^2 = .7854$ and an *adjusted* $R^2 = .7787$ which still falls below the adjusted R^2 for the three parameter quantum model, and so the γ parameter is making a useful contribution in this application.

In summary, comparing the two key models on the basis of fitting the means, we find that the quantum model with $\gamma \neq 0$ produces an increase in adjusted R-square over the Markov model when the two models are fit to the means. However, the next section provides a Hierarchical Bayesian estimation of the key quantum parameter to determine whether or not its posterior distribution lies near zero or within a quantum regime.

4   Hierarchical Bayesian Model Comparison

4.1   Log Likelihood for Each Person

The Bayesian model estimation was computed using the 33 choice trials observed from each person. On each trial, a gamble was presented and the person made both a plan for an outcome and a final choice after observing that same outcome. For person i on trial t we observe a data pattern $X_i(t) = [x_{TT}(t), x_{TR}(t), x_{RT}(t), x_{RR}(t)]$ defined by $x_{ij}(t) = 1$ if event (i,j) occurs and otherwise zero, where TT is the event "planned to take gamble and finally did take the gamble," TR is the event "planned to take gamble but changed and finally rejected gamble." RT is the event "planned to reject the gamble but changed and finally did take the gamble" and RR is the event "planned to reject gamble and finally did reject the gamble." The data for the 33 trials from a single person is represented by the 33 tuple $X_i = [X_i(1), ..., X_i(33)]$. Finally, the data for all 100 participants is defined by the 4×100 tuple $X = [X_1, ..., X_{N=100}]$.

Two allow for possible dependencies between a pair of choices within a single trial, an additional memory recall parameter was included in each model. For both models, it was assumed that there is some probability m, $0 \leq m \leq 1$ that the person simply recalls and repeats the planned choice for the final choice, and there is some probability $1 - m$ that the person forgets or ignores the planned choice when making the final choice. After including this memory parameter, the prediction for each event becomes

$$p_{TT} = p(T|plan) \cdot (m \cdot 1 + (1 - m) \cdot p(T|final)) \tag{12}$$
$$p_{TR} = p(T|plan) \cdot (1 - m) \cdot p(R|final)$$
$$p_{RT} = p(R|plan) \cdot (1 - m) \cdot p(T|final)$$
$$p_{RR} = p(R|plan) \cdot (m \cdot 1 + (1 - m) \cdot p(R|final))$$

Using these definitions for each model, the log likelihood function for the 33 trials from a single person can be expressed as

$$\ln L\left(X_i\left(t\right)\right) = \sum x_{jk}\left(t\right) \cdot \ln\left(p_{jk}\right) \tag{13}$$
$$\ln L\left(X_i\right) = \sum_{i=1}^{33} \ln L\left(X_i\left(t\right)\right).$$

The predictions p_{jk} used in the formulas shown above depend on the four model parameters $\theta_i = [a_i, b_i, m_i, \gamma_i]$ for person i. Therefore, the likelihood of the data for person i given the model parameters is then equal to $L\left(X_i|\theta_i\right) = \exp\left(\ln L\left(X_i\right)\right).$

4.2   Grid Analysis of Log Likelihood Function

Each model has four parameters $\theta_i = (a, b, m, \gamma)$, a risk aversion parameter, a loss aversion parameter, a memory parameter, and a choice model parameter. The first three parameters were common across both models and they only differ with respect to the fourth parameter. We used a fine grid of 21 points per parameter.

$$a \in [.400, .45, ..., .85, .90, .95, ..., 1.35, 1.40], \tag{14}$$
$$b \in [.50, .60, ..., 1.40, 1.50, 1.60, ...2.40, 2.50], \tag{15}$$
$$m \in [.00, .05, ..., .45, .500, .55, ..., .95, 1.00], \tag{16}$$
$$\gamma \in [-5.00, -4.5, ..., -.5, 0.0, .5, ..., 4.5, 5.00] \text{ (quantum)}. \tag{17}$$

This grid generated 21^4 combinations, and we evaluated the log likelihood function for each model at each combination. These ranges were chosen on the basis of past fits of these models. The risk aversion parameter ranges from risk aversion to risk seeking; the loss aversion parameter ranges across loss insensitivity to loss sensitivity; and the memory parameter ranges from no recall to perfect recall. The key γ parameter ranges from positive to negative values for the quantum model. Define $[a_i, b_i, m_i, \gamma_i] = [\theta_{i1}, \theta_{i2}, \theta_{i3}, \theta_{i4}] = \theta_i$ as the 4-tuple of parameters from a single person i, and define $\theta = [\theta_1, .., \theta_N]$ as the $4 \cdot N$ tuple of the four parameters for $N = 100$ participants.

4.3 Hierarchical Parameters

The hierarchical parameters are used to determine the distribution of θ_i across individuals. Define $\pi = [\pi_1, \pi_2, \pi_3, \pi_4]$ as a 4-tuple containing four hierarchical parameters, where π_j is the hierarchical parameter used to determine the distribution of θ_{ij} across the individuals i. Each hierarchical parameter was evaluated by a grid of 19 points $\pi_j \in [.05, .10, ..., .90, .95]$ which generated a grid of 19^4 combinations.

Define $r(\pi)$ as the prior distribution over the hierarchical parameters. We assumed an independent uniform so that $r(\pi) = 19^{-4}$. Define $q(\theta_i | \pi_i)$ as the prior distribution over model parameter θ_i given the hierarchical parameter π_i. For this prior we assumed an independent binomial distribution across the 21 values of each model parameter

$$q(\theta_i | \pi) = \prod_{j=1}^{4} q(\theta_{ij} | \pi_j), \quad q(\theta_{ij} = \theta_k | \pi_j) = \binom{21}{k} \cdot \pi_j^k \cdot (1 - \pi_j)^{21-k}. \quad (18)$$

The joint distribution of data and parameters then equals

$$p(\pi, \theta, X) = r(\pi) \cdot \prod_{i=1}^{N=100} q(\theta_i | \pi) \cdot L(X_i | \theta_i). \quad (19)$$

We marginalize over θ to obtain the joint distribution of hierarchical parameters and data

$$p(\pi, X) = \sum_{\theta} p(\pi, \theta, X). \quad (20)$$

Finally, we obtain the posterior distribution over the hierarchical parameters

$$p(\pi | X) = \frac{p(\pi, X)}{\sum_{\pi} p(\pi, X)}. \quad (21)$$

The posterior distribution for each hierarchical parameter is plotted in Figure 1 shown below. The top left distribution indicates that the risk aversion hierarchical parameter distribution is located below .50, which implies that the mean of the risk aversion parameter equals .6518, indicating somewhat strong risk aversion, which is a common finding in the literature. The top right distribution indicates that the loss aversion hierarchical parameter distribution is located above .50, which implies that the mean of the loss aversion equals 1.97, higher sensitivity to losses, which is also a common finding in the literature. The bottom left distribution indicates that the hierarchical memory parameter is slightly above .50, which implies that the mean of the memory parameter equals .5932, so that a little more than half the time people were simply recalling their previous choices. The bottom right distribution shows the hierarchical distribution for the key quantum parameter. According to the Markov model, this should be located around .50 to produce a mean value equal to zero. Contrary to this expectation, the entire distribution lies below .50, which implies a mean value equal to −2.67.

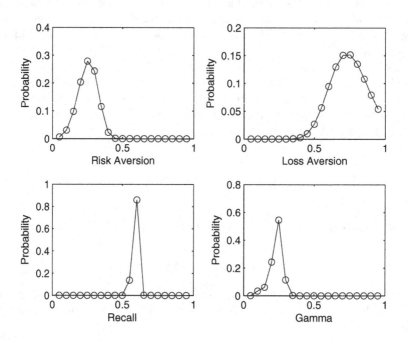

Fig. 1. Posterior distribution of hierarchical parameters of the quantum decision model

5   Conclusions

This paper presents the first hierarchical Bayesian estimation of the parameters used in a quantum decision model. A classic Markov model is a special case of the quantum model when the key quantum parameter is zero. The posterior distribution of the key quantum parameter was entirely below the value expected by the Markov model, providing strong evidence that the parameter lies within a quantum regime. Of course, it is much too soon to conclude that the quantum model is always superior to a Markov model. The models need to be compared using other data sets from various other experiments. Even within the same data set, various other prior distributions need to be examined. Further, with the two stage gambling paradigm, the learned model could be used to predict the next result with cross-validation methods. But the surprising lesson learned from this model comparison exercise was that contrary to expectations, there is clear evidence for the quantum model parameter.

References

1. Barkan, R., Busemeyer, J.R.: Modeling Dynamic Inconsistency with a Changing Reference Point. Journal of Behavioral Decision Making 16, 235–255 (2003)
2. Berger, J.O.: Statistical Decision Theory and Bayesian Analysis. Springer, New York (1985)
3. Busemeyer, J.R., Wang, Z., Lambert-Mogiliansky, A.: Comparison of Markov and Quantum Models of Decision Making. Journal of Mathematical Psychology 53(5), 423–433 (2009)
4. Khrennikov, A.Y., Haven, E.: Quantum Mechanics and Violations of the Sure Thing Principle: The use of Probability Interference and Other Concepts. Journal of Mathematical Psychology 53(5), 378–388 (2009)
5. Lambert-Mogiliansky, A., Zamir, S., Zwirn, H.: Type Indeterminacy: A Model of the 'KT' (Kahneman-Tversky)-Man. Journal of Mathematical Psychology 53(5), 349–361 (2009)
6. Pothos, E., Busemeyer, J.: A Quantum Probability Explanation for Violations of 'Rational' Decision Theory. Proceedings of the Royal Society B 276(1165), 2171–2178 (2009)
7. Tversky, A., Shafir, E.: The Disjunction Effect in Choice Under Uncertainty. Psychological Science 3, 305–309 (1992)
8. Yukalov, V., Sornette, D.: Decision Theory with Prospect Interference and Entanglement. Theory and Decision 70, 283–328 (2010)
9. Yukalov, V., Sornette, D.: Processing Information in Quantum Decision Theory. Entropy 11(4), 1073–1120 (2009)

Many Paths Lead to Discovery:
Analogical Retrieval of Cancer Therapies

Trevor Cohen[1], Dominic Widdows[2], Lance De Vine[3], Roger Schvaneveldt[4],
and Thomas C. Rindflesch[5]

[1] University of Texas School of Biomedical Informatics at Houston
[2] Microsoft Bing
[3] Queensland University of Technology
[4] Arizona State University
[5] National Library of Medicine

Abstract. This paper addresses the issue of analogical inference, and its potential role as the mediator of new therapeutic discoveries, by using disjunction operators based on quantum connectives to combine many potential reasoning pathways into a single search expression. In it, we extend our previous work in which we developed an approach to analogical retrieval using the Predication-based Semantic Indexing (PSI) model, which encodes both concepts and the relationships between them in high-dimensional vector space. As in our previous work, we leverage the ability of PSI to infer predicate pathways connecting two example concepts, in this case comprising of known therapeutic relationships. For example, given that *drug x* TREATS *disease z*, we might infer the predicate pathway *drug x* INTERACTS_WITH *gene y* ASSOCIATED_WITH *disease z*, and use this pathway to search for drugs related to another disease in similar ways. As biological systems tend to be characterized by networks of relationships, we evaluate the ability of quantum-inspired operators to mediate inference and retrieval across multiple relations, by testing the ability of different approaches to recover known therapeutic relationships. In addition, we introduce a novel complex vector based implementation of PSI, based on Plate's Circular Holographic Reduced Representations, which we utilize for all experiments in addition to the binary vector based approach we have applied in our previous research.

Keywords: Distributional Semantics, Vector Symbolic Architectures, Literature-based Discovery, Abductive Reasoning.

1 Introduction

The field of Literature-based Discovery (LBD) has been an important application area for quantum-inspired methodologies in recent years [1,2]. In particular, the ability of quantum-inspired approaches to measure implicit relatedness between composite representations of concepts holistically offers advantages in scalability and efficiency over rule-based approaches that require the decomposition of conceptual representations into their atomic components. In previous work, we have shown that these holistic approaches can be used to facilitate analogical retrieval across a set of object-relation-object triplets, or predications extracted from the biomedical literature, to solve simple

J.R. Busemeyer et al. (Eds.): QI 2012, LNCS 7620, pp. 90–101, 2012.

proportional analogy problems of the form "*A* is to *B* as *?* is to *C*" [2]. This mechanism provides the means to infer the predicate pathway connecting a disease to a drug that is known to treat it, and also to use the vector representation of this pathway to search for treatments connected to some other disease in the same way. However, the identification and re-use of individual pathways is of limited utility for the discovery of new therapies, as drugs tend to activate multiple pathways and targets simultaneously [3]. This suggests that modeling analogical retrieval across multiple pathways may facilitate the identification of novel therapeutic relationships. In this paper, we use quantum models of disjunction and superposition to achieve this end, allowing us to combine many compound stimuli to perform searches that would be brittle and computationally prohibitive using traditional symbolic methods. In doing so, we create a superposition of compound systems that has not been (and probably cannot be) represented as a product of two individual simple systems, a phenomenon known in the quantum literature as "entanglement". It is our hypothesis that modeling multiple pathways will improve the quality of analogical retrieval, and we evaluate this hypothesis by comparing the extent to which retrieval across individual and multiple pathways facilitates recovery of a held out set of cancer therapies. We evaluate these approaches in both binary and complex vector space, leveraging recent enhancements to the Semantic Vectors package [4].

2   Background

Distributional models of language, such as Latent Semantic Analysis (LSA) [5] derive human-like estimates of the semantic relatedness between terms from large volumes of unannotated natural language text. A desirable property of some distributional models is the ability to learn meaningful associations between terms that do not co-occur directly in the text concerned. This ability has been termed *indirect inference* and it has been argued that it is essential to LSA's human-like performance on a number of cognitive tasks [5]. Indirect inference is also a fundamental concern of the field of Literature-based Discovery (LBD), which aims to promote scientific discovery by identifying meaningful connections between terms, and concepts, in the scientific literature that have not yet occurred together in any published document [6], and several authors have explored the ability of distributional models to facilitate discoveries of this nature [7,8,9]. A limitation of the use of these models for LBD is that they capture general relatedness between terms or concepts only, without encoding the nature of the relationships concerned. As economic constraints limit the number of candidate therapies that can be advanced for further testing, there is a pressing need for the development of methods that selectively emphasize plausible therapeutic hypotheses. In recognition of the limitations of general relatedness, LBD researchers have recently begun exploring the notion of a *discovery pattern*, a sequence of relationship types that suggests a potential discovery [10]. For example, if a certain drug were known to inhibit a gene associated with a particular disease, it would follow that this drug may be a potential candidate therapy for this disease. These patterns have largely been pursued using rule-based approaches in which concepts, and the relationships between them, are represented as discrete entities each of which must be explored stepwise to find a pathway from treatment to disease (see for example [11]). However, given the rapid expansion of the number of logical connections between concepts in the biomedical literature [12,13], the development of methods to directly identify meaningful connections across specific patterns of relationships is a desirable alternative. To this end, we have developed PSI [2,14,15], which encodes concepts and their relations as vectors in high-dimensional space, facilitating efficient search and indirect inference without the need to unpack and explore individual relationships. In previously published work, we have shown that PSI can be used to infer relationship paths (such as INHIBITS-ASSOCIATED WITH) from one concept to another, and that these inferred pathways can be used to direct search through predication space for concepts related to a third concept in the same way [2]. However, the identification and re-use of individual pathways is of limited utility for discovery of new therapies, as drugs tend to activate multiple pathways simultaneously [3]. In this paper, we evaluate the utility of the PSI model as a means to identify therapeutic relationships by accommodating drug-disease relationships that include multiple relationship paths. In some cases, the quantum disjunction operator [16] is applied to measure the relatedness between concepts that are connected across multiple relationship paths, and in others we use superposition of vectors to achieve this end. In the section that follows, we introduce the fundamental operations that mediate PSI, and the notation used to describe them. We then illustrate the way in which analogy occurs in PSI space, and proceed to describe the empirical component of this work, in which we use analogical relations drawn from one disease, or set of diseases, to seek treatments for another.

3   Mathematical Structure and Methods

The methods in this paper all use high-dimensional vectors to represent concepts. There are many ways of generating such representations. Ours is based upon the Random Indexing paradigm using terminology as described in [9] and developed in [2], in which *semantic vectors* are built as superpositions of randomly generated *elemental vectors*, during the process of training. Throughout this paper we will write $E(X)$ and $S(X)$ for the elemental and semantic vectors associated with the concept X. In addition to concept vectors, we include vectors for relations. For example, $E(R)$ would denote the elemental vector for the relation R. Many relationships are directional, and we will use R_{inv} to denote the inverse of R, so that A R B and B R_{inv} A carry the same external meaning (though they may in some cases be represented by different vectors). To encode typed relations into high-dimensional vector spaces, we utilize two members of a family of representational approaches collectively known as Vector Symbolic Architectures [17]. VSAs originated from Smolenksy's tensor-product based approach [18], but differ from it in that they depend on vector operations that produce products of the same dimensionality as the component vectors. The VSAs we will use in our experiments are Kanerva's Binary Spatter Code (BSP) [19], which uses high-dimensional binary vectors as a representational unit, and Plate's Circular Holographic Reduced Representation (CHRR) [20], which uses circular vectors, vectors in which each dimension represents an angle between $-\pi$ and π. CHRRs have recently been used to encode information related to word order in a distributional model [21]. Before we discuss further distinctions between these models, we will describe the fundamental operations of VSAs, which are common to both of them. The primary operations facilitated by VSAs are *binding* and *bundling*. Binding is a multiplication-like operator through which two vectors are combined to form a third vector C that is dissimilar from either of its component vectors A and B. We will use the symbol "$\otimes$" for binding, and the symbol "$\oslash$" for the inverse of binding throughout this paper. It is important that this operator be invertible: if C = A $\otimes$ B, then A $\oslash$ C = A $\oslash$ (A $\otimes$ B) = B. In some models, this recovery may be approximate, but the robust nature of the representation guarantees that A $\oslash$ C is similar enough to B that B can easily be recognized as the best candidate for A $\oslash$ C in the original set of concepts. Thus the invertible nature of the bind operator facilitates the retrieval of information encoded during the binding process. Bundling is an addition-like operator, through which superposition of vectors is achieved. For example, vector addition followed by normalization is a commonly employed bundling operator. Bundling results in a vector that is maximally similar to its component vectors. We will write the usual "+" for bundling, and the computer science "+=" for "bundle the left hand side with the right hand side and assign the outcome to the symbol on the left hand side." So for example, $S(A) += E(B)$ could also be expressed as $S(A) = S(A) + E(B)$, and is a standard operation in training. Table 1 summarizes the differences between the binary (BSP) and complex (CHRR) vector implementations used in this work.

Table 1. Comparison between CHRR and BSP

Implementation	Complex/Circular	Binary
Semantic vectors $S(X)$	Complex (circular) vectors $d\ O(1000)$	Binary vectors $d\ O(10{,}000)$
Elemental vectors $E(X)$	Dense complex $[-\pi, \pi]$	Dense binary $\{0,1\}$
Bundling (Superposition)	Pairwise vector sum	Majority vote
Binding	Convolution (mod 2π addition of angles)	Pairwise XOR (mod 2 addition)
Release	Convolution with inverse	Pairwise XOR

In the case of the spatter code, pairwise exclusive or (XOR) is used as a binding operator: $X \otimes Y = X \text{ XOR } Y$. As it is its own inverse, the binding and decoding processes are identical ($\otimes = \oslash$). For bundling, the spatter code employs a majority vote: if the component vectors of the bundle have more ones than zeros in a dimension, this dimension will have a value of one, with ties broken at random (for example, bundling the vectors 011 and 010 may produce either 010 or 011 with equal probability). In the case of CHRR, binding is accomplished using circular convolution, accomplished by pairwise multiplication: $X \otimes Y = \{X_1 Y_1, X_2 Y_2, \ldots X_{n-1} Y_{n-1}, X_n Y_n\}$, which is equivalent to addition of the phase angles of the circular vectors concerned, as they are of unit length. The inverse of binding is obtained by binding to the inverse of the vector concerned: $X \oslash Y = X \otimes Y^{-1}$, where the inverse of a vector Y, Y^{-1} is the vector with a phase angle that when added to that of Y produces a phase angle of 0. As each dimension in a circular vector can be represented as a vector on the unit circle, superposition is accomplished in a pairwise manner by adding the unit circle vectors in a given dimension, and normalizing the result for each circular component of the vector. In the implementation used in our experiments, normalization is delayed until after training has concluded, so that the sequence in which superposition occurs is not relevant. Once a vector representation for a concept has been built up by binding and/or bundling, it is possible to apply an operator that reverses the binding process to the vector as a whole, allowing us to direct search in PSI space without explicitly representing the individual relations of a concept. This property is appealing for the purpose of modeling analogy, as similarity is measured on the basis of a superposed product without the need to decompose it [20].

Predication-Based Semantic Indexing: PSI takes as input sets of concept-relation-concept triplets, or predications. For these experiments, as well as those in our previous work, the PSI space is derived from a set of 22,669,964 predications extracted from citations added to MEDLINE over the past decade by the SemRep natural language processing system [22], which extracts predications from biomedical text using domain knowledge in the Unified Medical Language System [23]. For example, the predication "fluoxetine TREATS Major Depressive Disorder" (MDD) is extracted from "patients who have been successfully treated with fluoxetine for major depression." In a recent evaluation of SemRep, Kilicoglu et al. report .75 precision and .64 recall (.69 f-score) [24]. The first step in PSI is the generation of semantic and elemental vectors for each concept, $S(C)$ and $E(C)$. We also generate elemental vectors for each relation, or predicate $E(P)$. We then encode each predication in the set by binding $E(C_1)$ to $E(P)$ and bundling this into $S(C_2)$. The reverse of this process is also performed. In practice statistical weighting metrics are used to decrease the influence of frequently occurring concepts, and in some cases predicates. In the implementation we utilized for these experiments, we used inverse document frequency (*idf*) as a global weighting metric, and log(1+frequency of predication) as a local metric. For example, the predication "thalidomide INHIBITS cyclooxygenase 2" (cox2) would be encoded as follows:

$$S(\text{thalidomide})+=E(\text{INHIBITS}) \otimes E(\text{cox2}) \times idf(\text{cox2}) \times gw$$
$$S(\text{cox2})+=E(\text{INHIBITS}_{\text{inv}}) \otimes E(\text{thalidomide}) \times idf(\text{thalidomide}) \times gw$$
$$idf(\text{C}) = \log \frac{\text{total predications}}{\text{predications containing C}}$$
$$gw = \log(1 + \text{occurrences of thalidomide INHIBITS cox2})$$

For the sake of brevity, we will describe future encoding operations without explicitly referring to *idf* or *gw*. This process is repeated across all of the predications in the database, to generate a set of trained semantic vectors for each concept.

Analogical Retrieval: As the binding process is invertible, it is possible to retrieve a dual-predicate path connecting two concepts:

Training:

$$S(\text{multiple\_myeloma})(\text{MM})+=E(\text{ASSOCIATED\_WITH}) \otimes E(\text{cox2})$$
$$S(\text{thalidomide})+=E(\text{INHIBITS}) \otimes E(\text{cox2})$$

Inference:

$$S(\text{MM}) \oslash S(\text{thalidomide}) \approx E(\text{ASSOCIATED\_WITH}) \otimes E(\text{cox2})$$
$$\oslash \, (E(\text{INHIBITS}) \otimes E(\text{cox2}))$$
$$\approx E(\text{ASSOCIATED\_WITH}) \oslash E(\text{INHIBITS})$$
$$\otimes \, E(\text{cox2}) \oslash E(\text{cox2})$$
$$\approx E(\text{ASSOCIATED\_WITH}) \oslash E(\text{INHIBITS})$$

These inferred relationships can then be used to find concepts relating to a third concept in the same way that these cue concepts relate to one another. The ability of VSAs to capture relational similarity has led to their utilization as a means to model aspects of analogical thought [25,20,26]. In previous work, we have shown that this facility of VSAs can be used to solve proportional analogy problems, by inferring predicate paths between cue concepts, and using the vector representations of these paths to direct search through predication space [2]. This is accomplished with either the retrieved path (e.g. $E(\text{ASSOCIATED\_WITH}) \oslash E(\text{INHIBITS})$) or the noisy approximation of it derived from the cue concept vectors (e.g. $S(\text{MM}) \oslash S(\text{thalidomide})$). The vector representations of these inferred paths can be applied to another concept to direct search through PSI space to facilitate analogical retrieval as follows:

Training:

$$S(\text{fluoxetine}) += E(\text{INHIBITS}) \otimes E(\text{serotonin})$$
$$S(\text{MDD}) += E(\text{ASSOCIATED\_WITH}) \otimes E(\text{serotonin})$$

Inference:

$$S(\text{MDD}) \oslash (E(\text{ASSOCIATED\_WITH}) \oslash E(\text{INHIBITS}))$$
$$\approx E(\text{ASSOCIATED\_WITH}) \otimes E(\text{serotonin})$$
$$\oslash \, (E(\text{ASSOCIATED\_WITH}) \oslash E(\text{INHIBITS}))$$
$$\approx E(\text{ASSOCIATED\_WITH}) \oslash E(\text{ASSOCIATED\_WITH})$$
$$\otimes \, E(\text{INHIBITS}) \otimes E(\text{serotonin})$$
$$\approx E(\text{INHIBITS}) \otimes E(\text{serotonin}) \approx S(\text{fluoxetine})$$

4 Multiple Pathways and Quantum Disjunction

In previous work [2], we restricted our study of analogical retrieval to proportional analogies in which a single predicate path (consisting of one or two predicates) inferred from a cue pair (e.g. $S(\text{MM}) \oslash S(\text{thalidomide})$) is used to direct search toward concepts connected to a third target concept (e.g. $S(\text{MDD})$ in the same way as the cue pair relate to one another (e.g. z INHIBITS y, y ASSOCATED_WITH x), thereby solving a proportional analogy problem of the form "what relates to MDD as thalidomide relates to MM". However, analogies used in science tend to have more complex structure than this [27], and drugs tend to be connected to the diseases they treat across networks involving multiple biological entities [3]. Consequently, in this paper we evaluate the ability of PSI to perform analogical inference and retrieval across multiple predicate paths. In order to do so, we require a way to measure the similarity between an individual vector, representing a potential treatment, and a set of vectors representing the permitted paths from the target disease to this vector. One approach we evaluate in this paper involves comparing candidate therapies to the superposition of a set of inferred predicate paths. However, as we would like to identify both treatments that are strongly connected across a single path (such as INHIBITS:ASSOCIATED_WITH) and treatments that are connected across multiple paths (such as INHIBITS:ASSOCIATED_WITH; INTER-ACTS_WITH:CAUSES), we also utilize for this purpose the span of vectors, described in logic as the quantum disjunction operator by Birkhoff and Von Neumann [28] and applied to information retrieval by Widdows and Peters [16]. This operator measures the proportion of a vector (in our case a treatment) that can be projected onto a subspace spanned by a set of component vectors (in our case the predicate paths of interest bound to the disease of interest). In addition, we introduce a binary vector approximation of this operator, compared with the continuous implementation in Table 2.

Table 2. Continuous and Binary Implementations of Quantum Disjunction

Implementation Steps	Continuous	Binary
(1) Component vectors	Real/complex vectors $d\,O(1000)$	Binary vectors $d\,O(10,000)$
(2) Orthogonalize vectors	A - A's projection on B such that $\cos(\hat{A},B) = 0$	Introduce/eliminate identical dimensions until $HD(\hat{A},B) = \frac{d}{2}$.
(3) Projection	Project into subspace	Compare with component vectors
(4) Comparison	Cosine of angle between projection and original vector	Count of overlap with orthogonalized component vectors

5   Evaluation

To evaluate PSI's ability to mediate analogical inference, we utilize the same set of 22,669,964 predications as in our previous work. From this, we extract predications involving predicates in the set {AFFECTS; AUGMENTS; CAUSES; DISRUPTS; INHIBITS; PREDISPOSES; STIMULATES; ASSOCIATED_WITH; COEXISTS_WITH; INTERACTS_WITH}, which were selected on the basis of their potential as justification for therapeutic hypotheses. Predications with the predicate TREATS, and any predications involving a direct relationship between a pharmaceutical substance (UMLS semantic type "**phsu**") and neoplastic process (UMLS semantic type "**neop**", which represents types of cancer), were excluded from training. In addition, predications involving a concept with a global frequency greater than or equal to 100,000 were excluded, as these concepts tend to be general in nature and relatively uninformative. From the remaining predications, we generated two PSI spaces, one of which utilized binary vectors with dimension 32,000, and one of which utilized complex vectors with dimension of 4,000. We will refer to these spaces as BSP and CHRR respectively, in accordance with the methodology used to generate them. As a test set, we extracted 1,158 types of cancer (or neoplastic processes: UMLS semantic type "**neop**") with the prerequisite that each extracted neoplastic process occur in a TREATS relationships with a pharmaceutical substance represented in our spaces. Inclusion in the set does not, however, guarantee that a dual-predicate pathway between the cancer concerned and this treatment exists. We use this set to evaluate analogical retrieval, with the following approaches.

Collective Cues: This is an approach we have pursued in our recent work [29], in which dual-predicate pathways are inferred from a set of 48,204 known TREATS relationships between diseases or syndromes (UMLS semantic type "**dsyn**") and pharmaceutical substances (UMLS semantic type "**phsu**"). For each pair, the dual-predicate path connecting the concepts concerned is inferred by generating the composite cue vector $S(\text{dysn})$ $\oslash S(\text{phsu})$ and searching through the set of vectors generated by pairwise combination of the vectors representing individual predicate paths, $E(\text{PRED1}) \oslash E(\text{PRED2})$. From the original set of seventeen predicate vectors (7 directional x 2 = 14 + 3 that commute = 17), a set of 136 binary ($\frac{17 \times 16}{2}$) and a set of 272 complex (17×16) dual-predicate path vectors were generated. With complex vectors, twice as many paths are generated, as unlike XOR, the convolution operator is not its own inverse - the order of application of operators is of importance. Paths connecting pharmaceutical substances and diseases or syndromes were inferred by retrieving dual-predicate path vectors with a similarity to the composite cue vector $S(\text{dysn}) \oslash S(\text{phsu})$ greater than 1 SD above the mean similarity between 1000 randomly generated vectors of the same vector type and dimensionality. The number of times each possible predicate path was retrieved with a similarity above this threshold to the cue vector was counted, and the five most popular paths for both binary and complex vector spaces were retained. These paths are illustrated in Table 3. Most paths are readily interpretable, as the ASSOCIATED_WITH predicate links diseases to related biological entities, and a drug that interacts with such entities may be a plausible therapy. Some pathways are more difficult to interpret, and we refer the interested reader to a related publication [29] concerned primarily with identification, interpretation and application of such pathways. Of interest for our present purposes, directionality of the predicate paths is encoded in the complex case only. So complex pathways are easier to interpret, and binary pathways are less constrained.

Individual Cues: Cues in this case consist of other neoplastic processes drawn from the set. For each neoplastic process, we draw at random another neoplastic process, *cue_neop*, and retrieve all of its TREATS relationships from the predication database. The dual predicate paths are compared to the subspace derived from this set of treatments using the quantum disjunction operator. The components of this subspace (prior to orthogonalization) consist of the set $\{ S(\text{cue\_neop}) \oslash S(\text{treatment}_1) ...S(\text{cue\_neop}) \oslash S(\text{treatment}_n) \}$. Only pathways with an association strength above empirically determined thresholds of 6SD (binary vectors) and 2.5SD (complex vectors) above the mean pairwise relatedness between 1000 randomly generated vectors of the same type and dimensionality are retained. Random cue selection is repeated until an example with more than one above-threshold predicate path is found.

Table 3. Most Popular Predicate Paths in Binary and Complex Space

Binary	Count	Complex	Count
ASSOCIATED_WITH COEXISTS_WITH	925	COEXISTS_WITH ASSOCIATED_WITH	900
ASSOCIATED_WITH INTERACTS_WITH	201	ASSOCIATED_WITH INTERACTS_WITH	827
ASSOCIATED_WITH INHIBITS	82	ASSOCIATED_WITH INHIBITS	284
COEXISTS_WITH CAUSES	71	ASSOCIATED_WITH COEXISTS_WITH	264
CAUSES-INV INTERACTS_WITH	69	COEXISTS_WITH AFFECTS	248

Application of Pathways: To evaluate the ability of our models to infer (i.e. rediscover) TREATS relationships pertinent to the types of cancer under evaluation, we generate a composite cue vector, or subspace, from the vector representing the target neoplastic process, $S(\text{target\_neop})$, using three approaches. In the first of these, which we will term MAX, only the most strongly associated predicate path is utilized. The cue vector is constructed as $S(\text{target\_neop}) \oslash E(\text{predicate path}_1)$. In the second, which we will term SUP, all of the relevant predicate paths ($n=5$ for composite cues, and $n >= 2$ for individual cues) are superposed to generate a composite cue vectors constructed as $S(\text{target\_neop}) \oslash E(\text{predicate path}_1) + S(\text{target\_neop}) \oslash E(\text{predicate path}_2) + ... + S(\text{target\_neop}) \oslash E(\text{predicate path}_n)$. In the third approach, which we will designate SUB, the same set of vectors used to generate SUP are combined, but rather than superposing these we generate a subspace from them using the quantum disjunction operator. For each of the 1,158 target neoplasms, the MAX, SUP and SUB cues are compared with the semantic vectors for all of the pharmaceutical substances in the PSI space ($n = 16,337$). For each of the three cue types we retrieve all of the pharmaceutical substances with a similarity to the composite cues above a series of statistically determined thresholds of association for each of the 1,158 target neoplasms. This approach is used rather than a fixed number of nearest neighbors, as we anticipate that only a subset of target neoplasms will be connected in accordance with the dual predicate pathway cues. With a threshold, concepts connected in this way should be selectively retrieved.

6   Results and Discussion

Figures 1 and 2 show the results of our experiments in binary and complex space respectively. The y axis shows the total number of rediscovered therapeutic relationships at a given threshold for the set of 1,158 neoplastic processes. The x axis shows the mean number of candidate therapies retrieved at this threshold, so higher threshold values correspond to lower values on the x axis. Therefore, one interpretation of the results in Figure 1 (left) is that the binary SUB model recovered approximately two treatments

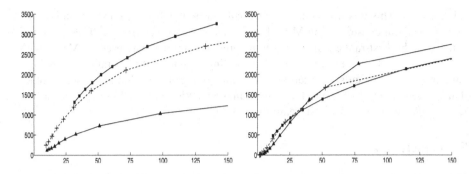

Fig. 1. Binary Vector Results. Left: Collective Cues. Right: Individual Cues. ■=SUB; +=SUP; ▲=MAX. Y axis = no. discoveries. X axis = mean no. retrieved.

per disease in the test set while returning on average sixty results per search. However, this is not to say that treatments were found for every test case. The most productive models returned treatments in only around one third of the cases, even at the lowest thresholds tested. It may be the case that this approaches the proportion of this test set for which TREATS relationships corresponding to dual-predicate paths exist, and that models incorporating longer paths are required to recover the remaining treatments.

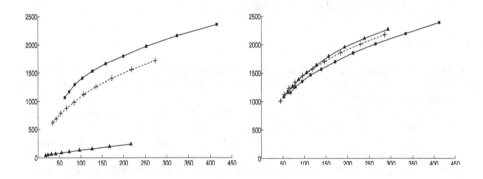

Fig. 2. Complex Vector Results. Left: Collective Cues. Right: Individual Cues. A. ■=SUB; +=SUP; ▲=MAX. Y axis = no. discoveries. X axis = mean no. retrieved.

With respect to the collective cues (left), there is a clear pattern of improved recovery for the models that capture connectedness across multiple pathways, with the quantum disjunction based SUB (■) model retrieving more treatments than the SUP (+) model, and both of these retrieving considerably more than MAX (▲). With individual cues (right) the distinction is less clear, with SUP and, in the binary case, SUB having a slight advantage over MAX at higher thresholds only, and MAX most productive at lower thresholds. This can be explained in part by the ASSOCIATED_WITH:INTERACTS_WITH pattern, which captures drug-gene-disease relationships. This was the second-ranked path for both collective cue sets, and consequently was not considered by MAX in these cases. However, this predicate path was usually the highest-ranked, and as such the predominant pathway used by MAX, with individual cues. One interpretation of this finding is that tight constraints on analogical retrieval are particularly hazardous when mapping from one domain (diseases other than cancer) to another. Overall, the quantum disjunction based SUB model with collective cues recovered the most treatments.

7   Conclusion

In this paper, we evaluate the ability of the PSI model to mediate retrieval across multiple relationships holistically and efficiently, without decomposing the representation of either the cue or the target. We find that models that facilitate retrieval across multiple predicate paths are better able to recover therapeutic relationships when the scope of these paths is relatively broad. The best performance was obtained with the quantum disjunction operator using collective cues derived from diseases other than cancer. As the predicate pathways concerned were not readily retrieved from individual cancer cues, the advantages of this model can be attributed to the application of relations derived from another domain, the hallmark of scientific analogy [27].

Acknowledgments. This research was supported by the US National Library of Medicine grant R21 LM010826, and the Intramural Research Program of the National Institute of Health, National Library of Medicine.

References

1. Bruza, P.: Semantic space: Bridging the divide between cognitive science, information processing technology and quantum mechanics. In: Proc. Inform. Symp. on Inform. Tech. (ITsim 2008), pp. 1–9 (2008)
2. Cohen, T., Widdows, D., Schvaneveldt, R., Rindflesch, T.C.: Finding Schizophrenia's Prozac Emergent Relational Similarity in Predication Space. In: Song, D., Melucci, M., Frommholz, I., Zhang, P., Wang, L., Arafat, S. (eds.) QI 2011. LNCS, vol. 7052, pp. 48–59. Springer, Heidelberg (2011)
3. Dudley, J., Schadt, E., et al.: Drug discovery in a multidimensional world: systems, patterns, and networks. J. Cardiovasc Transl. Res. 3(5), 438–447 (2010)
4. Widdows, D., Cohen, T., De Vine, L.: Real, complex, and binary semantic vectors. In: Proc. Sixth Intl. Symp. on Quantum Interactions, Paris, France (2012)
5. Landauer, T., Dumais, S.: A solution to plato's problem: The latent semantic analysis theory of acquisition, induction, and representation of knowledge. Psych. Review 104, 211–240 (1997)
6. Swanson, D.R.: Fish oil, raynaud's syndrome, and undiscovered public knowledge. Perspect Biol. Med. 30(1), 7–18 (1986)
7. Gordon, M.D., Dumais, S.: Using latent semantic indexing for literature based discovery. Journal of the American Society for Information Science 49, 674–685 (1998)
8. Cole, R.J., Bruza, P.D.: A Bare Bones Approach to Literature-Based Discovery: An Analysis of the Raynaud's/Fish-Oil and Migraine-Magnesium Discoveries in Semantic Space. In: Hoffmann, A., Motoda, H., Scheffer, T. (eds.) DS 2005. LNCS (LNAI), vol. 3735, pp. 84–98. Springer, Heidelberg (2005)

9. Cohen, T., Schvaneveldt, R., Widdows, D.: Reflective random indexing and indirect inference: A scalable method for discovery of implicit connections. Journal of Biomedical Informatics 43, 240–256 (2010)
10. Hristovski, D., Friedman, C., Rindflesch, T., Peterlin, B.: Literature-based knowledge discovery using natural language processing. In: Bruza, P., Weeber, M. (eds.) Literature Based Discovery, pp. 133–152. Springer, Heidelberg (2008)
11. Ahlers, C., Hristovski, D., Kilicoglu, H., Rindflesch, T.: Using the Literature-Based discovery paradigm to investigate drug mechanisms. In: AMIA Annu. Symp. Proc., pp. 6–10 (2007)
12. Wren, J.: The 'open discovery' challenge. In: Literature-Based Discovery, pp. 39–55 (2008)
13. Swanson, D.R.: Medical literature as a potential source of new knowledge. Bulletin of the Medical Library Association 78 (1990)
14. Cohen, T., Schvaneveldt, R., Rindflesch, T.: Predication-based semantic indexing: Permutations as a means to encode predications in semantic space. In: AMIA Annu. Symp. Proc., pp. 114–118 (2009)
15. Cohen, T., Widdows, D., Schvaneveldt, R.W., Rindflesch, T.C.: Logical leaps and quantum connectives: Forging paths through predication space. In: Proc. AAAI Fall Symp. on Quantum Informatics for Cognitive, Social, and Semantic Processes, pp. 11–13 (2010)
16. Widdows, D., Peters, S.: Word vectors and quantum logic experiments with negation and disjunction. In: Proc. 8th Math. of Language Conference, Bloomington, Indiana (2003)
17. Gayler, R.W.: Vector symbolic architectures answer jackendoff's challenges for cognitive neuroscience. In: Slezak, P. (ed.) ICCS/ASCS International Conference on Cognitive Science, pp. 133–138. University of New South Wales, Sydney (2004)
18. Smolensky, P.: Tensor product variable binding and the representation of symbolic structures in connectionist systems. Artificial Intelligence 46(1-2), 159–216 (1990)
19. Kanerva, P.: Binary Spatter-Coding of Ordered k-tuples. In: Vorbrüggen, J.C., von Seelen, W., Sendhoff, B. (eds.) ICANN 1996. LNCS, vol. 1112, Springer, Heidelberg (1996)
20. Plate, T.A.: Holographic Reduced Representation: Distributed Representation for Cognitive Structures. CSLI Publications, Stanfpord (2003)
21. De Vine, L., Bruza, P.: Semantic oscillations: Encoding context and structure in complex valued holographic vectors. In: Proc. AAAI Fall Symp. on Quantum Informatics for Cognitive, Social, and Semantic Processes (2010)
22. Rindflesch, T.C., Fiszman, M.: The interaction of domain knowledge and linguistic structure in natural language processing: interpreting hypernymic propositions in biomedical text. Journal of Biomedical Informatics 36, 462–477 (2003)
23. Bodenreider, O.: The unified medical language system (UMLS): integrating biomedical terminology. Nucleic Acids Research 32, D267 (2004) (database Issue)
24. Kilicoglu, H., Fiszman, M., Rosemblat, G., Marimpietri, S., Rindflesch, T.C.: Arguments of nominals in semantic interpretation of biomedical text. In: Proceedings of the 2010 Workshop on Biomedical Natural Language Processing, pp. 46–54 (2010)
25. Eliasmith, C., Thagard, P.: Integrating structure and meaning: A distributed model of analogical mapping. Cognitive Science 25(2), 245–286 (2001)
26. Kanerva, P.: What we mean when we say "What's the dollar of mexico?": Prototypes and mapping in concept space. In: Proc. AAAI Fall Symp. on Quantum Informatics for Cognitive, Social, and Semantic Processes (2010)
27. Holyoak, K.J., Thagard, P.: Mental Leaps: Analogy in Creative Thought. MIT Press (1995)
28. Birkhoff, G., Neumann, J.V.: The logic of quantum mechanics. The Annals of Mathematics 37(4), 823–843 (1936)
29. Cohen, T., Widdows, D., Schvaneveldt, R., Davies, P., Rindflesch, T.: Discovering discovery patterns with predication-based semantic indexing. Journal of Biomedical Informatics (July 2012) [epub ahead of print]

Emergence and Instability of Individual Identity

Ariane Lambert-Mogiliansky[1] and Jerome R. Busemeyer[2]

[1] Paris School of Economics, Paris, France
[2] Indiana University, USA
alambert@pse.ens.fr, jbusemey@indiana.edu

Abstract. The Type Indeterminacy model is a theoretical framework that uses some elements of quantum formalism to model the constructive preference perspective suggested by Kahneman and Tversky. In a dynamic decision context, type indeterminacy provides a framework for investigating the emergence and evolution of identity as the outcome of the interaction between multiple potential selves (eigentypes). We define a dynamic game among the selves with individual identity (preferences) as the state variable. In the Markov perfect equililibrium of the game, identity arises as "a relational property" that does not pre-exist the decision context. The approach allows to characterize generic personality types and derive some comparitive static results.

Keywords: indeterminacy, decision-making, identity.

1 Introduction

The idea that an individual's choice of action (behavior) determines her inner characteristics (preference, attitudes and beliefs) rather than (exclusively) the other way around has been present in people's mind throughout history and has been addressed in philosophy, psychology as well as more recently in economics. Nevertheless the dominating view in particular in economics, is based on a postulate: individuals are endowed with an identity (preferences, attitudes and beliefs) that explains their behavior. This postulate is hard to reconcile with a host of experimental evidence that behavior shapes identity. For a systematic review of experimental evidences see [3].

Psychologists developed several theories to account for these experimental facts. In particular self-perception theory which is based on two postulates: 1. *"individual come to "know" their own attitude and other internal states partially by inferring them from observations of their own behavior and/or the circumstances in which behavior occurs. 2. Thus the individual is functionally in the same position as an outside observer, an observer who must necessarily rely upon those same external cues to infer the individual inner state."* (p. 2 in [3]). Self-perception theory does not clearly give up the classical postulate. Nevertheless we argue that its own postulates are fully consistent with the hypothesis of (quantum) indeterminacy which overturns the classical postulate of pre-existing identity, attitudes and preferences.

J.R. Busemeyer et al. (Eds.): QI 2012, LNCS 7620, pp. 102–113, 2012.
© Springer-Verlag Berlin Heidelberg 2012

Recently Benabou and Tirole address the issue of identity in a series of papers (e.g., [4, 5]). They write "When contemplating choices, (people) take into account what kind of a person each alternative would make them" and the desirability of those self-views" ([5] p. 806-807). A common feature to Benabou and Tirole's and our approach is that todays' behavior affects tomorrows' identity i.e., effective preferences. In the last section we argue that the three assumptions they use are equivalent to assuming (quantum) type indeterminacy.

Under the last decade scholars from social sciences and psychology have contributed to the development of a "quantum-like" decision theory based on the premises of (non-classical) indeterminacy (see e.g., [8–14, 20, 21]). This line of research has shown itself very fruitful to explain a wide variety of behavioral phenomena ranging from cognitive dissonance to preferences reversal, the inverse fallacy or the disjunction effect.

The starting point for our approach is that we depart from the classical dogma that individuals are endowed with preferences and attitudes that motivate their behavior. Instead, we propose that the motivational underpinning of behavior is intrinsically uncertain i.e., indeterminate. It is only at the moment the individual selects an action that a specific type(preferences) is actualized. It is not merely revealed but rather determined in the sense that prior to the choice, there is an irreducible multiplicity of potential types. This idea, imported from Quantum Mechanics to the context of decision and game theory, is very much in line with Tversky and Simonson (in [19]), according to whom "There is a growing body of evidence that supports an alternative conception according to which preferences are often constructed not merely revealed in the elicitation process. These constructions are contingent on the framing of the problem, the method of elicitation, and the context of the choice".

The basic model of static decision-making with Type Indeterminate agents, the TI-model, is formulated in [21]. As we consider dynamic individual optimization, the TI-model induces a game among potential incarnations of the individual. In each period these potential incarnations represent conflicting desires or propensities to act. We formulate the decision problem in terms of a game between a multiplicity of (one-period lived) players, the selves. They are linked to each other through two channels: (i) the selves share a common interests in the utility of the future incarnations of the individual and (ii) they are connected to each other in a process of state transition (which captures indeterminacy). In each period the current selves form intentions to act. One action is played by the individual but the whole profile of (intended) actions matters to tomorrow's identity by force of the state transition process. This creates a strategic concern among contemporaneous selves. In particular when the selves pool, the individual's preferences are unchanged while if they choose different actions preferences are modified. We define a Markov Perfect Equilibrium among the selves where the state variable is the individual's identity. The model features the emergence of identity as the corollary of individual action which itself obtains as the result from the interaction between conflicting selves in a given decision context.

Identity is "a relational property" (see [6]) that does not pre-exist the decision context but is created anew each time the individual is called upon to act.

2   The Model

The kind of situations we have in mind is a sequence of (at least) two consecutive decision situations (DS). An example is as follows. Alice must decide whether to keep to her rutin work or accept a challenging task. The second decision situation is between a week of thalasso therapy or a week vacation in the family house. The two situations appeal to different but related (in a sense to be made clear below) type characteristics: the first DS appeals to her preference toward risk: cautious (θ_1) risk loving (θ_2). The second decision situation appeals to her attitude toward others: (τ_1) egoistic versus generous/empathetic (τ_2). We next develop the general theory and return to the two options example to illustrate some implications.

2.1   The Players

In each period the individual faces a Decision Situation (DS) A^t corresponding to a finite set of available actions in period t. We restrict the one-period players' strategy set to pure actions. The possible preferences over the profiles of actions (one action for each self) are denoted by $e_{M,i} \in E_M$, where $M \in \mathcal{M}$ ($\mathcal{M}$ is the set of all complete measurements) corresponds to an elicitation procedure that fully reveals the preferences in A_t. A choice in DS A^t is generally a coarse measurement. We refer to the $e_{M,i}$ as the selves or the "eigentypes" of M.[1] They are the players of our game.

In each period t the individual is represented by his state or type (we use the terms interchangeably), a vector $|s^t\rangle \in S$, where S is a (finite) $n-$dimensional Hilbert space and the bracket $|.\rangle$ denotes a (ket) vector in Dirac's notation which is standard when dealing with indeterminacy. The eigentypes $e_{M,i}$ of M are associated with the eigenvector $\left|e_{M,i}\right\rangle$ of the operator which form a basis of the state space. The state vector can therefore be expressed as a superposition[2]: $|s^t\rangle = \sum_{i=1}^{n} \lambda_i^t \left|e_{M,i}\right\rangle$, $\lambda_i \in \mathbb{R}$, $\sum_i (\lambda_i^t)^2 = 1$. This formulation means that the individual cannot generally be identified with a single true self. Instead he is intrinsically "conflicted" which is expressed by the multiplicity of the potential selves. The coefficients λ_i, also called amplitude of probability, provides a measure of the relative strength of potential self $e_{M,i}$.

We assume throughout this chapter that there is common knowledge among the players (selves) about the current state, the utility function of all players and about the state transition process (see below). We also assume that the individual is aware of his own indeterminacy and act consistently within the

---

[1] An eigentype corresponds to an eigenvalue of the operator.

[2] A superposition is simply a linear combination such that the square of the coefficients sum up to 1.

cognitive limitations implied by indeterminacy.[3] This hypothesis is captured in an assumption of rationality (in a way to be defined below) and common knowledge of rationality *at the level of the selves*.

2.2   Identity: The Ephemeral Outcome of Interacting Selves

In each period, the selves form intentions to play and eventually *one* action is taken by the individual. Decision-making is modelled as the measurement of individual preferences and it is associated with a transition process from the initial state and (intended) actions to a new state. The rules that govern the state transition process reflect the intrinsic indeterminacy of the individual's type or preferences. It features the minimal perturbation principle that defines a measurement operation which is formalized by the von Neumann (or its stringent version Luder's) projection postulate: if the initial state is t and the chosen action is a_1 then the new state is the normalized projection of t onto the eigenspace belonging to a_1.[4]

Formally, a transition process is a function from the initial state and (intended) actions to a new state. It can be decomposed into an outcome mapping $\mu_{A^t} : \mathbb{S} \to \Delta A$ where ΔA is the unit simplex of actions and a transition mapping $\tau_{M,a} : \mathbb{S} \to \mathbb{S}$. The first mapping defines the probability for the possible choices of action when an individual in state s is confronted with *DS A*. The second mapping $\tau_{M,a}$ indicates where the state transits as we confront the individual with *DS A* and obtain outcome a.

Let the initial state be $\left|s^t\right\rangle = \sum_i \lambda_i^t \left|e_{M,i}^t\right\rangle$. The standard Hilbert space formulation yields that if we, for instance, observe action a_1, the state transits onto

$$\left|s^{t+1}\right\rangle = \sum_{j=1} \lambda_j'^t \left|e_{M,,j}^t\right\rangle \tag{1}$$

where $\lambda_j' = \dfrac{\lambda_j}{\sqrt{\sum_{k^t} \lambda_k^2 \left(s_k^* = a_j\right)}}$ and $\sum_{k^t} \lambda_k^2 \left(s_k^* = a_j^t\right)$ is the sum over the probabilities for the selves who pool in choosing a_j. This is of course equivalent to Bayesian updating i.e., the state transition seems purely informational. The value of this more general formulation comes when dealing with a sequence of non-commuting *DS*. To see that the formal equivalence breaks down, we have to express $\left|s^{t+1}\right\rangle$ in terms of $\left|e_{N,i}\right\rangle$ where N is the new (non-commuting) measurement in period $t+1$ corresponding to *DS* A^{t+1} and $\left|e_{N,i}\right\rangle$ are its eigenvectors. The eigenvectors of N also form a (alternative) basis of the state space. And this is where the earlier mentioned correlations between selves from different periods enter into play.

---

[3] Type indeterminacy corresponds to cognitive limitations in the following sense. An individual cannot have simultaneous determined preferences in incompatible decision situations. Hence he cannot have determined preferences over the universal set of alternatives as requested in classical rational decision theory.

[4] We talked about "eigenspace" associated with an eigenvalue "a" of a measurement operator if the eigenvalue is degenerate i.e., if several linearly independent vectors yield the same outcome of the measurement.

The correlations link the two sets of basis vectors: the eigenvectors of M can be written as linear combinations of the eigenvectors of N with the correlations as the coefficients of superposition - see below.

These correlations captures the extent of overlap between the states.[5] In a classical world *all* distinct *atomic* states are orthogonal. So in a classical world either type characteristics are mutually exclusive or they can be combined. The novelty with indeterminacy is that type characteristics can overlap in the sense that they are non-orthogonal atomic states. For instance, in our example the risk-loving type and the cautious type are orthogonal but the risk-loving type and the egoistic type are not. Nevertheless, the three are complete descriptions of the individual i.e., they are atomic states.

Let B_{MN} denote the basis transformation matrix that links the two non-compatible type characteristics M and N: $|e_{M,i}\rangle = \sum_j \gamma_{ij} |e_{N,j}\rangle$ where γ_{ij} are the elements of the basis transformation matrix $\gamma_{ij} = \langle e_{N,j} | e_{M,i} \rangle$.[6] Substituting into (1) and collecting the terms we write

$$|s^{t+1}\rangle = \sum_j \left(\sum_i \lambda'_i \gamma_{ij} \right) |e_{N,i}\rangle = \sum_i \eta_i^{t+1} |e_{N,i}\rangle .$$

According to Bohr's rule the probability for eigentype $|e_{N,1}\rangle$ (if the agent is confronted with DS A^{t+1} that (coarsely) measures type characteristics N) is

$$TP : p\left(e_{N,1} \middle| s^{t+1} \right) = \left(\sum_i \lambda'_i \gamma_{1i} \right)^2 \tag{2}$$

TP is *not* a conditional probability formula where the γ_{ij}^2 are statistical correlations between the eigentypes at the two stages. The probabilities for the N-eigentypes depend on the M-eigentypes' *play* in DS A^t. When no player chooses the same action, the choice of a_i^t separates out a single player (some $e_{M,i}$), the sum in parenthesis involves *one* term only. While when several players pool in choosing the same action, the term in parenthesis involves several terms. As a consequence, the probabilities for the different players are given by the square of a sum, implying cross terms called interference effects - and not the sum of squares (as we would have in a classical setting). Since the amplitudes of probability can be negative numbers, the interference effect may be negative or positive.

We note that the state transition process is deterministic by the, earlier mentioned, von Neumann's postulate which says that under the impact of a measurement a pure state transits into another pure state. In this chapter we are

---

[5] "In physics, the expression transition probability generally refers to dynamical instability. Our use of the term is not directly related to instability rather we follow von Neuman's terminology. The transition probability between two states is meant to represent intuitively a measure of their overlapping. Actual transition from one state to another is triggered by a measurement." [2].

[6] $\langle e_{N,,j} | e_{M,i} \rangle$ is a scalar product.

only dealing with pure types. If we observe a_1^t (as the result of applying A_t) the state

$$\left|s^t\right\rangle = \sum_i \lambda_i^t \left|e_{M,i}\right\rangle \text{ transits onto } \left|s^{t+1}\right\rangle = \sum_{j=1} \lambda_j^{\prime t} \left|e_{M,,j}\right\rangle = \sum_i \eta_i^{t+1} \left|e_{N,i}\right\rangle.$$

that is $\left|s^{t+1}\right\rangle$ is a pure state. Yet, predictions on the outcome of (applying) A^{t+1} are probabilistic because of indeterminacy i.e., $\left|s^{t+1}\right\rangle$ is a superposed state.

2.3   Utility

When dealing with multiple selves, the question as to how to relate the utility of the selves (here the players) to that of the individual has no self-given answer.[7] We adopt the following definition of the utility of self (or player) $e_{M,i}$ of playing of a_i^t when the $-i$ other t−period players play $\mathbf{a}_{-i}^t$

$$U_{e_{M,i}}(a_i^t) + \delta_{e_{M,i}} \sum_{i=t}^{T} EU(s^{i+1}\left(a_i^t, \mathbf{a}_{-i}^t; s^t \middle| a^t = a_i^t\right)) \tag{3}$$

where a^t denotes the actual play of the individual.

The utility for $e_{M,i}$ of playing a_i^t is made of two terms. The first term is the utility in the current period evaluated by player $e_{M,i}$. This term only depends on the action chosen by $e_{M,i}$. The second term is the expected utility of the individual evaluated by the future selves conditional on $a^t = a_i^t$. The second term depends indirectly on the whole profile of (intended) actions in the current period through the state transition process $s^{t+1}\left(\mathbf{a}_i^t; s^t\right)$. The summation term in (3) can be collapsed into a single term $EU^T(s^{t+1}\left(\mathbf{a}^t; s^t\right)) = \sum_{i=t}^{T} EU^*(s^{i+1}\left(\mathbf{a}^t; s^t\right))$. Which is the expected utility when all future selves in all periods play an equilibrium pure strategy.[8] Utility thus writes

$$U_{e_{M,i}}(a_i^t; s^t) + \delta_{e_{M,i}} EU^T(s^{t+1}\left(\mathbf{a}^t; s^t \middle| a^t = a_i^t\right)) \tag{4}$$

in each period the payoff relevant history of play is captured by the state variable representing the current state or identity. The formulation in (4) means that he maximizes utility conditional on surviving. A self is defined as rational when he maximizes his conditional utility which is well-defined for any sequence of DS.

2.4   The Equilibrium

In each period, the current selves move simultaneously. They know the current state resulting from the previous (actual and intended) play. We have common

---

[7] One reason is that while the selves are incarnations of the same individual, they are short-lived. Another is that they might not recognize the "legitimacy" of some future possible incarnations. For instance a current compassionate self may not value the utility of a future spiteful incarnation.

[8] For the case when there exist mutiple equilibria, we assume that the current selves share the same beliefs about which equilibrium is played.

knowledge among the selves about the payoff functions of all selves current and future and common knowledge of rationality. We restrict ourselves to Markov strategies: a strategy for *a self* is a function $S \to A^t$ from the current state to the set of actions available at period t.

Definition 1. *A Markov Perfect Equilibrium of the game is characterized by* a_i^{t*} :

$$a_i^{t*} = \arg\max_{a_i \in A^t} U_{e_{M,i}}(a_i^t; s^t) + \delta_{e_{M,i}} \sum_{\tau=t+1}^{T} EU^*(s^\tau (\mathbf{a}^t; s^t)).$$

in all periods $t = 1, ...T$ *and for all* $e_{M,i}$, $M \in \mathcal{M}$, $i = 1, ...n$.

The equilibrium is found by backward induction in a standard way.[9] The novelty lies in the technology for the state transition process which captures indeterminacy. So in particular the state variable are the preferences themselves and they evolve in a non-monotonic way reflecting the dynamics of measurement operations and the correlations between non-commuting *DS*.

Remark 1. For the case all DS commute with each other, the model is the one of an individual who does not initially know his preferences and learns through Bayesian updating as he observes the actions he takes.

In the TI-model, the concern for identity arises exclusively as a consequence of the non-commutativity of successive *DS*. But we should keep in mind that the kind of preference instability that we describe in the next section does not apply within a sequence of commuting *DS*.

Remark 2. For the special case with $\delta_{e_{M,i}} = 0$ for all selves in all periods, we are back in the basic TI-model. There is no self-control. For $\delta_{e_{M,i}} \neq 0$ for some selves in some periods, the equilibrium path of action may exhibit some extent of self-control. The model suggests a classification of individual traits and behavior as we show below.

The case with $\delta_{e_{M,i}} = 1$, for all selves in all periods, is interesting because a classical agent would not face any self-control problem. In contrast, for a type indeterminate decision-maker, the issue of self management arises - see example below.

2.5   Generic Personalities

The 2 types, two actions and two periods case with non-commuting *DS* allows to illustrate some basic comparative statics results. For the ease of presentation we

---

[9] Although we know that a MPE exists in mixed strategies (cf theorem 13.1 [16]), we have no proof of existence for the case we restrict ourselves to pure strategies as we do here.

shall use the following notation. The potential types relevant to the first choice are: $e_{M,i}^t = \theta_i$, $i = 1, 2$ and to the second and last choice $e_{M,i}^{t+1} = \tau_i, i = 1, 2$.

$$|\theta_1\rangle = \alpha_1 |\tau_1\rangle + \alpha_2 |\tau_2\rangle$$
$$|\theta_2\rangle = \beta_1 |\tau_1\rangle + \beta_2 |\tau_2\rangle$$

where $\begin{pmatrix} \alpha_1 & \alpha_2 \\ \beta_1 & \beta_2 \end{pmatrix}$ is a rotation matrix. Since time ends after period 2, the τ_i- eigentype act with no concern for future identity. Our focus will be on the behavior of the θ_i-eigentypes. The τ_i eigentypes are associated with a utility corresponding to their optimal choice, $U^* (\tau_1)$ we assume $U^* (\tau_2) > U^* (\tau_1)$.

The TI-model distinguishes between two situations characterized by the sign of the interference effect applying to the high utility option $U^* (\tau_2)$. Interference effects are the signature of indeterminacy. When the individual is in a superposed state $|s\rangle$ both θ eigentypes are simultaneously present in his mind and they interact. The sign of interferences effect depends on the operators associated with the decisions. It is a structural properties of the state space which is common to all individuals. Each individual is characterized by his state, a vector in a potentially very high dimensional space. Whether interference effects are positive or negative is an empirical question.

Self-Control by Inner Agreement. In this section we assume, that the interference effects (IE) favor the high utility option x_2. We shall see that a positive IE is a factor that favors behavioral (and intertemporal) consistency. Assume we have $EU (\theta_2) < EU (\theta_1) < EU (t)$. We recall that by definition the first DS as a measurement of type characteristics θ[10] so we must also have: $U_{\theta_1} (a_1) > U_{\theta_1} (a_2)$ and $U_{\theta_2} (a_1) < U_{\theta_2} (a_2)$ where $\{a_1, a_1\}$ is the action set in $DS1$. The $\theta-$selves have conflicting short-run interests.

When considering a sequence of non-commuting DS, the model distinguishes between two classes of individuals: the balanced individual, an individual whose selves manage to agree on a common choice, and the conflicted individual whose selves make separating choice more precisely:

Definition 2. *A balanced individual is characterized by a MPE that is a pooling equilibrium. It obtains whenever*

$$U_{\theta_1} (a_1) + \delta_1 EU (\theta_1) \leq U_{\theta_1} (a_2) + \delta_1 EU (t) \tag{5}$$

or

$$U_{\theta_2} (a_2) + \delta_2 EU (\theta_2) \leq U_{\theta_2} (a_1) + \delta_2 EU (t) \tag{6}$$

or both. Otherwise, the individual is conflicted i.e., her inner equilibrium is characterized by separation.

The inequalities (5) or (6) capture the selves' incentives to refrain from choosing their preferred action (exerting self restraint) given that the other self chooses

---

[10] This means that when considered in isolation, DS1 separates between the $\theta-$types.

his preferred first period action. When an inequality is falsified it is a dominating strategy for that self to choose his preferred first period action. Since we have conflict of interest, when neither of them holds, the choices are separating. This means that the first period action triggers state transition onto one of the eigentypes i.e., identity is modified. As a consequence, behavior will exhibit inconsistency (e.g., preference reversal). So this suggests that individuals who are quite extreme in their judgment and have clear-cut preferences also exhibit behavioral inconsistency. Recall that this applies to non-commuting DS. So in particular in a sequence DS1-DSA-DS1 where DSA commutes with DS1, the individual that we characterized as conflicted, will not exhibit any behavioral instability.

In contrast the balanced individual is characterized by selves who are willing to reach an agreement, they make a pooling choice. This occurs at the expenses of one of the selves who chooses to forego his preferred option in period 1. This is an instance of self-control. The balanced individual has no clear-cut preferences, he retains the freedom to value options from different perspectives. A pooling MPE, triggers no state transition. If the selves were pooling in all periods, the individual would simply behave as a an individual endowed with stable but stochastic preferences. He does not qualify as behaviorally or dynamically inconsistent.

We would like to emphasize that our model features self-control by *means of identity management*. In this respect we stand closer to Benabou and Tirole ([5]). In particular, we do not address the question related to taking actions (commitment) to limit future behavior as in Gul and Pesendorfer ([17, 18]) and Fudenberg and Levine ([15]).

Definition 3 allows us to derive some simple comparative statics. For that purpose we write the inequalities as follows: $U_{\theta_i}(a_i) - U_{\theta_i}(a_j) \leq (>) \gamma_i [EU(t) - EU(\theta_i)]$.

Proposition 1. *i. The larger γ_i, $i = 1, 2$ the more likely we are dealing with a balanced type.*

ii. The larger the interference effect, the more likely we have pooling.

iii. The larger $[U_{\theta_i}(a_i) - U_{\theta_i}(a_j)]$, more likely the individual will turn out a conflicted person.

(i) The coefficients γ_i captures the weight put by self θ_i on the individual's identity relative to the self's utility. Quite naturally it also reads as a discounting factor. An individual composed of impatient selves behaves erratically as a conflicted person. The more patient and or the more concerned by identity the selves are the more likely we are dealing with a balanced individual (cf. Benabou Tirole ([5], Prop. 2.c).

(ii) The interference effect is preserved when the types pool but it is lost when they separate. In our context, the IE increases the probability for the type associated high utility alternative, this creates incentives to pool. Note further that we have $EU(t) - EU(\theta_2) > EU(t) - EU(\theta_1)$, so, if the cost of foregoing the preferred alternative are the same for both selves, an individual who exerts self-control through identity management will choose to "behave well" in the first period in order to "behave well" in the second period (cf. Benabou and Tirole ([5], Prop. 2.d).

(iii) The utility difference $[U_{\theta_i}(a_i) - U_{\theta_i}(a_j)]$ is the cost of foregoing the preferred action. It captures the degree of conflict between the selves. Not surprisingly, when the potential selves have strong preferences, they will have a hard time agreeing (pooling) and the individual is likely to behave as a conflicted individual.

Positive IE with respect to the type associated with the high utility alternative, means that indeterminacy with respect to DS1 is generally advantageous for the individual.[11] Under these circumstances, we are likely to observe a significant extent of individuals behaving as balanced persons. Pooling occurs most of the time on the action preferred by the first period eigentype most closely related to the preferred eigentype in period 2.

The correlation between DS and the associated interference effect can be viewed as the hardware of the mind. A conjecture is that preferences traits that are in some sense "close" while distinct, are expected to be associated with non-commuting DS. So for instance cautiousness and altruism are neither the same trait nor orthogonal, instead they could be described as "over-lapping". What the sign of IE concerns, we could expect the hardware of the human mind to evolve toward an efficient structure from a survival point of view.

When considering the mind as a whole, we are likely to have personal traits related to operators characterized by positive IE and other by negative IE. So it is in place to ask what behavior do we expect when the relevant interference effect is negative for the high utility alternative? In the next sub-section we briefly consider such a case.

Negative interference effect: agreeing to disagree Consider the case when $EU(t) < EU(\theta_2) < EU(\theta_1)$ which obtains in the example by inversing the signs of β_1 and α_2. The selves' incentives are described unambiguously by the inequalities

$$U_{\theta_1}(a_1) + \delta_1 EU(\theta_1) > U_{\theta_1}(a_2) + \delta_1 EU(t) \tag{7}$$

and

$$U_{\theta_2}(a_2) + \delta_2 EU(\theta_2) > U_{\theta_2}(a_1) + \delta_2 EU(t). \tag{8}$$

This implies that both types prefer separation in DS1. So we have a case of "agreement to disagree". With respect to DS linked by negative interference effects, the individual behaves as a conflicted person.

---

[11] With positive IE we may also have

$$EU(\theta_2) < EU(t) < EU(\theta_1)$$

if e.g., the initial state is strongly skewed toward θ_2 e.g., $\lambda_2 = \sqrt{.9}$. The only pooling equilibrium would be on a_1 and the only condition would be that (5) is not verified. This reflect the fact that the magnitude of the IE depends on the initial state.

3 Discussion

In this section we discuss the relation between the present work and some of the literature in economics. There exists a vast theoretical literature pioneered by Strotz ([26]) dealing with inner conflict and leading to time inconsistency. A large share of this literature has focused on inconsistency that arises because the individual does not discount the future at a constant rate. A contribution of this chapter is to demonstrate that there exists other sources of inner conflict i.e., not related to time preferences. A type indeterminate individual is in each period characterized by a multiplicity of conflicting selves (competing desires). All selves are equally rational and care about the future expected utility of the individual. This allows formalizing the "inner bargaining" (cf [1]) as a sequential game and characterize the circumstances when individual behavior exhibits preference instability and intertemporal inconsistency.

Our approach brings us close to the questions investigated in Benabou and Tirole ([4, 5]). They depart from homo economicus by assuming 1. imperfect self-knowledge; 2. imperfect recall; 3. imperfect will power. These three assumptions are in many respect equivalent with giving up the classical dogma of a pre-existing (deterministic) individual identity and replacing it by indeterminacy. Indeterminacy implies imperfect knowledge because of intrinsic uncertainty: there exists no "true preferences" to be learned. Indeterminacy implies imperfect recall because no type is the true type forever. Indeterminacy implies "imperfect will power" because it implies multiple selves both simultaneously (multiplicity of potentials) and dynamically (by force of the non-commutativity of decision situations). Moreover, in a world of indeterminate agents, actions aimed at shaping one's identity are fully justified from an instrumental point of view. In particular there is no need for any additional concerns about self-image (as in Benabou and Tirole or the diagnostic utility theory (see [7]).

Our results including some comparative statics are in many respects similar to those in Benabou and Tirole and consistent with a host of empirical data including those mentioned in the Introduction. The contribution of this chapter is to propose an alternative explanation in terms of a fundamental characteristics of the mind: its intrinsic indeterminacy. The postulate stating the existence of a true self together with the hypothesis that we ignore it and keep forgetting about it, is in itself not very convincing. In addition Benabou and Tirole have to assume imperfect control. But as we argued above those hypotheses are *in effect* intimately related to the one single hypothesis of type indeterminacy.

References

1. Ainslie, G.: The Breakdown of Will. Cambridge University Press, Cambridge (2001)
2. Beltrametti, E.G., Cassinelli, G.: The logic of Quantum Mechanics. In: Rota, G.C. (ed.) Encyclopedia of Mathematics and its Applications, vol. 15. Addison-Wesley, Boston (1981)

3. Bem, D.J.: Self Perception theory. Advances in Experimental Social Psychology 6, 1–62 (1972)
4. Benabou, R., Tirole, J.: Willpower and personal rules. J. of Pol. Economy 112(4), 848–886 (2004)
5. Benabou, R., Tirole, J.: Identity, morals and taboos: beleifs as assets. The Quarterly Journal of Economics 126, 805–855 (2011)
6. Bitbol: Reflective metaphysics: understanding quntum mechanics from a kantian viewpoint. Philosophica 83, 53–83 (2010)
7. Bodner, R., Prelec, D.: Self-signaling and diagnostic utility in everyday decision making. Psychol. Econ. Decis. 1, 105–126 (2003)
8. Busemeyer, J.R., Wang, Z., Townsend, J.T.: Quantum dynamics of human decision-Making. J. Math. Psychol. 50, 220–241 (2006)
9. Busemeyer, J.R.: Quantum information processing explanation for interaction between inferences and decisions. In: Proceedings of the Quantum Interaction Symposium, Arlington, Virginia Fall 2010. AAAI Press, Menlo Park (2010)
10. Busemeyer, J., Lambert-Mogiliansky, A.: An Exploration of Type Indeterminacy in Strategic Decision-Making. In: Bruza, P., Sofge, D., Lawless, W., van Rijsbergen, K., Klusch, M. (eds.) QI 2009. LNCS, vol. 5494, pp. 113–127. Springer, Heidelberg (2009)
11. Danilov, V.I., Lambert-Mogiliansky, A.: Measurable systems and behavioral sciences. Math. Soc. Sci. 55, 315–340 (2008)
12. Danilov, V.I., Lambert-Mogiliansky, A.: Expected utility under non-classical uncertainty. Theory Decis., 25–47 (2009)
13. Deutsch, D.: Quantum theory of propability and decisions. Proc. R. Soc. Lond. A 455, 3129–3137 (1999)
14. Franco, R.: The conjunction fallacy and interference effects (2007) arXiv:0708.3948v1
15. Fudenberg, D., Levine, D.K.: A dual self model of impulse control. Am. Econ. Rev. 96, 1449–1476 (2006)
16. Fudenberg, D., Tirole, J.: Game Theory. MIT Press, Cambridge (1991)
17. Gul, F., Pesendorfer, W.: Temptation and self control. Econometrica 69, 1403–1436 (2001)
18. Gul, F., Pesendorfer, W.: Self control and the theory of consumption. Econometrica 72, 110–158 (2004)
19. Kahneman, D., Tversky, A.: Choices, Values and Frames. Cambridge University Press (2000)
20. Khrennikov, A.: Ubiquitous Quantum Structure—From Psychology to Finance. Springer, Heidelberg (2010)
21. Lambert-Mogiliansky, A., Zamir, S., Zwirn, H.: Type indeterminacy—A model of the KT(Khaneman Tversky)- man. J. Math. Psychol. 53, 349–361 (2009)
22. McIntosh, D.: Foundation of Human Society. University of Chigago Press, Chicago (1969)
23. Maskin, E.S., Tirole, J.: Markov perfect equilibrium. J. Econ. Theory 100, 191–219 (2001)
24. la Mura, P.: Correlated equilibria of classical strategies with quantum Signals. Int. J. Quantum Inf. 3, 183–188 (2005)
25. Peleg, B., Yaari, M.: On the existence of a consistent Course of Action when tastes are changing. Rev. Econ. Stud. 40, 391–401 (1973)
26. Strotz, R.H.: Myopya and time inconsistency in dynamic utility maximization. Rev. Econ. Stud. 23, 165–180 (1956)

Entanglement of Conceptual Entities in Quantum Model Theory (QMod)

Diederik Aerts and Sandro Sozzo

Center Leo Apostel (CLEA), Vrije Universiteit Brussel (VUB),
Pleinlaan 2, 1050 Brussels, Belgium
{diraerts,ssozzo}@vub.ac.be

Abstract. We have recently elaborated *Quantum Model Theory* (*QMod*) to model situations where the quantum effects of contextuality, interference, superposition, entanglement and emergence, appear independently of the microscopic nature of the entities giving rise to these situations. We have shown that QMod models without introducing linearity for the set of the states. In this paper we prove that QMod, although not using linearity for the state space, provides a method of identification for entangled states and an intuitive explanation for their occurrence. We illustrate this method for entanglement identification with concrete examples.

Keywords: Quantum cognition, QMod, entanglement, concept combination.

1 Introduction

We have recently presented *Quantum Model Theory* (*QMod*) [1], a modeling theory worked out to describe situations entailing effects, such as, *interference*, *contextuality*, *emergence* and *entanglement*, which are typical of the micro-world but also occur at macroscopic level and even outside physics [2–5]. *QMod* rests on a generalization of the standard Hilbert space quantum formalism, namely the *State Context Property* (*SCoP*) formalism [6], developed in Brussels when investigating the structure of concepts, and how they combine to form sentences and texts [7–9]. The SCoP formalism was further used to analyze aspects of concepts and inspired contextual approaches [7, 10–18]. However, the SCoP formalism is very general, hence *QMod* has been developed to be a formalism closer to the complex Hilbert space of standard quantum theory but, at the same time, general enough to cope with the modeling of the main quantum effects identified in the domains different from the micro-world.

QMod makes it possible to describe not only concepts and their combinations, but any kind of entity in which the above quantum effects play a relevant role. Furthermore, it is a generalization of classical and quantum theory in a very similar way to how the relativistic manifold formalism is a generalization of special relativity.

J.R. Busemeyer et al. (Eds.): QI 2012, LNCS 7620, pp. 114–125, 2012.
© Springer-Verlag Berlin Heidelberg 2012

In this paper we focus on entanglement and emergence, and show that these effects find a very natural description in *QMod*. We first repeat in Sec. 2 the representation theorem which we proved in [1], and which shows how one can construct a real or complex representation for a general entity. Then, we apply this theorem to model three specific examples in Sec. 3. In the first example, we consider the concept *The Animal Acts*, which is a combination of the concepts *Animal* and *Acts*. By using the experimental data collected in [18] we analyze the entanglement between these two concepts (Sec. 3.1). In the second example, we consider the entity *Vessel of Water*, and show that states of this entity can be prepared which are not product states, i.e. they are entangled (Sec. 3.3). In the third example, we finally show that our *QMod* representation coincides with the standard quantum representation in the case of the entanglement between two genuine quantum entities (Sec. 3.4).

2 A Representation Theorem

In this section we resume the essentials of the representation theorem proved in detail in [1] that are needed to attain our results in the following sections. Let us begin with the abstract description of an entity in *QMod*. An entity is a collection of aspects of reality that hang together in such a way that different states exist without loosing the possibility of identification of the same entity in each of these states. Sometimes only one state exists, this is then the limiting case, and we say that the entity is a situation, in this case

Definition 1. *We consider an entity S that can be in different states, and denote states by $p, q, \ldots$, and the set of states by Σ. Different measurements can be performed on the entity S being in one of its states, and we denote measurements by $e, f, \ldots$, and the set of measurements by $\mathcal{M}$. With a measurement $e \in \mathcal{M}$ and the entity in state p, corresponds a set of possible outcomes $\{x_1, x_2, \ldots, x_j, \ldots, x_n\}$, and a set of probabilities $\{\mu(x_j, e, p)\}$, where $\mu(x_j, e, p)$ is the limit of the relative frequency of the outcome x_j, the situation being repeated where measurement e is executed and the entity S is in state p. We denote the final state corresponding to the outcome x_j by means of p_j.*

Let us now come to the representation theorem. It states that it is always possible to realize the situation in Def. 1 by means of a specific mathematical structure using a space of real numbers where the probabilities are derived as Lebesgue measures of subsets of real numbers. Moreover, a complex number realization exists as well, where the probabilities are calculated by making use of a scalar product similar to the one used in the quantum formalism [1].

Theorem 1. *Consider a measurement $e \in \mathcal{M}$ and a state $p \in \Sigma$, and the set of probabilities $\{\mu(x_j, e, p)\}$, where $\{x_1, \ldots, x_j, \ldots, x_n\}$ is the set of possible outcomes given e and p. Then, it is possible to work out a representation of this situation in $\mathbb{R}^n$ where the probabilities are given by Lebesgue measures of appropriately defined subsets of $\mathbb{R}^n$, and a representation in $\mathbb{C}^m$ where the measurement is modeled within the mathematical formalism of standard quantum theory defined on $\mathbb{C}^m$ as a complex Hilbert space.*

We do not repeat here the steps of the construction required to prove Th. 1 (see again [1]), for the sake of brevity, but we will apply this construction to specific cases. We limit ourselves to observe that Th. 1 is an application of the *hidden measurement approach* elaborated in Brussels during the eighties and nineties of the foregoing century, with the aim of formulating a contextual hidden variable model for quantum theory [19–28]. With the theorem above we have constructed a representation of the collection of states and experiments that lead to the same set of outcomes. In this sense, the $\mathbb{R}^n$ model and the $\mathbb{C}^m$ that we have constructed is a model for the interaction between state and experiment. The set of outcomes constitutes a context in which this interaction takes place. In the next section we investigate in detail the examples to show the relevance of our representation theorem for the modeling of entanglement.

3   Entanglement in QMod

The representation theorem of *QMod* stated in Sec. 2 can be applied to specific entities and situations to show that entanglement, hence quantum structures, appear if suitable conditions are satisfied.

3.1   Entanglement of Two Concepts

The first example that we take into account is a combination of two concepts.

Let us consider the example of the entity which is the concept *Animal*, and let e be a measurement where a person is asked to choose between the animal being a *Horse* or a *Bear*, hence e is associated with two outcomes $\{H, B\}$. We consider only one state for *Animal*, namely the ground state which is the state where animal is just animal, i.e. the bare concept, and let us denote it by p. Let us denote by $\mu(H, e, p)$ the probability that *Horse* is chosen when e is performed, and by $\mu(B, e, p)$ the probability that *Bear* is chosen in the same measurement. The following mathematical construction can now be elaborated.

For the measurement e we consider the vector space $\mathbb{R}^2$ and its canonical basis $\{(1, 0), (0, 1)\}$. The state p is contextually represented with respects to the measurement e by the vector $v(e, p) = (\mu(H, e, p), \mu(B, e, p))$ in $\mathbb{R}^2$. We introduce the vector $\lambda = (r, 1 - r)$, with $0 \leq r \leq 1$, such that for $(r, 1 - r)$ contained in the convex closure of $(1, 0)$ and $(\mu(H, e, p), \mu(B, e, p))$, we get outcome *Bear*, while for $(r, 1 - r)$ contained in the convex closure of $(\mu(H, e, p), \mu(B, e, p))$ and $(0, 1)$ we get *Horse*. Let us calculate the respective lengths and see that we re-obtain the correct probabilities. Denoting the length of the piece of line from $(1, 0)$ to $(\mu(H, e, p), \mu(B, e, p))$ by d, we have $\frac{d}{\sqrt{2}} = \mu(B, e, p)$, and $\frac{\sqrt{2} - d}{\sqrt{2}} = \mu(H, e, p)$.

We can also construct a quantum mathematics model in $\mathbb{C}^2$. Therefore we consider the vector $w(e, p) = (\sqrt{\mu(H, e, p)} e^{i\alpha(e, p)_H}, \sqrt{\mu(B, e, p)} e^{i\alpha(e, p)_B})$ in $\mathbb{C}^2$. We have $\mu(H, e, p) = |\langle(1, 0)|w(e, p)\rangle|^2$ and $\mu(B, e, p) = |\langle(0, 1)|w(e, p)\rangle|^2$, which shows that also the $\mathbb{C}^2$ construction gives rise to the correct probabilities.

Now, we want to introduce explicitly the data that we collected in an experiment that we performed on test subjects and that is described in detail in [18].

Of the 81 persons that we asked to choose between *Horse* and *Bear* as good exemplars of the concept *Animal*, 43 chose for *Horse*, and 38 for *Bear*. Calculating the relative frequencies gives rise to probabilities $\mu(H, e, p) = 0.53$ and $\mu(B, e, p) = 0.47$. Hence

$$v(e, p) = (0.53, 0.47) \quad w(e, p) = (0.73 \, e^{i\alpha(e,p)_H}, 0.68 \, e^{i\alpha(e,p)_B}) \tag{1}$$

are the vectors that represent the state of the concept *Animal* with respect to this measurement and these data in $\mathbb{R}^2$ and in $\mathbb{C}^2$, respectively.

We consider now the entity which is the concept *Acts*, where *Acts* denotes here the action of emitting a sound, and the measurement f, where a person is invited to choose between *Growls* or *Whinnies*. Hence we have two outcomes $\{G, W\}$. Also for the concept *Acts* we consider only one state, the ground state, which we denote by q. The probabilities $\mu(G, f, q)$ and $\mu(W, f, q)$ are respectively the probability that *Growls* is chosen when f is performed, and the probability that *Whinnies* is chosen in the same experiment. We again make the construction in $\mathbb{R}^2$ and $\mathbb{C}^2$ for the respective probabilities, giving rise to the vectors $v(f, q) = (\mu(G, f, q), \mu(W, f, q))$ and $w(f, q) = (\sqrt{\mu(G, f, q)} e^{i\alpha(f,q)_G}, \sqrt{\mu(W, f, q)} e^{i\alpha(f,q)_W})$. The respective constructions allow one to reproduce the correct probabilities also in this case.

Turning again to the data collected in the experiment described in [18], of the 81 persons there were 39 choosing *Growls* and 42 choosing *Whinnies*. This leads to $\mu(G, f, q) = 0.48$ and $\mu(W, f, q) = 0.52$. Hence the vectors

$$v(f, q) = (0.48, 0.52) \quad w(f, q) = (0.69 \, e^{i\alpha(f,q)_G}, 0.72 \, e^{i\alpha(f,q)_W}) \tag{2}$$

are the vectors that represent the state of the concept *Acts* with respect to this measurement and the collected data in $\mathbb{R}^2$ and in $\mathbb{C}^2$, respectively.

We consider now the combination of both entities, hence the conceptual combination *The Animal Acts*, and again only one state, namely its ground state, which we denote r. Let g be an experiment with four possible outcomes, namely *Horse* and *Growls* are chosen, *Horse* and *Whinnies* are chosen, *Bear* and *Growls* are chosen, or *Bear* and *Whinnies* are chosen. The set of possible outcomes is then $\{HG, HW, BG, BW\}$, and the corresponding probabilities are $\mu(HG, g, r)$, $\mu(HW, g, r)$, $\mu(BG, g, r)$ and $\mu(BW, g, r)$.

If we develop the mathematical construction explained in our representation theorem, we need to consider $\mathbb{R}^4$, and $\mathbb{C}^4$ and the corresponding simplex in $\mathbb{R}^4$. This is the crucial aspect that makes it possible to model entanglement, as our analysis will show.

We firstly recall that $\mathbb{R}^4$ is isomorphic to $\mathbb{R}^2 \otimes \mathbb{R}^2$, and $\mathbb{C}^4$ is isomorphic to $\mathbb{C}^2 \otimes \mathbb{C}^2$, and it are these isomorphisms that allow the modeling of entanglement in a straightforward way. The canonical basis of $\mathbb{R}^2 \otimes \mathbb{R}^2$ and of $\mathbb{C}^2 \otimes \mathbb{C}^2$ is

$$h_1 = (1, 0) \otimes (1, 0) \quad h_2 = (1, 0) \otimes (0, 1) \tag{3}$$

$$h_3 = (0, 1) \otimes (1, 0) \quad h_4 = (0, 1) \otimes (0, 1) \tag{4}$$

Hence, we have

$$v(g,r) = \mu(HG,g,r)h_1 + \mu(HW,g,r)h_2 + \mu(BG,g,r)h_3 + \mu(BW,g,r)h_4 \quad (5)$$
$$w(g,r) = \sqrt{\mu(HG,g,r)}e^{i\alpha(g,r)_{HG}}h_1 + \sqrt{\mu(HW,g,r)}e^{i\alpha(g,r)_{HW}}h_2$$
$$+\sqrt{\mu(BG,g,r)}e^{i\alpha(g,r)_{BG}}h_3 + \sqrt{\mu(BW,g,r)}e^{i\alpha(g,r)_{BW}}h_4 \quad (6)$$

and can prove the following theorem.

Theorem 2. $v(g,r)$ *equals the product state* $v(e,p) \otimes v(f,q)$ *(and then also* $w(g,r)$ *equals the product state* $w(e,p) \otimes w(f,q)$*) iff the probabilities satisfy*

$$\mu(HG,g,r) = \mu(H,e,p)\mu(G,f,q) \quad \mu(HW,g,r) = \mu(H,e,p)\mu(W,f,q) \quad (7)$$
$$\mu(BG,g,r) = \mu(B,e,p)\mu(G,f,q) \quad \mu(BW,g,r) = \mu(B,e,p)\mu(W,f,q) \quad (8)$$

Proof. We have

$$v(e,p) \otimes v(f,q) = (\mu(H,e,p),\mu(B,e,p)) \otimes (\mu(G,g,q),\mu(W,g,q))$$
$$= \mu(H,e,p)\mu(G,g,q)h_1 + \mu(H,e,p)\mu(W,g,q)h_2$$
$$+\mu(B,e,p)\mu(G,g,q)h_3 + \mu(B,e,p)\mu(W,g,q)h_4. \quad (9)$$

Analogously, we have

$$w(e,p) \otimes w(f,q) = \sqrt{\mu(H,e,p)\mu(G,f,q)}e^{i\alpha(e,p)_H}e^{i\alpha(f,q)_G}h_1$$
$$+ \sqrt{\mu(H,e,p)\mu(W,f,q)}e^{i\alpha(e,p)_H}e^{i\alpha(f,q)_W}h_2$$
$$+ \sqrt{\mu(B,e,p)\mu(G,f,q)}e^{i\alpha(e,p)_B}e^{i\alpha(f,q)_G}h_3$$
$$+ \sqrt{\mu(B,e,p)\mu(W,f,q)}e^{i\alpha(e,p)_B}e^{i\alpha(f,q)_W}h_4. \quad (10)$$

$\square$

Let us now consider the data that we collected in the experiment described in [18], and see that we encountered there an entangled state. From the 81 persons that participated in the experiment, there were 4 persons that chose *The Horse Growls*, 51 persons that choose *The Horse Whinnies*, 21 persons that choose *The Bear Growls*, and 5 persons that chose *The Bear Whinnies*. This leads to probabilities $\mu(HG,g,r) = 0.05$, $\mu(HW,g,r) = 0.63$, $\mu(BG,g,r) = 0.26$ and $\mu(BW,g,r) = 0.06$. This means that

$$v(g,r) = 0.05\ h_1 + 0.63\ h_2 + 0.26\ h_3 + 0.06\ h_4 \quad (11)$$
$$w(g,r) = 0.22\ e^{i\alpha(g,r)_{HG}}h_1 + 0.79\ e^{i\alpha(g,r)_{HW}}h_2$$
$$+0.51\ e^{i\alpha(g,r)_{BG}}h_3 + 0.25\ e^{i\alpha(g,r)_{BW}}h_4 \quad (12)$$

are the vectors that represent the state of the concept *The Animal Acts* with respect to this measurement and the collected data in $\mathbb{R}^4$ and $\mathbb{C}^4$, respectively. It is easy to check that the vectors in (11) and (12) represent a state that is not a product state in the sense that the probabilities corresponding to the joint measurement are not equal to the products of the probabilities corresponding to the component measurements. What is however much more conclusive with respect to the state of *The Animal Acts* being a state of entanglement, is that it can be proven that no component probabilities can possibly exist that give rise to the experimental values measured for the joint probabilities. This result is stated by means of the following theorem.

Theorem 3. *There do not exist numbers* a_1, a_2, b_1, b_2 *contained in the interval* $[0, 1]$, *such that* $a_1 + a_2 = 1$, *and* $b_1 + b_2 = 1$, *and such that* $a_1 b_1 = 0.05$, $a_2 b_1 = 0.63$, $a_1 b_2 = 0.26$ *and* $a_2 b_2 = 0.06$.

Proof. Let us suppose that such numbers do exist. From $a_2 b_1 = 0.63$ follows that $(1 - a_1) b_1 = 0.63$, and hence $a_1 b_1 = 1 - 0.63 = 0.37$. This is in contradiction with $a_1 b_1 = 0.05$. $\square$

It is important to observe that in case we do not have the equalities (7) and (8) for the probabilities satisfied, and hence are in a situation of entanglement, we can model this within the $\mathbb{R}^2 \otimes \mathbb{R}^2$ tensor product space, and also in the $\mathbb{C}^2 \otimes \mathbb{C}^2$ tensor product space. It is just that in this case the vectors $v(g, r)$ and $w(g, r)$ will not be product vectors, but entangled vectors, i.e. the sum of product vectors, as can be seen in (5) and (11). We also recall that we do not need any linear structure at all for the global set of states Σ, it is only the representation of this set of states due to the representation theorem 1 presented in section 2, and proven in [1], which is a space of real numbers or contains a linear structure as a complex space. But, what is most important of all to recall is that this 'local contextual real-space or complex-linear structure' can always be realized independent of the entity and situation considered. The analogy with how general relativity has been mathematically constructed as a generalization of special relativity can now be very well illustrated. Indeed, the real-space or linear structure is only local, for a fixed set of outcomes. Therefore, the formalism we propose is a generalization of standard quantum mechanics in the sense that, when the real space representation is used, no linearity at all is involved, and when the complex space representation is used, linearity is present only locally. Moreover, even in the latter representation, it is not necessarily the case that also globally the set of states can be made into a linear vector space. Only when this can be done, hence when all the local linearities join into one global linearity, the formalism we propose reduces to the standard quantum theoretical formalism. Another way of expressing the above is that *QMod* is realized by means of a 'contextual linear formalism'.

3.2   Entanglement of General Entities

The real and complex representations of a state of a compound entity in terms of the corresponding representations of the states of the component entities that we have constructed in Sec. 3.1 for two concepts can be extended to two general entities. In the following theorem we make this construction, for the sake of completeness, and indicate how entangled states can be identified.

Theorem 4. *Entangled states can be identified for general compound entities modeled in QMod*

Proof. Let S and T be two entities in the states p and q, respectively, and let the measurements e and f be performed on S and T, respectively. Suppose that $\{x_1, \ldots, x_n\}$ is the set of outcomes of e and $\{y_1, \ldots y_n\}$ is the set of outcomes of f, and denote by $\mu(x_j, e, p)$, $\mu(y_k, f, q)$ the corresponding probabilities. Finally, let

$$v(e, p) = (\mu(x_1, e, p), \ldots, \mu(x_n, e, p)) \tag{13}$$
$$v(f, q) = (\mu(y_1, f, q), \ldots, \mu(y_n, f, q)) \tag{14}$$

$$w(e, p) = (\sqrt{\mu(x_1, e, p)}e^{i\alpha(e,p)_1}, \ldots, \sqrt{\mu(x_n, e, p)}e^{i\alpha(e,p)_n}) \tag{15}$$
$$w(f, q) = (\sqrt{\mu(y_1, f, q)}e^{i\alpha(f,q)_1}, \ldots, \sqrt{\mu(y_n, f, q)}e^{i\alpha(f,q)_n}) \tag{16}$$

be the contextual representations of (e, p) and (f, q) in $\mathbb{R}^n$ and $\mathbb{C}^n$, respectively. Finally, let U be the compound entity made up of S and T, in the state r. Let the measurement of g on U consisting of a measurement of e on S and f on T so that the set of possible outcomes of g is $\{(x_1, y_1), \ldots, (x_j, y_k) \ldots, (x_n, y_n)\}$, and the set of corresponding probabilities $\{\mu((x_j, y_k), g, r)\}$. By repeating the procedure of Sec. 3.1, we can write

$$v(g, r) = \sum_{j,k} \mu((x_j, y_k), g, r) h_{jk} \tag{17}$$
$$w(g, r) = \sum_{jk} \sqrt{\mu((x_j, y_k), g, r)}e^{i\alpha(g,r)_{jk}} h_{jk} \tag{18}$$

where $\{h_{jk} | j, k \in \{1, \ldots, n\}\}$ is the canonical basis of $\mathbb{R}^n \otimes \mathbb{R}^n$, which is a n^2 dimensional real space, hence isomorphic to $\mathbb{R}^{n^2}$. Moreover, reasoning as in Theorem 2, we get that $v(g, r) = v(e, p) \otimes v(f, q)$ and $w(g, r) = w(e, p) \otimes w(f, q))$ iff the probabilities satisfy

$$\mu((x_j, y_k), g, r) = \mu(x_j, e, p)\mu(y_k, f, q) \tag{19}$$

In case (19) is not satisfied, r is an entangled state.   □

3.3   Entanglement of Two Vessels of Water

Let us come to the second example. We consider two vessels of water, each containing a volume of water, between 0 and 20 liters. We call the state of the left vessel p and the state of the right vessel q. We consider measurements e and f for the left and the right vessel respectively, that consist in pouring out the water by means of a siphon, collecting it in reference vessels, where we can read of the volume of collected water. We attribute the outcome M if the volume is more than 10 liters and the outcome L if it is less than 10 liters. We introduce the probabilities $\mu(M, e, p)$ and $\mu(L, e, p)$ for the outcomes M and L of e on the left vessel, and the probabilities $\mu(M, f, q)$ and $\mu(L, f, q)$ for the outcomes M and L of f on the right vessel.

We then consider the joint entity consisting of the two vessels of water and denote the state of this joint entity by r. The measurement g consists in pouring out the water of the left vessel with the siphon, and also of the right vessel, with another siphon. Volumes of water are collected at left and at right in two reference vessels, and four outcomes are considered $\{MM, LM, ML, LL\}$. The outcome MM corresponds to left as well as right vessel giving rise to the collection of more than 10 liters, and outcome LL corresponds to left as well as right vessel giving rise to the collection of less than 10 liters. The other two outcomes ML (LM) correspond to the left vessel giving rise to more (less) than 10 liters and right vessel giving rise to less (more) than 10 liters. The probabilities $\{\mu(MM, g, r), \mu(LM, g, r), \mu(ML, g, r), \mu(LL, g, r)\}$ correspond to these four outcomes. Obviously, if nothing extra happens between the two vessels, the joint probabilities will be product probabilities, which means that we have

$$\mu(MM, g, r) = \mu(M, e, p)\mu(M, f, q) \tag{20}$$

$$\mu(LM, g, r) = \mu(L, e, p)\mu(M, f, q) \tag{21}$$

$$\mu(ML, g, r) = \mu(M, e, p)\mu(L, f, q) \tag{22}$$

$$\mu(LL, g, r) = \mu(L, e, p)\mu(L, f, q). \tag{23}$$

This shows that there is no entanglement, and that in the local contextual model in $\mathbb{R}^2 \otimes \mathbb{R}^2$ and $\mathbb{C}^2 \otimes \mathbb{C}^2$, we can represent the state r by means of product states $v(e, p) \otimes v(f, q)$ and $w(e, p) \otimes w(f, q)$.

Let us propose a situation which is more concretely defined, and allows us to derive some numerical values for the probabilities. Thus, we suppose that, for each vessel, the states of different volume are equally probable. As a consequence of this extra hypothesis, the numerical values for all the probabilities are determined from reasons of symmetry, and we have

$$\mu(M, e, p) = \mu(L, e, p) = \mu(M, f, q) = \mu(L, f, q) = \frac{1}{2} \tag{24}$$

$$\mu(MM, g, r) = \mu(LM, g, r) = \mu(ML, g, r) = \mu(LL, g, r) = \frac{1}{4}. \tag{25}$$

We want to consider now another state of the two vessels, and show that this new state is entangled. It is a state where we connect the two vessels of water by a tube, such that they form 'connected vessels of water', and we put exactly 20 liters of water in the whole of the connected vessels. Let us denote this state by s. Knowing that the measuring of the volume of each vessel consist of pouring out the water by a siphon, for the state s, we find that the volume of both vessels, i.e. the water being collected by the siphons, is strictly correlated. Indeed, if we find less than 10 liters in the left vessel, we find more than 10 liters in the right vessel, and vice versa. This means that we never get outcome MM and LL, and hence we have $0 = \mu(MM, g, s) = \mu(LL, g, s)$, while $1 = \mu(ML, g, s) + \mu(LM, g, s)$. Let us investigate whether s is an entangled state. To this aim, we suppose that s is a product state, and see what follows from this hypothesis. If s is a product state we have

$$0 = \mu(M, e, p)\mu(M, f, q) = \mu(L, e, p)\mu(L, f, q) \tag{26}$$

which implies that $\mu(M, e, p) = 0$ and $\mu(L, f, q) = 0$ or $\mu(M, f, q) = 0$ and $\mu(L, e, p) = 0$. Hence, this means that the left vessel contains with certainty less than 10 liters, and the right vessel contains with certainty more than 10 liters, or vice versa. Suppose we have $\mu(M, e, p) = 0$ and $\mu(L, f, q) = 0$. Then $\mu(L, e, p) = 1$ and $\mu(M, f, q) = 1$, but hence $\mu(LM, g, r) = \mu(L, e, p)\mu(M, f, q) = 1$ and $\mu(ML, g, r) = 0$. This is only possible if the siphon of the left vessel would pour out no water at all, and all the water would be poured out by the siphon of the right vessel. This is very improbable, not to say impossible, and hence in case of a realistic situation we have both $\mu(LM, g, r)$ and $\mu(ML, g, r)$ different from zero, which means that s is an entangled state.

Let us again introduce an extra hypothesis that will allow us to derive numerical values for the probabilities in the state s, and prove that s is entangled. Thus, we suppose that both siphons are chosen at random to be applied to the left or to the right, and also all other parameters involved in applying the siphons are chosen at random, e.g. the starting time of siphoning is at random. In this case, we have probability one half that the left siphon will pour out more than 10 liters – and in this case the right siphon pours out less than 10 liters – and probability one half that the right siphon will pour out more than 10 liters of water – and in this case the left siphon pours out less than 10 liters. This means that

$$\mu(ML, g, s) = \mu(LM, g, s) = \frac{1}{2}. \tag{27}$$

If we compare (25) with (27), we see that if the extra hypothesis is satisfied, the state s is not a product state. Hence s is an entangled state. Again, like in the case of the example *The Animal Acts*, we can show that no component probabilities can exist to give rise to these joint probabilities.

Theorem 5. *There do not exist numbers a_1, a_2, b_1, b_2 contained in the interval $[0, 1]$, such that $a_1 + a_2 = 1$, and $b_1 + b_2 = 1$, and such that $a_1 b_1 = 0$, $a_2 b_1 = 0.5$, $a_1 b_2 = 0.5$ and $a_2 b_2 = 0$.*

Proof. Let us suppose that such numbers do exist. From $a_2 b_1 = 0.5$ follows that $(1 - a_1)b_1 = 0.5$, and hence $a_1 b_1 = 1 - 0.5 = 0.5$. This is in contradiction with $a_1 b_1 = 0$. $\qquad \square$

The entangled states that we identity in the way shown above do not contain already the best known characteristic of entanglement, namely the violation of Bell-type inequalities. The reason for this is that locally, hence if only one measurement context is considered, Bell-type inequalities cannot even be defined. Different measurement contexts need to be confronted with each other to come to an investigation of the violation of Bell-type inequalities. In [18] we show that for the data with respect to the combination of concepts *Animal* and *Acts*, in effect, also Bell-type inequalities are violated in case more measurement contexts are considered for this entity *The Animal Acts*. That the vessel of water example also violates Bell-type inequalities of more measurement contexts are considered was shown by one of the authors in earlier work [29, 30]. In forthcoming work we will show how the consideration of different contexts on *QMod* allows the identification of compatibility and non compatibility, again without the necessity of linearity. It will also be proven that the violation of Bell-type inequalities is due to the presence of both aspects entanglement and non compatibility.

3.4   Entanglement of Two Quantum Entities

We conclude this paper by illustrating how $QMod$ works for two genuine quantum entities. In particular, let S be a spin-1/2 quantum particle in the pure state p, and let e_u be a spin measurement along direction u to be performed on S. As we know, the standard quantum representations of p and e_u are given by the unit vector $|\psi\rangle$ and by the self-adjoint operator (up to a factor $\hbar/2$) $\boldsymbol{\sigma} \cdot \boldsymbol{u}$, respectively ($\sigma_i$ are the Pauli matrices). The measurement e_u is associated with the set of outcomes $\{+1, -1\}$. Let us denote by $\mu(+1, e_u, p)$ $(\mu(-1, e_u, p))$ the probability of getting outcome $+1$ (-1) when measuring e_u on S in the state p. The $QMod$ representations in $\mathbb{R}^2$ and $\mathbb{C}^2$ can be constructed at once, as follows.

The state p is contextually represented with respects to the measurement e_u by the vector $v(e_u, p) = (\mu(+1, e_u, p), \mu(-1, e_u, p))$ in the canonical basis $\{(1, 0), (0, 1)\}$ of $\mathbb{R}^2$. Let $\lambda = (r, 1 - r)$, $0 \leq r \leq 1$, be the vector such that, for $(r, 1 - r)$ contained in the line between $(1, 0)$ and $(\mu(+1, e_u, p), \mu(-1, e_u, p))$ $((\mu(+1, e_u, p), \mu(-1, e_u, p))$ and $(0, 1))$, we get outcome $+1$ (-1). As usual, if we denote by d the distance between $(1, 0)$ to $(\mu(+1, e_u, p), \mu(-1, e_u, p))$, we get the right probabilities, that is, $\frac{d}{\sqrt{2}} = \mu(+1, e_u, p)$, and $\frac{\sqrt{2} - d}{\sqrt{2}} = \mu(-1, e_u, p)$.

As expected, the $QMod$ representation in $\mathbb{C}^2$ coincides with the standard quantum representation. We choose as basis $\{|+_u\rangle = (1, 0), |-_u\rangle = (0, 1)\}$ of the Hilbert space $\mathbb{C}^2$, the eigenvectors of $\boldsymbol{\sigma} \cdot \boldsymbol{u}$, which means that $\boldsymbol{\sigma} \cdot \boldsymbol{u} = \sigma_z$, is the self-adjoint operator representing the spin measurement along direction u (or, with other words, we have chosen the z-direction of our three dimensional coordination system along u). We then have $|w(e_u, p)\rangle = \sqrt{\mu(+1, e_u, p)}e^{i\alpha(e_u, p)+}|+_u\rangle + \sqrt{\mu(-1, e_u, p)}e^{i\alpha(e_u, p)-}|-_u\rangle$. The quantum probabilities are given by $\mu(+1, e_u, p) = |\langle +_u|w(e, p)\rangle|^2$ and $\mu(-1, e_u, p) = |\langle -_u|w(e, p)\rangle|^2$.

Now, let S and T be two spin-1/2 quantum particles in the pure states p and q, respectively, let the spin measurements e_u and f_w along directions u and w be performed on S and T, respectively, so that $\{+1, -1\}$ is the set of outcomes of both e_u and f_w, and denote by $\mu(+1, e_u, p)$, $\mu(-1, e_u, p)$, $\mu(+1, f_w, q)$ and $\mu(-1, f_w, q)$ the corresponding probabilities. Finally, let

$$v(e_u, p) = (\mu(+1, e_u, p), \mu(-1, e_u, p)) \quad v(f_w, q) = (\mu(+1, f_w, q), \mu(-1, f_w, q))$$

$$|w(e_u, p)\rangle = \sqrt{\mu(+1, e_u, p)}e^{i\alpha(e_u, p)+}|+_u\rangle + \sqrt{\mu(-1, e_u, p)}e^{i\alpha(e_u, p)-}|-_u\rangle$$
$$|w(f_w, q)\rangle = \sqrt{\mu(+1, f_w, q)}e^{i\alpha(f_w, q)+}|+_w\rangle + \sqrt{\mu(-1, f_w, q)}e^{i\alpha(f_w, q)-}|-_w\rangle$$

be the contextual representations of (e_u, p) and (f_w, q) in $\mathbb{R}^2$ and $\mathbb{C}^2$, respectively. Finally, let U be the compound entity made up of S and T, in the state r. Let the measurement of g on U consisting of a measurement of e_u on S and f_w on T so that the set of possible outcomes of g is $\{(+1,+1),(+1,-1),(-1,+1),(-1,-1)\}$, and the corresponding probabilities $\mu((x_j,y_k),g,r)$, $x_j,y_k = \pm 1$. We have

$$v(g,r) = (\mu((+1,+1),g,r),\mu((+1,-1),g,r),\mu((-1,+1),g,r),\mu((-1,-1),g,r)) \in \mathbb{R}^4$$

$$\begin{aligned}
|w(g,r)\rangle = &\sqrt{\mu((+1,+1),g,r)}e^{i\alpha(g,r)++}|+_u\rangle \otimes |+_w\rangle \\
&+ \sqrt{\mu((+1,-1),g,r)}e^{i\alpha(g,r)+-}|+_u\rangle \otimes |-_w\rangle \\
&+ \sqrt{\mu((-1,+1),g,r)}e^{i\alpha(g,r)-+}|-_u\rangle \otimes |+_w\rangle \\
&+ \sqrt{\mu((-1,-1),g,r)}e^{i\alpha(g,r)--}|-_u\rangle \otimes |-_w\rangle \in \mathbb{C}^4
\end{aligned}$$

We get from Theorem 2 that $v(g,r) = v(e_u,p) \otimes v(f_w,q)$ and $|w(g,r)\rangle = |w(e_u,p)\rangle \otimes |w(f_w,q)\rangle$ iff $\mu((x_j,y_k),g,r) = \mu(x_j,e_u,p)\mu(y_k,f_w,q)$, $x_j,y_k = \pm 1$.

The entanglement of two quantum entities identified in *QMod* obviously coincides with the quantum entanglement recognized in standard quantum theory.

References

1. Aerts, D., Sozzo, S.: Quantum Model Theory (QMod): Modeling Contextual Emergent Entangled Interfering Entities. In: Busemeyer, J.R., Dubois, F., Lambert-Mogiliansky, A. (eds.) QI 2012. LNCS, vol. 7620, pp. 126–137. Springer, Heidelberg (2012)
2. Aerts, D.: Quantum Structure in Cognition. J. Math. Psych. 53, 314–348 (2009)
3. Aerts, D.: Quantum Particles as Conceptual Entities: A Possible Explanatory Framework for Quantum Theory. Found. Sci. 14, 361–411 (2010)
4. Aerts, D.: Interpreting Quantum Particles as Conceptual Entities. Int. J. Theor. Phys. 49, 2950–2970 (2010)
5. Aerts, D.: A Potentiality and Conceptuality Interpretation of Quantum Physics. Philosophica 83, 15–52 (2010)
6. Aerts, D.: Being and Change: Foundations of a Realistic Operational Formalism. In: Aerts, D., Czachor, M., Durt, T. (eds.) Probing the Structure of Quantum Mechanics: Nonlinearity, Nonlocality, Probability and Axiomatics, pp. 71–110. World Scientific, Singapore (2002)
7. Gabora, L., Aerts, D.: Contextualizing Concepts Using a Mathematical Generalization of the Quantum Formalism. J. Exp. Theor. Art. Int. 14, 327–358 (2002)
8. Aerts, D., Gabora, L.: A Theory of Concepts and Their Combinations I: The Structure of the Sets of Contexts and Properties. Kybernetes 34, 167–191 (2005)
9. Aerts, D., Gabora, L.: A Theory of Concepts and Their Combinations II: A Hilbert Space Representation. Kybernetes 34, 192–221 (2005)
10. Gabora, L.: Cultural Evolution Entails (Creativity Entails (Concept Combination Entails Quantum Structure)). In: Bruza, P., Lawless, W., van Rijsbergen, K., Sofge, D. (eds.) Proceedings of the Association for the Advancement of Artificial Intelligence (AAAI) Spring Symposium 8: Quantum Interaction, March 26-28, pp. 106–113. Stanford University, Stanford (2007)
11. Nelson, D.L.: Entangled Associative Structures and Context. In: Bruza, P., Lawless, W., van Rijsbergen, K., Sofge, D. (eds.) Proceedings of the Association for the Advancement of Artificial Intelligence (AAAI) Spring Symposium 8: Quantum Interaction, March 26-28. Stanford University, Stanford (2007)

12. Gabora, L., Rosch, E., Aerts, D.: Toward an Ecological Theory of Concepts. Ecol. Psych. 20, 84–116 (2008)
13. Flender, C., Kitto, K., Bruza, P.: Beyond Ontology in Information Systems. In: Bruza, P., Sofge, D., Lawless, W., van Rijsbergen, K., Klusch, M. (eds.) QI 2009. LNCS, vol. 5494, pp. 276–288. Springer, Heidelberg (2009)
14. Gabora, L., Aerts, D.: A Model of the Emergence and Evolution of Integrated Worldviews. J. Math. Psych. 53, 434–451 (2009)
15. D'Hooghe, B.: The SCOP-formalism: An Operational Approach to Quantum Mechanics. In: AIP Conference Proceedings, vol. 1232, pp. 33–44 (2010)
16. Aerts, D., Czachor, M., Sozzo, S.: A Contextual Quantum-based Formalism for Population Dynamics. In: Proceedings of the AAAI Fall Symposium (FS-10-08), Quantum Informatics for Cognitive, Social, and Semantic Processes, pp. 22–25 (2010)
17. Veloz, T., Gabora, L., Eyjolfson, M., Aerts, D.: Toward a Formal Model of the Shifting Relationship between Concepts and Contexts during Associative Thought. In: Song, D., Melucci, M., Frommholz, I., Zhang, P., Wang, L., Arafat, S. (eds.) QI 2011. LNCS, vol. 7052, pp. 25–34. Springer, Heidelberg (2011)
18. Aerts, D., Sozzo, S.: Quantum Structure in Cognition: Why and How Concepts Are Entangled. In: Song, D., Melucci, M., Frommholz, I., Zhang, P., Wang, L., Arafat, S. (eds.) QI 2011. LNCS, vol. 7052, pp. 116–127. Springer, Heidelberg (2011)
19. Aerts, D.: A Possible Explanation for the Probabilities of Quantum Mechanics. J. Math. Phys. 27, 202–210 (1986)
20. Aerts, D.: Quantum Structures due to Fluctuations of the Measurement Situations. Int. J. Theor. Phys. 32, 2207–2220 (1993)
21. Aerts, D.: Quantum Structures, Separated Physical Entities and Probability. Found. Phys. 24, 1227–1259 (1994)
22. Aerts, D.: Quantum Structures: An Attempt to Explain Their Appearance in Nature. Int. J. Theor. Phys. 34, 1165–1186 (1995)
23. Aerts, D., Aerts, S.: The Hidden Measurement Formalism: Quantum Mechanics as a Consequence of Fluctuations on the Measurement. In: Ferrero, M., van der Merwe, A. (eds.) New Developments on Fundamental Problems in Quantum Physics, pp. 1–6. Springer, Dordrecht (1997)
24. Aerts, D., Aerts, S., Coecke, B., D'Hooghe, B., Durt, T., Valckenborgh, F.: A Model with Varying Fluctuations in the Measurement Context. In: Ferrero, M., van der Merwe, A. (eds.) New Developments on Fundamental Problems in Quantum Physics, pp. 7–9. Springer, Dordrecht (1997)
25. Aerts, D., Aerts, S., Durt, T., Lévêque, O.: Classical and Quantum Probability in the ϵ-model. Int. J. Theor. Phys. 38, 407–429 (1999)
26. Aerts, S.: Hidden Measurements from Contextual Axiomatics. In: Aerts, D., Czachor, M., Durt, T. (eds.) Probing the Structure of Quantum Mechanics: Nonlinearity, Nonlocality, Probability and Axiomatics, pp. 149–164. World Scientific, Singapore (2002)
27. Aerts, S.: The Born Rule from a Consistency Requirement on Hidden Measurements in Complex Hilbert Space. Int. J. Theor. Phys. 44, 999–1009 (2005)
28. Aerts, S.: Quantum and Classical Probability as Bayes-optimal Observation (2006), http://uk.arxiv.org/abs/quant-ph/0601138
29. Aerts, D.: Example of a macroscopical situation that violates Bell inequalities. Lettere al Nuovo Cimento 34, 107–111 (1982)
30. Aerts, D.: A mechanistic classical laboratory situation violating the Bell inequalities with $2\sqrt{2}$, exactly 'in the same way' as its violations by the EPR experiments. Helvetica Physica Acta 64, 1–23 (1991)

Quantum Model Theory (QMod): Modeling Contextual Emergent Entangled Interfering Entities

Diederik Aerts and Sandro Sozzo

Center Leo Apostel (CLEA), Vrije Universiteit Brussel (VUB),
Pleinlaan 2, 1050 Brussels, Belgium
{diraerts,ssozzo}@vub.ac.be

Abstract. In this paper we present *Quantum Model Theory* (*QMod*), a theory we developed to model entities that entail the typical quantum effects of *contextuality, superposition, interference, entanglement* and *emergence*. The aim of *QMod* is to put forward a theoretical framework that is more general than standard quantum mechanics, in the sense that, for its complex version it only uses this quantum calculus locally, i.e. for each context corresponding to a measurement, and for its real version it does not need the property of 'linearity of the set of states' to model the quantum effect. In this sense, *QMod* is a generalization of quantum mechanics, similar to how the general relativity manifold mathematical formalism is a generalization of special relativity. We prove by means of a representation theorem that *QMod* can be used for any entity entailing the typical quantum effects mentioned above. Some examples of application of QMod in concept theory and macroscopic physics are also considered.

Keywords: Quantum modeling, contextuality, interference, QMod.

1 Introduction

Over the years it has become clear that quantum structures do not only appear within situations in the micro-world, but also arise in the macro-world [1–7]. In this respect, more recently [4–7], four major effects have been put forward which also appear in macroscopic situations, and give rise to the presence of quantum structures. These effects are 'interference', 'contextuality', 'emergence' and 'entanglement'. Sometimes it has been possible to use the full quantum apparatus of linear operators in complex Hilbert space to model these effects as they appear in macroscopic situations. But, in quite some occasions a formalism more general than standard quantum theory in complex Hilbert space is needed.

When investigating the structure of concepts, and how they combine to form sentences and texts, we already proposed a generalization of the standard quantum formalism, which we called a *State Context Property*, or *SCoP*, formalism, specifically designed to model concepts and their combinations [8]. This generalization was inspired by work on quantum axiomatics [9], and later also used to

J.R. Busemeyer et al. (Eds.): QI 2012, LNCS 7620, pp. 126–137, 2012.

analyze aspects of concepts, or inspire contextual approaches [10–18]. However, the SCoP formalism is very general, which led us to reflect about a formalism closer to the complex Hilbert space of standard quantum theory, more specific and hence mathematically more efficient than SCoP, but at the same time general enough to cope with the modeling of the main quantum effects identified in the domains different from the micro-world.

In this article we aim to propose a general modeling theory capable of modeling situations in which the effects of contextuality, emergence, entanglement and interference appear. We will call this modeling theory *Quantum Model Theory*, or *QMod*. It is not just a broad modeling scheme, because a specific powerful mathematical representation theorem is the heart of it. It is due to this representation theorem that the mathematical structure of *QMod* contains the potential to describe entanglement and emergence. We will see that the standard quantum mechanical formalism is a special case of *QMod*, where emergence and entanglement are consequences of respectively the linear structure of the Hilbert space and the tensorproduct procedure for compound quantum systems. In *QMod* no linearity is needed in principle, although it can be introduced if useful. This is the fundamental reason why *QMod* constitutes a powerful and helpful generalization of the quantum formalism. We will also see that *QMod* is a concretization of SCoP in a specific way when it is used to model concepts and their combinations. However, *QMod* is not only meant to model concepts and their combinations, like it was the case for SCoP. It aims at modeling all situations of entities where the effects of interference, contextuality, emergence and entanglement play a role, and in this sense it is more general than SCoP in its applications.

Proceeding by analogy, we could say that *QMod* is a generalization of classical and quantum theory in a very similar way to how the general relativistic manifold formalism is a generalization of special relativity. Indeed, general relativity theory assumes that, for each point of space-time, hence locally, space-time can be considered operationally in an Euclidean way. Similarly, *QMod* assumes that, whenever a given measurement is considered, hence again locally, the probabilities are defined operationally and locally for this one measurement, and for an arbitrary set of states of the considered entity. For one fixed state and when an event space is defined on the set of outcomes, one can, for example, assume Kolmogorov's axioms to be valid. Remark that since an arbitrary set of states is considered locally, the probability structure will not be a single Kolmogorovian probability space, but set of Kolmogorovian models, one for each state. Of course, we expect the overall general probability model to be non-Kolmogorovian in *QMod* if different measurements and different states are considered, as we expect that a non-Euclidean model arises if different points of space-time are considered in general relativity theory.

For the sake of completeness, let us briefly resume the content of this paper. We introduce the essentials of *QMod* in Sec. 2, where we prove a representation theorem providing the steps needed to construct a quantum modeling. More specifically, the representation theorem states that any entity that can be described by means of its states, its contexts and specifically corresponding operationally defined probabilities admits a mathematical modeling in $\mathbb{R}^n$ and $\mathbb{C}^m$, with n and m suitably chosen. Successively, we supply in Sec. 3 applications that illustrate how *QMod* concretely works. Indeed, we firstly consider a conceptual entity (Sec. 3.1), then a macroscopic entity (Sec. 3.2). These two examples admit real and complex representations in $\mathbb{R}^2$ and $\mathbb{C}^2$, respectively. Finally, an abstract example in three dimensions (Sec. 3.3) is provided which admits a real representation in $\mathbb{R}^3$ and a complex representation in $\mathbb{C}^3$. The treatment of a specific quantum effect, namely interference, concludes the paper (Sec. 4). The latter allows one to understand how a mixed state differs from a superposition state within *QMod* [19–26].

2   A Representation Theorem

Let us introduce the fundamental notions we need for our purposes. We will model 'entities' where the notion of entity is to be understood in its most general sense. An entity is a collection of aspects of reality that hang together in such a way that different states exist without loosing the possibility of identification of the same entity in each of these states. Sometimes only one state exists, this is then the limiting case, and the entity is then just a situation. Let us right away give two examples that we will be using in the course of this article to illustrate different aspects of the quantum modeling scheme we introduce.

A first example of an entity that we consider is the concept *Animal*. The concept *Animal* can indeed be in different states, for example *Ferocious Animal* and *Sweet Animal* are two such possible states, and many more exists. Each time an adjective is put in front of the concept *Animal* another state of *Animal* is realized. But also each sentence, or paragraph, or piece of text, surrounding the concept *Animal*, places it in a different state. Also exemplars of the concept *Animal*, such as *Horse* and *Bear* can be considered to be states of the concept *Animal*. So clearly a large set of different states exist for the concept *Animal*. A second example of an entity that we consider is a *Vessel of Water*. Different volumes of water that the vessel can contain are different states of the *Vessel of Water*.

Along with the notions of entity and state we introduce the notions of measurement and outcome. A measurement consists of a specific context that is realized for the entity being able to be in different states, which is the reason that in some cases, e.g. in SCoP, we use the term 'context' to indicate the measurement or measurement context. This context affects generally the state of the entity in different ways and as a consequence different outcomes to the measurement defined by this context can occur for a specific state of the entity. Usually the state of the entity is changed by the measurement, and the resulting state after the measurement on the entity can be identified with each of the outcomes. If this is the case, such an outcome can also be represented by this state. This is in fact why we did not introduce the notion of outcome in SCoP, because contexts, i.e. measurements in SCoP, always change a state of a concept into different possible new states, and hence the outcomes of this measurement context are identified with these states in the case of SCoP. Now, we explicitly want to introduce the notion of outcome in *QMod*, because we also want to be able to model situations where the state after a measurement is not identified. We also introduce the notion of probability of occurrence of an outcome, a measurement being performed, with the entity being in a state, as the limit of the relative frequency of this outcome by repetition. It is for this limit of relative frequency for a fixed state, after defining events related to the outcome set, for which Kolmogorov's axioms of probability can be supposed to be valid. In the case of SCoP, this probability is a transition probability from the state before the measurement context to the state after the measurement context.

Definition 1 (Entity, State, Measurement, Outcome, Probability). *We consider the situation of an entity S that can be in different states, and denote states by $p, q, \ldots$, and the set of states by Σ. Different measurements can be performed on the entity S being in one of its states, and we denote measurements by $e, f, \ldots$, and the set of measurements by $\mathcal{M}$. With a measurement $e \in \mathcal{M}$ and the entity in state p, corresponds a set of possible outcomes $\{x_1, x_2, \ldots, x_j, \ldots, x_n\}$, and a set of probabilities $\{\mu(x_j, e, p)\}$, where $\mu(x_j, e, p)$ is the limit of the relative frequency of the outcome x_j, the situation being repeated where measurement e is performed and the entity S is in state p. We denote the final state corresponding to the outcome x_j by means of p_j.*

The following theorem proves that it is always possible to realize the above introduced situation by means of a specific mathematical structure making use of a space of real numbers where the probabilities are derived as Lebesgue measures of subsets of real numbers. We also prove that on top of this real number realization a complex number realization exists, where the probabilities are calculated by making use of a scalar product similar to the one used in the quantum formalism.

Theorem 1 (Representation theorem). *Let us consider a measurement $e \in \mathcal{M}$ and a state $p \in \Sigma$, and introduce the set $\{\mu(x_j, e, p) \mid j = 1, \ldots, n\}$ of probabilities, where $\{x_1, \ldots, x_j, \ldots, x_n\}$ is the set of possible outcomes given e and p. Then, it is possible to work out a representation of this situation in $\mathbb{R}^n$ where the probabilities are given by Lebesgue measures of appropriately defined subsets of $\mathbb{R}^n$, and a representation in $\mathbb{C}^m$ where the measurement is modeled in an analogous way as this is the case in the mathematical formalism of standard quantum theory defined on $\mathbb{C}^m$ as a complex Hilbert space.*

Proof. We introduce the space $\mathbb{R}^n$, and its canonical basis $h_1 = (1, \ldots, 0, \ldots, 0)$, $h_2 = (0, 1, 0, \ldots, 0)$, $\ldots$, $h_j = (0, \ldots, 1, \ldots)$, $\ldots$, $h_n = (0, \ldots, 1)$. The situation of the measurement e and state p can be represented by the vector

$$v(e, p) = \sum_{j=1}^{n} \mu(x_j, e, p) h_j \tag{1}$$

which is a point of the simplex $S_n(e)$, the convex closure of the canonical basis $\{h_1, \ldots, h_j, \ldots, h_n\}$ in $\mathbb{R}^n$. We call $A_j(e, p)$ the convex closure of the vectors

$\{h_1, h_2, \ldots, h_{j-1}, v(e,p), h_{j+1}, \ldots, h_n\}$. We use this configuration to construct a micro-dynamical model for the measurement dynamics of e for the entity in state p. This micro-dynamics is defined as follows, a vector λ contained in the simplex $S_n(e)$, hence we have

$$\lambda = \sum_{j=1}^{n} \lambda_j h_j \quad 0 \leq \lambda_j \leq 1 \quad \sum_{j=1}^{n} \lambda_j = 1 \tag{2}$$

determines the dynamics of the measurement e on the state p in the following way. If $\lambda \in A_j(e,p)$, and is not one of the boundary points (hence λ is contained in the interior of $A_j(e,p)$), then the measurement e gives with certainty, hence deterministically, rise to the outcome x_j, with the entity being in state p. If λ is a point of the boundary of $A_j(e,p)$, then the outcome of the experiment e, the entity being in state p, is not determined. Let us prove that from the above construction we can derive the probabilities $\mu(x_j, e, p)$ from just Lebesgue measuring the sets of relevant real numbers as subsets of $S_n(e)$. Of course, we make the hypothesis that the micro-dynamical modeling of the measuring process is such that the vector λ is chosen at random in the simplex $S_n(e)$ with a randomness modeled by the Lebesque measure on this simplex. Then, following the formulation of the micro-dynamics of the measurement process e for S being in state p, we have that the $\mu(x_j, e, p)$, being the probability to obtain outcome x_j, is given by the Lebesgue measure of the set of vectors λ that are such that this outcome is obtained deterministically, hence this are the λ contained in $A_j(e,p)$, divided by the Lebesgue measure of the total set of vectors λ, which are the λ contained in $S_n(e)$. This means that

$$\mu(x_j, e, p) = \frac{m(A_j(e,p))}{m(S_n(e))}. \tag{3}$$

To calculate the Lebesgue measures, let us introduce the following notations. If $h_1, h_2, \ldots, h_n$ are vectors in $\mathbb{R}^n$, we denote by $M(h_1, h_2, \ldots, h_n)$ the $n \times n$ matrix, where $M_{jk} = (h_j)_k$. We denote by $\det(h_1, h_2, \ldots, h_n)$ the determinant of this matrix $M(h_1, h_2, \ldots, h_n)$, and by $Par(h_1, h_2, \ldots, h_n)$ the parallelepiped spanned by the n vectors. If we consider the two parallelepipeds $Par(h_1, h_2, \ldots, h_n)$ and $Par(h_1, h_2, \ldots, h_{j-1}, v(e,p), h_{j+1}, \ldots, h_n)$, then they are constructions with the same heights over bases which are the simplexes $S_n(e)$ and $A_j(e,p)$. This means that the volumes of these parallelepipeds, as n dimensional subsets of $\mathbb{R}^n$, are equal to the volumes of the simplexes $S_n(e)$ and $A_j(e,p)$, multiplied by the same constant number $c(n)$, which is a number depending on the global dimension n. Now, the volumes of the two parallelepipeds, let us denote them $m(Par(h_1, h_2, \ldots, h_n))$ and $m(Par(h_1, h_2, \ldots, h_{j-1}, v(e,p), h_{j+1}, \ldots, h_n))$ can be calculated by means of the determinants of their matrices, and hence we can also calculate the volumes of the simplexes by these determinants. More specifically we have

$$m(S_n(e)) = c(n)m(Par(h_1, h_2, \ldots, h_n)) \tag{4}$$

$$m(Par(h_1, h_2, \ldots, h_n)) = \det \begin{pmatrix} h_1 \ldots h_j \ldots h_n \end{pmatrix} \tag{5}$$

$$m(A_j(e,p)) = c(n)m(Par(h_1, h_2, \ldots, v(e,p), \ldots, h_n)) \tag{6}$$

$$m(Par(h_1, h_2, \ldots, v(e,p), \ldots, h_n)) = \det \begin{pmatrix} h_1 \ldots v(e,p) \ldots h_n \end{pmatrix} \tag{7}$$

and calculating the determinants of the matrices we get

$$\det \begin{pmatrix} h_1 \ldots h_j \ldots h_n \end{pmatrix} = 1 \tag{8}$$

$$\det \begin{pmatrix} h_1 \ldots v(e,p) \ldots h_n \end{pmatrix} = \mu(x_j, e, p). \tag{9}$$

From (4) and (6) follows that

$$\frac{m(A_j(e,p))}{m(S_n(e))} = \frac{m(Par(h_1, h_2, \ldots, v(e,p), \ldots, h_n))}{m(Par(h_1, h_2, \ldots, h_n))}. \tag{10}$$

And from (5), (7), (8) and (9) follows (3).

For the quantum representation we introduce a set of orthogonal projection operators $\{M_k \mid k = 1, \ldots, n\}$ on a complex Hilbert $\mathbb{C}^m$ space, with $n \leq m \leq n^2$, that form a spectral family. This means that $M_k \perp M_l$ for $k \neq l$ and $\sum_{k=1}^n M_k = \mathbb{1}$, and we take the M_k such that they are diagonal matrices in $\mathbb{C}^m$. More concretely, each M_k is a matrix with 1's at some of the diagonal places, and zero's everywhere else. The number of 1's is between 1 and n, for each M_k, and the collections of 1's hang together, their mutual intersections being empty, and the union of all of them being equal to the collection of 1's of the unit matrix $\mathbb{1}$. The state is represented by a vector $w(e,p)$ of $\mathbb{C}^m$, such that

$$\mu(x_k, e, p) = \langle w(e,p) \mid M_k \mid w(e,p) \rangle = \| M_k \mid w(e,p) \rangle \|^2. \tag{11}$$

A possible solution is

$$w(e,p) = \sum_{j=1}^m a_j e^{i\alpha(e,p)_j} h_j \quad \text{with} \quad a_j = \frac{1}{b}\sqrt{\mu(x_j, e, p)} \tag{12}$$

where h_j is the canonical basis of $\mathbb{C}^m$, and b is the dimension of the projector M_k if h_j is such that $M_k h_j = h_j$. But this is not the only solution, and it might also not be the appropriate solution for the situation we want to model. It shows however that a solution exists, which proves that it is always possible to built this local quantum model.   □

The above theorem is an application of the 'hidden measurement' approach that we elaborated in our Brussels research group during the eighties and nineties of the foregoing century, with the aim of formulating a contextual hidden variable model for quantum theory [2, 27–32].

With the above theorem we have constructed a representation of the collection of states and experiments that lead to the same set of outcomes. In this sense, the

$\mathbb{R}^n$ model and the $\mathbb{C}^m$ model that we have constructed are models for the inter-action between state and experiment. The set of outcomes constitutes a context in which this interaction takes place.

Concluding this section, it is important to observe that the representation theorem proved above allows one to identify some quantum–like aspects without the necessity of assuming an underlying linear structure. This aspect will manifestly emerge from the treatment of entanglement in a forthcoming paper [33], where we prove that the tensorproduct structure appears already on the level of the real space description, and that it is possible to identify entangled states of an entity without the need of linearity. Although we mentioned also the effect of 'emergence' as one of the characteristic quantum effect, we do not consider 'emergence' here or in [33], but give it explicitly attention in [34]. One could say that *QMod* is a generalization of standard quantum mechanics in the sense that, when the real space representation is used, no linearity at all is at play, and when the complex space representation is used, linearity is present only locally. We do not insist on this point, for the sake of brevity, and refer to [33] for a detailed analysis of the linearity issue.

3   Applications of *QMod*

QMod can be applied to the modeling of any type of entity that can be described by a set of states, a set of contexts and probabilities defined for outcomes. In the following, we consider some relevant examples that show how our construction works. As we have anticipated at the end of the previous section, these examples will be employed in the description of entanglement in *QMod* in a forthcoming paper [33].

3.1   Concepts

Let us consider the example of the entity which is the concept *Animal*. We consider a measurement e, where a person is asked to choose between the animal being a *Horse* or a *Bear*, hence there are two outcomes $\{H, B\}$. We consider only one state for *Animal*, namely the ground state which is the state where animal is just animal, i.e. the bare concept, and let us denote it p. Let us denote by $\mu(H, e, p)$ the probability that *Horse* is chosen when e is performed, and by $\mu(B, e, p)$ the probability that *Bear* is chosen.

Let us now work out a mathematical construction put forward in the representation theorem proven in Sec. 2. For the measurement e we consider the vector space $\mathbb{R}^2$ and its canonical basis $\{(1, 0), (0, 1)\}$. The state p is contextually represented with respects to the measurement e by the vector $v(e, p) = (\mu(H, e, p), \mu(B, e, p))$ in $\mathbb{R}^2$. We introduce the vector $\lambda = (r, 1 - r)$, with $0 \leq r \leq 1$, such that for $(r, 1 - r)$ contained in the convex closure of $(1, 0)$ and $(\mu(H, e, p), \mu(B, e, p))$, we get outcome *Bear*, while for $(r, 1 - r)$ contained in the convex closure of $(\mu(H, e, p), \mu(B, e, p))$ and $(0, 1)$ we get *Horse*. Let us calculate the respective lengths and see that we re-obtain the correct probabilities. Denoting the length of the piece of line from $(1,0)$ to $(\mu(H,e,p),\mu(B,e,p))$ by d, we have $\frac{d}{\sqrt{2}} = \mu(B,e,p)$, and $\frac{\sqrt{2}-d}{\sqrt{2}} = \mu(H,e,p)$.

We can also construct a quantum mathematics model in $\mathbb{C}^2$. Therefore we consider the vector $w(e,p) = (\sqrt{\mu(H,e,p)}e^{i\alpha(e,p)_H}, \sqrt{\mu(B,e,p)}e^{i\alpha(e,p)_B})$ in $\mathbb{C}^2$. We have $\mu(H,e,p) = |\langle(1,0)|w(e,p)\rangle|^2$ and $\mu(B,e,p) = |\langle(0,1)|w(e,p)\rangle|^2$, which shows that also the $\mathbb{C}^2$ construction gives rise to the correct probabilities.

3.2   Vessel of Water

As a second example, we consider an entity S that is a vessel of water containing a volume of water between 0 and 20 liters. Suppose that we are in a situation where we lack knowledge about the exact volume contained in the vessel, and call p the state describing this situation. We consider a measurement e for the vessel that consists in pouring out the water by means of a siphon, collecting it in a reference vessel, where we can read of the volume of collected water. We attribute outcome M if the volume is more than 10 liters and the outcome L if it is less than 10 liters, hence the set of outcomes for e is $\{M,L\}$. We introduce the probabilities $\mu(M,e,p)$ and $\mu(L,e,p)$ for the outcomes M and L, respectively. As in the case of concepts, we construct a mathematical representation in $\mathbb{R}^2$ and its canonical basis $\{(1,0),(0,1)\}$. The state p is contextually represented with respects to the measurement e by the vector $v(e,p) = (\mu(M,e,p),\mu(L,e,p))$ in $\mathbb{R}^2$. The simplex $A_M(e,p)$ is the line connecting the points $(\mu(M,e,p),\mu(L,e,p))$ and $(0,1)$, while the simplex $A_L(e,p)$ is the line connecting the points $(1,0)$ and $(\mu(M,e,p),\mu(L,e,p))$. We introduce the vector $\lambda = (r,1-r)$, with $0 \leq r \leq 1$, such that for $(r,1-r)$ contained in the convex closure of $(1,0)$ and $(\mu(M,e,p),\mu(L,e,p))$, we get outcome L, while for $(r,1-r)$ contained in the convex closure of $(\mu(M,e,p),\mu(L,e,p))$ and $(0,1)$ we get M. Let us calculate the respective lengths and see that we find back the correct probabilities. Denoting the length of the piece of line from $(1,0)$ to $(\mu(M,e,p),\mu(L,e,p)) = (1/2,1/2)$ by d, we have $\frac{d}{\sqrt{2}} = \mu(L,e,p)$, an $\frac{\sqrt{2}-d}{\sqrt{2}} = \mu(M,e,p)$. Thus, $d = \frac{\sqrt{2}}{2}$ allows one to recover the right probabilities.

The quantum mathematics model in $\mathbb{C}^2$ can be constructed as follows. We consider the orthogonal projection operators $M_M = \begin{pmatrix} 1 & 0 \\ 0 & 0 \end{pmatrix}$ and $M_L = \begin{pmatrix} 0 & 0 \\ 0 & 1 \end{pmatrix}$, and the vector $w(e,p) = (\sqrt{\mu(M,e,p)}e^{i\alpha(e,p)_M}, \sqrt{\mu(L,e,p)}e^{i\alpha(e,p)_L})$ in $\mathbb{C}^2$. We have $\mu(M,e,p) = \langle w(e,p)|M_M|w(e,p)\rangle$ and $\mu(L,e,p) = \langle w(e,p)|M_L|w(e,p)\rangle$, which also gives rise to the correct probabilities.

3.3   Illustration in Three Dimensions

Let S be an entity and let us consider the situation where the measurement e on S has three possible outcomes $\{x_1,x_2,x_3\}$. We denote by $\mu(x_1,e,p)$, $\mu(x_2,e,p)$ and $\mu(x_3,e,p)$ the probabilities for these outcomes to occur, performing the measurement e, the entity being in state p. The construction leading to the representation theorem takes then place in $\mathbb{R}^3$. We have represented the canonical basis vectors $h_1 = (1,0,0)$, $h_2 = (0,1,0)$ and $h_3 = (0,0,1)$ of $\mathbb{R}^3$ in Fig. 1, and also drawn the simplexes $S_3(e)$, $A_1(e,p)$, $A_2(e,p)$ and $A_3(e,p)$.

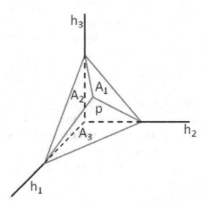

Fig. 1. A simple 3-dimensional picture showing the construction needed for the representation theorem

We now introduce the vector $v(e,p) = \mu(x_1,e,p)h_1 + \mu(x_2,e,p)h_2 + \mu(x_3,e,p)h_3 = (\mu(x_1,e,p), \mu(x_2,e,p), \mu(x_3,e,p))$. We have that $A_1(e,p)$, $A_2(e,p)$ and $A_3(e,p)$ are the convex closures of $\{v(e,p), h_2, h_3\}$, $\{h_1, v(e,p), h_3\}$ and $\{h_1, h_2, v(e,p)\}$, respectively. Then, let the point λ belonging to the simplex $S_3(e)$ be defined as $\lambda = \lambda_1 h_1 + \lambda_2 h_2 + \lambda_3 h_3 = (\lambda_1, \lambda_2, \lambda_3)$, with $0 \leq \lambda_1, \lambda_2, \lambda_3 \leq 1$ and $\lambda_1 + \lambda_2 + \lambda_3 = 1$. Finally, measurement e gives outcome x_j with certainty when S is in state p if and only if $\lambda \in A_j(e,p)$, and $\mu(x_j,e,p) = m(A_j(e,p))/m(S_3(e))$.

Coming to the quantum representation in $\mathbb{C}^3$, we introduce the orthogonal projection operators

$$M_1 = \begin{pmatrix} 1 & 0 & 0 \\ 0 & 0 & 0 \\ 0 & 0 & 0 \end{pmatrix} \quad M_2 = \begin{pmatrix} 0 & 0 & 0 \\ 0 & 1 & 0 \\ 0 & 0 & 0 \end{pmatrix} \quad M_3 = \begin{pmatrix} 0 & 0 & 0 \\ 0 & 0 & 0 \\ 0 & 0 & 1 \end{pmatrix}, \tag{13}$$

and the vector $w(e,p) = (\sqrt{\mu(x_1,e,p)}e^{i\alpha}, \sqrt{\mu(x_2,e,p)}e^{i\beta}, \sqrt{\mu(x_3,e,p)}e^{i\gamma})$. Then, we have $\mu(x_j,e,p) = \langle w(e,p)|M_j|w(e,p)\rangle = \| M_j|w(e,p)\rangle \|^2$, $j = 1, 2, 3$.

4   Interference and Superposition

The results obtained in the previous sections can be applied at once to a typical quantum phenomenon, namely, interference [19–26].

To investigate a situation of interference in our general modeling scheme we introduce a measurement e with an outcome set $\{x_1, \ldots, x_j, \ldots, x_n\}$, and sets of probabilities $\{P(x_j,e,p)|\ j = 1 \ldots n\}$, $\{P(x_j,e,q)|\ j = 1 \ldots n\}$ and

$\{P(x_j, e, r)| \ j = 1 \ldots n\}$ with respect to states p, q and r. We now wonder how the probabilities with respect to r are related to the probabilities with respect to p and the ones with respect to q, in case r is a superposition state of p and q. Let us consider this situation. Hence, we suppose that the vector $w(e, r)$ is a linear combination of the vectors $w(e, p)$ and $w(e, q)$, more specifically $w(e, r) = ae^{i\alpha}w(e, p) + be^{i\beta}w(e, q)$. From this follows that

$$
\begin{aligned}
w(e, r) &= \sum_{j=1}^{n} \sqrt{P(x_j, e, r)} e^{i\alpha(e,r)_j} h_j \\
&= \sum_{j=1}^{n} (ae^{i\alpha} \sqrt{P(x_j, e, p)} e^{i\alpha(e,p)_j} + be^{i\beta} \sqrt{P(x_j, e, q)} e^{i\alpha(e,q)_j}) h_j \quad (14)
\end{aligned}
$$

and hence

$$
\sqrt{P(x_j, e, r)} e^{i\alpha(e,r)_j} = \sqrt{a^2 P(x_j, e, p)} e^{i(\alpha(e,p)_j + \alpha)} + \sqrt{b^2 P(x_j, e, q)} e^{i(\alpha(e,q)_j + \beta)}
$$

which leads to

$$
\begin{aligned}
P(x_j, e, r) &= (\sqrt{a^2 P(x_j, e, p)} e^{-i(\alpha(e,p)_j + \alpha)} + \sqrt{b^2 P(x_j, e, q)} e^{-i(\alpha(e,q)_j + \beta)}) \cdot \\
&\quad (\sqrt{a^2 P(x_j, e, p)} e^{i(\alpha(e,p)_j + \alpha)} + \sqrt{b^2 P(x_j, e, q)} e^{i(\alpha(e,q)_j + \beta)}) \\
&= a^2 P(x_j, e, p) + b^2 P(x_j, e, q) \\
&\quad + 2ab \sqrt{P(x_j, e, p) P(x_j, e, q}\cos(\alpha(e,p)_j - \alpha(e,q)_j + \alpha - \beta). \quad (15)
\end{aligned}
$$

The third term of Eq. (15) is the *interference term*. If this term is different from zero, which is generally the case, the vector $v(e, r)$ is not located on the line segment between the vectors $v(e, p)$ and $v(e, q)$.

References

1. Aerts, D.: Example of a macroscopical situation that violates Bell inequalities. Lett. N. Cim. 34, 107–111 (1982)
2. Aerts, D.: A Possible Explanation for the Probabilities of Quantum Mechanics. J. Math. Phys. 27, 202–210 (1986)
3. Aerts, D., Durt, T., Grib, A., Van Bogaert, B., Zapatrin, A.: Quantum structures in macroscopical reality. Int. J. Theor. Phys. 32, 489–498 (1993)
4. Aerts, D.: Quantum Structure in Cognition. J. Math. Psych. 53, 314–348 (2009)
5. Aerts, D.: Quantum Particles as Conceptual Entities: A Possible Explanatory Framework for Quantum Theory. Found. Sci. 14, 361–411 (2009)
6. Aerts, D.: Interpreting Quantum Particles as Conceptual Entities. Int. J. Theor. Phys. 49, 2950–2970 (2010)
7. Aerts, D.: A Potentiality and Conceptuality Interpretation of Quantum Physics. Philosophica 83, 15–52 (2010)
8. Aerts, D., Gabora, L.: A Theory of Concepts and Their Combinations I&II. Kybernetes 34, 167–191, 192–221 (2005)

9. Aerts, D.: Being and Change: Foundations of a Realistic Operational Formalism. In: Aerts, D., Czachor, M., Durt, T. (eds.) Probing the Structure of Quantum Mechanics: Nonlinearity, Nonlocality, Probability and Axiomatics, pp. 71–110. World Scientific, Singapore (2002)

10. Gabora, L., Aerts, D.: Contextualizing Concepts Using a Mathematical Generalization of the Quantum Formalism. J. Exp. Theor. Art. Int. 14, 327–358 (2002)

11. Nelson, D.L.: Entangled Associative Structures and Context. In: Bruza, P., Lawless, W., van Rijsbergen, K., Sofge, D. (eds.) Proceedings of the Association for the Advancement of Artificial Intelligence (AAAI) Spring Symposium 8: Quantum Interaction, March 26-28. Stanford University, Stanford (2007)

12. Gabora, L., Rosch, E., Aerts, D.: Toward an Ecological Theory of Concepts. Ecol. Psych. 20, 84–116 (2008)

13. Flender, C., Kitto, K., Bruza, P.: Beyond Ontology in Information Systems. In: Bruza, P., Sofge, D., Lawless, W., van Rijsbergen, K., Klusch, M. (eds.) QI 2009. LNCS, vol. 5494, pp. 276–288. Springer, Heidelberg (2009)

14. Gabora, L., Aerts, D.: A Model of the Emergence and Evolution of Integrated Worldviews. J. Math. Psych. 53, 434–451 (2009)

15. D'Hooghe, B.: The SCOP-formalism: An Operational Approach to Quantum Mechanics. In: AIP Conference Proceedings, vol. 1232, pp. 33–44 (2010)

16. Aerts, D., Czachor, M., Sozzo, S.: A Contextual Quantum-based Formalism for Population Dynamics. In: Proceedings of the AAAI Fall Symposium (FS-10-08), Quantum Informatics for Cognitive, Social, and Semantic Processes, pp. 22–25 (2010)

17. Veloz, T., Gabora, L., Eyjolfson, M., Aerts, D.: Toward a Formal Model of the Shifting Relationship between Concepts and Contexts during Associative Thought. In: Song, D., Melucci, M., Frommholz, I., Zhang, P., Wang, L., Arafat, S. (eds.) QI 2011. LNCS, vol. 7052, pp. 25–34. Springer, Heidelberg (2011)

18. Aerts, D., Sozzo, S.: Quantum Structure in Cognition: Why and How Concepts Are Entangled. In: Song, D., Melucci, M., Frommholz, I., Zhang, P., Wang, L., Arafat, S. (eds.) QI 2011. LNCS, vol. 7052, pp. 116–127. Springer, Heidelberg (2011)

19. Young, T.: On the Theory of Light and Colours. Phil. Trans. Roy. Soc. 92, 12–48 (1802); Reprinted in part in: Crew, H. (ed.): The Wave Theory of Light, New York (1990)

20. de Broglie, L.: Ondes et Quanta. Comptes Rendus 177, 507–510 (1923)

21. Schrödinger, E.: Quantizierung als Eigenwertproblem(Erste Mitteilung). Ann. Phys. 79, 361–376 (1926)

22. de Broglie, L.: La Nouvelle Dynamique des Quanta. In: Proceedings of the Solvay Conference-1928, Electrons et Photons, pp. 105–132 (1928)

23. Jönsson, C.: Elektronen Interferenzen an Mehreren Künstlich Hergestellten Feinspalten. Zeit. Phys. 161, 454–474 (1961)

24. Feynman, R.P.: The Feynman Lectures on Physics. Addison-Wesley, New York (1965)

25. Jönsson, C.: Electron Diffraction at Multiple Slits. Am. J. Phys. 4, 4–11 (1974)

26. Arndt, M., Nairz, O., Vos-Andreae, J., Keller, C., van der Zouw, G., Zeilinger, A.: Wave-particle Duality of C_{60} Molecules. Nature 401, 680–682 (1999)

27. Aerts, D.: Quantum Structures due to Fluctuations of the Measurement Situations. Int. J. Theor. Phys. 32, 2207–2220 (1993)

28. Aerts, D.: Quantum Structures, Separated Physical Entities and Probability. Found. Phys. 24, 1227–1259 (1994)

29. Aerts, D., Aerts, S.: The Hidden Measurement Formalism: Quantum Mechanics as a Consequence of Fluctuations on the Measurement. In: Ferrero, M., van der Merwe, A. (eds.) New Developments on Fundamental Problems in Quantum Physics, pp. 1–6. Springer, Dordrecht (1997)

30. Aerts, D., Aerts, S., Coecke, B., D'Hooghe, B., Durt, T., Valckenborgh, F.: A Model with Varying Fluctuations in the Measurement Context. In: Ferrero, M., van der Merwe, A. (eds.) New Developments on Fundamental Problems in Quantum Physics, pp. 7–9. Springer, Dordrecht (1997)

31. Aerts, S.: Hidden Measurements from Contextual Axiomatics. In: Aerts, D., Czachor, M., Durt, T. (eds.) Probing the Structure of Quantum Mechanics: Nonlinearity, Nonlocality, Probability and Axiomatics, pp. 149–164. World Scientific, Singapore (2002)

32. Aerts, S.: The Born Rule from a Consistency Requirement on Hidden Measurements in Complex Hilbert Space. Int. J. Theor. Phys. 44, 999–1009 (2005)

33. Aerts, D., Sozzo, S.: Entanglement of Conceptual Entities in Quantum Model Theory (QMod). In: Busemeyer, J.R., Dubois, F., Lambert-Mogiliansky, A. (eds.) QI 2012. LNCS, vol. 7620, pp. 114–125. Springer, Heidelberg (2012)

34. Aerts, D., Gabora, L., Sozzo, S.: How Concepts Combine: A Quantum Theoretic Modeling of Human Though. Accepted for publication in Topics in Cognitive Science (2012)

Quantum-Like Representation
of Irrational Inference

Masanari Asano[1], Irina Basieva[2], Andrei Khrennikov[2],
Masanori Ohya[1], and Yoshiharu Tanaka[2]

[1] Department of Information Sciences, Tokyo University of Science
Yamasaki 2641, Noda-shi, Chiba, 278-8510 Japan
[2] International Center for Mathematical Modeling in Physics and
Cognitive Sciences, Linnaeus University, S-35195, Växjö, Sweden

Abstract. In this paper we develop a general quantum-like representation of decision making. Here *quantum-like representation* is based on linear algebra, the von Neumann-Lüders projection postulate, Born's rule, and the quantum representation of the state space of a composite system by the tensor product. Our approach generalizes in a natural way the classical Bayesian inference and explains irrational (non-Bayesian) inference biased by psychological factors. For the mathematical description of irrational inference, we use the *lifting map*, which is important concept to discuss a general quantum dynamics called adaptive dynamics.

Keywords: quantum-like cognitive model, (non-)Bayesian inference, lifting map.

1 Introduction

Recently *quantum-like cognitive models* [2–6, 8–13, 17, 18, 21, 25–31, 33, 37] attracted a new wave of interest as a consequence of developed research in cognitive psychology and economics. This research is related to the problem of *"irrational decision making"* in games of the Prisoner's Dilemma type [3, 4, 6]. It was shown that in cognitive psychology some experimental studies produce statistical data [14–16, 38, 39] which cannot be described by classical probability theory. In particular, the process of decision making generating these data cannot be reduced to the classical Bayesian updating. Therefore a number of quantum-like models of decision making was proposed, see above references.

In this paper we introduce a general quantum-like model of decision making, which represents in a natural way the classical Bayesian inference, see Sec. 3. We remark that our model is not about updating on the basis of classical probabilistic mixtures: an event preceding updating has occurred with probability p and not occurred with probability $(1 - p)$. The state of the brain is really in a superposition, cf. [8, 9, 37]. Further, we mathematically discuss irrational inference "biased" by psychological factors. In our formalism, a psychological factor is described as an "environment" affecting to the "main system" that provides the usual Bayesian inference. For this description, we use the *lifting*

J.R. Busemeyer et al. (Eds.): QI 2012, LNCS 7620, pp. 138–147, 2012.

map [1], which describes a general form of quantum dynamics so-called *adaptive dynamics* [34, 35]. Lastly, we will discuss an example of irrationality seen in *taxi problem* [23]. It is known that in this problem, people frequently get a false solution with neglecting the base rate, see, e.g., [7, 19, 24, 36]. Some researchers have proposed that the base-rate effect has its root in the *inverse fallacy* [22, 32, 41]. Our model will strongly support the latter proposition.

2 Bayesian Inference

Bayesian inference is a method of statistical inference in which Bayes' theorem is used to calculate how the degree of belief in a proposition changes due to evidence. Usually, its method is explained like follows: Let us consider the event system denoted by $S_1 = \{A, B\}$ where the events A and B are mutually exclusive. A decision-making entity, which is called Alice hereafter, has a belief for the occurrence of the event A (or B). In the philosophy of Bayesian probability, the degree of belief is represented by probability, $P(A)$ (or $P(B)$) which is called *prior probabilities*. Here, another event system $S_2 = \{C, D\}$ is introduced. Alice knows that this event system S_2 is correlated with S_1, and she can estimate the conditional probabilities $P(C|A)$, $P(C|B)$, $P(D|A)$ and $P(D|B)$ for the events C and D. In such situation, Alice can *update* her beliefs for the events A and B, when she sees an "evidence" of the occurrence of the event C or D. The updated belief is calculated by Bayes' theorem: If Alice sees the occurrence of C, she can update $P(A)$ to

$$P(A|C) = \frac{P(C|A)P(A)}{P(C|A)P(A) + P(C|B)P(B)}.$$

If Alice sees the occurrence of D, she can update $P(A)$ to

$$P(A|D) = \frac{P(D|A)P(A)}{P(D|A)P(A) + P(D|B)P(B)}.$$

These conditional probabilities are called the *posterior probabilities*.

3 Quantum-Like Representation

In this section, the process of Bayesian inference is represented in the mathematical framework of quantum mechanics.

Let us consider the situation that Alice estimates prior probabilities $P(A)$ and $P(B)$ for the events A and B. Many physicists might not feel the need of quantum mechanics to explain this situation, or they might use the following description in the term of density operator;

$$\rho = P(A)|A\rangle\langle A| + P(B)|B\rangle\langle B|,$$

where $\{|A\rangle, |B\rangle\}$ are a set of orthogonal basis defined on Hilbert space $\mathcal{H} = \mathbb{R}^2$, and the values of $P(A)$ and $P(B)$ are given as the eigen values of ρ. The states

$|A\rangle\langle A|$ and $|B\rangle\langle B|$ correspond to the events A and B. Here, we have to stress that this ρ is just a statistical description for the event system S_1, and it does not represent the *uncertainty* that Alice feels on the occurrence of event in S_1. We represent the uncertainty by the *quantum superposition*;

$$\rho = |\phi\rangle\langle\phi|, \quad |\phi\rangle = p_A |A'\rangle + p_B |B'\rangle,$$

where p_A (p_B) are real positive numbers satisfying $p_A^2 = P(A)$ ($p_B^2 = P(B)$), and $\{|A'\rangle, |B'\rangle\}$ are orthogonal basis on $\mathcal{H} = \mathbb{C}^2$. It should be noted that the states $|A'\rangle\langle A'|$ and $|B'\rangle\langle B'|$ does *not* mean the events A and B, and these are *subjective* events relating with Alice's decision-making;

Event A': Alice judges "the event A will occur"
Event B': Alice judges "the event B will occur".
The state vector $|\phi\rangle$ represents that Alice is fluctuated between two conflicting tendencies of judgments A' and B'. The values of p_A and p_B are degrees of these tendencies.

In the theory of Bayesian inference, the correlation with another event system $S_2 = \{C, D\}$ is assumed, and the conditional probabilities $P(C|A)$, $P(C|B)$, $P(D|A)$ and $P(D|B)$ are given. The uncertainty that Alice feels for S_1 is correlated with the uncertainty for S_2, and such situation is represented in the following state vector on $\mathcal{H}_1 \otimes \mathcal{H}_2 = \mathbb{C}^2 \otimes \mathbb{C}^2$.

$$\begin{aligned}
|\Phi\rangle = &\, p_A |A'\rangle \otimes (p_{C|A} |C'\rangle + p_{D|A} |D'\rangle) \\
&+ p_B |B'\rangle \otimes (p_{C|B} |C'\rangle + p_{D|B} |D'\rangle),
\end{aligned} \quad (1)$$

where $p_{C|}$ and $p_{D|}$ are real positive numbers with $p_{C|}^2 = P(C|\cdot)$ and $p_{D|}^2 = P(D|\cdot)$. We call this vector *prediction state vector*.

The process of Bayesian inference is explained as follows: When Alice obtains an evidence of the occurrence of the event C in S_2, for example, she recognizes "the event C occurred" and then the possibility of D' is *vanished*. In our formalism, such vanish is represented as the *reduction of the prediction state* $\theta = |\Phi\rangle\langle\Phi|$ by the projection operator $M_{C'} = I \otimes |C'\rangle\langle C'|$:

$$\frac{M_{C'}\theta M_{C'}}{\mathrm{tr}(M_{C'}\theta)} \equiv \theta_{C'}. \quad (2)$$

For the state $\theta_{C'}$, one can calculate

$$\mathrm{tr}(M_{A'}\theta_{C'}) = \frac{p_{C|A}^2 \cdot p_A^2}{p_{C|A}^2 \cdot p_A^2 + p_{C|B}^2 \cdot p_B^2}$$

where $M_{A'} = |A'\rangle\langle A'| \otimes I$. This value is equal to the posterior probability $P(A|C)$.

4   Biased Bayesian Inference

As mentioned in the previous section, the reduction of the prediction state θ provides a rational inference consistent with the standard Bayesian scheme. In real situations, we empirically know that our behavior is sometime "irrational" and at the background, there is some psychological situation such that disturbs the rational process. Our main purpose in this paper is to describe an irrational inference in the quantum-like formalism. As a mathematical way to do this, we use an important concept in the quantum information theory, so-called *lifting map*, $\mathcal{E}^* : \mathcal{S}(\mathcal{H}) \mapsto \mathcal{S}(\mathcal{H} \otimes \mathcal{K})$. A role of this map is to extend a main system in $\mathcal{S}(\mathcal{H})$ to a compound system combined with an environment in $\mathcal{S}(\mathcal{K})$: It is useful to discuss a state change induced by a correlation with environment system, and it is closely related to the theory of open system dynamics. We consider the following lifting map

$$\mathcal{E}^*_{\sigma,V}(\theta) = V\theta \otimes \sigma V^*. \tag{3}$$

Here, $\theta \in \mathcal{S}(\mathcal{H})$ is a prediction state, and $\sigma \in \mathcal{S}(\mathcal{K})$ implies a psychological situation biasing rational process of inference, in other words, a generator of psychological biases. The operator V on $\mathcal{H} \otimes \mathcal{K}$ is assumed to be isometry $VV^* = I$ and specifies all possible psychological biases from σ. We define the form of V as

$$V = \sum_{i=1}^{dim(\mathcal{K})} V_i \otimes |f_i\rangle \langle f_i|, \tag{4}$$

where $V_i \in B(\mathcal{H})$ is a isometry operator and $\{|f_i\rangle\}$ is a set of orthogonal basis on $\mathcal{K}$. We call V_i *bias* and call f_i *psychological factor of bias-V_i*. A decision-making entity can hold various kinds of factors to make various psychological biases. The degree of factor f_i is given by the diagonal part of σ, $\langle f_i| \sigma |f_i\rangle$. Further, psychological factors are influenced each other in a decision-making entity's mental, and such correlations are represented in non-diagonal parts of σ. We define the *biased prediction* state $\theta_{\sigma,V}$ by

$$\theta_{\sigma,V} \equiv \mathrm{tr}_{\mathcal{K}} \mathcal{E}^*_{\sigma,V}(\theta), \tag{5}$$

and define the *biased posterior probability* as

$$P_{\sigma,V}(A|C) \equiv \frac{\mathrm{tr}(M_{C'} M_{A'} M_{C'} \theta_{\sigma,V})}{\mathrm{tr}(M_{C'} \theta_{\sigma,V})}. \tag{6}$$

The value of the biased posterior probability is generally different from the standard one estimated by Bayes' rule.

In the next section, we focus on an example of irrational inference called the *inverse fallacy*, which is well known in psychology and cognitive science. A decision-making entity with the inverse fallacy estimates his biased posterior probability as $P(C|A)$, not $P(A|C)$. Such simple fallacy will be explained in a simple case of our model: We consider the case that the state σ has a unique factor f_k, that is, $\sigma = |f_k\rangle \langle f_k|$. Then, by using the bias $V_k = L$, the biased prediction $\theta_{\sigma,V}$ is written as

$$\theta_{\sigma,V} = L\theta L^* \equiv \theta_L. \tag{7}$$

5   Inverse Fallacy

Bayesian inference is a most objective way of inference which is consistent with probability theorem. However, in psychology, it is known that people frequently use *heuristics* beyond the objective way. The *inverse fallacy* is induced in such heuristics. In this section, we focus on the inverse fallacy seen in the *taxi problem* [23].

5.1   Taxi Problem

A witness sees a crime involving a taxi in a town. The witness says that the taxi is blue. It is known from previous research that witnesses are correct 80 % of the time when making such statements. The police also know that 85% of the taxis in the town are green, the other 15% being blue. What is the probability that a blue taxi was involved in the crime?

This problem is solved as follow: Let H and $\neg H$ be events "a blue taxi was involved in the crime" and "a green taxi was involved in the crime". Let D be the event "the witness says that the taxi was blue". The "base rates" $P(H) = 0.15$, $P(\neg H) = 0.85$ and the conditional probabilities $P(D|H) = 0.8$, $P(D|\neg H) = 0.2$ are given. The solution, the posterior probability $P(H|D)$, is calculated by Bayes' rule:

$$P(H|D) = \frac{P(D|H)P(H)}{P(D|H)P(H) + P(D|\neg H)P(\neg H)} \approx 0.41.$$

Kahneman and Tversky set subjects to solve this problem and found that their majority answered "0.8" which is the value of $P(D|H)$ [23]. From this result, such subjects seem to mix up $P(D|H)$ and $P(H|D)$.

5.2   Bias Operator Making Inverse Fallacy

We discuss the bias operator L such that the biased prediction state θ_L of Eq. (7) satisfies

$$P_L(H|D) = \frac{\mathrm{tr}(M_{H'} M_{D'} M_{H'} \theta_L)}{\mathrm{tr}(M_{H'} \theta_L)} = P(D|H). \qquad (8)$$

To find such bias L, let us consider the following events,

$$E : \text{The witness is correct,} \qquad (9)$$

$$\neg E : \text{The witness is not correct.} \qquad (10)$$

From the sentence in the taxi problem, one can answer the values of probabilities for these events; $P(E) = 0.8$ and $P(\neg E) = 0.2$. The event E is interpreted as the sum event of $H \wedge D$ and $\neg H \wedge \neg D$; $E = (H \wedge D) \vee (\neg H \wedge \neg D)$. Similarly, $\neg E = (H \wedge \neg D) \vee (\neg H \wedge D)$. Here, note that the prediction state $\theta = |\Phi\rangle \langle \Phi|$ is given by

$$|\Phi\rangle = p_H |H'\rangle \otimes (p_{D|H} |D'\rangle + p_{\neg D|H} |\neg D'\rangle)$$
$$+ p_{\neg H} |\neg H'\rangle \otimes (p_{D|\neg H} |D'\rangle + p_{\neg D|\neg H} |\neg D'\rangle). \qquad (11)$$

From $p_E = p_{D|H} = p_{\neg D|\neg H}$ and $p_{\neg E} = p_{D|\neg H} = p_{\neg D|H}$, this form is rewritten as

$$|\Phi\rangle = p_E(p_H |H'\rangle \otimes |D'\rangle + p_{\neg H} |\neg H'\rangle \otimes |\neg D'\rangle)$$
$$+ p_{\neg E}(p_H |H'\rangle \otimes |\neg D'\rangle + p_{\neg H} |\neg H'\rangle \otimes |D'\rangle)$$
$$\equiv p_E |E'\rangle + p_{\neg E} |\neg E'\rangle \tag{12}$$

We consider the bias operator L that transforms the vector $|E'\rangle$ and $|\neg E'\rangle$ as

$$L |E'\rangle = \cos(\lambda - \omega) |H'\rangle \otimes |D'\rangle + \sin(\lambda - \omega) |\neg H'\rangle \otimes |\neg D'\rangle,$$
$$L |\neg E'\rangle = \cos(\lambda - \tilde{\omega}) |H'\rangle \otimes |\neg D'\rangle + \sin(\lambda - \tilde{\omega}) |\neg H'\rangle \otimes |D'\rangle. \tag{13}$$

Here, λ is a constant satisfying $\cos \lambda = p_H$ and $\sin \lambda = p_{\neg H}$. Further, let us consider the case of $\omega - \tilde{\omega} = \frac{\pi}{2}$. Then, the biased prediction state $\theta_L = L |\Phi\rangle \langle \Phi| L^* = |\Phi_L\rangle \langle \Phi_L|$ is described as

$$|\Phi_L\rangle = \cos(\lambda - \omega) |D'\rangle \otimes (p_E |H'\rangle + p_{\neg E} |\neg H'\rangle)$$
$$- \sin(\lambda - \omega) |\neg D'\rangle \otimes (p_{\neg E} |H'\rangle - p_E |\neg H'\rangle). \tag{14}$$

In the above form, the meanings of $P(E)$ and $P(\neg E)$ are biased: In the classical discussion, the probabilities $P(E)$ and $P(\neg E)$ correpond to the conditional $P(D|H) = P(\neg D|\neg H)$ and $P(D|\neg H) = P(D|\neg H)$. Nevertheless, these $P(E)$ and $P(\neg E)$ in Eq. (14) look like the conditional probabilities $P(H|D) = P(\neg H|\neg D)$ and $P(\neg H|D) = P(H|\neg D)$. It seems that the events H ($\neg H$) and D ($\neg D$) are mixed up. Actually, one can easily check that the biased posterior probability explains the inverse fallacy;

$$P_L(H|D) = P(E) = P(D|H).$$

5.3   Irrational Updating

Most people who solve the taxi problem by the heuristics will *not* calculate posterior probability by Bayes rule, which is represented as a reduction of prediction state by a projection operator in our formalism. They will achieve the false solution directly and intuitively. We assume, they bias their prediction in which the estimation for the possibility of the event $\neg D$ is almost not considered. Such a prediction vector is described as

$$|\Phi_L\rangle \approx |D'\rangle \otimes (\sqrt{P(E)} |H'\rangle + \sqrt{P(\neg E)} |\neg H'\rangle).$$

This corresponds to the form of Eq. (14) with $\omega \approx \lambda$. People in such situation will find the solution (but the false solution $P(E)$) directly, and they will not feel the occasion of calculating posterior probability.

In a sense, the bias from the ideal $|\Phi\rangle$ to the above $|\Phi_L\rangle$ is a kind of "updating". We call it "irrational updating". The irrational updating L biases $|E\rangle$ and $|\neg E\rangle$ as

$$L |E\rangle \approx |H'\rangle \otimes |D'\rangle, \quad L |\neg E\rangle \approx |\neg H'\rangle \otimes |D'\rangle.$$

These imply that in Alice's brain doing the irrational updating, the event E is identified with $H \wedge D$ ($\neg E$ is identified with $\neg H \wedge D$).

Conventionally, the inverse fallacy is understood as the result of tendency to undervalue the base rate information $P(H)$, $P(\neg H)$ [7, 19, 24, 36]. However, some researchers have proposed that the base-rate effect was in fact originating from the inverse fallacy [22, 32, 41]. Our model will strongly support the latter proposition, because, in our model, the inverse fallacy is represented in the term of the bias operator L, which biases the base rate information, see Eq. (13).

Further, it should be noted that the base rate is completely neglected in the irrational updating. This base rate neglect is different from the *normative base rate neglect* such that $P(H)$ and $P(\neg H)$ are regarded as $\frac{1}{2}$. This point is consistent with the claim by Villejoubert and Mandel [40]: They pointed out that the normative base rate and inverse fallacies are different. It is important that our model can explain the normative base rate neglect by using the bias operator L with $\omega = \tilde{\omega} = \lambda - \frac{\pi}{4}$ in Eq. (13), and then, the biased prediction vector $|\Phi_L\rangle$ is given by

$$|\Phi_L\rangle = \sqrt{\frac{1}{2}}|H'\rangle \otimes (\sqrt{P(D|H)}\,|D'\rangle + \sqrt{P(\neg D|H)}\,|\neg D'\rangle)$$

$$+ \sqrt{\frac{1}{2}}|\neg H'\rangle \otimes (\sqrt{P(D|\neg H)}\,|D'\rangle + \sqrt{P(\neg D|\neg H)}\,|\neg D'\rangle).$$

Here, remind the taxi problem, where $P(D|H) = P(\neg D|\neg H)$ and $P(\neg D|H) = P(D|\neg H)$. The biased posterior probability calculated from such $|\Phi_L\rangle$ is $P_L(H|D) = P(D|H)$ that is same with the result of inverse fallacy. It is difficult to find the difference between the normative base rate and the inverse fallacies in the term of probability. On the other hand, our quantum-like representation distinguishes them mathematically in the term of bias operator.

5.4   Conclusion

In this paper, we defined a general framework to describe non-Bayesian inference in terms of the lifting map, where the concept of bias operator is important, see Eq. (3). A bias operator represents a psychological factor disturbing a Bayesinan inference, and the operator L of Eq. (13) is an example, which makes the inverse fallacy. Further, in Sec.5.3, we pointed out that a bias operator provides an inference without calculation of a posterior probability. Such an inference might be related to the problem of heuristics. To show the availability of our approach, we have to find bias operators that can explain other fallacies well-known in the cognitive science, for example, the violation of sure thing principle or the conjunction fallacy, and we also have to analyze the consistency with experimental results for these fallacies. These are our issues in the future.

Acknowledgements. One of the authors (Irina Basieva) is supported by the post-doc fellowship of Swedish Institute; two authors (Irina Basieva and Andrei

Khrennikov) were supported by visiting fellowships at QBIC, Tokyo University of Science. The authors thank I. Yamato, T. Matsuoka and R. Belavkin for numerous fruitful discussions.

References

1. Accardi, L., Ohya, M.: Compound channels, transition expectations and liftings. Applied Mathematics Optimization 39, 33–59 (1991)
2. Accardi, L., Khrennikov, A., Ohya, M.: Quantum Markov model for data from Shafir-Tversky experiments in cognitive psychology. Open Systems and Information Dynamics 16, 371–385 (2009)
3. Asano, M., Khrennikov, A., Ohya, M.: Quantum-like model for decision making process in two players game, A Non-Kolmogorovian model. Found. Phys. 41, 538–548 (2010)
4. Asano, M., Ohya, M., Tanaka, Y., Khrennikov, A., Basieva, I.: On application of Gorini-Kossakowski-Sudarshan-Lindblad equation in cognitive psychology. Open Systems & Information Dynamics 18(1), 55–69 (2011)
5. Asano, M., Ohya, M., Tanaka, Y., Khrennikov, A., Basieva, I.: Quantum-like Representation of Bayesian Updating. In: Proceedings of the International Conference on Advances in Quantum Theory. American Institute of physics, vol. 1327, pp. 57–62 (2011)
6. Asano, M., Ohya, M., Tanaka, Y., Khrennikov, A., Basieva, I.: Quantum-like Dynamics of Decision-Making. Physica A (2011), doi:10.1016
7. Bar-Hillel, M.: The base rate fallacy in probability judgments. Acta Psychologica 44, 211–233 (1980)
8. Busemeyer, J.R., Wang, Z., Townsend, J.T.: Quantum dynamics of human decision making. J. Math. Psychology 50, 220–241 (2006)
9. Busemeyer, J.R., Wang, Z., Lambert-Mogiliansky, A.: Empirical Comparison of Markov and quantum models of decision making. J. Math. Psychology 53, 423–433 (2009)
10. Busemeyer, J.R., Trueblood, J.: Comparison of Quantum and Bayesian Inference Models. In: Bruza, P., Sofge, D., Lawless, W., van Rijsbergen, K., Klusch, M. (eds.) QI 2009. LNCS (LNAI), vol. 5494, pp. 29–43. Springer, Heidelberg (2009)
11. Busemeyer, J.R., Pothos, E.M., Franco, R., Trueblood, J.S.: A quantum theoretical explanation for probability judgment errors. Psychological Review 118, 193–218 (2011)
12. Cheon, T., Takahashi, T.: Classical and quantum contents of solvable game theory on Hilbert space. Phys. Lett. A 348, 147–152 (2006)
13. Cheon, T., Takahashi, T.: Interference and inequality in quantum decision theory. Phys. Lett. A 375, 100–104 (2010)
14. Conte, E., Khrennikov, A., Todarello, O., Federici, A., Zbilut, J.P.: Mental states follow quantum mechanics during perception and cognition of ambiguous figures. Open Systems and Information Dynamics 16, 1–17 (2009)
15. Conte, E., Todarello, O., Federici, A., Vitiello, F., Lopane, M., Khrennikov, A., Zbilut, J.P.: Some remarks on an experiment suggesting quantum-like behavior of cognitive entities and formulation of an abstract quantum mechanical formalism to describe cognitive entity and its dynamics. Chaos, Solitons and Fractals 31(5), 1076–1088 (2007)

16. Croson, R.: The Disjunction Effect and Reason-Based Choice in Games. Organizational Behavior and Human Decision Processes 80, 118–133 (1999)
17. Danilov, V.I., Lambert-Mogiliansky, A.: Measurable systems and behavioral sciences. Mathematical Social Sciences 55(3), 315–340 (2008)
18. Danilov, V.I., Lambert-Mogiliansky, A.: Expected utility theory under non-classical uncertainty. Theory and Decision 68(1), 25–47 (2010)
19. Dawes, R.M., Mirels, H.L., Gold, E., Schiavo, M.D.: Equating inverse probabilities in implicit personality judgments. Psychological Science 4, 396–400 (1979)
20. Franco, R.: The inverse fallacy and quantum formalism. In: Proceedings of the the Second Interaction Symposium (QI 2008), pp. 94–98 (2008)
21. Franco, R.: The conjunction fallacy and interference effects. J. Math. Psychol. 53, 415–422 (2009)
22. Hamm, R.M.: Explanation for common responses to the blue/green cab probabilistic inference word problem. Psychological Reports 72, 219–242 (1993)
23. Kahneman, D., Tversky, A.: Subjective probability: A judgment of representativeness. Cognitive Psychology 3, 430–454 (1972)
24. Kahneman, D., Tversky, A.: On the psychology of prediction. Psychological Review 80, 237–251 (1973)
25. Khrennikov, A.: Classical and quantum mechanics on information spaces with applications to cognitive, psychological, social and anomalous phenomena. Found. of Physics 29, 1065–1098 (1999)
26. Khrennikov, A.: On quantum-like probabilistic structure of mental information. Open Systems and Information Dynamics 11(3), 267–275 (2004)
27. Khrennikov, A.: Quantum-like brain: Interference of minds. BioSystems 84, 225–241 (2006)
28. Khrennikov, A., Haven, E.: Quantum mechanics and violations of the sure-thing principle: the use of probability interference and other concepts. Journal of Mathematical Psychology 53, 378–388 (2009)
29. Khrennikov, A.: Quantum-like model of cognitive decision making and information processing. Biosystems 95, 179–187 (2009)
30. Khrennikov, A.: Contextual approach to quantum formalism. Fundamental Theories of Physics. Springer, Heidelberg (2009)
31. Khrennikov, A.: Ubiquitous quantum structure: from psychology to finance. Springer, Heidelberg (2010)
32. Koehler, J.J.: The base rate fallacy reconsidered: Descriptive, normative and methodological challenges. Behavioral and Brain Sciences 19, 1–53 (1996)
33. Lambert-Mogiliansky, A., Zamir, S., Zwirn, H.: Type Indeterminacy: A model of the KT (Kahneman-Tversky)-man. J. Math. Psychol. 53(5), 349–361 (2009)
34. Ohya, M.: Adaptive Dynamics and its Applications to Chaos and NPC Problem. In: QP-PQ: Quantum Probability and White Noise Analysis, Quantum Bio-Informatics 2007, vol. 21, pp. 181–216 (2007)
35. Ohya, M., Volovich, I.: Mathematical foundations of quantum information and computation and its applications to nano- and bio-systems. Springer, Heidelberg (2011)
36. Pollard, P., St Evans, J.B.T.: The role of representativeness in statistical inference. In: St Evans, J.B.T. (ed.) Thinking and Reasoning, pp. 309–330. Routledge and Kegan Paul, London (1983)
37. Pothos, E.M., Busemeyer, J.R.: A quantum probability explanation for violation of rational decision theory. Proc. Royal. Soc. B 276, 2171–2178 (2009)

38. Shafir, E., Tversky, A.: Thinking through uncertainty: nonconsequential reasoning and choice. Cognitive Psychology 24, 449–474 (1992)
39. Tversky, A., Shafir, E.: The disjunction effect in choice under uncertainty. Psychological Science 3, 305–309 (1992)
40. Villejoubert, G., Mandel, D.: The inverse fallacy: An account of deviations from Bayes's theorem and the additivity principle. Memory and Cognition 30(2), 171–178 (2002)
41. Wolfe, C.R.: Information seeking on Bayesian conditional probability problems: A fuzzy-trace theory account. Journal of Behavioral Decision Making 8, 85–108 (1995)

Type Indeterminacy in Privacy Decisions: The Privacy Paradox Revisited

Christian Flender and Günter Müller

Institute of Computer Science and Social Studies
University of Freiburg
Freiburg, Germany
{flender, mueller}@iig.uni-freiburg.de

Abstract. The paper at hand aims to provide a rational explanation of why people generously give away personal data while at the same time being highly concerned about their privacy. For many years, research has come up with attempts to untangle the privacy paradox. We provide a thorough literature review on privacy decisions in socio-economic scenarios and identify explanatory gaps. To explain paradoxical behavior in privacy decision making we illuminate (1) generous data disclosure and (2) high valuation of privacy as two non-commuting observations of incompatible preferences (types). Abstract risk awareness of privacy threats and concrete privacy decisions are not interchangeable, i.e. disclosing personal data prior to becoming aware of privacy risks does not equal the raising of risk awareness before revealing personal information. Privacy decisions do not commute as subjects may alter their preferences indeterminately, i.e. at the time an actual decision is made, in response to discomfort arising from conflicting preferences.

Keywords: Privacy, Indeterminacy, Noncommutativity.

1 Introduction

The unprecedented success of recent internet services dealing with personal data fulfills the need of many companies to know their customers. As companies progress in transforming their business by incorporating the collection, storage, and analysis of vast amounts of consumer data, opportunities for addressing the right target groups with their individual preferences rises. However, consumers becoming increasingly transparent with regard to their preferences also raise concerns over the erosion of their privacy. Many surveys witness serious privacy concerns of consumers[1]. This appears paradoxical as they easily forget about their fears provided the right circumstances like entertainment, attention, or comfort are given, i.e. the benefits received in return for data disclosure. Moreover, the disparity between stated preferences and actual behavior, i.e. the privacy paradox, may not only turn out to be disadvantageous for consumers.

---

[1] cf. https://www.cdt.org/privacy/guide/surveyinfo.php

J.R. Busemeyer et al. (Eds.): QI 2012, LNCS 7620, pp. 148–159, 2012.

Also for service providers this may have negative consequences. Consumers confronted with their paradoxical behavior, e.g. when finding out about their personal data being used without consent, may react with resentment, which may cause damage to customer relationships[1].

Economically, the privacy paradox is of high relevance. Discrepancies between attitudes and actual decisions may affect economic welfare[2,3]. A potential threat to welfare stems from consumers becoming increasingly aware of such discrepancies. As a consequence an erosion of trust may threaten markets for services based on the collection and dissemination of personal data. For instance, trust is likely to erode once consumers find out that provided contact information will be used for unwanted marketing phone calls or past purchase orders will serve as input for price discrimination. Accordingly, for many years research in economics, psychology, and social studies, has been addressing privacy decision making as its object of investigation. However, it occurred only recently that attempts to describe human decision making with the tools borrowed from quantum theory emerged, e.g. [4,5], thereby offering a new perspective of phenomena like the privacy paradox.

From this perspective, we provide a rational explanation of why people generously give away personal data while at the same time being highly concerned about their privacy. We argue that observations of abstract risk awareness of privacy threats and concrete privacy decisions are not interchangeable, i.e. they do not commute. Prior to that we come up with a thorough literature review on privacy decisions in socio-economic scenarios and identify explanatory gaps. The paper is structured as follows.

In the next section we review empirical studies and explanatory attempts related to the privacy paradox. Literature stems from several fields like privacy economics, cognitive psychology, and information systems, and its review is structured along three descriptive dimensions (1) incomplete information, (2) bounded rationality, (3) and decision biases. Then, in section 3, we come up with a formalization of the privacy paradox. By means of a numerical example representative for conflicting privacy observations, we show that stated preferences and actual behavior interfere, i.e. abstract risk awareness and concrete privacy decisions do not commute. Finally, in section 4, we speculate about how our results may contribute to transparency and trust on markets of recent internet services and give an outlook towards future work.

2 Explanatory Gap: The Privacy Paradox

According to Westin (1967) privacy refers to each individual's right to control, edit, manage, and delete information about them and decide when, how, and to what extent information is communicated to others[6]. There are several studies showing that individuals are quite clear about their valuation and desired level of privacy. However, when observed in practical situations people's willingness to disclose personal data stands in stark contrast to their own privacy claims.

2.1 Empirical Observations

In the US several polls and surveys support the claim that people care about their privacy[2]. Given the success of companies like Google and Facebook as well as the amount and sensitivity of data disclosed in exchange for using their services, the privacy paradox appears intuitively evident. Beyond intuition, there are quite a few behavioral studies witnessing the privacy paradox. As one of the main schools of privacy research, behavioral economics studies how individual, social, cognitive and emotional biases influence privacy decision making.

Spiekermann et al. (2001) conducted an experiment with data from 171 participants and compared their self-reported privacy preferences with actual data disclosure[7]. The authors analyzed questionnaire answers to discern privacy preferences and log files to analyze behavior and found that participants did not live up their self-reported privacy attitudes when it comes to interactions with an anthropomorphic shopping bot. Risk awareness was determined by clustering users according to their level of concern. 76% of participants care about their privacy. 30% are privacy fundamentalists, 26% profiling averse (avoidance of disclosure of hobbies, interests, health data, etc.), and 20% identity concerned (avoidance of disclosure of name, address, and email). Only 24% are marginally concerned.

Norberg et al. (2007) demonstrate the existence of the privacy paradox within two experimental studies[8]. Their hypothesis draws from individuals' consideration of risks and trust. The authors are interested in the degree to which privacy attitudes or intentions might influence actual disclosure behavior. As opposed to risks, they assume that trust directly influences privacy behavior. Risk considerations have an influence on stated preferences but influence is not strong enough to have an effect on actual behavior. As environmental factor trust has stronger effects on actual behavior and outweighs privacy concerns. In contrast, when asked about intentions to provide personal information it is the other way round and risk outweighs trust. Privacy intentions or attitudes and actual data disclosure are paradox as risk awareness dominates in abstract decision situations and reliance upon trustworthiness dominates in concrete decision making processes. In their studies the authors found support of risks significantly influencing privacy intentions. However, they didn't find trust having an effect on actual behavior as expected. Nonetheless, Dwyer et al. (2007) showed that trust and usage goals affect people's willingness to disclose personal information in online social networks[9]. They found that Facebook users expressed greater trust in Facebook than MySpace users did in MySpace. According to this higher level of trust Facebook users were more willing to disclose data on the site.

Sheehan and Hoy (1999) conducted a study to investigate linkages between E-mail users' privacy concerns and their change of behavior[10]. The authors found that with an increase in privacy concern actual behavior changed. In particular, respondents with increased privacy awareness were more likely to provide incomplete information to web sites, or to request removal from mailing lists. Although they do not claim to have found a causal relationship between stated

---

[2] cf. https://www.cdt.org/privacy/guide/surveyinfo.php

concerns and actual privacy decisions, the authors revealed a clear correlation between the two observations.

With regard to trade-offs between costs and benefits Sayre and Horne (2000) examined privacy decision making in an offline context[11]. They found that people are willing to give away their personal information in exchange for small discounts in a grocery store. Here the assumption is that consumers trade benefits (small discounts) for the costs (risks associated with personal data disclosure). A trade-off is calculated according to an individual's utility function which takes as input costs and benefits.

Awad and Krishnan (2006) deduce benefits from the degree a service is personalized and fits consumer needs[12]. In contrast, costs are driven by perceived privacy risks. Personalized product recommendations of online shops are beneficial to consumers in the sense of reduced search efforts. On the other hand, consumers often don't know about the way their data is used and protected. This lack of knowledge incurs costs due to the risks that have to be taken into account. In privacy decisions users are constantly balancing the costs and benefits of data disclosure and concealment according to their primary goal of maximizing utility.

In line with trading costs and benefits three major attempts have been put forth to explain paradoxical behavior in privacy decision making[13,14]. In the following incomplete information, bounded rationality, and decision biases such as immediate gratification affecting users' perception will be discussed with regard to their explanatory shortcomings.

2.2 Incomplete Information

According to homo oeconomicus, the prototype of an economic man, consumers maximize their utility with rational decisions based on available information. Consumers under- or overestimate the value of their privacy due to incomplete information about the costs and benefits of data disclosure. For instance, since consumers often are not even aware about their data being collected at all, they do have incomplete information about the market value of their personal data. Also users do not know about consequences of their data being used for profiling or linkage with other data sources. From the background of complete information about the value of their data (benefits) and potential risks (costs) consumers would be able to calculate the right balance between costs and benefits and maximize utility. Incomplete information prevents users from acting rationally and maximizing utility. Nevertheless, from their subjective point of view and within their limited boundaries of reasoning, data disclosure may appear rational for users themselves. From an objective third person's point of view, i.e. having complete information, privacy behavior may appear contradictory, cost-neglecting, and irrational.

Others have argued against the assumption of complete information. Acquisti and Grossklags (2009) share the view that incomplete information complicates privacy decision making[15]. Subjects have to consider multiple layers of outcomes and associated probabilities and not just deterministic outcomes. This leads to highly imprecise estimates of the likelihood and consequences of adverse events. Eventually, privacy threats and protection modes are ignored altogether. The authors favor the view that in most privacy decision making situations it is unrealistic to assume the existence of known or unknown probabilities or subjective beliefs for probabilities over outcomes. Besides acting on incomplete information people posses no consistent preferences between alternatives, they do not chose the utility maximizing option, they do not discount future events consistently, and they do not know the probability distributions over outcomes. Instead, individuals' rationality is bounded, heuristics are applied for privacy decisions and biases affect consumers' behavior whenever they compare alternatives, perceive risks, and discount values. In contrast to risk-awareness where probabilities of possible random outcomes are objectively known, uncertain and ambiguous decision outcomes are not pre-determined and thus probabilities cannot be objectively known.

2.3 Bounded Rationality

Bounded rationality states that human decision making is bounded by nature and so decisions often result in wrong or biased conclusions[16]. Consumers under- or overestimate the risk of data disclosure. Underestimating risks due to limited cognitive abilities explains paradoxical behavior in privacy decision making. Like the possibility of having complete information, bounded rationality assumes the possibility of unbounded rationality leading to objectively right and unbiased conclusions. Privacy decisions resulting in wrong or biased conclusions are essentially irrational as outcomes are not Pareto-optimal and thus inefficient. Again, from a subjective point of view, disclosing personal data despite privacy concerns may appear quite rational to the subjects themselves. This confusion of ontological and epistemological categories, i.e. subjective and objective rationality, however, is problematic. There are no truly rational decisions based on all facts for or against all possible courses of action. Cumulative aggregations of facts about the world, by themselves, are meaningless[17]. To capture significance or involvement, they must be assigned relevance. However, such an assignment of relevance just adds more meaningless facts, a problem that very quickly leads to infinite regress. Facts are essentially meaningless because they are indeterminate up to the point in time an actual decision is made. Nevertheless, uncertain and ambiguous outcomes may have an effect on privacy decision making. As put forth by Tversky and Kahnemann (1981), the way a problem or question is framed affects how subjects respond[18]. For instance, Acquisti and Grossklags (2005) showed impacts on willingness to accept or reject a privacy-related offer when consequences of the offer are re-framed in uncertain or ambiguous terms[19].

2.4 Decision Biases

Other attempts to explain the privacy paradox refer to decision biases. For instance, the time frame costs and benefits are perceived lead to decision biases. In observations of hyperbolic discounting subjects prefer rewards that arrive sooner[20], e.g. benefits derived from using a search engine, compared to long-term risks such as potential data breaches. Such immediate gratification is stronger than future privacy concerns. For instance, the chance to socialize with peer group members immediately beyond restrictions of analogous communication overweighs potential privacy threats.

Besides biases related to time frames the tangibility of decision factors plays a role in privacy decision making. Privacy, i.e. the right to informational self-determination, is less tangible than risks associated with physical harm such as becoming ill or having an accident. Acquisti (2004) presents a model on privacy behavior grounded in the tendency to trade-off privacy costs and benefits in a way that may be inconsistent with privacy intentions leading to damages in the future[21]. Users draw less attention to privacy risks which require their active intervention, or prevention, than to risks they are exposed to more passively but which they can imagine more illustratively.

In [15] several other biases are suggested to drive privacy decision making. For instance, the valence effect refers to the tendency to overestimate the likelihood of favorable events. People tend to think privacy harms to other users is more likely than to themselves. Rational ignorance is another effect that occurs when costs of learning are higher than potential benefits gained from a decision. For example, consumers may consider costs for reading privacy policies too high compared to the expected benefit of using a service.

As technical mean to influence biases in privacy decision making privacy statements are meant to foster consumers to act in accordance with their privacy preferences. However, studies show that simply stating privacy guidelines does not avoid the privacy paradox[22]. To reduce discrepancies between stated preferences and actual behavior privacy statements do not have an impact on most users' behavior. Rather simplified social interaction appears to influence privacy decision biases. Drawing from[7] Berendt et al. (2005) argue that simplifying communication plays a role for opinion change in privacy decision making. They refer to ELIZA, an electronic psychotherapist developed by Joseph Weizenbaum in the 1960s, who, in the course of interaction, became a trusted interaction partner. This appears to be in accordance with one of the basic drivers in human communication and language acquisition, i.e. cooperative behavior in terms of sharing attitudes and informing others helpfully[23].

From a sociological point of view, peer group pressure plays an important role in privacy decision making. People disclose information to conform and in conforming they pose threats to their privacy. Opting out becomes hardly possible if exclusion from the group is undesirable. For instance, members of social groups using social networks as their primary communication medium put pressure on their peer group members to do likewise, i.e. share information and conform to social norms. Peer group members not conforming to communication and information sharing rituals are sanctioned with attention deprivation and exclusion from the social group. Opting out and privacy protection becomes increasingly difficult the more group members agree on information sharing as a basic principle constituting their affiliation. Social desirability biases may contaminate intentions to disclose personal information in such a way that stated preferences are not predictive for actual disclosure behavior anymore[24].

In summary, there are several fruitful attempts to explain the privacy paradox. Incomplete information measures privacy decision outcomes from the background of complete knowledge of all relevant facts. Bounded rationality measures decision outcomes from the background of decisions made without cognitive limitations. Eventually, decision biases consider social, cognitive and emotional factors influencing privacy decision making. Several explanatory gaps can be derived from the forgoing discussion.

Explanatory attempts discussed so far consider uncertainty to be inherent in privacy decision making. However, preferences guiding privacy decisions often are not merely revealed but realized only when the decision is made. In such cases uncertainty is not due to lack of information where costs and benefits are assumed to be out there readily determined though not yet known. Rather uncertain events are indeterminate[25]. Thus distinctions between complete and incomplete information as well as bounded and unbounded rationality become obsolete. Privacy decisions based on preferences which are not due to lack of information and cognitive limitations are inherently context-dependent. Explanatory attempts taking decision biases into account point to the right direction by explaining paradoxical behavior with dependence upon contextual factors. The disparity between stated preferences and actual behavior is not a contradiction but depends on the psychological and sociological context. Thus from the background of a high valuation of privacy personal data disclosure is not necessarily irrational. In the next section, we describe stated preferences and actual behavior as two non-commuting observations of incompatible preferences (types).

3   Indeterminacy and Noncommutativity

More recently several attempts to describe human decision making with the tools borrowed from quantum theory emerged[4,5] thereby offering a new perspective of phenomena like the privacy paradox. This new perspective allows incorporating effects like indeterminacy, i.e. the outcome of a decision making process is determined at the time the decision is made but not prior to it, and noncommutativity, i.e. two decisions A and B are not interchangeable, in descriptions of privacy decision making. These effects are common in daily situations[26] but hardly considered in behavioral studies of privacy. To our best knowledge quantum effects haven't been considered in a privacy context yet.

In the context of information technology, the quantum formalism has been applied for several descriptions of indeterminate and contextual phenomena. Bruza et al. (2008) entangles words and their meanings[27]. In their work they show that in certain contextual situations, the semantics of words represented as vectors combine in a way that instances of combined words are neither typical for one nor the other constituent. Piworawski and Lalmas (2009) come up with a vector model for information retrieval based on quantum interaction[28]. Flender et al. (2009) applies quantum effects to data and process models and describes how part-whole relationships and view updates appear under a new light[29,30]. One of the earliest approaches to a generalization of quantum effects is the model of a State-Context-Property (SCoP)-System and can be found in Aerts and Gabora (2005)[31,32].

With their contribution to behavioral economics, Lambert-Mogiliansky et al. (2009) present an approach to modeling decision situations in which preferences (types) of agents emerge indeterminately as the outcome of an interaction process between agent and environment[25]. According to quantum theory, decision situations are modeled as observables, i.e. linear operators. The decision making itself is analogous to the measurement process in quantum experiments. It projects the initial state of an agent into the subspace of the preference space associated with the eigenvalue corresponding with the choice made, i.e. the type or preference is not revealed as it wasn't determined prior to the choice; rather it is constructed with the choice made. The authors come up with an example from cognitive psychology showing that cognitive dissonant behavior can be modeled in terms of type indeterminacy. Their example draws from a study about workers in risky industries neglecting safety regulations. Before starting a risky job, however, workers were reasonably averse to risk. In cognitive psychology, this phenomenon is called cognitive dissonance[33]. People modify their types or preferences in response to discomfort arising from conflicting preferences, e.g. not using safety tools despite high risk awareness. Both decision situations can be modeled as observables with eigenvalues of two choices. Job seekers are either adventurous (1) or habit prone (2) whereas workers are either risk-averse (1) or risk-loving (2) when it comes to applying safety measures at work. Lambert-Mogiliansky et al. (2009) showed that both decision situations do not commute and thus preferences are incompatible.

In the following we consider the privacy paradox in a similar fashion. For a complete description of the privacy paradox stated preferences and actual behavior are necessary but mutually exclusive observations. Privacy behavior is not irrational due to incomplete information about risks or limited cognitive capacity. The disparity between the two decisions comes from the fact that subjects are not in the same state. Like in the job seeking example, the situation where consumers make a decision about their valuation of privacy is represented by an operator that does not commute with the operator representing the situation where consumers actually disclose or conceal data.

Two decision situations involving a sequence of two non-commuting privacy decisions are given. For each decision there are two choices. For an observable X there is a decision about privacy valuation to be made. Choice x_1 stands for a high valuation, choice x_2 refers to a low valuation. Another observable refers to Y. Here subjects disclose personal data with choice y_1, or they conceal personal data with choice y_2.

In a first scenario users are confronted with decision situation Y. Either they disclose data (y_1) or they refrain from disclosure (y_2). The initial state of the user X is written in terms of a linear superposition of two eigenvectors representing choices. Superposition states afford to get actualized in relation to a specific context, or observation.

$$|\psi\rangle = a_1|x_1\rangle + a_2|x_2\rangle \tag{1}$$

where $a_1^2 + a_2^2 = 1$. The vectors can be written in terms of eigenvectors of Y.

$$|x_1\rangle = b_{11}|y_1\rangle + b_{12}|y_2\rangle \tag{2}$$
$$|x_2\rangle = b_{21}|y_1\rangle + b_{22}|y_2\rangle \tag{3}$$

The superposition state $|\psi\rangle$ is now written in terms of of eigenvectors of Y.

$$|\psi\rangle = (a_1 b_{11} + a_2 b_{21})|y_1\rangle + (a_1 b_{12} + a_2 b_{22})|y_2\rangle \tag{4}$$

The probability that a subject discloses personal data is expressed as follows.

$$\mathbf{Pr}_Y(y_1) = \langle y_1|\psi\rangle^2 = (a_1 b_{11} + a_2 b_{21})^2$$
$$= a_1^2 b_{11}^2 + a_2^2 b_{21}^2 + 2a_1 a_2 b_{11} b_{21} \tag{5}$$

In a second scenario users first value their privacy (X), then they decide if they disclose personal data (Y).

$$\mathbf{Pr}_{YX}(y_1) = \mathbf{Pr}_X(x_1)\mathbf{Pr}_Y(y_1|x_1) + \mathbf{Pr}_X(x_2)\mathbf{Pr}_Y(y_1|x_2)$$
$$= a_1^2 b_{11}^2 + a_2^2 b_{21}^2 \tag{6}$$

Now we can give a formal representation of the privacy paradox.

$$\mathbf{Pr}_{YX}(y_1) < \mathbf{Pr}_Y(y_1) \tag{7}$$

The privacy paradox occurs in case of a positive interference between both decision situations, i.e. $2a_1 a_2 b_{11} b_{21} > 0$. In quantum physics, the interference effect occurs due to matter and energy both exhibiting wave-like and particle-like properties but not both at the same time, i.e., not within the same context. In different contexts or experimental arrangements some matter seems more particle-like than wave-like. With reduced values of energy (change of context) the same matter will be more likely to show wave-like qualities than particle-like properties. All the information about a particle is encoded in its wave function, which is analogous to the amplitude of a wave at each point in space. This function evolves according to a differential equation (the Schrödinger equation) and so gives rise to interference. Interference occurs when the interaction of two or more waves, e.g., one wave representing observer and the other one standing for the observed system, influences their direction of propagation characterized by crests and troughs. When two or more waves reach the same point in space at the same time, they either add up (the crests arrive together which is called in-phase) or cancel each other out (the crest from one wave meets a trough from another wave which is called out-of-phase). The state of a wave-like property is called superposition or potentiality state and represented as a vector $|\psi\rangle$. Its linear combination, the superposition or addition of two or more states, resembles an interference pattern typical of waves.

We assume data is disclosed $|\psi\rangle = |y_1\rangle$. Moreover, we assume that most users disclose personal data while at the same time being highly concerned about their privacy. This assumption is reasonable as empirical studies witness generous data disclosure despite high risk awareness (cf. section 2). Let $\mathbf{Pr}(x_1|\psi) = 0.8$ and $\mathbf{Pr}(x_2|\psi) = 0.2$. Accordingly, $|a_1| = \sqrt{0.8}$ and $|a_2| = \sqrt{0.2}$ and likewise $|b_{11}| = \sqrt{0.8}$ and $|b_{21}| = \sqrt{0.2}$.

In order to get the probability of y_1 in Y we use (5).

$$1 = \langle y_1|\psi\rangle^2 = a_1^2 b_{11}^2 + a_2^2 b_{21}^2 + 2a_1 a_2 b_{11} b_{21}$$
$$= 0.64 + 0.04 + 2a_1 a_2 b_{11} b_{21}$$
$$= 0.68 + 2a_1 a_2 b_{11} b_{21} \tag{8}$$

(8) implies that the interference effect is positive and equals $1 - 0.68 = 0.32$. In context X the probability for disclosing data is given by (6). It is the same sum as in (5), but without the interference term.

$$\mathbf{Pr}_{YX}(y_1) = 0.68 \tag{9}$$

The privacy paradox occurs due to $\mathbf{Pr}_Y(y_1) > \mathbf{Pr}_{YX}(y_1)$. The choices between low/high privacy valuation and data disclosure/concealment are observations of two incompatible types (or preferences) represented by two noncommuting observables. Privacy valuation refers to an abstract perception of risk. The decision to disclose data refers to a motivational perception of concrete benefits. The two modes are incompatible, the subject is cognitively dissonant.

4 Transparency and Trust

Our economy increasingly relies on personal data. Many service providers offer their services for free and collect personal data in exchange. At the same time consumers become increasingly transparent with regard to their preferences and this raises concerns over the erosion of their privacy. Moreover, the disparity between stated preferences and actual behavior, i.e. the privacy paradox, may not only turn out to be disadvantageous for consumers. Also for service providers this may have negative consequences. Consumers confronted with their paradoxical behavior, e.g. when finding out about their personal data being used without consent, may react with resentment, which may cause damage to customer relationships[1].

From an economic point of view, the challenge is to find the right balance of measures to ensure trusted relationships between market participants. There are several options to handle privacy. Ensuring privacy through law usually lacks behind and privacy-enhancing technology is hardly accepted. Policy makers suggest providing more information about possible privacy threats will help them to make better decisions. Such information may be provided by companies, peers, or consumer advocacy groups. However, it is questionable that even with complete transparency and unbounded rationality individuals would act consistently.

As proposed here abstract risk awareness of privacy threats and concrete privacy decisions are not interchangeable, i.e. disclosing personal data prior to becoming aware of privacy risks does not equal the raising of risk awareness before revealing personal information. Privacy decisions do not commute as subjects may alter their preferences indeterminately, i.e. at the time an actual decision is made. Signaling consumers that there is uncertainty in their privacy decisions which is not due to lack of information but indeterminacy may prevent them from reacting with resentment once they find out about the state of their privacy.

In the near future we will look at transparency mechanisms bearing the potential to reduce the disparity between stated preferences and actual behavior. Privacy statements were not found to be effective[22]. They rather suggest an information surfeit.

References

1. Adams, A.: The Implications of Users' Multimedia Privacy Perceptions on Communication and Information Privacy Policies. In: Proceedings of Telecommunications Policy Research Conference (1999)
2. Akerlof, G., Dickens, W.: The Economic Consequences of Cognitive Dissonance. The American Economic Review 72, 307–319 (1982)
3. Müller, G., Flender, C., Peters, M.: Vertrauensinfrastruktur und Privatheit als ökonomische Fragestellung. In: Internet Privacy - Eine multidisziplinäre Bestandsaufnahme - A Multidisciplinary Analysis, pp. 143–189. Springer (2012)
4. Busemeyer, J., Wang, Z., Townsend, J.: Quantum Dynamics of Human Decision Making. Journal of Mathematical Psychology 50, 220–241 (2006)
5. Busemeyer, J.R., Lambert-Mogiliansky, A.: An Exploration of Type Indeterminacy in Strategic Decision-Making. In: Bruza, P., Sofge, D., Lawless, W., van Rijsbergen, K., Klusch, M. (eds.) QI 2009. LNCS, vol. 5494, pp. 113–127. Springer, Heidelberg (2009)
6. Westin, A.: Privacy and Freedom. Atheneum, New York (1967)
7. Spiekermann, S., Grossklags, J., Berendt, B.: E-Privacy in 2nd Generation E-Commerce: Privacy Preferences vs. Actual Behavior. In: Proceedings of the 3rd ACM Conference on Electronic Commerce, pp. 38–47. ACM (2001)
8. Norberg, P., Horne, D., Horne, D.: The Privacy Paradox: Personal Information Disclosure Intentions vs. Behaviors. Journal of Consumer Affairs 41, 100–126 (2007)
9. Dwyer, C., Hiltz, S., Passerini, K.: Trust and Privacy Concern Within Social Networking Sites: A Comparison of Facebook and MySpace. In: Proceedings of AMCIS 2007 (2007)
10. Sheehan, K., Hoy, M.: Flaming, Complaining, Abstaining: How Online Users Respond to Privacy Concerns. Journal of Advertising, 37–51 (1999)
11. Sayre, S., Horne, D.: Trading Secrets for Savings: How Concerned are Consumers About Club Cards as a Privacy Threat? Advances in Consumer Research 27, 151–155 (2000)
12. Awad, N., Krishnan, M.: The Personalization Privacy Paradox: An Empirical Evaluation of Information Transparency and the Willingness to be Profiled Online for Personalization. MIS Quarterly, 13–28 (2006)
13. Acquisti, A., Grossklags, J.: Privacy and Rationality in Individual Decision Making. IEEE Security & Privacy 3, 26–33 (2005)

14. Deuker, A.: Addressing the Privacy Paradox by Expanded Privacy Awareness –
    The Example of Context-Aware Services. In: Bezzi, M., Duquenoy, P., Fischer-
    Hübner, S., Hansen, M., Zhang, G. (eds.) IFIP AICT 320. IFIP AICT, vol. 320,
    pp. 275–283. Springer, Heidelberg (2010)
15. Acquisti, A., Grossklags, J.: What Can Behavioral Economics Teach Us About
    Privacy? Digital Privacy: Theory, Technologies and Practices, 363–380 (2009)
16. Simon, H.: Models of Bounded Rationality: Empirically Grounded Economic Rea-
    son. The MIT Press (1997)
17. Dreyfus, H.L.: What Computers Still Can't Do: A Critique of Artificial Reason.
    MIT Press (1992)
18. Tversky, A., Kahneman, D.: The Framing of Decisions and the Psychology of
    Choice. Science 211, 453–458 (1981)
19. Acquisti, A., Grossklags, J.: Uncertainty, Ambiguity and Privacy. In: Fourth An-
    nual Workshop Economics and Information Security (WEIS 2005), MA, pp. 2–3
    (2005)
20. Acquisti, A., Grossklags, J.: Losses, Gains, and Hyperbolic Discounting: An Exper-
    imental Approach to Information Security Attitudes and Behavior. In: 2nd Annual
    Workshop on Economics and Information Security - WEIS, vol. 3 (2003)
21. Acquisti, A.: Privacy in Electronic Commerce and the Economics of Immediate
    Gratification. In: Proceedings of the 5th ACM Conference on Electronic Commerce,
    pp. 21–29. ACM (2004)
22. Berendt, B., Günther, O., Spiekermann, S.: Privacy in E-Commerce: Stated Pref-
    erences vs. Actual Behavior. Communications of the ACM 48, 101–106 (2005)
23. Tomasello, M.: Origins of Human Communication. The MIT Press (2008)
24. Milne, G.: Consumer Participation in Mailing Lists: A Field Experiment. Journal
    of Public Policy & Marketing, 298–309 (1997)
25. Lambert Mogiliansky, A., Zamir, S., Zwirn, H.: Type Indeterminacy: A Model
    of the KT (Kahneman-Tversky)-Man. Journal of Mathematical Psychology 53,
    349–361 (2009)
26. Atmanspacher, H.: Quantenphysik und Quantenalltag. In: Die Welt im Bild: Wel-
    tentwürfe in Kunst, Literatur und Wissenschaft seit der Frühen Neuzeit, pp.
    293–305. Fink, Paderborn (2010)
27. Bruza, P., Kitto, K., Nelson, D., McEvoy, K.: Entangling Words and Meaning. In:
    Proceedings of QI 2008. University of Oxford (2008)
28. Piwowarski, B., Lalmas, M.: Structured Information Retrieval and Quantum The-
    ory. In: Bruza, P., Sofge, D., Lawless, W., van Rijsbergen, K., Klusch, M. (eds.)
    QI 2009. LNCS, vol. 5494, pp. 289–298. Springer, Heidelberg (2009)
29. Flender, C., Kitto, K., Bruza, P.: Beyond Ontology in Information Systems. In:
    Bruza, P., Sofge, D., Lawless, W., van Rijsbergen, K., Klusch, M. (eds.) QI 2009.
    LNCS, vol. 5494, pp. 276–288. Springer, Heidelberg (2009)
30. Flender, C.: A Quantum Interpretation of the View-update Problem. In: Proceed-
    ings of the 21st Australasian Conference on Database Technologies, vol. 104, pp.
    67–74 (2010)
31. Aerts, D., Gabora, L.: A State-Context-Property Model of Concepts and their
    Combinations I: The Structure of the Sets of Contexts and Properties. Kyber-
    netes 34(1&2), 167–191 (2005)
32. Aerts, D., Gabora, L.: A State-Context-Property Model of Concepts and their
    Combinations II: A Hilbert Space Representation. Kybernetes 34(1&2), 192–221
    (2005)
33. Festinger, L.: A Theory of Cognitive Dissonance. Stanford University Press (1957)

Adaptive Dynamics and Its Application to Context Dependent Systems Breaking the Classical Probability Law

Masanari Asano[1], Irina Basieva[2], Andrei Khrennikov[2], Masanori Ohya[1], Yoshiharu Tanaka[1], and Ichiro Yamato[3]

[1] Department of Information Sciences, Tokyo University of Science, Yamasaki 2641, Noda-shi, Chiba, 278-8510 Japan
[2] International Center for Mathematical Modeling in Physics and Cognitive Sciences, Linnaeus University, S-35195, Växjö, Sweden
[3] Department of Biological Science and Technology, Tokyo University of Science Yamasaki 2641, Noda-shi, Chiba, 278-8510 Japan

Abstract. There exist several phenomena (systems) breaking the classical probability laws. In this report, we present a new mathematical formula to compute the probability in those context dependent systems by using the concepts of the adaptive dynamics and the lifting.

Keywords: classical probability law, quantum probability, adaptive dynamics, quantum channel, lifting map.

1   Introduction

Several phenomena (systems) breaking the usual probability laws in such as quantum interference in cognitive science, the game of prisoner's dilemma (PD game), the lactose-glucose interference in *E. coli* growth have been considered[1]–[13]. The PD game was considered by taking account of the players' minds [13, 14]. The lactose-glucose interference is studied by the quantum interference [15].

These phenomena (systems) will require us to change the usual probability law. One of our trials is to make a new rule of probability which is the updating the Bayesian law [16]. It is important to notice that these phenomena are contextual dependent, so that they are adaptive to the surroundings.

In such systems, the conditional probability can not be defined in usual mathematical framework. It is well-known that in quantum systems the conditional probability does not exist (see the section 3) in the sense of classical systems, so that the naive total probability law should be reconsidered. Same situation is occurred even in non-quantum systems.

Let us consider a simple and intuitive example: When one takes sugar S and chocolate C and he is asked whether it is sweet (1) or not so (0). Then the simple classical probability law may not be satisfied, that is,

$$P(C = 1) \neq P(C = 1|S = 1)P(S = 1) + P(C = 1|S = 0)P(S = 0)$$

J.R. Busemeyer et al. (Eds.): QI 2012, LNCS 7620, pp. 160–171, 2012.

because the LHS $P(C = 1)$ will be very close to 1 but the RHS will be less than $\frac{1}{2}$. After taking very sweet sugar, he will taste the chocolate is not so sweet. Taking sugar changes his taste, i.e., the situation of the tongue changes. The conditional probability should be defined on the basis of such a change, so that it is observable-adaptive quantity. The $P(C = i|S = j)$ should be written as $P_{\text{adap}}(C = i|S = j)$ and its proper mathematical description (definition) should be given, that is, we will give a mathematical formula to compute the LHS and the RHS above.

In this report, we present a mathematical framework for the study of these context dependent systems.

2   Adaptive Dynamics

The idea of the adaptive dynamics has implicitly appeared in series of papers [18, 19, 21–27] for the study of compound dynamics, chaos and the SAT algorithm. The name of the adaptive dynamics was deliberately used in [28]. The AD has two aspects, one of which is the "observable-adaptive" and another is the "state-adaptive". *The observable-adaptive dynamics is a dynamics characterized as follows: (1) Measurement depends on how to see an observable to be measured. (2)The interaction between two systems depends on how a fixed observable exists. The state-adaptive dynamics is a dynamics characterized asfollows: (1)Measurement depends on how the state to be used exists. (2)The correlation between two systems interaction depends on how the state of at least one of the systems at one instant exists.* The idea of observable-adaptivity comes from studying chaos. We claimed that any observation will be unrelated or even contradicted to mathematical universalities such as taking limits, sup, inf, etc. Observation of chaos is a result due to taking suitable scales of, for example, time, distance or domain, and it will not be possible in the limiting cases. Examples of the observable-adaptivity are used to understand chaos [19, 26] and examine the violation of Bell's inequality, namely the chameleon dynamics of Accardi [29]. The idea of the state-adaptivity is implicitly started in constructing a compound state for quantum communication [17, 18, 20, 21]. Examples of the state-adaptivity are seen in an algorithm solving NP complete problem, i.e., a pending problem for more than 30 years asking whether there exists an algorithm solving a NP complete problem in polynomial time, as discussed [23, 24, 27].

3   Conditional Probability and Joint Probability in Quantum Systems

The conditional probability and the joint probability do not generally exist in quantum system, which is an essential difference from classical system. First of all, let us fix the notations to be used throughout in this paper. We will review these facts for the sequel uses.

Let $\mathcal{H}$, $\mathcal{K}$ be the Hilbert spaces describing the system of interest, $\mathcal{S}(\mathcal{H})$ be the set of all states or probability measures on $\mathcal{H}$, $\mathcal{O}(\mathcal{H})$ be the set of all observables or events on $\mathcal{H}$ and $\mathcal{P}(\mathcal{H}) \subset \mathcal{O}(\mathcal{H})$ be the set of projections in $\mathcal{O}(\mathcal{H})$.

In classical probability, the joint probability for two events A and B is $\mu(A \cap B)$ and the conditional probability is defined by

$$\frac{\mu(A \cap B)}{\mu(B)}.$$

In quantum probability, if the von Neumann-Lüder projection rule is correct, after a measurement of $F \in \mathcal{P}(\mathcal{H})$, a state ρ is considered to be

$$\rho_F = \frac{F\rho F}{\mathrm{tr}\rho F}.$$

When we observe an event $E \in \mathcal{P}(\mathcal{H})$, the expectation value becomes

$$\mathrm{tr}\rho_F E = \frac{\mathrm{tr}F\rho FE}{\mathrm{tr}\rho F} = \frac{\mathrm{tr}\rho FEF}{\mathrm{tr}\rho F}. \tag{1}$$

This expectation value can be a candidate of the *conditional probability in QP (quantum probability)*.

There is another candidate for the conditional probability in QP, which is a direct generalization of CP (classical probability).

This alternative expression of joint probability and the conditional probability in QP are expressed as

$$\varphi(E \wedge F) \quad \text{and} \quad \frac{\varphi(E \wedge F)}{\varphi(F)}, \tag{2}$$

where φ is a state (a measure) and $\wedge$ is the meet of two events (projections) corresponding to $\cap$ in CP, and for the state describing by a density operator, we have

$$\varphi(\cdot) = \mathrm{tr}\rho(\cdot).$$

We ask when the above two expressions (1) and (2) in QP are equivalent. From the next proposition, $\varphi(\cdot \wedge F)/\varphi(F)$ is not a probability measure (state) on $\mathcal{P}(\mathcal{H})$.

Proposition 1. *(1) When E commutes with F, the above two expressions are equivalent, namely,*

$$\frac{\varphi(FEF)}{\varphi(F)} = \frac{\varphi(E \wedge F)}{\varphi(F)}.$$

(2) When $EF \neq FE$, $\frac{\varphi(\cdot \wedge F)}{\varphi(F)}$ is not a probability on $\mathcal{P}_{\mathcal{H}}$, so that the above two expressions are not equivalent.

Proof. (1) $EF = FE$ implies $E \wedge F = EF$ and $FEF = EFF = EF^2 = EF$, so that

$$\frac{\varphi(E \wedge F)}{\varphi(F)} = \frac{\varphi(FEF)}{\varphi(F)} = \frac{\varphi(EF)}{\varphi(F)}.$$

(2) Put $K_\varphi(E \mid F) \equiv \frac{\varphi(E \wedge F)}{\varphi(F)}$ and put $z \in linsp\{x, y\}$, $z \neq x, y$ for any $x, y \in \mathcal{H}$. Take the projections $P_x = |x\rangle\langle x|$, $P_y = |y\rangle\langle y|$, $P_z = |z\rangle\langle z|$ such that $(P_x \vee P_y) \wedge P_z = P_z$ and $P_x \wedge P_z = 0 = P_y \wedge P_z$. Then

$$K_\varphi(P_x \vee P_y \mid P_z) = K_\varphi(P_z \mid P_z) \neq 0, \quad K_\varphi(P_x \mid P_z) + K_\varphi(P_y \mid P_z) = 0.$$

Therefore

$$K_\varphi(P_x \vee P_y \mid P_z) \neq K_\varphi(P_x \mid P_z) + K_\varphi(P_y \mid P_z)$$

so that $K_\varphi(\cdot \mid P_z)$ is not a probability measure on $\mathcal{P}_\mathcal{H}$.

In CP, the joint distribution for two random variables f and g is expressed as

$$\mu_{f,g}(\Delta_1, \Delta_2) = \mu\left(f^{-1}(\Delta_1) \cap g^{-1}(\Delta_2)\right)$$

for any Borel sets $\Delta_1, \Delta_2 \in B(\mathbb{R})$. The corresponding quantum expression is either

$$\varphi_{A,B}(\Delta_1, \Delta_2) = \varphi(E_A(\Delta_1) \wedge E_B(\Delta_2)) \quad \text{or} \quad \varphi(E_A(\Delta_1) \cdot E_B(\Delta_2))$$

for two observables A, B and their spectral measures $E_A(\cdot)$, $E_B(\cdot)$ such that

$$A = \int aE_A(da), \quad B = \int bE_B(da).$$

It is easily checked that neither one of the above expressions satisfies neither the condition of probability measure nor the marginal condition unless $AB = BA$, so that they can not be the joint quantum probability in the classical sense.

Let us explain the above situation, as an example, in a physical measurement process. When an observable A has a discrete decomposition like

$$A = \sum_k a_k F_k, \quad F_i \perp F_j \ (i \neq j),$$

the probability obtaining a_k by measurement in a state ρ is

$$p_k = \mathrm{tr}\rho F_k$$

and the state ρ is changed to a (conditional) state ρ_k such that

$$\rho_k = \frac{F_k \rho F_k}{\mathrm{tr}\rho F_k}.$$

After the measurement of A, we will measure a similar type observable B (i.e., $B = \sum_j b_j E_j$, $(E_i \perp E_j \ (i \neq j))$) and the probability obtaining b_j after we have obtained the above a_k for the measurement of A is given by

$$p_{jk} = (\mathrm{tr}\rho F_k)(\mathrm{tr}\rho_k E_j) = \mathrm{tr}\rho F_k E_j F_k = P_\rho(E_j|F_k)\mathrm{tr}\rho F_k., \tag{3}$$

where $P_\rho(E_j|F_k) = \mathrm{tr}\rho_k E_j$. This p_{jk} satisfies

$$\sum_{j,k} p_{jk} = 1, \quad \sum_j p_{jk} = \mathrm{tr}\rho F_k = p_k, \tag{4}$$

but not

$$\sum_k p_{jk} = \text{tr}\rho E_j$$

unless $E_j F_k = F_k E_j$ $(\forall j, k)$ so that p_{jk} is not considered as a joint quantum probability distribution. More intuitive expression breaking the usual classical probability law is the following:

$$p_{jk} = P(B=b_j \,|\, A=a_k)P(A=a_k) \text{ and } P(B=b_j) \neq \sum_k P(B=b_j \,|\, A=a_k)P(A=a_k)$$

Therefore we conclude in quantum system that the above two candidates can not satisfy the properties of both conditional and joint probabilities in the sense of classical system.

The above discussion shows that the order of the measurement of two observables A and B is essential and it gives us a different expectation value, hence the state changes.

4   Lifting and Joint Probability

In order to partially solve the difficulty of the nonexistence of joint quantum distribution, the notion of compound state satisfying the marginal condition is useful. In this section we discuss a bit general notion named "lifting"[27] to discuss new scheme of probability containing both classical and quantum.

Definition 1. *Let $\mathcal{A}_1, \mathcal{A}_2$ be C^*-algebras and let $\mathcal{A}_1 \otimes \mathcal{A}_2$ be a fixed C^*-tensor product of $\mathcal{A}_1$ and $\mathcal{A}_2$. A lifting from $\mathcal{A}_1$ to $\mathcal{A}_1 \otimes \mathcal{A}_2$ is a weak $*$-continuous map*

$$\mathcal{E}^* : \mathcal{S}(\mathcal{A}_1) \to \mathcal{S}(\mathcal{A}_1 \otimes \mathcal{A}_2)$$

If $\mathcal{E}^*$ is affine and its dual is a completely positive map, we call it a linear lifting; if it maps pure states into pure states, we call it pure.

The algebras $\mathcal{A}_1, \mathcal{A}_2$ can be considered as two systems of interest, for instance, $\mathcal{A}_1$ is an objective system for a study and $\mathcal{A}_2$ is the subjective system or the surrounding of $\mathcal{A}_1$.

Note that to every lifting from $\mathcal{A}_1$ to $\mathcal{A}_1 \otimes \mathcal{A}_2$ we can associate two channels: one from $\mathcal{A}_1$ to $\mathcal{A}_1$, defined by

$$\Lambda^* \rho_1(A_1) \equiv (\mathcal{E}^* \rho_1)(A_1 \otimes 1) \quad ; \quad \forall A_1 \in \mathcal{A}_1$$

another from $\mathcal{A}_1$ to $\mathcal{A}_2$, defined by

$$\Lambda^* \rho_1(A_2) \equiv (\mathcal{E}^* \rho_1)(1 \otimes A_2) \quad ; \quad \forall A_2 \in \mathcal{A}_2$$

In general, a state $\varphi \in \mathcal{S}(\mathcal{A}_1 \otimes \mathcal{A}_2)$ such that

$$\varphi \,|_{\mathcal{A}_1 \otimes 1} = \rho_1 \quad ; \quad \varphi \,|_{1 \otimes \mathcal{A}_2} = \rho_2$$

is called a compound state of the states $\rho_1 \in S(\mathcal{A}_1)$ and $\rho_2 \in S(\mathcal{A}_2)$. Remark here that the above compound state is nothing but the joint probability in CP.

The following problem is important in several applications: Given a state $\rho_1 \in S(\mathcal{A}_1)$ and a channel $\Lambda^* : S(\mathcal{A}_1) \to S(\mathcal{A}_2)$, find a standard lifting $\mathcal{E}^* : S(\mathcal{A}_1) \to S(\mathcal{A}_1 \otimes \mathcal{A}_2)$ such that $\mathcal{E}^* \rho_1$ is a compound state of ρ_1 and $\Lambda^* \rho_1$. Several particular solutions of this problem have been proposed by Ohya, Ceccini and Petz, however an explicit description of all the possible solutions to this problem is still missing, which might be related to find a new scheme of probability theory.

However it is not true that one can resolve the difficulty of quantum probability if one can solve this problem. The compound state corresponds to the joint probability in classical systems, but there is still ambiguity to define the conditional state in quantum systems. As pointed out in Introduction, the usual conditional probability meets an inadequacy to interpret a certain phenomenon, in which it is important not to manage to set the conditional state by mimicking the classical one but to make a mathematical rule to set new treatment of probabilistic aspects of such a phenomenon.

Definition 2. *A lifting from $\mathcal{A}_1$ to $\mathcal{A}_1 \otimes \mathcal{A}_2$ is called non-demolition for a state $\rho_1 \in S(\mathcal{A}_1)$ if ρ_1 is invariant for Λ^* i.e., if for all $a_1 \in \mathcal{A}_1$*

$$(\mathcal{E}^* \rho_1)(a_1 \otimes 1) = \rho_1(a_1)$$

The idea of this definition being that the interaction with system 2 does not alter the state of system 1.

Definition 3. *A transition expectation from $\mathcal{A}_1 \otimes \mathcal{A}_2$ to $\mathcal{A}_1$ is a completely positive linear map $\mathcal{E}^* : \mathcal{A}_1 \otimes \mathcal{A}_2 \to \mathcal{A}_1$ satisfying*

$$\mathcal{E}^*(1_{\mathcal{A}_1} \otimes 1_{\mathcal{A}_2}) = 1_{\mathcal{A}_1}.$$

Let an initial state (resp. input signal) is changed (resp. transmitted) to the final state (resp. output state) due to a dynamics Λ^* (resp. channel). Here $\mathcal{A}_1$ (resp. $\mathcal{A}_2$) is interpreted as the algebra of observables of the input (resp. output) system and $\mathcal{E}^*$ describes the interaction between the input and the output. If $\rho_1 \in S(\mathcal{A}_1)$ is the initial state, then the state $\rho_2 = \Lambda^* \rho_1 \in S(\mathcal{A}_2)$ is the output state.

In several important applications, the state ρ_1 of the system before the interaction (preparation, input signal) is not known and one would like to know this state knowing only $\Lambda^* \rho_1 \in S(\mathcal{A}_2)$, i.e., the state of the apparatus after the interaction (output signal). From a mathematical point of view this problem is not well posed, since the map Λ^* is usually not invertible. The best one can do in such cases is to acquire a control on the description of those input states which have the same image under Λ^* and then choose among them according to some statistical criterion.

Let us show some important examples of liftings and channels below

Example 1. : **Isometric lifting.**

Let $V : \mathcal{H}_1 \to \mathcal{H}_1 \otimes \mathcal{H}_2$ be an isometry $V^*V = 1_{\mathcal{H}_1}$. Then the map

$$\mathcal{E} : x \in \mathbf{B}(\mathcal{H}_1) \otimes \mathbf{B}(\mathcal{H}_2) \to V^*xV \in \mathbf{B}(\mathcal{H}_1)$$

is a transition expectation in the sense of Accardi, and the associated lifting maps a density matrix w_1 in $\mathcal{H}_1$ into

$$\mathcal{E}^*w_1 = Vw_1V^*$$

in $\mathcal{H}_1 \otimes \mathcal{H}_2$. Liftings of this type are called isometric. Every isometric lifting is a pure lifting. In this case the channel $\Lambda^* : \mathcal{H}_1 \to \mathcal{H}_1$ is given by $\mathrm{tr}_{H_2}\mathcal{E}^*$.

Example 2. Quantum measurement: If a measuring apparatus is prepared by an positive operator valued measure $\{Q_n\}$ then the state ρ changes to a state $\Lambda^*\rho$ after this measurement, $\rho \to \Lambda^*\rho = \sum_n Q_n\rho Q_n$.

Example 3. Reduction (Open system dynamics): If a system Σ_1 interacts with an external system Σ_2 described by another Hilbert space $\mathcal{K}$ and the initial states of Σ_1 and Σ_2 are ρ_1 and ρ_2, respectively, then the combined state θ_t of Σ_1 and Σ_2 at time t after the interaction between two systems is given by

$$\theta_t \equiv U_t(\rho_1 \otimes \rho_2)U_t^*,$$

where $U_t = \exp(-itH)$ with the total Hamiltonian H of Σ_1 and Σ_2. A channel is obtained by taking the partial trace w.r.t. $\mathcal{K}$ such as

$$\rho_1 \to \Lambda^*\rho_1 \equiv \mathrm{tr}_{\mathcal{K}}\theta_t.$$

Example 4. : **The compound lifting.**

Let $\Lambda^* : \mathcal{S}(\mathcal{A}_1) \to \mathcal{S}(\mathcal{A}_2)$ be a channel. For any $\rho_1 \in \mathcal{S}(\mathcal{A}_1)$ in the closed convex hull of the external states, fix a decomposition of ρ_1 as a convex combination of extremal states in $\mathcal{S}(\mathcal{A}_1)$

$$\rho_1 = \int_{\mathcal{S}(\mathcal{A}_1)} \omega_1 d\mu$$

where μ is a Borel measure on $\mathcal{S}(\mathcal{A}_1)$ with support in the extremal states, and define

$$\mathcal{E}^*\rho_1 \equiv \int_{\mathcal{S}(\mathcal{A}_1)} \omega_1 \otimes \Lambda^*\omega_1 d\mu$$

Then $\mathcal{E}^* : \mathcal{S}(\mathcal{A}_1) \to \mathcal{S}(\mathcal{A}_1 \otimes \mathcal{A}_2)$ is a lifting, nonlinear even if Λ^* is linear, and it is a nondemolition type.

The most general lifting, mapping $\mathcal{S}(\mathcal{A}_1)$ into the closed convex hull of the extremal product states on $\mathcal{A}_1 \otimes \mathcal{A}_2$ is essentially of this type. This nonlinear nondemolition lifting was first discussed by Ohya to define the compound state and the mutual entropy for quantum information communication [18, 20]. The above is a bit more general because we shall weaken the condition that μ is concentrated on the extremal states used in [18].

Therefore once a channel is given, by which a lifting of convex product type can be constructed. For example, the von Neumann quantum measurement process is written, in the terminology of lifting, as follows: Having measured a compact observable $A = \sum_n a_n P_n$ (spectral decomposition with $\sum_n P_n = I$) in a state ρ, the state after this measurement will be

$$\Lambda^* \rho = \sum_n P_n \rho P_n$$

and a lifting $\mathcal{E}^*$, of convex product type, associated to this channel Λ^* and to a fixed decomposition of ρ as $\rho = \sum_n \mu_n \rho_n$ ($\rho_n \in \mathcal{S}(\mathcal{A}_1)$) is given by :

$$\mathcal{E}^* \rho = \sum_n \mu_n \rho_n \otimes \Lambda^* \rho_n.$$

Finally we note that a channel is determined by a lifting and coversely a lifting is constructed by a channel.

5   New Views of Probability Both in Classical and Quantum Systems

In this section, I will discuss how to use the concept of lifting to explain phenomena breaking the usual probability law.

Let $\mathcal{A}, \mathcal{B}$ be C*-algebras describing the systems for a study, more specifically, let $\mathcal{A}, \mathcal{B}$ be the sets of all obserbales in Hilbert spaces $\mathcal{H}$, $\mathcal{K}$; $\mathcal{A} = \mathcal{O}(\mathcal{H})$, $\mathcal{B} = \mathcal{O}(\mathcal{K})$. Let $\mathcal{E}^*$ be a lifting from $\mathcal{S}(\mathcal{H})$ to $\mathcal{S}(\mathcal{H} \otimes \mathcal{K})$, so that its dual map $\mathcal{E}$ is a mapping from $\mathcal{A} \otimes \mathcal{B}$ to $\mathcal{A}$. There are several liftings for various different cases to be considered: (1) If $\mathcal{K}$ is $\mathbb{C}$, then the lifting $\mathcal{E}^*$ is nothing but a channel from $\mathcal{S}(\mathcal{H})$ to $\mathcal{S}(\mathcal{H})$. (2) If $\mathcal{H}$ is $\mathbb{C}$, then the lifting $\mathcal{E}^*$ is a channel from $\mathcal{S}(\mathcal{H})$ to $\mathcal{S}(\mathcal{K})$. Further $\mathcal{K}$ or $\mathcal{H}$ can be decomposed as $\mathcal{K} = \otimes_i \mathcal{K}_i$ (resp. $\oplus_i \mathcal{K}_i$), and so for $\mathcal{H}$, so that $\mathcal{B}$ can be $\otimes_i \mathcal{B}_i$ (resp. $\oplus_i \mathcal{B}_i$) and so for $\mathcal{A}$.

The adaptive dynamics is considered that the dynamics of a state or an observable after an instant (say the time t_0) attached to a system of interest is affected by the existence of some other observable and state at that instant. Let $\rho \in \mathcal{S}(\mathcal{H})$ and $A \in \mathcal{A}$ be a state and an obserbable before t_0, and let $\sigma \in \mathcal{S}(\mathcal{H} \otimes \mathcal{K})$ and $Q \in \mathcal{A} \otimes \mathcal{B}$ be a state and an observable to give an effect to the state ρ and the observable A. In many cases, the effect to the state is dual to that to the observable, so that we will discuss the effect to the state only. This effect is described by a lifting $\mathcal{E}^*_{\sigma Q}$, so that the state ρ becomes $\mathcal{E}^*_{\sigma Q} \rho$ first, then it will be $\text{tr}_{\mathcal{K}} \mathcal{E}^*_{\sigma Q} \rho \equiv \rho_{\sigma Q}$. The adaptive dynamics is the whole process such as

$$\textit{Adaptive Dynamics}: \ \rho \Rightarrow \mathcal{E}^*_{\sigma Q} \rho \Rightarrow \rho_{\sigma Q} = \text{tr}_{\mathcal{K}} \mathcal{E}^*_{\sigma Q} \rho$$

That is, what we need is how to construct the lifting for each problem to be studied. The expectation value of another observable $B \in \mathcal{A}$ or $\mathcal{A} \otimes \mathcal{B}$ in the adaptive state $\rho_{\sigma Q}$ is

$$tr \rho_{\sigma Q} B = \text{tr}_{\mathcal{H}} \text{tr}_{\mathcal{K}} B \mathcal{E}^*_{\sigma Q} \rho.$$

Now suppose that there are two quantum event systems $A = \{a_k \in \mathbb{R}, F_k \in \mathcal{A}\}$ and $B = \{b_j \in \mathbb{R}, E_j \in \mathcal{B}\}$, where we dot not assume F_k, E_j are projections but they satisfy the conditions $\sum_k F_k = I, \sum_j E_j = I$ as POVM (positive operator valued measure) corresponding to the partition of a probability space in classical system. Then the "joint-like" probability obtaining a_k and b_j might be given by the *formula*

$$P(a_k, b_j) = \text{tr} F_k \boxdot E_j \mathcal{E}^*_{\sigma Q} \rho, \tag{5}$$

where $\boxdot$ is a certain operation (relation) between A and B, more generally one can take a certain operator function $f(F_k, E_j)$ instead of $F_k \boxdot E_j$. If σ, Q are independent from any F_k, E_j and the operation $\boxdot$ is the usual tensor product $\otimes$ so that A and B can be considered in two independent systems or to be commutative, then the above "joint-like" probability becomes the joint probability. However if not such a case, e.g., Q is related to A and B, the situation will be more subtle. Therefore the problem is how to set the operation $\boxdot$ and how to construct the lifting $\mathcal{E}^*_{\sigma Q}$ in order to describe the particular problems associated to systems of interest.

5.1   State Change of Tongue for Sweetness

The first problem is not so sophisticated but very simple and common one. As considered in Introduction, when one takes sugar S and chocolate C and he is asked whether it is sweet (1) or not so (0). Then the simple classical probability law may not be satisfied, that is,

$$P(C = 1) \neq P(C = 1|S = 1)P(S = 1) + P(C = 1|S = 0)P(S = 0)$$

because the LHS $P(C = 1)$ will be very close to 1 but the RHS will be less than $1/2$. Here we start from the following neutral pure state ρ because we consider two sweet things. Let e_1 and e_0 be the orthogonal vectors describing sweet and non-sweet states, respectively. *The initial state of tongue is neutral such as*

$$\rho \equiv |x\rangle \langle x|,$$

where $x = \frac{1}{\sqrt{2}}(e_0 + e_1)$. It is enough for us to take the Hilbert space $\mathbb{C}^2$ for this problem, so that e_0 and e_1 can be set as $\binom{1}{0}$ and $\binom{0}{1}$, respectively.

When one takes "sugar", the operator corresponding to taking "sugar" will be given as

$$S = \begin{pmatrix} \lambda_0 & 0 \\ 0 & \lambda_1 \end{pmatrix},$$

where $|\lambda_0|^2 + |\lambda_1|^2 = 1$. This operator can be regarded as the square root of the sugar state σ_S;

$$\sigma_S = |\lambda_0|^2 E_0 + |\lambda_1|^2 E_1, \ E_0 = \begin{pmatrix} 1 \\ 0 \end{pmatrix}(10), E_1 = \begin{pmatrix} 0 \\ 1 \end{pmatrix}(01).$$

Taking sugar, he will taste that it is sweet with the probability $|\lambda_1|^2$ and non-sweet with the probability $|\lambda_0|^2$, so $|\lambda_1|^2$ should be much higher than $|\lambda_0|^2$ for a usual sugar. This comes from the following change of the neutral initial tongue (i.e., non-adaptive) state:

$$\rho \to \rho_S = \Lambda_S^*(\rho) \equiv \frac{S^* \rho S}{\text{tr}\,|S|^2 \rho},$$

which is the state when he takes the sugar. This is similar to the usual expression of state change in quantum dynamics, although it is adaptive for sugar. Note here that if we kill the subjectivity (personal character?) of one's tongue, then the state of tongue can be understood as

$$\bar{\rho}_S \equiv E_0 \rho_S E_0 + E_1 \rho_S E_1,$$

which is the unread objective state as usual in quantum measurement. We can use the above two expressions ρ_S and $\bar{\rho}_S$ which give us the same result for the computation of the probability.

For some time duration, the tongue becomes dull to sweetness, so the tongue state can be written by means of a certain "exchanging" operator $X = \begin{pmatrix} 0 & 1 \\ 1 & 0 \end{pmatrix}$ such that

$$\rho_S^a = X \rho_S X,$$

where "a" means the adaptive change: This operation by X is given in the situation S_{sug} that he took the sugar. Then similarly as sugar, when one takes a chocolate, the state will be $\rho_{S \to C}^a$ given by

$$\rho_{S \to C}^a = \Lambda_C^*(\rho_S^a) \equiv \frac{C^* \rho_S^a C}{\text{tr}\,|C|^2 \rho_S^a},$$

where C will be given as

$$C = \begin{pmatrix} \mu_0 & 0 \\ 0 & \mu_1 \end{pmatrix}$$

with $|\mu_0|^2 + |\mu_1|^2 = 1$. Common experience tells us that $|\lambda_1|^2 \geq |\mu_1|^2 \geq |\mu_0|^2 \geq |\lambda_0|^2$ and the first two are much larger than the last two.

As discussed in Sec. 4, the adaptive set $\{\sigma, Q\}$ is the set $\{S \,(=\sigma_S), X, C\}$, we introduce the following *nonlinear demolition* lifting:

$$\mathcal{E}_{\sigma Q}^*(\rho)(= \mathcal{E}_{S\,(=\sigma_S)XC}^a(\rho)) \equiv \rho_S \otimes \rho_{S \to C}^a = \Lambda_S^*(\rho) \otimes \Lambda_C^*(X\Lambda_S^*(\rho)X),$$

which implies the joint probabilities $P(S = j, C = k)\ (j, k = 0, 1)$ as

$$P(S = j, C = k) = \text{tr} E_j \otimes E_k \mathcal{E}_{\sigma Q}^*(\rho).$$

The probability that one tastes sweetness of the chocolate after tasting sugar is

$$P(S = 1, C = 1) + P(S = 0, C = 1) = \frac{|\lambda_0|^2 |\mu_1|^2}{|\lambda_0|^2 |\mu_1|^2 + |\lambda_1|^2 |\mu_0|^2}.$$

Note that this probability is much less than

$$P(C = 1) = \mathrm{tr}E_1\Lambda_C^*(\rho) = |\mu_1|^2,$$

which is the probability of sweetness tasted by the neutral tongue ρ. In this sense, it seems that the usual probability law

$$P(C = 1) = P(S = 1, C = 1) + P(S = 0, C = 1)$$

is not satisfied. As mentioned in the introduction, this violoation of law is natural, because the probability of LHS and the one of RHS are estimated in the different situations denoted by $S_{\neg sug}$ and S_{sug}, that is, $P_{S_{\neg sug}}(C = 1) \neq P_{S_{sug}}(C = 1)$.

The double-slit experiment in quantum mechanics and others are discussed by A. Khrennikov and Y. Tanaka in this conference. It is possible to explain these context-dependent phenomena by taking proper adaptive dynamics.

References

1. Khrennikov, A.: On Quantum-Like Probabilistic Structure of Mental Information. Open Systems and Information Dynamics 11(3), 267–275 (2004)
2. Khrennikov, A.: Quantum-like brain:"Interference of minds". BioSystems 84, 225–241 (2006)
3. Fichtner, K.-H., Fichtner, L., Freudenberg, W., Ohya, M.: On a quantum model of the recognition process. QP-PQ:Quantum Prob. White Noise Analysis 21, 64–84 (2008)
4. Busemeyer, J.B., Wang, Z., Townsend, J.T.: Quantum dynamics of human decision making. J. Math. Psychology 50, 220–241 (2006)
5. Busemeyer, J.R., Matthews, M., Wang, Z.: A Quantum Information Processing Explanation of Disjunction Effects. In: Sun, R., Myake, N. (eds.) The 29th Annual Conference of the Cognitive Science Society and the 5th International Conference of Cognitive Science, pp. 131–135. Erlbaum, Mahwah (2006)
6. Busemeyer, J.R., Santuy, E., Lambert-Mogiliansky, A.: Comparison of Markov and quantum models of decision making. In: Bruza, P., Lawless, W., van Rijsbergen, K., Sofge, D.A., Coeke, B., Clark, S. (eds.) Quantum interaction: Proceedings of the Second Quantum Interaction Symposium, pp. 68–74. College Publications, London (2008)
7. Accardi, L., Khrennikov, A., Ohya, M.: The problem of quantum-like representation in economy, cognitive science, and genetics. In: Accardi, L., Freudenberg, W., Ohya, M. (eds.) Quantum Bio-Informatics II: From Quantum Information to Bio-Informatics, pp. 1–8. WSP, Singapore (2008)
8. Accardi, L., Khrennikov, A., Ohya, M.: Quantum Markov Model for Data from Shafir-Tversky Experiments in Cognitive Psychology. Open Systems and Information Dynamics 16, 371–385 (2009)
9. Conte, E., Khrennikov, A., Todarello, O., Federici, A., Zbilut, J.P.: Mental States Follow Quantum Mechanics during Perception and Cognition of Ambiguous Figures. Open Systems and Information Dynamics 16, 1–17 (2009)
10. Khrennikov, A., Haven, E.: Quantum mechanics and violations of the sure-thing principle: the use of probability interference and other concepts. Journal of Mathematical Psychology 53, 378–388 (2009)

11. Khrennikov, A.: Ubiquitous quantum structure: from psychology to finance. Springer, Heidelberg (2010)
12. Khrennikov, A.: Contextual approach to quantum formalism. Fundamental Theories of Physics. Springer, Heidelberg (2009)
13. Asano, M., Ohya, M., Khrennikov, A.: Quantum-Like Model for Decision Making Process in Two Players Game. Foundations of Physics 41(3), 538–548 (2010)
14. Asano, M., Ohya, M., Tanaka, Y., Khrennikov, A., Basieva, I.: On application of Gorini-Kossakowski-Sudarshan-Lindblad equation in cognitive psychology. Open Systems & Information Dynamics 18(1), 55–69 (2011)
15. Basieva, I., Khrennikov, A., Ohya, M., Ichiro, Y.: Quantum-like interference effect in gene expression: glucose-lactose destructive interference. Syst. and Synth. Biol. 5(1-2), 59–68 (2010)
16. Asano, M., Ohya, M., Tanaka, Y., Khrennikov, A., Basieva, I.: Quantum-like Representation of Bayesian Updating. In: American Institute of Physics 1327: Proceedings of the International Conference on Advances in Quantum Theory, pp. 57–62 (2011)
17. Ohya, M.: Note on quantum proability. L. Nuovo Cimento 38(11), 203–206 (1983)
18. Ohya, M.: On compound state and mutual information in quantum information theory. IEEE Trans. Information Theory 29, 770–777 (1983)
19. Ohya, M.: Complexities and their applications to characterization of chaos. International Journal of Theoretical Physics 37(1), 495–505 (1998)
20. Ohya, M.: Some aspects of quantum information theory and their applications to irreversible processes. Rep. Math. Phys. 27, 19–47 (1989)
21. Accardi, L., Ohya, M.: Compound Channels, Transition Expectations, and Liftings. Appl. Math. Optim. 39, 33–59 (1999)
22. Inoue, K., Ohya, M., Sato, K.: Application of chaos degree to some dynamical systems. Chaos, Soliton & Fractals 11, 1377–1385 (2000)
23. Ohya, M., Volovich, I.V.: New quantum algorithm for studying NP-complete problems. Rep. Math. Phys. 52(1), 25–33 (2003)
24. Ohya, M., Volovich, I.V.: Mathematical Foundations of Quantum Information and Computation and Its Applications to Nano-and Bio-systems. Springer (2011)
25. Inoue, K., Ohya, M., Volovich, I.V.: Semiclassical properties and chaos degree for the quantum baker's map. Journal of Mathematical Physics 43(1) (2002)
26. Kossakowski, A., Ohya, M., Togawa, Y.: How can we observe and describe chaos? Open System and Information Dynamics 10(3), 221–233 (2003)
27. Accardi, L., Ohya, M.: A Stochastic Limit Approach to the SAT Problem. Open Systems and Information Dynamics 11, 1–16 (2004)
28. Ohya, M.: Adaptive Dynamics and its Applications to Chaos and NPC Problem. QP-PQ: Quantum Probability and White Noise Analysis Quantum Bio-Informatics 21, 181–216 (2007)
29. Accardi, L.: Urne e camaleonti: Dialogo sulla realta, le leggi del caso e la teoria quantistica. Il Saggiatore (1997) (English edition, World Scientific 2002; japanese edition, Makino 2002, russian edition, Regular and Chaotic dynamics 2002)
30. Asano, M., Ohya, M., Tanaka, T., Khrennikov, A., Basieva, I.: Quantum-like Representation of Bayesian Updating. In: American Institute of Physics 1327: Proceedings of the International Conference on Advances in Quantum Theory, pp. 57-62 (2011)
31. Inada, T., Kimata, K., Aiba, H.: Mechanism responsible for glucose-lactose diauxie in Escherichia coli challenge to the cAMP model. Genes and Cells 1, 293–301 (1996)
32. Asano, M., Ohya, M., Tanaka, Y., Khrennikov, A., Basieva, I.: Quantum-like Bayesian Updating. TUS preprint (2011)

Modelling Word Activation in Semantic Networks: Three Scaled Entanglement Models Compared

David Galea[1], Peter Bruza[1], Kirsty Kitto[1], and Douglas Nelson[2]

[1] Queensland University of Technology, Brisbane, Australia
[2] University of South Florida, Tampa, USA

Abstract. Modelling how a word is activated in human memory is an important requirement for determining the probability of recall of a word in an extra-list cueing experiment. Previous research assumed a quantum-like model in which the semantic network was modelled as entangled qubits, however the level of activation was clearly being overestimated. This paper explores three variations of this model, each of which are distinguished by a scaling factor designed to compensate the overestimation.

1 Introduction

A crucial aspect of producing models that predict the probability of recall is modelling the activation of a target word in memory prior to cuing. Much evidence shows that for any individual seeing or hearing a word activates words related to it through prior learning. Seeing "planet" activates the associates "earth", "moon", and so on, because "planet-earth", "planet-moon", "moon-space" and other associations have been acquired in the past. This activation aids comprehension, is implicit, and provides rapid, synchronous access to associated words. Therefore, some models of activation fundamentally rely on the probabilities of such associations.

Conventionally, the way in which words are represented in memory is modelled using a semantic network comprising the target word and its most common associates in a directed weighted graph (see Fig. 1 for an example). However, the notion of relational weighting has been challenged with an alternative viewpoint which suggests only the existence of a relationship between the words in the graph is required in the model (i.e., a 1 or 0 representing the presence or absence of a link). This $\{1, 0\}$ measure often seems to provide a better practical predictor of activation level than the weighted probability measure. Theoretically the use of the $\{1, 0\}$ measure implies that, when a link is activated, it is activated regardless of how strongly it is represented in its local network (i.e., strength of activation is not important). Activation must provide extremely fast access to the entirety of its semantic links regardless of their strength because relatively weaker meanings are often what are needed in the immediate future for a given context [7]. In our view, the strength of a link becomes critically important when one word is used

J.R. Busemeyer et al. (Eds.): QI 2012, LNCS 7620, pp. 172–183, 2012.

as a cue for recalling a related word because it can activate many words other than the one needed. In this case, the strength of the link between the cue and its target word is critical in determining success. Hence, we think of activation as being all or none for each link, and strength as varying along a continuum when using a cue to sample related information in the semantic network.

Three models are proposed and tested to identify whether this binary semantic network representation would provide a better model of activation that the Spooky-action-at-a-distance model, which is based on the links in the semantic network being weighted. Given that no existing knowledge exists surrounding the nature between Spooky-action-at-a-distance[4], and the new "all or none" approach to link weights, both the average activation, average error (when fitted against a Probability of Recall), and correlation with probability of recall will be performed.

2   Activation Models

In order to aid in understanding the implementation of the three models consider the following situation of a hypothetical target with two associates, a single associate-to-target and associate-to-associate links, all of which can be represented using the Markov Chain Matrix as given in Table 1.

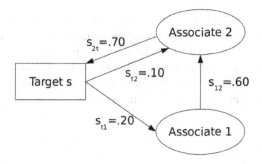

Fig. 1. A hypothetical target with two associates and single associate-to-target and associate-to-associate links [4]

Table 1. Matrix corresponding to hypothetical target shown in Fig. 1. Free association probabilities are obtained by finding the row of interest(the cue) and running across to the associate word obtained [2].

	Target (t)	Associate 1 (a_1)	Associate 2 (a_2)
Target (t)		0.2	0.1
Associate 1 (a_1)			0.6
Associate 2 (a_2)	0.7		

2.1 Spooky Action at a Distance

The Spooky-action-at–distance model of target activation is computed via the following formula:

$$S(T) = \sum_i S_{T,i} + \sum_i S_{i,T} + \sum_i \sum_j S_{i,j} \tag{1}$$

where,

$$S_{i,T} = Pr(\text{Word}_i \mid T) \ , \ S_{T,i} = Pr(\text{Word}_i|T) \ , \ S_{i,j} = Pr(\text{Word}_i \mid \text{Word}_j) \tag{2}$$

and,

$$\text{Word}_{i,j} \in \text{Target Associates}$$

Noting that $S_{i,T}$, $S_{T,i}$ and $S_{i,j}$ represent free association probabilities, i.e. $S_{i,j} = Pr(\text{Word}_i \mid \text{Word}_j)$ represents the probability that Word_i is produced when Word_j is used as cue in free association experiments [1]. Taking the example from Fig. 1,

$$S(T) = (0.1 + 0.2) + (0 + 0.7) + (0.6 + 0) = 1.6.$$

2.2 Entanglement Activation Model

One method used to model activation is to view a target's network as a composite quantum system as discussed by [6]. Using the example of Fig. 1 to view a target's association network, this would translate into a quantum system modelled by three qubits. Fig. 2 depicts this system, where each word is in a superposed state of being activated (denoted by the basis state $|1\rangle$) or not activated (denoted by the basis state $|0\rangle$). Thus the states of the words in the associative network are represented as,

$$|t\rangle = \bar{\pi}_t |0\rangle + \pi_t |1\rangle \ , \ |a_1\rangle = \bar{\pi}_{a_1} |0\rangle + \pi_{a_1} |1\rangle \ , \ |a_2\rangle = \bar{\pi}_{a_2} |0\rangle + \pi_{a_2} |1\rangle \tag{3}$$

While the amplitudes of the respective qubits can be derived from the matrix depicted in Table 1. Consider the column associate a_2. The two non-zero values in this column represent the level and the number of times associate a_2 is recalled in a free association experiment. Intuitively, the more non-zero entries and the

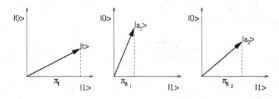

Fig. 2. Three bodied quantum system of words [1]

Table 2. Matrix corresponding to hypothetical target system shown in Fig. 1 where all of the link weightings not equal to zero have been set to 1

	Target (t)	Associate 1 (a_1)	Associate 2 (a_2)
Target (t)	0	1	1
Associate 1 (a_1)	0	0	1
Associate 2 (a_2)	1	0	0

higher the values, the more a_2 is activated. [6] formalized this by taking the square root of the average of these values as being the amplitude. For example $\pi_{a_2} = \sqrt{0.35}$. In the "all or none" approach, we no longer consider the strength of the relationships in ascribing the amplitudes, rather the existence (or non-existence) of a relationship. Consequently, the original semantic network depicted in Table 1 now takes the form in Table 2. The intuition behind entanglement activation is that the target t "activates its associative structure in synchrony" [2]. This intuition is modelled using an entangled state,

$$\psi'_t = \sqrt{p_0}\,|000\rangle + \sqrt{p_1}\,|111\rangle, \tag{4}$$

which represents a situation in which the entire associative structure is either completely activated ($|111\rangle$) or not activated at all ($|000\rangle$). The entanglement model is fundamentally different to the existing models found in the psychological literature (predominantly that of the spreading activation model as well as the spooky-action-at-a-distance model) as it models the target and its associative network as a non-separable structure [3].

The question remains how to ascribe values to the probabilities p_0 and p_1. One approach is to assume the target is not activated. Given that p_1 refers to the probability of the target being activated, this reflects the strength of activation, namely $S(T)$ as proposed by [6]:

$$p_1 = S(T) = 1 - (1 - Pr(T)) \prod_i (1 - Pr(\text{Word}_i)). \tag{5}$$

Eq. 5 is known to overestimate activation, particularly as the number of words in the semantic network increases [6]. This paper will contribute three entanglement models, each of which suggests a different approach to re-scaling the activation, with the intention of alleviating this overestimation problem. Each model will retain Eq. 5's structure, however the $Pr(\text{Word}_i)$ (the square of the amplitude) is redefined for each of the three models according to a different scaling factor.

2.3   Entanglement Binary V1

The Entanglement Binary V1 Activation Model assumes that the $Pr(\text{Word}_i)$'s strength is scaled by the ratio of the number of associate to word links to the number of words (n) within the network, namely:

$$S(T) = 1 - (1 - Pr(T)) \prod_i (1 - Pr(\text{Word}_i)). \tag{6}$$

$$Pr(\text{Word}_i) = \frac{\#\{Pr(\text{Word}_i|Pr(\text{Word}_j)) \neq 0; \forall j \neq i\}}{n}. \tag{7}$$

Taking the example from Fig. 1, the target's and associate's probabilities are

	Target (t)	Associate 1 (a_1)	Associate 2 (a_2)
$Pr(\text{Word})$	$\frac{1}{3}$	$\frac{1}{3}$	$\frac{2}{3}$

and the corresponding probability of target activation is given by,

$$S(T) = 1 - \left(1 - \frac{1}{3}\right)\left(1 - \frac{1}{3}\right)\left(1 - \frac{2}{3}\right) = 0.851851852. \tag{8}$$

2.4 Entanglement Binary V2

The Entanglement Binary V2 Activation Model assumes that the $Pr(\text{Word}_i)$'s strength is scaled by ratio of the number of associate to word links to the total number of possible links within the network (excluding self resonant links), i.e.,

$$S(T) = 1 - (1 - Pr(T)) \prod_i (1 - Pr(\text{Word}_i)). \tag{9}$$

$$Pr(\text{Word}_i) = \frac{\#\{Pr(\text{Word}_i|Pr(\text{Word}_j)) \neq 0; \forall j \neq i\}}{n(n-1)} \tag{10}$$

Taking the example from Fig. 1, the target's and sssociate's probabilities are:

	Target (t)	Associate 1 (a_1)	Associate 2 (a_2)
$Pr(\text{Word})$	$\frac{1}{3(3-1)}$	$\frac{1}{3(3-1)}$	$\frac{2}{3(3-1)}$

and the corresponding probability of target activation is given by

$$S(T) = 1 - \left(1 - \frac{1}{6}\right)\left(1 - \frac{1}{6}\right)\left(1 - \frac{2}{6}\right) = 0.537037037. \tag{11}$$

2.5 Entanglement Binary V3

The Entanglement Binary V3 Activation Model assumes that the $Pr(\text{Word}_i)$'s strength is scaled by the ratio of the number of associate to word links with the number of actual links within the network m (excluding self resonant links),i.e.,

$$S(T) = 1 - (1 - Pr(T)) \prod_i (1 - Pr(\text{Word}_i)) \tag{12}$$

$$Pr(\text{Word}_i) = \frac{\#\{Pr(\text{Word}_i|Pr(\text{Word}_j)) \neq 0; i \neq j\}}{m} \tag{13}$$

$$m = \#\{Pr(\text{Word}_i|\text{Word}_j) \neq 0; \forall i, j; i \neq j\}. \tag{14}$$

Taking the example from Fig. 1, the target's and associate's probabilities are

	Target (t)	Associate 1 (a_1)	Associate 2 (a_2)
$Pr(\text{Word})$	$\frac{1}{4}$	$\frac{1}{4}$	$\frac{2}{4}$

and the corresponding probability of target activation is now given by

$$S(T) = 1 - \left(1 - \frac{1}{4}\right)\left(1 - \frac{1}{4}\right)\left(1 - \frac{2}{4}\right) = 0.71875. \tag{15}$$

3   Analysis of Activation Models

The focus of this paper lies on modelling the activation for each of the three models and evaluating their performance against the Spooky-action-at-a-distance model as a baseline for comparison. This model was chosen as it is currently the best performing model for target activation in the literature.

The University of South Florida supplied the data set used for the testing, which was comprised of 4068 individual target-cue pairs, and a probability of recall of the target with respect to the cue. The probability of recall was established by human subjected in extra-list cuing experiments [5]. In the analysis to follow the probability of activation of a target $S(T)$ was computed using the Spooky-action-at-a-distance formula (1), and each of the the three entanglement models, equations (6),(9) and (12).

Two sets of analysis were performed for this process. The first area of analysis involved assessing the whether the binary network representations better suited modelling target activation. The mean probability of target activation was chosen as the figure for comparison pending all the three model's fitted values could be definitively shown to follow a Normal Distribution. A key feature of normality is that it allows for the standard measure of centrality, i.e. the mean, median and mode, coupled with the standard deviation to aid in understand the distribution of the results. Secondly, an analysis was performed on the error: probability of activation minus the probability of recall. As the cue process is ignored in this error analysis, a negative mean error would be expected for a good model of target activation model. This is because cue probabilities and target activation probabilities combine to estimate the probability of recall of the target given the cue. The purpose of the error analysis was to again seek a normal like distribution to justify the use of the mean as a characteristic for comparison, but furthermore to gain an understanding as to how the model compared to the observed data. Finally the activation probabilities of all models were correlated with the actual probability of recall.

3.1   Spooky Action at a Distance

The Spooky Action at a Distance Activation was computed against all test cases produced the results depicted in Table 3.

Here we observe that on average the activation is fairly low (Mean = 0.327), coupled with an almost matching median and low standard deviation is it fair

Table 3. Descriptive Statistics on Spooky-Activation-at-a-Distance

	Target Activation
Mean	0.3272031
Median	0.3030769
Standard Deviation	0.1431615
Range	1.6775
Minimum	0.0525
Maximum	1.73

to suppose that its distribution would be fairly centred, dense and akin to that of a true Normal Distribution. The maximum value of 1.73 is greater than 1, as unlike traditional activation models which are probabilistic; the activation level for this model is not a probability. However, as values greater than 1 were rarely observed, these were treated as flaws/outliers for the purposes of this analysis and the spooky activation modelled was thereby assumed to generate a probability of recall. To reinforce this, a further investigation was made into measuring the target activation against the probability of recall, the results of which are shown in Fig. 3, which indicates that there is strong evidence that the errors are Normally Distributed, and from which the original proposition to use the Mean (0.3272031) as a basis is supported.

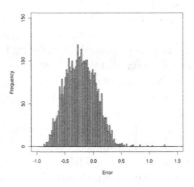

Fig. 3. Histogram of Spooky-Activation-at-a-Distance Activation Recall minus Probability of Recall ($\mu = -0.2196072$, $\sigma = 0.2679344$)

These results show why Spooky performs well in modelling activation — the underfitting of the probability of recall is to be expected in a good model.

3.2 Entanglement Binary V1

The Entanglement Binary V1 Model was computed against all test cases producing the results shown in Table 4.

Here we observe that on average the activation is extremely high (Mean = 0.9500141), coupled with an almost matching median and particularly low standard deviation implies that it would be fair to conclude that its distribution

Table 4. Descriptive Statistics on Entanglement Binary V1

	Target Activation
Mean	0.9500141
Median	0.9661007
Standard Deviation	0.04912377
Range	0.3276542
Minimum	0.67232
Maximum	0.9999742

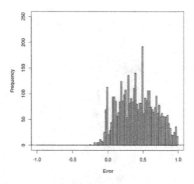

Fig. 4. Histogram of Entanglment Binary V1 probability of target activation minus Probability of Recall ($\mu = 0.420401, \sigma = 0.2643495$)

would be analogous to that of a Normal Distribution. The error anlaysis shown in Fig. 4 indicates that there is sufficient evidence that the errors are Normally Distributed, and from which the original proposition to use the Mean (0.9500141) as a basis is supported. The over-fitting of the probability of recall is is even worse than for the entanglement activation model reported in [6]. Clearly, using the number of associates (n) as a scaling factor in the entangled representation of the binary semantic network has not compensated for the overestimation documented in [6].

3.3   Entanglement Binary V2

The Entanglement Binary V2 Model was computed against all test cases producing the results depicted in Table 5.

Here we observe that on average the activation is quite low (Mean = 0.2285645), coupled with an almost matching median and particularly low standard deviation implies that it would be fair to conclude that its distribution would resemble that of a Normal Distribution. The target activation against the probability of recall error analysis is shown in Fig. 5, which indicates that there is strong evidence that the errors are Normally Distributed, and from which the original proposition to use the Mean (0.2285645) as a basis is supported. These results show a greater promise for development than that of the previous model.

Table 5. Descriptive Statistics on Entanglement Binary V2

	Target Activation
Mean	0.2285645
Median	0.2062454
Standard Deviation	0.0976225
Range	0.55611115
Minimum	0.07351845
Maximum	0.6296296

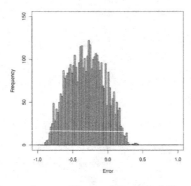

Fig. 5. Histogram of Entanglement Binary V2 probability of target activation minus Probability of Recall ($\mu = -0.3010487, \sigma = 0.2583977$)

Here, by scaling by the number of possible links between associates $n(n-1)$, the overestimation documented in [6] has been compensated, but the mean error is greater than that of Spooky-action-at-a-distance ($\mu = -0.3010487$ vs. $\mu = -0.2196072$).

3.4   Entanglement Binary V3

The Entanglement Binary V3 model was computed against all test cases producing the results shown in Table 7.

Table 6. Descriptive Statistics on Entanglement Binary V3

	Target Activation
Mean	0.6561066
Median	0.6529113
Standard Deviation	0.01069147
Range	0.0772161
Minimum	0.6415339
Maximum	0.71875

Here we observe that on average the activation is fairly strong (Mean = 0.6561066), coupled with an almost matching median and particularly low

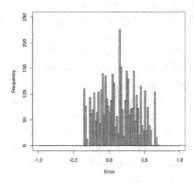

Fig. 6. Histogram of Entanglement Binary V3 Activation Recall vs Probability of Recall ($\mu = 0.1264935$, $\sigma = 0.2648446$)

Table 7. Descriptive Statistics on the PIER2 model

	V1	V2	V3	Spooky
ρ	0.1248266704	0.3473200375	0.0972704901	0.0104764534
Mean Error	-0.0330907371	0.191858518	-0.0079025998	-0.2307347387
St Dev Error	0.2572710404	0.2405896058	0.2603335278	0.26892291

standard deviation (relative to the mean) implies that it would be fair to conclude that its distribution would resemble that of a Normal Distribution.

The results of the error analysis are shown in Fig. 6, which indicates that there is strong evidence that the errors are Normally Distributed, and from which the original conjecture to use the Mean (0.6561066) is supported. V3 performs the best empirically as its average mean error is lowest for all models. The number of actual links (m) within the network appears to be a robust feature for scaling activation probabilities.

4 Discussion

The primary focus of this paper was to investigate whether the binary semantic network representation would lead to improved models of target activation. As stated previously the methods developed were to be benchmarked against the Spooky-action-at-a-Distance model; given its quantum nature, its origins in classical psychological modelling and its proven performance on empirical data [4].

The Entanglement Binary V1, V2 and V3 models all worked on generating probabilities of target activation by scaling the number of associate to word links to features based on the semantic network. All three exhibited relatively loose normal distributions, yet produced robust normal distributions when fitted against the Probability of Recall allowing us to use the mean as a basis for comparison. Given the respective averages are Spooky = 0.3272031 , Entanglement Binary V1 = 0.9500141 , V2 = 0.2285645, V3 = 0.6561066. We see that the V1,V3 overfit and V2 underfits with respect to probabilities of activation computed by the Spooky-action-at-a-distance baseline; however V3 is far more stable. When fitted against a Probability of Recall the respective average errors are Spooky = −0.2196072 , Entanglement Binary V1 = 0.420401 , V2 = −0.3010487, V3 = 0.1264935. As the error is proportional to the scaling method used, Entanglement Binary V1 and V2 scale too strongly and weakly respectively, whilst V3 not only outperforms V1 and V2 empirically, it also reduces the average error of Spooky by ∼ 30%.

5   Summary and Outlook

In summary, this article uses a binary semantic network representation for modelling the activation of words in memory as entangled states. A previously published entanglement model overestimated the level of activation. Three entanglement models were analysed with respect to mean level of activation and average error with respect to probability of recall. These models differed only in the means employed to scale the level of activation as a means of addressing the aforementioned propensity to overestimate. The well known Spooky-action-at-a-distance model of activation was used as a baseline for comparative performance. It was found that by scaling the level of activation by the actual number of links in the network significantly reduced the average error with respect to the probability of recall, even though this method still has a propensity to overestimate target activation. Therefore a significant step in the right direction has been taken and further work will consist of further tuning this factor in order to combat the overestimation problem.

We anticipate that future empirical analysis will be broadened to include the cue process. One way to pursue this is to use the well know PIER2 model [8] to generate estimates of the probability of recall. In this way the cue process is held constant and alternative models of activation can be manipulated as a parameter and their mean error with respect to the probability of recall used as a comparative performance measure. A preliminary analysis of binary activation models (V1, V2, V3) on the PIER2 model against the Spooky model which yielded the following results;

Using the correlation coefficient as a performance indicator, V2 is the most well behaved model, whereas taking the Mean Error, V3 is the best. Similar issues arise when comparing the distributions of the models and the need of a single or grouped set of performance indicators is required for the models to be properly assessed.

References

1. Bruza, P., Kitto, K., Nelson, D., McEvoy, C.: Extracting Spooky-Activation-at-a-Distance from Considerations of Entanglement. In: Bruza, P., Sofge, D., Lawless, W., van Rijsbergen, K., Klusch, M. (eds.) QI 2009. LNCS, vol. 5494, pp. 71–83. Springer, Heidelberg (2009)
2. Bruza, P., Kitto, K., Nelson, D., McEvoy, C.: Is there something quantum-like about the human mental lexicon? Journal of Mathematical Psychology 53, 362–377 (2009)
3. Busemeyer, J., Bruza, P.: Quantum cognition and decision. Cambridge University Press (in press, 2012)
4. Nelson, D., McEvoy, C., Pointer, L.: Spreading activation or spooky activation at a distance? Journal of Experimental Psychology:Learning, Memory and Cognition 29(1), 42–52 (2003)
5. Nelson, D., McEvoy, C., Schreiber, T.: The University of South Florida, word association, rhyme and word fragment norms. Behaviour Research Methods, Instruments and Computers 36, 408–420 (2004)
6. Galea, D., Bruza, P., Kitto, K., Nelson, D., McEvoy, C.: Modelling the Acitivation of Words in Human Memory: The Spreading Activation, Spooky-activation-at-a-distance and the Entanglement Models Compared. In: Song, D., Melucci, M., Frommholz, I., Zhang, P., Wang, L., Arafat, S. (eds.) QI 2011. LNCS, vol. 7052, pp. 149–160. Springer, Heidelberg (2011)
7. Kintsch, W.: The role of knowledge in discourse comprehension construction-integration model. Psychological Review 95, 163–182 (1988)
8. Nelson, D., McEvoy, C.: Implicitly activated memories: The missing links of remembering. In: Izawa, C., Ohta, N. (eds.) Human Learning and Memory: Advances in Theory and Applications, pp. 177–198. Erlbaum, New Jersey (2005)

Quantum Entanglement and the Issue of Selective Influences in Psychology: An Overview

Ehtibar N. Dzhafarov[1] and Janne V. Kujala[2]

[1] Purdue University
ehtibar@purdue.edu
[2] University of Jyväskylä
jvk@iki.fi

Abstract. Similar formalisms have been independently developed in psychology, to deal with the issue of selective influences (deciding which of several experimental manipulations selectively influences each of several, generally non-independent, response variables), and in quantum mechanics (QM), to deal with the EPR entanglement phenomena (deciding whether an EPR experiment allows for a "classical" account). The parallels between these problems are established by observing that any two noncommuting measurements in QM are mutually exclusive and can therefore be treated as analogs of different values of one and the same input. Both problems reduce to that of the existence of a jointly distributed system of random variables, one variable for every value of every input (in psychology) or every measurement on every particle involved (in an EPR experiment). We overview three classes of necessary conditions (some of them also sufficient under additional constraints) for the existence of such joint distributions.

Keywords: Bell-CHSH-Fine inequalities, cosphericity test, EPR paradigm, joint distribution criterion, linear feasibility test, non-commuting measurements, pseudo-quasi-metrics on random variables, quantum entanglement, selective influences.

1 Introduction

Given a set of inputs into a system and a set of stochastically non-independent outputs, what is the precise meaning and means of ascertaining that a given output *is not influenced* by a given input? This paper reviews the developments related to this question.

The problem can be illustrated on the following *diagram of selective influences*:

$$
\begin{array}{ccc}
\alpha^1 = \{w, x, y\} & \alpha^2 = \{x\} & \alpha^3 = \{w, z\} \\
\downarrow & \downarrow & \downarrow \\
A^1 & A^2 & A^3
\end{array}
\tag{1}
$$

J.R. Busemeyer et al. (Eds.): QI 2012, LNCS 7620, pp. 184–195, 2012.

A^1, A^2, and A^3 here are *random outputs*, w, x, y, z are *inputs* (usually referred to as *external factors* in psychology and as *measurement settings* in QM), and arrows indicate the relation "may influence": thus, the diagram does not say that A^2 is necessarily influenced by x, but rather that A^2 is not influenced by w, y, z. The diagram is shown in the *canonical form*, i.e., the inputs are redefined, $\{w, x, y\}$ into α^1, $\{x\}$ into α^2, etc., so that each output A^i may only be influenced by a single input α^i that may not influence other outputs. We say then, for brevity, that $\left(A^1, A^2, A^3\right)$ are *selectively influenced* by $\left(\alpha^1, \alpha^2, \alpha^3\right)$ and write this as

$$\left(A^1, A^2, A^3\right) \nleftrightarrow \left(\alpha^1, \alpha^2, \alpha^3\right). \tag{2}$$

Inputs $\left(\alpha^1, \alpha^2, \alpha^3\right)$ are treated as deterministic quantities, i.e., even if they are random variables, the joint distribution of the outputs is always conditioned on their specific values. Each input can have one of several values, and the joint distribution of $\left(A^1, A^2, A^3\right)$ is known for each *allowable treatment*, a combination of input values. Thus, if w, x, y, z are all binary, then $\alpha^1, \alpha^2, \alpha^3$ may be viewed as inputs with 8, 2, and 4 values, respectively, but the number of allowable treatments cannot exceed $16 < 8 \times 2 \times 4$. It can be less than 16 because some of the combinations may be physically impossible or simply not used or observed.

As a motivating example, consider a double-detection experiment in which two stimuli, say brief flashes, are presented simultaneously (right-left) or in a succession (first-second), each on one of two levels of intensity. The observer is asked to state, for each of the two *observation areas* (i.e., locations or time intervals), whether it contains a flash (Yes/No). The results of such an experiment are statistical estimates of 16 probabilities

$$p\left(A^1, A^2 | \alpha^1, \alpha^2\right) = \Pr\left[A^1 : \begin{cases} Yes \\ No \end{cases}, A^2 : \begin{cases} Yes \\ No \end{cases} \middle| \alpha^1 : \begin{cases} \alpha_1^1 \\ \alpha_2^1 \end{cases}, \alpha^2 : \begin{cases} \alpha_1^2 \\ \alpha_2^2 \end{cases}\right], \tag{3}$$

where α^i ($i = 1, 2$) is the input representing the ith observation area (with values α_1^i, α_2^i), and A^i is the response (Yes or No) to the ith observation area. Assume that A^1 and A^2 for a given $\left(\alpha_i^1, \alpha_j^2\right)$ are not independent (due to attention fluctuations, perceptual learning, fatigue, etc.) In what sense then can we say that $\left(A^1, A^2\right) \nleftrightarrow \left(\alpha^1, \alpha^2\right)$, and by what means can we find out if this is true?

Many empirical situations have precisely the same formal structure. In QM, an example is provided by the Bohmian version of the EPR paradigm [3]: two subatomic particles are emitted from a common source in such a way that they retain highly correlated spins as they run away from each other. An experiment may consist, e.g., in measuring the spin of electron 1 along one of two axes, α_1^1 or α_2^1, and (in another location but simultaneously in some inertial frame of reference) measuring the spin of electron 2 along one of two axes, α_1^2 or α_2^2. The outcome of a measurement on electron 1, A^1, is a random variable with two possible values, "up" or "down," and the same holds for A^2, outcome of a measurement on electron 2. The question here is: for $i = 1, 2$, can we say that A^i may only depend on α^i, even though A^1 and A^2 are not independent? What makes this situation formally identical with the double-detection example is that the measurements along different axes, α_1^i and α_2^i, are *noncommuting*, i.e., they cannot be performed on the ith particle simultaneously. This makes it possible to consider them (measurements performed, not to be confused with their recorded outcomes) as mutually exclusive values of input α^i. The results of such an experiment are described by (3), with Yes/No interpreted as spin up/down. In the original EPR paradigm [14] the non-commuting measurements are those of momentum and location, each with a continuum of possible values. Our parallel with the issue of selective influences requires that the measurements of the momentum and of the location of a given particle be interpreted as mutually exclusive values of one and the same input, "(measurement of the) momentum-location of the particle." This may be less intuitive than the analogous interpretation of the spins along different axes.

The question of selective influences cannot generally be decided based on the marginal distributions of the outputs alone. The most important example here is the classical CHSH experiment [4] where the marginal distributions of A^1 and A^2 (in the case of two electrons) remain constant, with $\Pr\left[spin\ up\right] = 1/2$. Examples from psychology are also readily available, especially if one adopts a copula view of the joint distributions. Thus, α^1 and α^2 may represent two stimuli presented in a succession (each having several values), and A^1, A^2 be *response times quantiles*. The marginal distributions then are always the same, unit-uniform.

2   A Historical Note

The issue of selective influences was introduced to psychology in Sternberg's influential paper [22], in the context of studying consecutive "stages" of information processing. Sternberg acknowledged that selective influences can hold even if the durations of the stages are not stochastically independent, but he lacked mathematical apparatus for dealing with this possibility. Townsend [24] proposed to formalize the notion of selectively influenced and stochastically interdependent random variables by the concept of "*indirect nonselectiveness*": the conditional distribution of the variable A^1 given any value a^2 of the variable A^2, depends on α^1 only, and, by symmetry, the conditional distribution of A^2 at any $A^1 = a^1$ depends on α^2 only. Under the name of "*conditionally selective influence*" this notion was mathematically characterized and generalized in [5]. Thus, if all combinations of values of inputs α^1, α^2 are allowable and random outputs A^1, A^2 are discrete, the diagram $\left(A^1, A^2\right) \overset{cond}{\leftarrow} \left(a^1, a^2\right)$, where $\overset{cond}{\leftarrow}$ means "is conditionally selectively influenced," holds if and only if $\Pr\left[A^1 = a^1, A^2 = a^2 \mid \alpha_x^1, \alpha_y^2\right]$ can be presented as

$$f_{12}\left(a^1, a^2\right) f_1\left(a^1, \alpha_x^1\right) f_2\left(a^2, \alpha_y^2\right) f\left(\alpha_x^1, \alpha_y^2\right), \tag{4}$$

for all values $\left(a^1, a^2\right)$ of $\left(A^1, A^2\right)$ at all treatments $\left(\alpha_x^1, \alpha_y^2\right)$. Conditional selectivity is a useful notion, but it is not a satisfactory formalization of the intuitive notion of selective influences. The reason is that $\left(A^1, A^2\right) \overset{cond}{\leftarrow} \left(a^1, a^2\right)$ can be shown [5] to violate the following obvious property of an acceptable definition: the marginal distributions of A^1 and A^2 do not depend on, respectively, α^2 and α^1 ("*marginal selectivity*" [25]).

A different approach to selective influences, reviewed below, is based on [6,7,9,10,11,12,19]. As it turns out[1] this approach parallels the development in QM of the issue of whether an EPR experiment can have a "classical" explanation (in terms of non-contextual local variables). The Joint Distribution Criterion which is at the heart of this development (see below) was indirectly introduced in the celebrated work of Bell [2], and explicitly in [15,16,23].

3   Basic Notions

Aimed at providing a broad overview of concepts and results, the content of this paper partially overlaps with that of several previous publications, especially [11,12,19].

Random variables are understood in the broadest sense, as measurable functions $X : V_s \to V$, with no restrictions on the sample spaces (V_s, Σ_s, μ_s) and the induced probability spaces (*distributions*) (V, Σ, μ). In particular, any set X of jointly distributed random variables (functions on the same sample space) is a random variable, and its distribution (V, Σ, μ) is referred to as the *joint distribution* of its elements. We use symbol $\sim$ in the meaning of "has the same distribution as." A random variable in the narrow sense is a special case of a random entity, with V a finite product of countable sets and intervals of reals, and Σ the smallest sigma-algebra containing the corresponding product of power sets and Lebesgue sigma-algebras. Note that a vector of random variables in the narrow sense is a random variable in the narrow sense.

Consider an indexed set $\alpha = \{\alpha^\lambda : \lambda \in \Lambda\}$, with each α^λ being a set referred to as a (deterministic) *input*, with the elements of $\{\lambda\} \times \alpha^\lambda$ called *input points*. Input points therefore are pairs of the form $x = (\lambda, w)$, with $w \in \alpha^\lambda$, and should not be confused with *input values* w. A nonempty set $\Phi \subset \prod_{\lambda \in \Lambda} \alpha^\lambda$ is called a set of *(allowable) treatments*. A treatment therefore is a function $\phi : \Lambda \to \bigcup_{\lambda \in \Lambda} \alpha^\lambda$ such that $\phi(\lambda) \in \alpha^\lambda$ for any $\lambda \in \Lambda$.

Let there be a collection of sets of random variables A_ϕ^λ ($\lambda \in \Lambda$, $\phi \in \Phi$), referred to as (random) *outputs*, with distributions $\left(V^\lambda, \Sigma^\lambda, \mu_\phi^\lambda\right)$. Let

$$A_\phi = \left\{A_\phi^\lambda : \lambda \in \Lambda\right\}, \ \phi \in \Phi, \tag{5}$$

be a random variable with a known distribution (the joint distribution of all A_ϕ^λ in A_ϕ) for every treatment $\phi \in \Phi$. We define

$$A^\lambda = \left\{A_\phi^\lambda : \phi \in \Phi\right\}, \ \lambda \in \Lambda, \tag{6}$$

with the understanding that A^λ is not generally a random variable, i.e., A_ϕ^λ for different ϕ are not necessarily jointly distributed. The definition of the relation

$$\left\{A^\lambda : \lambda \in \Lambda\right\} \nleftrightarrow \left\{\alpha^\lambda : \lambda \in \Lambda\right\}, \tag{7}$$

---

[1] This was first pointed out to us by Jerome Busemeyer (personal communication, November 2010), for which we remain deeply grateful.

interpreted as "for each $\lambda \in \Lambda$, A^λ may be influenced by α^λ only," can be given in three equivalent forms:

(SI$_1$) there are independent random variables C, $\{S^\lambda : \lambda \in \Lambda\}$, and functions

$$\left\{ R^\lambda \left(w, C, S^\lambda \right) : w \in \alpha^\lambda, \lambda \in \Lambda \right\}, \qquad (8)$$

such that, for any treatment $\phi \in \Phi$,

$$\left\{ R^\lambda \left(\phi\left(\lambda\right), C, S^\lambda \right) : \lambda \in \Lambda \right\} \sim A_\phi; \qquad (9)$$

(SI$_2$) there is a random variable C and functions

$$\left\{ P^\lambda \left(w, C \right) : w \in \alpha^\lambda, \lambda \in \Lambda \right\}, \qquad (10)$$

such that, for any treatment $\phi \in \Phi$,

$$\left\{ P^\lambda \left(\phi\left(\lambda\right), C \right) : \lambda \in \Lambda \right\} \sim A_\phi; \qquad (11)$$

(JDC) there is a set of jointly distributed random variables

$$H = \left\{ H_w^\lambda : w \in \alpha^\lambda, \lambda \in \Lambda \right\} \qquad (12)$$

(one random variable for every value of every input), such that, for any treatment $\phi \in \Phi$,

$$\left\{ H_{\phi(\lambda)}^\lambda : \lambda \in \Lambda \right\} \sim A_\phi. \qquad (13)$$

The latter statement constitutes the *Joint Distribution Criterion* (JDC) for selective influences, and H is called the JDC *(indexed) set*. The proof of the equivalence [10] obtains essentially by the definition of a joint distribution, which seems to have been overlooked in the earlier derivations [15,16]. If $\Lambda = \{1, \ldots, n\}$ and all outputs A^λ are random variables in the narrow sense, then C in SI$_2$ and $C, S^1, \ldots, S^n$ in SI$_1$ can also be chosen to be random variables in the narrow sense; moreover, their distribution functions can be chosen arbitrarily, provided they are continuous and strictly increasing on their domains, e.g., unit uniform [11].

Two important consequences of (7) are as follows:

1. *(nestedness)* any subset Λ' of Λ, $\{A^\lambda : \lambda \in \Lambda'\} \looparrowright \{\alpha^\lambda : \lambda \in \Lambda'\}$; in particular, $\{A^\lambda : \lambda \in \Lambda'\}$ may not depend on inputs outside Λ' *(complete marginal selectivity)*;
2. *(invariance with respect to input-value-specific transformations)* for any set of measurable functions $\{F_w^\lambda \left(a \right) : w \in \alpha^\lambda, \lambda \in \Lambda, a \in V^\lambda\}$,

$$\left(B^\lambda : \lambda \in \Lambda \right) \looparrowright \left\{ \alpha^\lambda : \lambda \in \Lambda \right\} \qquad (14)$$

where $B^\lambda = \left\{ B_\phi^\lambda : \phi \in \Phi \right\}$, and $B_\phi^\lambda = F_{\phi(\lambda)}^\lambda \left(A_\phi^\lambda \right)$.

These properties should be viewed as desiderata for any reasonable definition of selective influences.

In QM, SI_1 corresponds to the existence of a *"classical"* probabilistic explanation. In psychology, statement SI_1 combined with auxiliary assumptions was used in [8] and [20] to analyze the representability of same-different pairwise discrimination probabilities by means of *Thurstonian-type models* in which two stimuli being compared are mapped into random entities (distributed in some hypothetical space of mental images) that in turn are mapped (deterministically or probabilistically) into a response, "same" or "different." Statement SI_1 was also used to analyze the response time distributions for *parallel-serial networks of mental operations* with selectively influenced components [13]. Note that the representation of the outputs A^λ as functions of the corresponding inputs α^i and unobservable sources of randomness, A^λ-specific (S^λ) and common (C), includes as special cases all conceivable generalizations and combinations of *regression* and *factor analyses*, with our term "input" corresponding to the traditional "regressor," and the term "source of randomness" to the factor-analytic "factor." This observation alone shows the potentially unlimited sphere of applicability of SI_1.

Statement SI_2 (corresponding in QM to *"classical" determinsitic* explanation) and JDC turn out to be more convenient in dealing with certain foundational probabilistic issues [9] and for the construction of the working *tests* (*necessary conditions*) for selective influences [10,11,12,19]. The tests are discussed below.

The following is a table of correspondences between the general terminology used in dealing with the issue of selective influences, and that of QM in dealing with EPR.

Selective Probabilistic Causality (general)	Quantum Entanglement Problem
observed random output	outcome of a given measurement on a given particle
input (factor)	set of noncommuting measurements on a given particle
input value	one of noncommuting measurements on a given particle
joint distribution criterion	joint distribution criterion
diagram of selective influences	"classical" explanation
representation in the form SI_1	probabilistic "classical" explanation
representation in the form SI_2	deterministic "classical" explanation

4   Tests for Selective Influences

Let $H = \left\{ H_w^\lambda : w \in \alpha^\lambda, \lambda \in \Lambda \right\}$ be a *hypothetical* JDC-set, i.e., a set satisfying (13) but not necessarily jointly distributed. Denoting

$$\left\{ H_{\phi(\lambda)}^\lambda : \lambda \in \Lambda \right\} = H_\phi, \ \phi \in \Phi, \tag{15}$$

let $\mathcal{H}$ be a *set of constraints* imposed on possible distributions of H_ϕ. For instance, $\mathcal{H}$ may be the requirement that all H_ϕ^λ be composed of Bernoulli variables, or multivariate-normally distributed.

A statement $S\left(H_{\phi_1}, \ldots, H_{\phi_s}\right)$, with $\phi_1, \ldots, \phi_s \in \Phi$, is called a *test* for the relation (7) under constraints $\mathcal{H}$, if

1. (*observability*) its truth value only depends on the distributions of $H_{\phi_1}, \ldots, H_{\phi_s}$;
2. (*non-emptiness*) it is not true for all possible distributions of $H_{\phi_1}, \ldots, H_{\phi_s}$ satisfying $\mathcal{H}$,
3. (*necessity*) it is true if H is jointly distributed.

If $S\left(H_{\phi_1}, \ldots, H_{\phi_s}\right)$ is false for all distributions of $H_{\phi_1}, \ldots, H_{\phi_s}$ satisfying $\mathcal{H}$ unless H is jointly distributed, the test is called a *criterion* for (7). In the following we assume that $\mathcal{H}$ always includes the requirement of complete marginal selectivity: for any $\Lambda' \subset \Lambda$, the joint distribution of $\left\{A_{\phi(\Lambda')\cup\phi(\Lambda-\Lambda')}^\lambda : \lambda \in \Lambda'\right\}$ does not depend on $\phi(\Lambda - \Lambda')$. If this condition is violated, (7) is ruled out trivially.

4.1   Pseudo-Quasi-Distance Tests

A function $d : H \times H \to \mathbb{R}$ is a *pseudo-quasi-metric* (*p.q.-metric*) on H if, for any $H_1, H_2, H_3 \in H$,

(i) $d\left(H_1, H_2\right)$ only depends on the joint distribution of $\left(H_1, H_2\right)$,
(ii) $d\left(H_1, H_2\right) \geq 0$,
(iii) $d\left(H_1, H_1\right) = 0$,
(iv) $d\left(H_1, H_3\right) \leq d\left(H_1, H_2\right) + d\left(H_2, H_3\right)$.

The conventional *pseudometrics* (also called *semimetrics*) obtain by adding the property $d\left(H_1, H_2\right) = d\left(H_2, H_1\right)$; the conventional *quasimetrics* are obtained by adding the property $\Pr\left[H_1 = H_2\right] < 1 \Rightarrow d\left(H_1, H_2\right) > 0$. A conventional *metric* is both a pseudometric and a quasimetric.

A sequence of input points

$$x_1 = \left(\lambda_1, w_1\right), \ldots, x_l = \left(\lambda_l, w_l\right), \tag{16}$$

where $w_i \in \alpha^{\lambda_i}$ for $i = 1, \ldots, l \geq 3$, is called *treatment-realizable* if there are treatments $\phi^1, \ldots, \phi^l \in \Phi$ (not necessarily pairwise distinct), such that

$$\{x_1, x_l\} \subset \phi^1 \text{ and } \{x_{i-1}, x_i\} \subset \phi^i \text{ for } i = 2, \ldots, l. \tag{17}$$

If a JDC-set H exists, then for any p.q.-metric d on H we should have

$$d\left(H_{w_1}^{\lambda_1}, H_{w_l}^{\lambda_l}\right) = d\left(A_{\phi^1}^{\lambda_1}, A_{\phi^1}^{\lambda_l}\right) \tag{18}$$

and

$$d\left(H_{w_{i-1}}^{\lambda_{i-1}}, H_{w_i}^{\lambda_i}\right) = d\left(A_{\phi^i}^{\lambda_{i-1}}, A_{\phi^i}^{\lambda_i}\right), \ i = 2, \ldots, l, \tag{19}$$

whence

$$d\left(A_{\phi^1}^{\lambda_1}, A_{\phi^1}^{\lambda_l}\right) \leq \sum_{i=2}^{l} d\left(A_{\phi^i}^{\lambda_{i-1}}, A_{\phi^i}^{\lambda_i}\right). \tag{20}$$

This chain inequality constitutes a *p.q.-metric test* for selective influences. If this inequality is found not to hold for at least one treatment-realizable sequence of input points, selectivity (7) is ruled out [12].

It turns out that one needs to check the chain inequality only for *irreducible* treatment-realizable sequences $x_1, \ldots, x_l$, i.e., those with $x_1 \neq x_l$ and with the property that the only subsequences $\{x_{i_1}, \ldots, x_{i_k}\}$ with $k > 1$ that are subsets of treatments are pairs $\{x_1, x_l\}$ and $\{x_{i-1}, x_i\}$, for $i = 2, \ldots, l$. Inequality (20) is satisfied for all treatment-realizable sequences if and only if it holds for all irreducible sequences [12]. The situation is even simpler if $\Phi = \prod_{\lambda \in \Lambda} W^\lambda$ (all logically possible treatments are allowable). Then (20) is satisfied for all treatment-realizable sequences if and only if this inequality holds for all tetradic sequences of the form x, y, s, t, with $x, s \in \{\lambda_1\} \times \alpha^{\lambda_1}$, $y, t \in \{\lambda_2\} \times \alpha^{\lambda_2}$, $x \neq s$, $y \neq t$, $\lambda_1 \neq \lambda_2$ [10].

Order-distances constitute a special class of p.q.-metrics, defined as follows. Let the distribution of $H_w^\lambda \in H$ be $(V^\lambda, \Sigma^\lambda, \mu_w^\lambda)$. Let

$$R \subset \bigcup_{(\lambda_1, \lambda_2) \in \Lambda \times \Lambda} V^{\lambda_1} \times V^{\lambda_2}, \tag{21}$$

and let us write $a \preceq b$ for $(a, b) \in R$. Let R be a total order (transitive, reflexive, and connected). We assume that for any $(\lambda_1, \lambda_2) \in \Lambda \times \Lambda$, $\Pr\left[H_{w_1}^{\lambda_1} \preceq H_{w_2}^{\lambda_2}\right]$ is well-defined, i.e., $\{(a, b) : a \in V^{\lambda_1}, b \in V^{\lambda_2}, a \preceq b\}$ belongs to the product sigma-algebra over Σ^{λ_1} and Σ^{λ_2}. Then the function

$$D\left(H_{w_1}^{\lambda_1}, H_{w_2}^{\lambda_2}\right) = \Pr\left[H_{w_1}^{\lambda_1} \prec H_{w_2}^{\lambda_2}\right], \tag{22}$$

where $\prec$ is the strict order induced by $\preceq$, is well-defined, and it is a p.q.-metric on H, called order-distance [12].

As a simple example, consider the results of a CHSH type experiment with two spin axes per each of two entangled $1/2$-spin particles. Enumerate the spin axes $1, 2$ for either particle, enumerate the two outcomes (up and down) of each measurement $1, 2$ for particle 1 and $1', 2'$ for particle 2, and denote

$$\Pr\left[H_i^1 = k, H_j^2 = l'\right] = \Pr\left[A_{(i,j)}^1 = k, A_{(i,j)}^2 = l'\right] = p_{kl|ij}, \tag{23}$$

where $i, j, k, l \in \{1, 2\}$. Define the order-distance D_1 by putting $1 \simeq 1' \prec 2 \simeq 2'$, where $\simeq$ is equivalence induced by $\preceq$. We have then the chain inequality

$$\begin{aligned} p_{12|12} &= D_1(H_1^1, H_2^2) \\ &\leq D_1(H_1^1, H_1^2) + D_1(H_1^2, H_2^1) + D_1(H_2^1, H_2^2) = p_{12|11} + p_{21|21} + p_{12|22}. \end{aligned} \tag{24}$$

Consider next a similar inequality for the order-distance D_2 defined by $1 \simeq 2' \prec 2 \simeq 1'$:

$$\begin{aligned} p_{11|12} &= D_2(H_1^1, H_2^2) \\ &\leq D_2(H_1^1, H_1^2) + D_2(H_1^2, H_2^1) + D_2(H_2^1, H_2^2) = p_{11|11} + p_{22|21} + p_{11|22}. \end{aligned} \tag{25}$$

By simple algebra, denoting

$$\Pr\left[H_i^1 = k\right] = p_{k\cdot|i\cdot}, \ \Pr\left[H_j^2 = l'\right] = p_{\cdot l|\cdot j}, \tag{26}$$

the conjunction of (24) and (25) can be shown to be equivalent to

$$-1 \leq p_{11|11} + p_{11|21} + p_{11|22} - p_{11|12} - p_{1\cdot|2\cdot} - p_{\cdot1|\cdot1} \leq 0. \tag{27}$$

One derives analogously

$$\begin{aligned}
-1 &\leq p_{11|12} + p_{11|22} + p_{11|21} - p_{11|11} - p_{1\cdot|2\cdot} - p_{\cdot1|\cdot2} \leq 0, \\
-1 &\leq p_{11|21} + p_{11|11} + p_{11|12} - p_{11|22} - p_{1\cdot|1\cdot} - p_{\cdot1|\cdot1} \leq 0, \\
-1 &\leq p_{11|22} + p_{11|12} + p_{11|11} - p_{11|21} - p_{1\cdot|1\cdot} - p_{\cdot1|\cdot2} \leq 0.
\end{aligned} \tag{28}$$

The four double-inequalities (27)-(28) can be referred to as the *Bell-CHSH-Fine inequalities* [15,16], necessary and sufficient conditions for the CHSH type experiment to have a "classical" explanation.

4.2 Cosphericity Tests

Let the outputs A_ϕ^λ all be random variables in the narrow sense. Denote, for any distinct $\lambda_1, \lambda_2 \in \Lambda$ and any $\phi \in \Phi$ with $\phi(\lambda_1) = w_1$ and $\phi(\lambda_2) = w_2$,

$$\mathrm{Cor}\left[H_{w_1}^{\lambda_1}, H_{w_2}^{\lambda_2}\right] = \mathrm{Cor}\left[A_\phi^{\lambda_1}, A_\phi^{\lambda_2}\right] = \rho_{w_1 w_2}^{\lambda_1 \lambda_2}, \tag{29}$$

where Cor designates correlation. Let $\phi_1, \phi_2, \phi_3, \phi_4 \in \Phi$ be any treatments with

$$\begin{aligned}
\phi_1(\lambda_1) = \phi_2(\lambda_1) = w_1; \ &\phi_1(\lambda_2) = \phi_3(\lambda_2) = w_2 \\
\phi_4(\lambda_1) = \phi_2(\lambda_1) = w_1'; \ &\phi_4(\lambda_2) = \phi_3(\lambda_2) = w_2'.
\end{aligned} \tag{30}$$

Then, as shown in [19], if the components of H are jointly distributed,

$$\begin{aligned}
&\left| \rho_{w_1 w_2}^{\lambda_1 \lambda_2} \rho_{w_1 w_2'}^{\lambda_1 \lambda_2} - \rho_{w_1' w_2}^{\lambda_1 \lambda_2} \rho_{w_1' w_2'}^{\lambda_1 \lambda_2} \right| \\
&\leq \sqrt{1 - \left(\rho_{w_1 w_2}^{\lambda_1 \lambda_2}\right)^2} \sqrt{1 - \left(\rho_{w_1 w_2'}^{\lambda_1 \lambda_2}\right)^2} + \sqrt{1 - \left(\rho_{w_1' w_2}^{\lambda_1 \lambda_2}\right)^2} \sqrt{1 - \left(\rho_{w_1' w_2'}^{\lambda_1 \lambda_2}\right)^2},
\end{aligned} \tag{31}$$

This is the *cosphericity test* for (7), called so because geometrically (31) describes the possibility to place four points (w_1, w_2, w_1', w_2') on a unit sphere in 3D Euclidean space so that the angles between the corresponding radius-vectors have cosines equal to the correlations. Note that an outcome of this test does not allow to predict the outcome of the same test applied to nonlinearly input-value-specifically transformed random variables. Due to (14), this creates a multitude of cosphericity tests for one and the same initial set of outputs A_ϕ^λ.

In the all-important for behavioral sciences 2×2 factorial design ($\Lambda = \{1, 2\}$, each input is binary, and Φ consists of all four possible treatments), the cosphericity test is a criterion for $\left(A^1, A^2\right) \leftrightarrow \left(\alpha^1, \alpha^2\right)$ if (perhaps following some input-value-specific transformation) the outputs are bivariate normally distributed for all four treatments [19].

4.3 Linear Feasibility Test

The *Linear Feasibility Test* (LFT) is a criterion for selective influences in all situations involving finite sets of inputs/outputs, $\Lambda = \{1, \ldots, n\}$, with the ith input and ith output having finite sets of values, $\{1, \ldots, k_i\}$ and $\{1, \ldots, m_i\}$, respectively [11]. In other situations LFT can be used as a necessary condition because every set of possible values can be discretized. The distributions of $H_\phi = \left(H_{j_1}^1, \ldots, H_{j_n}^n \right)$ are represented by probabilities

$$\Pr\left[H_{j_1}^1 = a_1, \ldots, H_{j_n}^n = a_n \right] = \Pr\left[A_\phi^1 = a_1, \ldots, A_\phi^n = a_n \right], \tag{32}$$

with $\phi = (j_1, \ldots, j_n) \in \Phi$ and

$$(a_1, \ldots, a_n) \in \{1, \ldots, m_1\} \times \cdots \times \{1, \ldots, m_n\}. \tag{33}$$

We consider this probability the $[(a_1, \ldots, a_n), (j_1, \ldots, j_n)]$th component of the $m_1 \cdots m_n t$-vector P (with t denoting the number of treatments in Φ). The joint distribution of H in JDC, if it exists, is represented by probabilities

$$\Pr\left[H_1^1 = h_1^1 \ldots, H_{k_1}^1 = h_{k_1}^1, \ldots, H_1^n = h_1^n, \ldots, H_{k_n}^n = h_{k_n}^n \right], \tag{34}$$

with

$$\left(h_1^1, \ldots, h_{k_1}^1, \ldots, h_1^n, \ldots, h_{k_n}^n \right) \in \{1, \ldots, m_1\}^{k_1} \times \ldots \times \{1, \ldots, m_n\}^{k_n}. \tag{35}$$

We consider this probability the $\left(h_1^1, \ldots, h_{k_1}^1, \ldots, h_1^n, \ldots, h_{k_n}^n \right)$th component of the $(m_1)^{k_1} \cdots (m_n)^{k_n}$-vector Q. Consider now the Boolean matrix M with rows corresponding to components of P and columns to components of Q: let $M(r, c) = 1$ if and only if

1. row r corresponds to the $[(j_1, \ldots, j_n), (a_1, \ldots, a_n)]$th component of P,
2. column c to the $\left(h_1^1, \ldots, h_{k_1}^1, \ldots, h_1^n, \ldots, h_{k_n}^n \right)$th component of Q, and
3. $h_{j_1}^1 = a_1, \ldots, h_{j_n}^n = a_n$.

Clearly, the vector Q exists if and only if the system

$$MQ = P, \ Q \geq 0 \tag{36}$$

has a solution (is *feasible*). This is a linear programming task in the standard form (with a constant objective function). Let $\mathcal{L}(P)$ be a Boolean function equal to 1 if and only if this system is feasible. $\mathcal{L}(P)$ is known to be computable, its time complexity being polynomial [18].

The potential of JDC to lead to LFT and provide an ultimate criterion for the Bohmian entanglement problem has not been utilized in quantum physics until relatively recently, when LFT was proposed in [26,27] and [1]. But the essence of the idea can be found in [21]. Given a set of numerical (experimentally estimated or theoretical) probabilities, computing $\mathcal{L}(P)$ is always preferable to dealing with explicit inequalities as their number becomes very large even for moderate-size vectors P. The classical Bell-CHSH-Fine inequalities (27)-(28) for

$n = 2$, $k_1 = k_2 = 2$, $m_1 = m_2 = 2$ (assuming that the marginal selectivity equalities hold) number just 8, but already for $n = 2$, $k_1 = k_2 = 2$ with $m_1 = m_2 = 3$ (describing, e.g., an EPR experiment with two spin-1 particles, or two spin-$1/2$ ones and inefficient detectors), our computations yield 1080 inequalitiies equivalent to $\mathcal{L}(P) = 1$. For $n = 3$, $k_1 = k_2 = k_3 = 2$ and $m_1 = m_2 = m_3 = 2$, corresponding to the GHZ paradigm [17] with three spin-$1/2$ particles, this number is 53792. Lists of such inequalities can be derived "mechanically" from the format of matrix M using well-known facet enumeration algorithms (see, e.g., program lrs at http://cgm.cs.mcgill.ca/~avis/C/lrs.html). Once such a system of inequalities S is derived, one can use it to prove necessity (or sufficiency) of any other system S' by showing, with the aid of a linear programming algorithm, that S' is redundant when added to S (respectively, S is redundant when added to S').

Acknowledgments. This research has been supported by the NSF grant SES-1155956 to Purdue University and the Academy of Finland grant 121855 to University of Jyväskylä.

References

1. Basoalto, R.M., Percival, I.C.: BellTest and CHSH experiments with more than two settings. Journal of Physics A: Mathematical & General 36, 7411–7423 (2003)
2. Bell, J.: On the Einstein-Podolsky-Rosen paradox. Physics 1, 195–200 (1964)
3. Bohm, D., Aharonov, Y.: Discussion of Experimental Proof for the Paradox of Einstein, Rosen and Podolski. Physical Review 108, 1070–1076 (1957)
4. Clauser, J.F., Horne, M.A., Shimony, A., Holt, R.A.: Proposed experiment to test local hidden-variable theories. Physical Review Letters 23, 880–884 (1969)
5. Dzhafarov, E.N.: Conditionally selective dependence of random variables on external factors. Journal of Mathematical Psychology 43, 123–157 (1999)
6. Dzhafarov, E.N.: Unconditionally selective dependence of random variables on external factors. Journal of Mathematical Psychology 45, 421–451 (2001)
7. Dzhafarov, E.N.: Selective influence through conditional independence. Psychometrika 68, 7–26 (2003)
8. Dzhafarov, E.N.: Thurstonian-type representations for "same-different" discriminations: Probabilistic decisions and interdependent images. Journal of Mathematical Psychology 47, 229–243 (2003) see Dzhafarov, E.N.: Corrigendum to "Thurstonian-type representations for 'same–different' discriminations: Probabilistic decisions and interdependent images." Journal of Mathematical Psychology 50, 511 (2006)
9. Dzhafarov, E.N., Gluhovsky, I.: Notes on selective influence, probabilistic causality, and probabilistic dimensionality. Journal of Mathematical Psychology 50, 390–401 (2006)
10. Dzhafarov, E.N., Kujala, J.V.: The Joint Distribution Criterion and the Distance Tests for Selective Probabilistic Causality. Frontiers in Quantitative Psychology and Measurement 1, 151 (2010), doi: 10.3389/fpsyg.2010.0015
11. Dzhafarov, E.N., Kujala, J.V.: Selectivity in probabilistic causality: Where psychology runs into quantum physics. Journal of Mathematical Psychology 56, 54–63 (2012)

12. Dzhafarov, E.N., Kujala, J.V.: Order-distance and other metric-like functions on jointly distributed random variables. Proceedings of the American Mathematical Society (2011) (in press)
13. Dzhafarov, E.N., Schweickert, R., Sung, K.: Mental architectures with selectively influenced but stochastically interdependent components. Journal of Mathematical Psychology 48, 51–64 (2004)
14. Einstein, A., Podolsky, B., Rosen, N.: Can Quantum-Mechanical Description of Physical Reality be Considered Complete? Physical Review 47, 777–780 (1935)
15. Fine, A.: Joint distributions, quantum correlations, and commuting observables. Journal of Mathematical Physics 23, 1306–1310 (1982)
16. Fine, A.: Hidden variables, joint probability, and the Bell inequalities. Physical Review Letters 48, 291–295 (1982)
17. Greenberger, D.M., Horne, M.A., Zeilinger, A.: Going beyond Bell's theorem. In: Kafatos, M. (ed.) Bell's Theorem, Quantum Theory and Conceptions of the Universe, pp. 69–72. Kluwer, Dordrecht (1989)
18. Karmarkar, N.: A new polynomial-time algorithm for linear programming. Combinatorica 4, 373–395 (1984)
19. Kujala, J.V., Dzhafarov, E.N.: Testing for selectivity in the dependence of random variables on external factors. Journal of Mathematical Psychology 52, 128–144 (2008)
20. Kujala, J.V., Dzhafarov, E.N.: Regular Minimality and Thurstonian-type modeling. Journal of Mathematical Psychology 53, 486–501 (2009)
21. Pitowski, I.: Quantum Probability – Quantum Logic. Springer, Berlin (1989)
22. Sternberg, S.: The discovery of processing stages: Extensions of donders' method. Acta Psychologica 30, 276–315 (1969)
23. Suppes, P., Zanotti, M.: When are probabilistic explanations possible? Synthese 48, 191–199 (1981)
24. Townsend, J.T.: Uncovering mental processes with factorial experiments. Journal of Mathematical Psychology 28, 363–400 (1984)
25. Townsend, J.T., Schweickert, R.: Toward the trichotomy method of reaction times: Laying the foundation of stochastic mental networks. Journal of Mathematical Psychology 33, 309–327 (1989)
26. Werner, R.F., Wolf, M.M.: All multipartite Bell correlation inequalities for two dichotomic observables per site. arXiv:quant-ph/0102024v1 (2001)
27. Werner, R.F., Wolf, M.M.: Bell inequalities and entanglement. arXiv:quant-ph/0107093 v2 (2001)

Quantum-Like Behavior of Classical Systems

Thomas Filk[1,2,3]

[1] Institute for Physics, University of Freiburg, Hermann-Herder-Str. 3,
D-79104 Freiburg
[2] Parmenides Foundation for the Study of Thinking, Munich
[3] Institute of Frontier Areas in Psychology and Mental Health, Freiburg
`thomas.filk@physik.uni-freiburg.de`

Abstract. Bohmian mechanics is an example for a classical theory with
a (Newtonian) ontology which reproduces all features of quantum mechanics. It is often used as a "classical" formulation of quantum mechanics, but in this article we invert the argument: Bohmian mechanics proves
that there are classical systems which can show a quantum-like behavior;
in particular, such models are able to explain non-classical probabilities.
We analyze the general structure of Bohmian-type models and argue,
that neural processes related to the correlates of mental states are likely
to follow a dynamics which is similar to this class of models. Therefore,
it may not be too surprising that cognitive phenomena under certain
circumstances show a quantum-like behavior.

Keywords: Non-classical probability, Bohmian mechanics, Neural correlates of mental processes.

1 Introduction

One of the fundamental laws of probability theory states that the probability
of the union of two disjoint events E_1 and E_2 (i.e., the probablity for the event
$E_1 \cup E_2$ which is interpreted as "E_1 OR E_2") is equal to the sum of the single
probabilities:

$$P(E_1 \cup E_2) = P(E_1) + P(E_2) \qquad (\text{if} \quad E_1 \cap E_2 = \emptyset)\,. \tag{1}$$

This law seems to be violated in quantum theory: pure states can be represented
by vectors in a Hilbert space, events are associated with amplitudes derived from
the scalar product of such vectors, and the probability is equal to the absolute
square of such amplitudes.

For instance, in the famous double-slit experiment one first determines the
amplitudes $\psi_1(x)$ and $\psi_2(x)$ associated to the processes where a particle propagates through one of the possible slits (slit 1 or slit 2, respectively) and hits the
screen at position x, and then one obtains the probability for a hit at x for the
case that both slits are open and the particle can propagate through "slit 1 OR
slit 2" according to

$$P_{1\&2}(x) = \frac{1}{2}|\psi_1(x) + \psi_2(x)|^2\,. \tag{2}$$

J.R. Busemeyer et al. (Eds.): QI 2012, LNCS 7620, pp. 196–206, 2012.

This way of calculating probabilities — adding amplitudes associated to disjoint events and determining the probability from the absolute square of the sum of amplitudes — is sometimes called *quantum probability*.[1] In general, amplitudes are complex valued and the intesity, calculated as the absolute square of the sum of amplitudes, can exhibit constructive and destructive interference leading to many of the counter-intuitive effects in quantum mechanics. In the following, whenever probabilities seem to violate eq. (1), we speak of non-classical probabilities, while the special case of eq. (2) is called quantum probability.

Non-classical probabilities have also been observed in many situations related to human behavior (see, e.g., [1, 14, 2, 8–10] as well as the special issue in the Journal of Mathematical Psychology [17]). As quantum theory is the most prominent scientific theory for which a consistent non-classical probability calculus is known to exist, the mathematical formalism of quantum theory seems to be a natural structure to apply also to these situations. The obvious question — why should the formalism of quantum theory be applicable to psychological or social systems — remains unanswered and gives rise to many speculations.

Several attemps have been made to explain a quantum-like behavior for cognitive processes. One explanation is based on the assumption that quantum mechanics actually does play a prominent role in cognitive processes (for a review of this and other "quantum approaches to consciousness" see, e.g., [3]). A second type of explanation is based on the observation that quantum theory on the one hand and consciousness on the other share common conceptual notions and, therefore, are likely to exhibit similar phenomena, even though this does not imply a direct relation between the two [13]. A third explanation utilizes non-trivial partitions of the state space of complex classical systems due to a limited and/or biased epistemic access [5, 4].

In this article, I will propose a new and promising explanation of why a fundamentally classical system can exhibit quantum-like behavior and, in particular, non-classical probabilities. The explanation is based on a very general class of models among which so-called Bohmian mechanics is a special case. In general, Bohmian mechanics is considered as a classical interpretation of quantum mechanics, however, here we invert the argument by noticing that Bohmian mechanics is a classical (Newtonian) theory which reproduces all known effects of quantum mechanics. This implies that there exist classical models which show quantum-like behavior. The main purpose of this article will be to extract from this type of classical models the general features which allow them to appear quantum-like and to argue why it is not unlikely that similar features are realized in cognitive processes and their neural correlates in the brain.

Bohmian mechanics was developed by David Bohm [7] in 1952 as a counterexample for a famous theorem of John von Neumann [19], according to which an extension of quantum mechanics by so-called hidden variables, which could

---

[1] We should remark that this expression is also used for several related but not identical mathematical structures: It can denote the attribution of positive operator valued measures (POVMs) to events, it can also refer to the expectation value functional for random variables which are elements of non-commutative C^*-algebras.

explain the non-deterministic behavior of quantum theory as a statistical effect, is not possible. Already in 1927 Louis de Broglie proposed a simplified version of this model [11], however, based on a detailed analysis of the measurement process in the framework of this model, Bohm could prove that this "classical" model is able to reproduce all observed effects of quantum theory. The main objective against Bohmian mechanics — the non-locality of the quantum potential — shall not concern us in this context, because I will use Bohmian-type models only on a phenomenological level as a possible explanation of non-classical probabilities.

In Section 2, I will briefly introduce the main concepts and ideas of Bohm's model, while a sketch of the mathematics is put into an Appendix. In Section 3, I will generalize Bohm's model by extracting the essential features necessary to develop the probability calculus related to this type of models. I will show that there exists a broad spectrum of non-classical probabilities which can be obtained in this way. Finally, in Section 4, I will speculate about how this type of dynamics may possibly be realized in neural processes such that mental states and mental events exhibit a non-classical behavior with respect to probabilities. The final conclusions not only summarize the main content of this article but also extend the speculations to other fields of applications.

2   Bohmian Mechanics

This section describes the essential concepts of Bohmian mechanics. A brief sketch of the mathematics is given in the Appendix. The reader who is interested in the mathematical details is referred to the standard literature (e.g., [7, 16, 12, 15]).

The essential ideas of Bohmian mechanics can be summarized as follows:

1. The wave function $\psi(x)$ serves as a "guidance field"[2] (sometimes also called "pilot wave") for a particle, i.e., particles are assumed to exist in the sense of Newtonian mechanics, but their trajectories $q(t)$ are determined by Schrödinger's wave function. Wave functions have a similar ontology as the potential energy in classical mechanics.

2. The dynamics of a particle in the background of the Schrödinger field — i.e., it's trajectory $q(t)$ — is such that the probability density $P(q)$ of finding a particle in a particular location q is equal to the absolute square of the wave function: $P(q) = |\psi(q)|^2$.

3. The dynamics of wave functions is determined by Schrödinger's equation. Wave functions can be superimposed leading to interference patterns. The trajectories of the particles follow these interference patterns, which leads to the observed probabilities for particle detection. Quantum probability (in the sense mentioned in the introduction) follows immediately from this dynamics.

---

[2] This expression was first used in the context of general relativity where it referred to the connection derived from a metric; in relativity the connection form determines the trajectories of particles.

While in standard quantum theory a (pure) state can be described by the wave function $\psi(x)$, in Bohmian mechanics a pure state is given by the pair $(\psi(x), q)$, i.e., in addition to the wave function also the position q of the particle is needed in order to fix a pure state of the system. The position q can only be determined by a measurement which, however, intervenes with the wave function. Furthermore, the uncertainty relations for observable quantities also hold in the framework of Bohmian mechanics, and as any measuring process is subject to the laws of physics (in this case the laws of Bohmian mechanics), it is not possible to determine the initial location q *and* the momentum $p = m\dot{q}$ simultaneously. In this sense $q(t)$ is a "hidden" variable. The ontologically pure states of Bohmian mechanics can never be measured or specifically prepared, or, in other words, the initial conditions for the hidden variable can never be known and utilized for future predictions beyond the limits set by the uncertainty relations.

For an N-particle system the wave function is an element of the N-fold tensor product of the single-particle Hilbert spaces, which makes the quantum potential to a field in configuration space. The same holds for the potential in Newtonian mechanics. Generalizations of the formalism to spin variables shall not concern us here (see, e.g., [6]). Bohm has proven that this extension of quantum mechanics reproduces all experimentally observable features of standard quantum mechanics. Actually, the most difficult part of the theory is the description of the measurement process.

The most prominent objective against Bohmian mechanics is related to "non-locality": in order to explain quantum correlations (and the observed violation of Bell's inequalities), the wave function (and, thereby, the quantum potential) has to change instantaneously everywhere in space as the result of a local measurement. As we are using Bohmian mechanics as a phenomenological model (e.g., describing specific neural processes), this objective against Bohmian mechanics shall not concern us here.

3   Classical Dynamics Which Looks Quantum

In this section we will generalize the concepts of Bohmian mechanics (Sect. 3.1), clarify the relation between "events" and "conditions" in these models (Sect. 3.2) and derive a generalized non-classical relation for probabilities (Sect. 3.3).

3.1   Conceptual Generalization of Bohmian Mechanics

In order for a classical theory to exhibit quantum features (and, in particular, the effects of quantum probability), Bohmian mechanics suggests the following ingredients (it should be emphasized that these are neither necessary nor sufficient conditions for observing non-classical behavior, they are merely a good starting point):

1. There are two dynamical entities: (1) a spatially extended "background activity" which can be described by a field $\psi(x)$ and which replaces the guiding

field (in more complicated situations one can even think of several types of background fields, i.e., $\psi(x)$ can be a multi-component field), and (2) a more localized entity for which the dynamics is "guided" by the background field. In Bohmian mechanics this second entity is the particle, but one can also think of a second type of activity which is also described by a field for which the support is more local.

2. The dynamics of the background activity can be quite general, but in order to mimick quantum probability, the dynamics of this field should be described by a linear equation such that with any two solutions $\psi_1(x)$ and $\psi_2(x)$ also (possibly normalized) superpositions $\alpha\psi_1(x) + \beta\psi_2(x)$ are a solution. Note, however, that this is not a necessary condition for the observation of "non-classical probabilities", it only makes the similarity to quantum mechanics more obvious.

   In order to observe interference patterns, the field should have the property to assume positive and negative values which, when superimposed, can cancel each other. Interference-like solutions, however, can also occur for non-linear equations.

3. The dynamics of the guided entity can also be quite general but it should be such that the probability of finding the guided entity at a location x is a function of the guiding (background) activity $\psi(x)$. In Bohmian mechanics this probability is proportional to the absolute square of the background activity.

   The correlates of this guided entity are observed, but indirectly the observation of this entity probes the background activity.

There are many examples of this type of dynamics, in particular in the realm of chemistry or biology: The background field can be the concentration $\rho(x)$ of some chemical or nutrition in a solution and the guided entity can be some bacterium which propagates along the gradient of increasing concentration of the nutrition. In many cases this leads to a "classical" probability for the location of the bacterium, in particular, if the probability of finding the bacterium is proportional to the concentration of the nutrition and this concentration follows a linear dynamics.

If, however, the probability $P(x)$ is a non-linear function of $\rho(x)$ and, in particular, if the dynamics of $\rho(x,t)$ is more complicated (one may think of two nutritious components which interact like in a Belousov-Zhabotinsky reaction) also the probability of finding a bacterium behaves non-classically and (in the case of the BZ reaction) even can show interference-like patterns.

3.2   Events and Conditions

We now elaborate on the relation between "events" E (the occurence or preparation of particular situations) and observed probabilities $P(E)$ in this class of models in more detail.

Strictly speaking, we should distinguish between two types of events which are associated to the two entities (the guided and the guiding entity) of Bohmian models. One type of events will be symbolized by "x" and refers to the "observation of the guided entity at location x". The other type of events will be symbolized by "E" and refers to the "contextual situation E which leads to the event x". In the case of the double-slit experiment, the event x denotes the registration of the particle at a position x on the screen, and E refers to the condition of the slits: "slit 1 open", "slit 2 open", "slit 1 and 2 open". $P_E(x)$ denotes the probability of detecting the particle at location x on the screen under the condition of situation E. Expressing it this way, $P_E(x)$ is a conditional probability for the event x with E being the condition. However, if we assume that the possible conditions E exhaust all possibilities for a particle to arrive at x and that disjoint conditions (like "slit 1 open" and "slit 2 open") do no interfer when fulfilled both, we arrive at

$$P_{E_1 \cup E_2}(x) = P_{E_1}(x) + P_{E_2}(x), \tag{3}$$

which is the analogue of eq. 1. This last assumption is not valid in quantum theory. The identification of a condition (one slit or both slits being open) with an "event" (the particle passes exactly one of the possible slits in the same way as it would do if the other slit were closed) is not justified in both, quantum theory and Bohmian mechanics: In standard quantum theory the assumption that "the particle passes one of the possible slits" is usually rejected and in Bohmian mechanics the assumption "as it would do if the other slit were closed" is wrong.

In a similar sense, the "set of all pet-fishes" may be the intersection of the "set of all fishes" and the "set of all pets". But asking questions like whether a guppy is a fish, a pet, or a pet-fish sets certain conditions, and the concept of "pet-fish" may induce interferences between the concepts of "fish" and "pet". This remark refers to the famous Pet-Fish experiment in psychology ([20]).

3.3 Non-classical Probabilities

In quantum mechanics and also in Bohmian mechanics, the result of the preparation of the system and the conditions E are mathematically encoded in the quantum state and can be described by a field $\psi_E(x)$. In general, the observed probability $P_E(x)$ of finding the guided entity at location x will be some function of the local value of the background field $\psi_E(x)$:

$$P_E(x) = F(\psi_E(x)). \tag{4}$$

In quantum mechanics we have $P_E(x) = |\psi_E(x)|^2$.

For two mutually exclusive conditions E_1 and E_2 corresponding the background fields $\psi_1(x)$ and $\psi_2(x)$, respectively, we consider the situation $E_1 \cup E_2$ ("E_1 OR E_2"), which shall be described by a background field

$$\psi_{1\&2}(x) = G(\psi_1(x), \psi_2(x)). \tag{5}$$

For quantum mechanics we simply have $G(\psi_1, \psi_2) = \psi_1 + \psi_2$ (up to a possible normalization), but for more general situations this function maybe non-linear.

The probability for the observation of the entity at location x is now given by:

$$P_{E_1 \cup E_2}(x) = F(G(\psi_1(x), \psi_2(x))).$$ (6)

In general, the right hand side is not equal to the sum $P_{E_1} + P_{E_2}$, and in these cases the probabilities follow a non-classical behavior.

4   A Bohmian Model for Cognitive Processes

In this section, I will speculate about a possible scenario for neural processes which may fall into the class of models discussed in this article. First, I identify the guiding and the guided entity:

1. Suppose the "guiding field" $\psi(x)$ describes the general activity of neural assemblies, i.e., essentially it is a measure for the local activity of populations of neurons. A specific situation E (e.g., an external stimulus) induces a neural activity described by $\psi_E(x)$.

2. The "guided entity" shall correspond to a particular class of neural activities to which I will refer as "neural correlates of mental states".[3] Whatever these special neural correlates of mental states are, it is conceivable to assume that they depend on the general neural activity $\psi(x)$ and that their dynamics is "guided" by this general activity. Whether these guided neural activities are related to the synchronization of firing patterns or realized in other ways is not important. What is important, and this seems to be a plausible assumption, is that these "neural correlates of mental states" are most likely to be found where the intensity of the general neural activity is high.

In many psychological experiments the observed reaction of a subject is related to the mental state of this subject. This means that what is observed are "cognitive events" which are assumed to be correlated to the guided neural activity of the proposed model. Therefore, in contrast to Bohmian versions of quantum theory where the position of the particle (the hidden variable) is measured directly, in psychological experiments only the mental correlates of the guided neural activity are observed. In the following we will neglect this additional feature. Relevant for the proposed scenario is only the existence of certain neural activities which are correlated to the mental states and that these particular neural activities are more or less localized within the general neural activity. (Localization does not necessarily refer to a 3-dimensional localization in the brain but can refer to an abstract configuration space: the "space of all possible mental states".)

This simple and quite general scenario fulfills all the requirements needed for a generalized Bohmian-type mechanics: Two activities, one of which can be described by a field and the other being dependend on this first activity in the sense that it is most likely to be found where the first activity is large. If there is

---

[3] Mental state is just a placeholder for any other concept — awareness, intentionality, consciousness, etc. — which may be relevant in the psychological context.

any non-linearity in the dependencies one can expect non-classical probabilities in the correlations between the experimental context and the observed reactions.

Up to now, the model only explains the observation of non-classical probabilities in cognitive systems. As mentioned in the introduction, many experiments support the observation of non-classical probabilities in cognitive processes. Whether they prove the validity of quantum probability (in the sense of eq. 2) may be a matter of debate. Of course, in order to close up with quantum theory and, in particular, to realize quantum probabilities, the dynamics for the neuronal activities $\psi(x)$ and the dependencies between this background activity and the guided activity should be made more precise.

However, we can refine the model in such a way that it even comes close to Bohmian mechanics. Let us assume that the local neuronal activity is not only described by a rate but also by a phase (as realized, e.g., by the phases of spiking trains). In this case the neural activity can be described by a complex field $\psi(x)$ where the amplitude corresponds to the firing rate and the angular argument to the phase. Such a field allows for superpositions in a similar way as the quantum mechanical wave function. In particular, two activities can "cancel" each other at locations where the neuronal activities are "out of phase" and reinforce each other at locations where they are synchronized. In order to make the similarity to quantum theory (almost) complete, the guided activities of the neural correlates of mental states should be such that they are found more likely in locations where this synchronization (in addition to the firing rate) is large and less likely in locations where this synchronization is low.

In our point of view, the proposed scenario comes close to a plausible description of the actual neuronal activities and their relations to mental states. Therefore, the occurrence of correlations which obey non-classical probabilities may find a surprising but natural explanation. Conversely, detailed measurements of the non-classical relations between probabilities may allow to draw conclusions about the dynamics of the guided neural correlates of mental states in the background neural activity.

5   Conclusions

We have shown that Bohmian-type models are quite general and can lead to non-classical probabilities, even though they are based on a classical ontology. In particular, it is not inconceivable that neural dynamics on the level of neuronal assemblies is similar to such a Bohmian-type model, which would explain the observation of non-classical probabilities with respect to particular situations in human behavior.

The general scenario suggested by Bohmian-type models — a guiding field and a guided entity — are very likely to be found also in other fields, in particular in the social or economic sciences. Public opinion, e.g., may guide individual opinions, etc. We already mentioned examples from chemistry, and it is not difficult to find also examples in evolutionary biology, developmental biology and population dynamics.

The main reason why "non-classical probabilities" usually are not considered as relevant for these situations seems to be that both, the guiding quantity as well as the guided quantity, can be observed, which makes the classical structure behind the observed pattern obvious. However, in quantum theory as well as in many cases in the cognitive sciences, only one part of the two entities is observed — the particle in case of quantum mechanics and mental aspects in case of psychological experiments. The observed quantity seems to behave non-classically because the dynamics of this quantity in the background of the underlying guiding field is neither observed nor known and, therefore, it is not possible to take this dynamics directly into account. However, indirectly it manifests itself in the occurence of non-classical probabilities.

Acknowledgement. I greatly profited from discussions with P. beim Graben and H. Atmanspacher. Furthermore, I acknowledge partial funding of this research by the Franklin Fetzer Trust.

References

1. Aerts, D., Aerts, S.: Applications of quantum statistics in psychological studies of decision processes. Foundations of Science, 85–97 (1994)
2. Aerts, D.: Quantum Structure in Cognition. Journal of Mathematical Psychology 53(5), 314–348 (2009)
3. Atmanspacher, H.: Quantum Approaches to Consciousness. Stanford Encyclopedia of Philosophy, http://plato.stanford.edu/entries/qt-consciousness/
4. Atmanspacher, H., Filk, T., beim Graben, P.: Can classical epistemic states be entangles? In: Bruza, P., et al. (eds.) Quantum Intercation - 2011, pp. 128–137. Springer, Berlin (2011)
5. beim Graben, P., Atmanspacher, H.: Complementarity in classical dynamical systems. Foundations of Physics 36, 291–306 (2006)
6. Bell, J.: On the Problem of Hidden Variables in Quantum Mechanics. Reviews of Modern Physics 38(3), 447–452 (1966)
7. Bohm, D.J.: A Suggested Interpretation of the Quantum Theory in Terms of "Hidden" Variables I & II. Phys. Rev. 85, 166 & 180 (1952)
8. Bruza, P.D., Kitto, K., Nelson, D., McEvoy, C.L.: Is there something quantum-like about the human mental lexicon? Journal of Mathematical Psychology 53, 362–377 (2009)
9. Busemeyer, J.R., Wang, Z., Townsend, J.T.: Quantum dynamics of human decision making. Journal of Mathematical Psychology 50, 220–241 (2006)
10. Busemeyer, J.R., Pothos, E., Franco, R., Trueblood, J.S.: A quantum theoretical explanation for probability judgement errors. Psychological Review 108, 193–218 (2011)
11. de Broglie, L.: Wave mechanics and the atomic structure of matter and of radiation. Le Journal de Physique et le Radium 8, 225 (1927); see also Bacciagaluppi, G., Valentini, A.: Quantum Theory at the Crossroads – Reconsidering the 1927 Solvay Conference. Cambridge University Press (2009)
12. Cushing, J.T., Fine, A., Goldstein, S.: Bohmian Mechanics and Quantum Theory: An Appraisal. Boston Studies in the Philosophy of Science, vol. 184. Springer, Netherlands (1996)

13. Filk, T., von Müller, A.: Quantum Physics and Consciousness: The Quest for a Common Conceptual Foundation. Mind and Matter 7(1), 59–79 (2009)
14. Gabora, L., Aerts, D.: Contextualizing concepts using a mathematical generalization of the quantum formalism. Journal of Experimental and Theoretical Artificial Intelligence, 327–358 (2002)
15. Holland, P.R.: The Quantum Theory of Motion — An Account of the DeBroglie-Bohm Causal Interpretation of Quantum Mechanics. Cambridge University Press (1993)
16. Jammer, M.: The Philosophy of Quantum Mechanics: The Interpretations of Quantum Mechanics in Historical Perspective. Wiley-Interscience, New York (1974)
17. Special Issue: Quantum Cognition; Journal of Mathematical Psychology 53(5) (2009)
18. Khrennikov, A.Y.: Classical and quantum mechanics on information spaces with applications to cognitive, psychological, social and anomalous phenomena. Foundations of Physics 29, 1065–1098 (1999)
19. von Neumann, J.: Mathematische Grundlagen der Quantenmechanik. Springer (1932); Mathematical Foundations of Quantum Mechanics. Princeton University Press (1952)
20. Osherson, D.N., Smith, E.E.: On the adequacy of prototype theory as a theory of concepts. Cognition 9, 35–58 (1981)

Appendix: A Sketch of Bohmian Mechanics

Starting point is Schrödinger's equation for a complex field $\psi(x,t)$:

$$i\hbar\frac{\partial \Psi(x,t)}{\partial t} = -\frac{\hbar^2}{2m}\Delta\Psi(x,t) + V(x)\Psi(x,t) \ . \tag{7}$$

We express the complex field in polar coordinates

$$\Psi(x,t) = R(x,t)\exp\left(\frac{i}{\hbar}S(x,t)\right) \tag{8}$$

where now $R(x,t)$ and $S(x,t)$ are real fields and satisfy the differential equations:

$$\frac{\partial R(x,t)}{\partial t} = -\frac{1}{2m}\Big(R(x,t)\Delta S(x,t) + 2\nabla R(x,t)\cdot\nabla S(x,t)\Big) \ , \tag{9}$$

$$\frac{\partial S(x,t)}{\partial t} = -\left[\frac{(\nabla S(x,t))^2}{2m} + V(x) - \frac{\hbar^2}{2m}\frac{\Delta R(x,t)}{R(x,t)}\right] \ . \tag{10}$$

Replacing the amplitude $R(x,t)$ by the absolute square of the wave function $P(x,t) = |\psi(x,t)|^2 = R(x,t)^2$ one obtains the differential equations:

$$\frac{\partial P(x,t)}{\partial t} = -\nabla\cdot\left(P(x,t)\frac{\nabla S(x,t)}{m}\right) \ , \tag{11}$$

$$\frac{\partial S(x,t)}{\partial t} = -\frac{(\nabla S(x,t))^2}{2m} - V(x) + \frac{\hbar^2}{4m}\left[\frac{\Delta P(x,t)}{P(x,t)} - \frac{1}{2}\frac{(\nabla P(x,t))^2}{P(x,t)^2}\right] \ . \tag{12}$$

The second equation is well-known in the Hamilton-Jacobi formulation of classical mechanics: the trajectories of particles are orthogonal to the surfaces of constant $S(x, t)$, and the velocity $v(x, t)$ of a particle (following a trajetory which at time t is at point x) is given by $v(x, t) = \nabla S(x, t)/m$. Using this expression, the differential equation for $P(x, t)$ assumes the form:

$$\frac{\partial P}{\partial t} + \nabla \cdot (Pv) = 0 \ . \tag{13}$$

This is a continuity equation for $P(x, t) = |\psi(x, t)|^2$.

Up to now, everything is completely within the framework of standard quantum theory. It is just a reformulation of Schrödinger's equation, and the continuity equation expresses the "conservation of probability" (the unitarity of time evolution). The essential step beyond standard quantum theory is the introduction of "hidden variables" $q(t)$ associated to the position of real, existing particles. $P(x, t)$ is now interpreted as the probability distribution for an ensemble of trajectories: for t fixed, $P(x, t)$ is the density of trajectories $\{q(t)\}$ in this ensemble at point x, and the continuity equation guarantees that this interpretation remains valid for all t. The Newtonian equation of motion corresponding to eq. (12) is

$$m \frac{\mathrm{d}^2 q}{\mathrm{d}t^2} = -\nabla \left(V(q(t)) - \frac{\hbar^2}{2m} \frac{\Delta R(q(t))}{R(q(t))} \right) \ , \tag{14}$$

where, apart from the classical potential $V(x)$, also the so-called quantum potential

$$U(x) = -\frac{\hbar^2}{2m} \cdot \frac{\Delta R}{R} = \frac{\hbar^2}{4m} \left[\frac{\Delta P}{P} - \frac{1}{2} \frac{(\nabla P)^2}{P^2} \right] \tag{15}$$

appears. This quantum potential is responsible for the non-classical patterns which are observed, e.g., the interference patterns in a double-slit experiment.

Connecting the Dots: Mass, Energy, Word Meaning, and Particle-Wave Duality

Sándor Darányi and Peter Wittek

Swedish School of Library and Information Science
University of Borås
Allégatan 1, 50190 Borås, Sweden
sandor.daranyi@hb.se, peterwittek@acm.org

Abstract. With insight from linguistics that degrees of text cohesion are similar to forces in physics, and the frequent use of the energy concept in text categorization by machine learning, we consider the applicability of particle-wave duality to semantic content inherent in index terms. Wave-like interpretations go back to the regional nature of such content, utilizing functions for its representation, whereas content as a particle can be conveniently modelled by position vectors. Interestingly, wave packets behave like particles, lending credibility to the duality hypothesis. We show in a classical mechanics framework how metaphorical term mass can be computed.

1 Introduction

The general idea to use physics, prominently both classical and quantum mechanics, to model phenomena crucial to managing society has lately made an interesting debut among significant research questions. To do so, the calculus being the same as in quantum mechanics, the trick is to switch the probability type from the variant pertinent in the subatomic domain to the other one which works in the macroworld [1]. By this, phenomena like financial market evolution (deterministic and stochastic models of markets), language evolution, or digital repositories handling term meaning fluctuations become available for extensive and application-oriented, testable research with implementable results.

At the same time, currently this intellectual tightrope walking is mostly theory development, with expected immediate practical implications. If one can show on new use cases such as e.g. media, health, and part text, part signal based science data that quantum-like modelling works, and yields at least as good or better results than the benchmark, then one will have to ask for the reason of this success. One explanation we have at this point is the metaphorically "energetic" nature of both language [2] and learning (decision making) [3]. Since we perceive this "energetic" nature based on macroworld observations also underpinned by microworld calculation methodology, the phenomenon must be underlying both classical mechanics (CM) and quantum mechanics (QM).

With this caveat, as a next phase in an ongoing thought experiment, below we will first cite arguments from linguistics to compare kinds of coherence in

J.R. Busemeyer et al. (Eds.): QI 2012, LNCS 7620, pp. 207–217, 2012.

language to types of forces in physics, and suggest the field concept as a possible unifying metaphor to represent word and sentence semantics both in the CM and QM frames of thought. Our first observation cites views calling for a regionally rather than exactly located kind of semantic content to be considered [4]. Secondly, mathematical objects with physical equivalents, such as sinusoids standing for e.g. electromagnetic waves and wavelets for impulses (outbursts), can be used to model the above regional distribution of semantic content [5,6], also demonstrated for the visible light part of the spectrum [7] – as if, in a sense, terms and documents had a wave nature. Thirdly, we will postulate that the same semantic content can be conceived both as a particle and a wave-packet, arguing for this quasi-dual nature as an essential property enabling new kinds of experiments.

The topic is heating up because of increasing interest in temporal dynamics [8,9,10,11] and its anticipated connection with the Hamiltonian, a typically quantum interaction (QI) consideration. As proposed earlier, in both CM and QM, it is the Hamiltonian which describes the energy stored in a system, and in order to approach it, finding a way to compute term "mass" is the key.

This paper is organized as follows: Section 2 outlines the concept of energy in machine learning, Section 3 interprets the Hamiltonian on the constituents of a term-document matrix and in Section 4 we consider the duality of semantic content representation. Section 5 is the discussion of some immediate implications of our observations, with Section 6 offering our brief conclusions.

2   Energy in Machine Learning

The metaphoric use of physics is based on the urge to find better models of text classification (TC) and information retrieval (IR) by means of machine learning (ML). We start with arguments from linguistics to compare kinds of coherence in language to types of force in physics.

As White suggests, linguistics, like physics, has four binding forces [12]:

- The strong nuclear force, which is the strongest "glue" in physics, corresponds to word uninterruptability (binding morphemes into words);
- Electromagnetism, which is less strong, corresponds to grammar and binds words into sentences;
- The weak nuclear force, being even less strong, compares to texture or cohesion (also called coherence), binding sentences into texts;
- Finally gravity as the weakest force acts like intercohesion or intercoherence which binds texts into literatures (i.e. documents into collections or databases).

Mainstream linguistics traditionally deals with Forces 1 and 2, while discourse analysis and text linguistics are particularly concerned with Force 3. The field most identified with the study of Force 4 is information science [12,13,14]. As the concept of force implies, referring here to attraction, it takes energy to keep things together, therefore the energy doing so is stored in agglomerations of observables of different kinds in different magnitudes, and can be released from such structures. A notable difference between physical and lingustic systems is that extracting work content, i.e. "energy" from symbols by reading or copying them does not annihilate symbolic content, however.

Looking now at the same problem from a different angle, in the above and related efforts, energy inherent in all four types can be the model of:

- A Type 2, i.e. electromagnetism-like attractive-repulsive binding force such as lexical attraction, a.k.a syntactic word affinity [15], also called sentence cohesion, such as by modelling dependency grammar by mutual information [16]. Once pointwise mutual information replaces mutual information, the nickname of the effect is "infomagnetism" [17]. In a TC and/or IR setting, a similar phenomenon is term dependence based on their co-occurrence;
- Decision making, such as in a classification process, both in a supervised and unsupervised manner;
- Information representation, such as conceiving documents as wave interference patterns [7,18].

Again from a different angle, the energy concept used in experiments of the above types can be mathematical or physical. For mathematical energy, at least three concepts are current:

- Signal energy in calculations, devoid of physical content (e.g. [6]. A typical consideration runs like this: "Signals that arise from strictly mathematical processes and have no apparent physical equivalent are commonly considered to represent some form of mathematical energy" [19];
- Loss functions in ML. These model the cost of a classification decision as an energy minimizing process;
- Local density of values within a mathematical object: "Energy of a (part of a) vector is calculated by summing up the squares of the values in the (part of the) vector" [20].

For physical energy as a model of content or processes, the applicability of the metaphor in ML pertains to all kinds of media, images included. With a focus mainly on clustering, its range is already strikingly broad, spanning the electromagnetic force [21], gravity [22,23], spin [24], waves [25], wavelets [26], and wave functions [27,28]. At the same time, the utilization of the energy concept in ML goes back to the use of potentials. In the examples cited above, there are two kinds thereof, Coulomb potential vs. gravitational potential, so that decision making (classification, categorization) is minimum or maximum seeking by gradient descent or ascent on a hypersurface, constructed from statistics describing the event space. Whereas gravitational force assumes energy from the mass of particles (i.e., documents) in a cluster, Coulomb potential presupposes the dipole nature of entities such as belonging to vs. not belonging to a class.

We have to mention here the inherent eigen conjecture in latent semantic methods, namely that terms have "mass", i.e. word meaning behaves as if it had an energetic nature [2]. This conjecture is now reinforced by the explicit consideration of mass in the kinetic part of dynamic quantum clustering (DQC) as well [28].

3   The Role of the Hamiltonian in Evolving Document Collections

Taking into consideration that $H = T + V$ is the Hamiltonian equation we want to interpret, where H is the Hamiltonian operator, T is the kinetic energy and V is the potential energy of a system, respectively, we argue that $AA^T = H$, that is, we treat the term co-occurrence matrix as the description of the total energy of the system. Thereby we also assume that our system is a conservative one. The same assumption was made by DQC [27,28,29].

Any update of AA^T results in an $A'A'^T$ state with its corresponding V' potential energy, whereas the difference between any two consecutive V' goes back partly to changes in document collection content reflected by different index term occurrence rates (a.k.a. term frequency), partly to changes in the proportion of referential meaning added to H by sense definitions and sense relations of index terms. Both T and V can be analyzed by comparing consecutive spectral decomposition of the same index term over periods.

It is key to the understanding of V to remember that the semantic interpretation of both A and AA^T goes back to term occurrences in context, and thereby to the distributional hypothesis of word meaning [30]. However, taking a broader view of the issue, it is clear that at least one more factor, i.e. referential meaning must play a role in interpreting the above matrices as well. Namely the reason *why* terms in a particular context co-occur goes back to their ontological meaning, in a referential relation with their occurrences in sentences. This external, hidden contribution can be measured e.g. by the inverse relationship between the number of intensions (features) of a word vs. its extensions (cardinality of the set of its examples) [31].

Next we bring arguments for the regional nature of semantic content. We will focus on Euclidean space, i.e. the vector space IR model (VSM) and its offsprings, where a natural concern is to ask, is semantic content exactly or inexactly located, i.e. regional? The answer depends on what one wants to model and by which mathematical objects; however, this ambiguity, the potentially dual nature of semantic content will be key to our conclusions.

4   Duality in Semantic Representation

4.1   The Regionality of Semantic Content – Wave-Like Representation

In linguistics, the regional nature of word semantics can be best observed on the overlap between word senses displayed as semantic fields [32,33]. Priss and Old model the underlying, language-independent conceptual regions by neighbourhood lattices [34]. Further the very concern itself is not new, IR and TC having assumed for a long time that the immediate neighbourhood [4] of relevant terms and documents contains related, and therefore important, information, which can be used for e.g. relevance feedback [35]. In a QI setting, Bruza and Woods ascribed word sense disambiguation to the collapse of meaning superpositions due to disambiguating local term context [36]. Further there is an argument in [37] about support vector machines (SVM) linked to quantum disjunctions, the link being regions, meant to solve the problem to be able to say that apple is a kind of fruit (apple is part of the fruit region, i.e. its hyponym), as opposed to modeling that apple and fruit have something to do with each other. SVMs do this by finding the separating hyperplane, but more research is needed to understand whether the separating hyperplane defines a region. Finally, instead of regions, [38] measure the distance between subspaces spanned by documents by projecting them into one another.

In vector models using position vectors content is usually exactly located. However, reinforcing Dyvik's and Priss and Old's argument, e.g. Erk also argues for the regionality of word meaning, i.e. its inexact location [4]. She departs from the fact that many models of categorization in psychology represent a concept as a region, characterized by feature vectors with dimension weights, and offers two computational models, both of which can host soft region boundaries. Using so-called type vectors as central vectors, each type vector comes with a vector β which defines the importance of each dimension, thus the type vector and its weight vector define a region. Here, regionality implies gradually decreasing similarity between document, query and term vectors. Another model, of sentence formation and called lexical attraction [15], deals with the likelihood of a syntactic relation decaying over distance like a force.

Regionality also manifests itself if term vectors are embedded into an L_2 space, assigning sums of sinusoids or wavelets to each term in the function space [39,40]. In these models the length of the period or the length of the support controls the inexactness of semantic content, and given that terms are arranged according to a semantic order, this representation may lead to improvement in classification performance.

Hence both terms and sentence components can be considered as having a regional interpretation or aspect as well. Interference (pattern) models using functions to represent semantic content implement this regionality expectation [18,7] – as do Erk's token vectors for monosemous vs. polysemous words. By these means, the question has to remain undecided. However, the applicability of the concepts of energy, the Hamiltonian, and regional, "smeared out" content beg for a thought experiment which compares exactly located content to particles, inexactly located content to waves, and invokes the parallel with particle-wave duality in QM.

4.2   Meaning and Mass – Particle-Like Representation

The attempt presented here goes back to CM with the implied argument that if QI methods work on language, terms must have "energies" and, in turn, related "mass" equivalents; but then, these must be observable in the much simpler Newtonian environment as well.

Following this train of thought, given that in CM, force is the product of mass and acceleration, $F = ma$ in Newton's 2nd law, we assume that similarity is a "glue", i.e. binding force, between entities in vector space [41]: the more similar two vectors are, the better they attract each other (which is different for example from electromagnetic attraction and repulsion).

Table 1. Evolution of an indexing vocabulary over time

$t = 0$	Doping	Football	Performance	Skiing	Training
d_1	5	2	0	0	0
d_2	4	0	0	3	1
d_3	0	0	4	0	5
d_4	6	0	2	0	0
d_5	0	3	0	0	4
$t = 1$					
d_1	5	2	0	0	0
d_2	4	0	0	3	1
d_3	0	0	4	0	5
d_4	6	0	2	0	0
d_5	0	3	0	0	4
d_6	2	3	0	1	1
d_7	1	0	0	4	5
$t = 2$					
d_1	5	2	0	0	0
d_2	4	0	0	3	1
d_3	0	0	4	0	5
d_4	6	0	2	0	0
d_5	0	3	0	0	4
d_6	2	3	0	1	1
d_7	1	0	0	4	5
d_8	5	6	1	1	0
d_9	2	1	1	3	0

Thinking back of Salton's dynamic library with its moving cluster centroids due to collection update (expansion) [42], we leave the question undecided here if an updated system is a closed or open one. With a conservative system in mind, we consider a vector space of many term-document matrices, representing consecutive updates of the same database with a fixed vocabulary over an increasing number of documents, so that all the documents and the terms will have temporal indices as well. This way term and document similarity can be computed as the cosine of two vectors with the same temporal index, and the dislocation (i.e. distance, x) of the same term due to database update will be the cosine of the two respective vectors with consecutive temporal indices. Assuming updates over units of time, term velocity (v) will be the same as the distance between two consecutive positions of the same term. Calculating term acceleration (a) equals the difference between term velocities over units of time. Table 1 shows a toy example of a growing document collection indexed by the same terms in three timesteps. Given this, we depart from Ehrenfest's theorem stating that the time-dependent expectation value of the position operator

$$\langle \psi(t)|x|\psi(t)\rangle = \int \psi(x,t)^* x\psi(x,t)dx$$

satisfies the equation

$$\frac{d^2\langle x(t)\rangle}{dt^2} = \langle \psi(t)|\nabla V(x)|\psi(t)\rangle.$$

This means that the expectation values of the position operator obey their corresponding classical equations of motion, that is, the centre of each wave packet rolls towards the nearest minimum of the potential according to Newton's 2nd law. Following this train of thought further, with term similarities at different times as attraction between them in a symmetric matrix, we insert term acceleration in the respective row and column headings and see that $|F|/|a| = m$ for every term at a given time, i.e. for every term pair compute their time-dependent masses.

We derive term "mass" the following way. Assuming unit time steps, we calculate term velocities between subsequent time steps based on the Euclidean distance between the term's vector at the respective time steps. We only care about the magnitude. The change in the velocity results in an acceleration value. At every time step, we regard the force that acts on a term as a sum of dissimilarities with every term except itself. This calculation is similar to an interaction potential that considers $n : n$ relations between particles (or agents) [1, p.157]. This is a considerable simplification as the force that changes the term distribution is at least partially external to an existing distributional pattern. Based on the absolute value of the acceleration and the force, term "mass" can be calculated (see Table 2).

Table 2. Calculation of term mass over t_0-t_1

	Doping	Football	Performance	Skiing	Training
v_1	9	9	0	25	36
v_2	49	49	4	16	0
a	40	40	4	-9	-36
F	1.56	1.28	1.24	1.35	1.37
m	0.039	0.032	0.31	0.15	0.038

5   Discussion

Immediate consequences of term representation by wave packets include the following:

– When describing the behaviour of index terms in a document collection expanding over time according to the CM frame of thought, all the numerical results for variables like force, acceleration or mass, are dimensionless, i.e. metaphoric. An explanation of the results can be to ascribe constant mass to terms like in [41] where term occurrences count as such, but variable density, $\rho = mV$. Here any word form would count as a unit container, hence $V = $ const., and variable term density is the result of variable forces acting on the system in different periods;

– In DQC, Gaussian wave packets model particles [28]. According to Eq 6.4, "the generalized Gaussian packet shows that the packet center moves along the classical trajectory for a particle starting with the given initial mean position and mean momentum". A wave packet (or wave train) is a short "burst" or "envelope" of wave action that travels as a unit and can be analyzed into, or can be synthesized from, an infinite set of component sinusoidal waves of different wavenumbers, with phases and amplitudes such that they interfere constructively only over a small region of space, and destructively elsewhere. Wave packets, while behaving as particles, can reversibly model sentences as word sequences. If a sentence happens to be a definition of a word sense, like in Wordnet, they model referential semantics charging words "from the outside", i.e. adding extra meaning to words in the term-document matrix whose only meaning this far was ascribed to the distributional hypothesis [30];

– The total energy of a classical mechanical or a QM system is described by the Hamiltonian operator, adding up its kinetic and potential energy. However, the Hamiltonian may or may not describe a quantum-like system. Further there are some subtle issues here and we must not jump to conclusions. Inexactly located semantic content suggests a distribution as well as some kind of an uncertainty; in a QL context both stem from the non-commutative nature of the operators. We only conjecture that the use of such non-commutative operators is an apt description for semantic content.

6   Conclusions

To further underpin the observation that language may be a quantum-like system, we sampled arguments in favour of a metaphorical use of classical and quantum mechanics to model the static and dynamic behaviour of word meaning. With energy as a concept frequently used in some form in text categorization and information retrieval, we contrasted two equally valid approaches to the representation of semantic content, by its exact vs. inexact location, and argued that they closely resemble particle-wave duality in QM. One cited example, wave packets, interestingly behave like particles, lending credibility to the duality hypothesis. Further we showed on a toy example in a classical mechanics framework how metaphorical term mass can be computed. Our future work will increasingly focus on the interpretation and practical use of the Hamiltonian of evolving semantic systems.

References

1. Khrennikov, A.: Ubiquitous quantum structure: from psychology to finance. Springer (2010)
2. Wittek, P., Darányi, S.: Spectral composition of semantic spaces. In: Proceedings of QI 2011, 5th International Quantum Interaction Symposium, Aberdeen, UK (2011)
3. LeCun, Y., Chopra, S., Hadsell, R.: A tutorial on energy-based learning. Predicting Structured Data, 1–59 (2006)
4. Erk, K.: Representing words as regions in vector space. In: Proceedings of CoNLL 2009, 13th Conference on Computational Natural Language Learning, Boulder, CO, USA, pp. 57–65 (2009)
5. Park, L., Palaniswami, M., Kotagiri, R.: Internet document filtering using Fourier domain scoring. LNCS, pp. 362–373 (2001)
6. Park, L.: Spectral Based Information Retrieval. PhD thesis, University of Melbourne (2003)
7. Dorrer, C., Londero, P., Anderson, M., Wallentowitz, S., Walmsley, I.: Computing with interference: all-optical single-query 50-element database search. In: Proceedings of QELS 2001, Quantum Electronics and Laser Science Conference, pp. 149–150 (2001)
8. Buriol, L., Castillo, C., Donato, D., Leonardi, S., Millozzi, S.: Temporal analysis of the wikigraph. In: Proceedings of WI 2006, 5th International Conference on Web Intelligence, Hong Kong, pp. 45–51 (2006)
9. Lin, Y., Sundaram, H., Chi, Y., Tatemura, J., Tseng, B.: Detecting splogs via temporal dynamics using self-similarity analysis. ACM Transactions on the Web 2(1) (2008)
10. Fujimura, K., Fujimura, S., Matsubayashi, T., Yamada, T., Okuda, H.: Topigraphy: visualization for large-scale tag clouds. In: Proceedings of WWW 2008, 17th International Conference on World Wide Web, Beijing, China, pp. 1087–1088 (2008)
11. Jurgens, D., Stevens, K.: Event detection in blogs using temporal random indexing. In: Proceedings of the Workshop on Events in Emerging Text Types, Wolverhampton, UK, pp. 9–16 (2009)
12. White, H.: Cross-textual cohesion and coherence. In: Proceedings of the Workshop on Discourse Architectures: The Design and Analysis of Computer-Mediated Conversation, Minneapolis, MN, USA (2002)
13. Foltz, P.W., Kintsch, W., Landauer, T.K.: The measurement of textual coherence with latent semantic analysis. Discourse Processes 25(2-3), 285–307 (1998)
14. Gärdenfors, P.: Conceptual spaces: The geometry of thought. The MIT Press (2000)
15. Beeferman, D., Berger, A., Lafferty, J.: A model of lexical attraction and repulsion. In: Proceedings of ACL 1997, 35th Annual Meeting of the Association for Computational Linguistics, Madrid, Spain, pp. 373–380 (1997)
16. Yuret, D.: Discovery of linguistic relations using lexical attraction. Arxiv preprint cmp-lg/9805009 (1998)
17. Hutchens, J.: Infomagnetism and sentence generation. Technical report, Artificial Intelligence (2001)
18. Azzopardi, L.: Wave motion: A new metaphor for 2d information visualization the exploration of a metaphor. Technical report, University of Newcastle (2000)
19. Bruce, E.: Biomedical signal processing and signal modeling. Wiley-Interscience (2001)

20. Wang, C., Wang, X.: Indexing very high-dimensional sparse and quasi-sparse vectors for similarity searches. The VLDB Journal 9(4), 344–361 (2001)
21. Chatterjee, A., Bhowmick, S., Raghavan, P.: FAST: Force-directed approximate subspace transformation to improve unsupervised document classification. In: Proceedings of 6th Text Mining Workshop held in Conjunction with SIAM International Conference on Data Mining, Atlanta, GA, USA (2008)
22. Giraud, C.: Gravitational clustering and additive coalescence. Stochastic Processes and Their Applications 115(8), 1302–1322 (2005)
23. Oyang, Y.-J., Chen, C.-Y., Yang, T.-W.: A Study on the Hierarchical Data Clustering Algorithm Based on Gravity Theory. In: Siebes, A., De Raedt, L. (eds.) PKDD 2001. LNCS (LNAI), vol. 2168, pp. 350–361. Springer, Heidelberg (2001)
24. Blatt, M., Wiseman, S., Domany, E.: Superparamagnetic clustering of data. Physical Review Letters 76(18), 3251–3254 (1996)
25. Xiao-dan, W., Dian-min, Y., Feng-li, L., Chao-hsien, C.: Distributed model based sampling technique for privacy preserving clustering. In: Proceedings of ICMSE 2007, International on Conference on Management Science and Engineering, pp. 192–197 (2007)
26. Sheikholeslami, G., Chatterjee, S., Zhang, A.: WaveCluster: a wavelet-based clustering approach for spatial data in very large databases. The VLDB Journal 8(3), 289–304 (2000)
27. Horn, D., Gottlieb, A.: The method of quantum clustering. In: Dietterich, T., Becker, S., Ghahramani, Z. (eds.) Advances in Neural Information Processing Systems, Vancouver, Canada, vol. 14, pp. 769–776 (2001)
28. Weinstein, M., Horn, D.: Dynamic quantum clustering: A method for visual exploration of structures in data. Physical Review E 80(6), 066117 (2009)
29. Di Buccio, E., Di Nunzio, G.M.: Envisioning Dynamic Quantum Clustering in Information Retrieval. In: Song, D., Melucci, M., Frommholz, I., Zhang, P., Wang, L., Arafat, S. (eds.) QI 2011. LNCS, vol. 7052, pp. 211–216. Springer, Heidelberg (2011)
30. Harris, Z.: Distributional structure. In: Harris, Z. (ed.) Papers in Structural and Transformational Linguistics. Formal Linguistics, pp. 775–794. Humanities Press, New York (1970)
31. Carnap, R.: Meaning and Necessity: A Study in Semantics and Modal Logic. University Of Chicago Press, Chicago (1947)
32. Lehrer, A.: Semantic fields and lexical structure. American Elsevier, New York (1975)
33. Dyvik, H.: Translations as a semantic knowledge source. In: Proceedings of HLT 2005, 2nd Baltic Conference on Human Language Technologies, Tallinn, Estonia (2005)
34. Priss, U., Old, L.: Conceptual exploration of semantic mirrors. In: Proceedings of ICFCA 2005, 3rd International Conference on Formal Concept Analysis, Lens, France (2005)
35. Rocchio, J.: Relevance feedback in information retrieval. In: Salton, G. (ed.) The SMART Retrieval System: Experiments in Automatic Document Processing, pp. 313–323. Prentice-Hall, Inc., Upper Saddle River (1971)
36. Bruza, P., Woods, J.: Quantum collapse in semantic space: interpreting natural language argumentation. In: Proceedings of QI 2008, 2nd International Symposium on Quantum Interaction, Oxford, UK (2008)
37. Widdows, D.: Semantic vector products: Some initial investigations. In: Proceedings of QI 2008, 2nd International Symposium on Quantum Interaction, Oxford, UK (2008)

38. Zuccon, G., Azzopardi, L.A., van Rijsbergen, C.J.: Semantic Spaces: Measuring the Distance between Different Subspaces. In: Bruza, P., Sofge, D., Lawless, W., van Rijsbergen, K., Klusch, M. (eds.) QI 2009. LNCS, vol. 5494, pp. 225–236. Springer, Heidelberg (2009)

39. Wittek, P., Darányi, S.: Representing word semantics for IR by continuous functions. In: Dominich, S., Kiss, F. (eds.) Proceedings of ICTIR 2007, 1st International Conference of the Theory of Information Retrieval, Budapest, Hungary, pp. 149–155 (2007)

40. Wittek, P., Tan, C.L.: Compactly supported basis functions as support vector kernels for classification. Transactions on Pattern Analysis and Machine Intelligence 33(10), 2039–2050 (2011)

41. Peng, L., Chen, Y., Yang, B., Chen, Z.: A novel classification method based on data gravitation. In: Proceedings of ICNNB 2005, International Conference on Neural Networks and Brain, Beijing, China, pp. 667–672 (2005)

42. Salton, G.: Dynamic information and library processing (1975)

Indiscernability and Mean Field, a Base of Quantum Interaction

Michel Gondran and Sébastien Lepaul

[1] University Paris Dauphine, Lamsade, 75 016 Paris, France
[2] EDF R et D, BP 408 - 92141 Clamart Cedex, France

Abstract. We study the convergence of the Schrödinger equation, when the Planck constant tends to 0. Our analysis leads us to introduce non-discerned particles in classical mechanics and discerned particles in quantum mechanics. These non-discerned particles in classical mechanics correspond to an action and a density which verify the statistical Hamilton-Jacobi equations. The indiscernability of classical particles provides a very simple and natural explanation to the Gibbs paradox. We then consider the case of a large number of identical non-discerned interacting particles modeled by a mean field. In classical mechanics these particles satisfy the mean field Hamilton-Jacobi equations. We show how the analysis of non-discerned particles in classical mechanics can be fruitfully applied to some other fields. In economics, we show that the theory of mean field games, where non-discerned agents are considered interacting with one another, is the analogue of mean field Hamilton-Jacobi equations.

Keywords: indiscernability, Gibbs paradox, mean field, mean field game, Hamilton-Jacobi equations.

1 Introduction

The idea that particles can be "indiscernable" has led to some notoriously difficult problems and misleading interpretations. In fact, the concept of indiscernability is at the origin of the Gibbs paradox (Gibbs, 1899): Indeed, *when one calculates the entropy of two mixed gases, the classical result for distinguishable particles is double the expected result. If the particles are considered indistinguishable, the correct result is recovered because of the indiscernability factor.* A common view is that the introduction of the indiscernability postulate for quantum particles provides a resolution of this paradox. Moreover, as noted by Greiner in this book on statistical mechanics, in addition to the Gibbs paradox, many situations of classical mechanics call for the notion of indistinguishable particles and distinguishable particles in quantum mechanics [1] p.134 : "*Hence, the Gibbs factor $\frac{1}{N!}$ is indeed the correct recipe for avoiding the Gibbs paradox. From now on we will therefore always take into account the Gibbs correction factor for indistinguishable states when we count the microstates. However, we want to emphasize that this factor is no more than a recipe to avoid the contradictions of classical statistical mechanics. In the case of distinguishable objects*

J.R. Busemeyer et al. (Eds.): QI 2012, LNCS 7620, pp. 218–226, 2012.
© Springer-Verlag Berlin Heidelberg 2012

(e.g., atoms which are localized at certain grid points), the Gibbs factor must **not** *be added. In classical theory the particles remain distinguishable. We will meet this inconsistency more frequently in classical statistical mechanics."*

By studying the convergence of the Schrödinger equation, when the Planck constant tends to 0, we argue in section 2 that indiscernability is a natural notion for classical mechanics, while the idea of discerned particles particles appears as appropriate notion in quantum mechanics. These non-discerned particles in classical mechanics correspond to an action and a density which satisfy the statistical Hamilton-Jacobi equations. The indiscernability of classical particles provides a very simple and natural explanation of the Gibbs paradox.

In section 3, we consider the case of a large number of identical non-discerned particles interacting with one another for which the interaction can be modeled by a mean field. In classical mechanics these particles satisfy the mean field Hamilton-Jacobi equations, the equations of physics at a mesoscopic scale. We show how the analysis of non-discerned particles in classical mechanics can be fruitfully applied to some other fields. In section 4, we show that in economics the theory of mean field game, where non-discerned agents are considered interacting with one another, is the analogue of mean field Hamilton-Jacobi equations. In section 5, we provide an application of mean field games to individuals who wish to form a community. We intend to apply our analysis to the field of humanity and social science rather economics.

2   The Two Limits of the Schrödinger Equation in the Semi-classical Approximation

Let us consider the wave function solution to the Schrödinger equation $\Psi(\mathbf{x}, t)$:

$$i\hbar \frac{\partial \Psi}{\partial t} = -\frac{\hbar^2}{2m} \triangle \Psi + V(\mathbf{x}, t)\Psi \tag{1}$$

$$\Psi(\mathbf{x}, 0) = \Psi_0(\mathbf{x}). \tag{2}$$

With the variable change $\Psi(\mathbf{x}, t) = \sqrt{\rho^{\hbar}(\mathbf{x}, t)} \exp(i\frac{S^{\hbar}(\mathbf{x}, t)}{\hbar})$, the Schrödinger equation can be decomposed into Madelung equations [2] (1926):

$$\frac{\partial S^{\hbar}(\mathbf{x}, t)}{\partial t} + \frac{1}{2m}(\nabla S^{\hbar}(\mathbf{x}, t))^2 + V(\mathbf{x}, t) - \frac{\hbar^2}{2m}\frac{\triangle\sqrt{\rho^{\hbar}(\mathbf{x}, t)}}{\sqrt{\rho^{\hbar}(\mathbf{x}, t)}} = 0 \tag{3}$$

$$\frac{\partial \rho^{\hbar}(\mathbf{x}, t)}{\partial t} + div(\rho^{\hbar}(\mathbf{x}, t)\frac{\nabla S^{\hbar}(\mathbf{x}, t)}{m}) = 0 \tag{4}$$

with initial conditions

$$\rho^{\hbar}(\mathbf{x}, 0) = \rho_0^{\hbar}(\mathbf{x}) \quad and \quad S^{\hbar}(\mathbf{x}, 0) = S_0^{\hbar}(\mathbf{x}). \tag{5}$$

We shall consider two cases *depending on the preparation procedures of the particles* [3,4].

Definition 1. - *The statistical semi-classical case where*
- *the initial probability density $\rho_0^\hbar(\mathbf{x})$ and the initial action $S_0^\hbar(\mathbf{x})$ are regular functions $\rho_0(\mathbf{x})$ and $S_0(\mathbf{x})$ not depending on $\hbar$.*
- *the interaction with the potential field $V(\boldsymbol{x}, t)$ can be described classically.*

This represents a set of non-interacting particles, prepared in the same way: a free particle beam in a linear potential, an electronic or C_{60} beam in the Young's slits diffraction, or an atomic beam in the Stern and Gerlach experiment.

Definition 2. - *The determinist semi-classical case where*
- *the initial probability density $\rho_0^\hbar(\mathbf{x})$ converges, when $\hbar \to 0$, to a Dirac distribution and the initial action $S_0^\hbar(\mathbf{x})$ is a regular function $S_0(\mathbf{x})$ not depending on $\hbar$.*
- *the interaction with the potential field $V(\boldsymbol{x}, t)$ can be described classically.*

This situation occurs when the wave packet corresponds to a quasi-classical coherent state, introduced in 1926 by Schrödinger [5].

THEOREM 1. *[3,4] For particles in the statistical semi-classical case, the probability density $\rho^\hbar(\boldsymbol{x}, t)$ and the action $S^\hbar(\boldsymbol{x}, t)$, solutions to the Madelung equations (3)(4)(5), converge, when $\hbar \to 0$, to the classical density $\rho(\boldsymbol{x}, t)$ and the classical action $S(\boldsymbol{x}, t)$, solutions to the statistical Hamilton-Jacobi equations:*

$$\frac{\partial S(\boldsymbol{x}, t)}{\partial t} + \frac{1}{2m}(\nabla S(\boldsymbol{x}, t))^2 + V(\boldsymbol{x}, t) = 0 \tag{6}$$

$$\frac{\partial \rho(\boldsymbol{x}, t)}{\partial t} + div\left(\rho(\boldsymbol{x}, t)\frac{\nabla S(\boldsymbol{x}, t)}{m}\right) = 0 \qquad \forall (\boldsymbol{x}, t) \tag{7}$$

$$\rho(\mathbf{x}, 0) = \rho_0(\mathbf{x}) \qquad and \qquad S(\boldsymbol{x}, 0) = S_0(\boldsymbol{x}). \tag{8}$$

The statistical Hamilton-Jacobi equations correspond to a set of independent classical particles, in a potential field $V(\mathbf{x}, t)$, and for which we only know, at the initial time, the probability density $\rho_0(\mathbf{x})$ and the velocity $\mathbf{v}(\mathbf{x}) = \frac{\nabla S_0(\mathbf{x}, t)}{m}$.

Definition 3. - *N identical particles, prepared in the same way, with the same initial density $\rho_0(\boldsymbol{x})$, the same initial action $S_0(\boldsymbol{x})$, and evolving in the same potential $V(\boldsymbol{x}, t)$ are called non-discerned.*

We refer to these particles as non-discerned and not as indistinguishable because, the knowledge of their initial positions give automatically the information on their trajectories. Nevertheless, when one counts them, they will have the same properties as the indistinguishable ones. Thus, if the initial density $\rho_0(\mathbf{x})$ is given, and one randomly chooses N particles, the N! permutations are strictly equivalent and correspond to the same configuration of indistinguishable particles. This indistinguishability of classical particles provides a very simple and natural explanation to the Gibbs paradox.

In the statistical semi-classical case, the uncertainty about the position of a quantum particle corresponds to an uncertainty about the position of a classical particle, whose initial density alone has been defined. *In classical mechanics, this uncertainity is removed by giving the initial position of the particle. It would illogical not to do the same in quantum mechanics.* We assume that for *the statistical semi-classical case,* a quantum particle is not well described by its wave function. One therefore needs to add its initial position and it follows that we introduce the so-called de Broglie-Bohm trajectories [6,7] with the velocity $\mathbf{v}^{\hbar}(\mathbf{x}, t) = \frac{1}{m}\nabla S^{\hbar}(\mathbf{x}, t)$.

The convergence study of the determinist semi-classical case is mathematically very difficult. We only study the example of a coherent state where an explicit calculation is possible.

For the two dimensional harmonic oscillator, $V(\mathbf{x}) = \frac{1}{2}m\omega^2\mathbf{x}^2$, coherent states are built [8] from the initial wave function $\Psi_0(\mathbf{x})$ which corresponds to the density and initial action $\rho_0^{\hbar}(\mathbf{x}) = (2\pi\sigma_{\hbar}^2)^{-1}e^{-\frac{(\mathbf{x}-\mathbf{x}_0)^2}{2\sigma_{\hbar}^2}}$ and $S_0(\mathbf{x}) = S_0^{\hbar}(\mathbf{x}) = m\mathbf{v}_0 \cdot \mathbf{x}$ with $\sigma_{\hbar} = \sqrt{\frac{\hbar}{2m\omega}}$. Here, $\mathbf{v}_0$ and $\mathbf{x}_0$ are still constant vectors and independent from $\hbar$, but $\sigma_{\hbar}$ will tend to 0 as $\hbar$. With initial conditions, the density $\rho^{\hbar}(\mathbf{x}, t)$ and the action $S^{\hbar}(\mathbf{x}, t)$, solutions to the Madelung equations (3)(4)(5), are equal to [8]:

$\rho^{\hbar}(\mathbf{x}, t) = (2\pi\sigma_{\hbar}^2)^{-1}e^{-\frac{(\mathbf{x}-\xi(t))^2}{2\sigma_{\hbar}^2}}$ and $S^{\hbar}(\mathbf{x}, t) = +m\frac{d\xi(t)}{dt}\cdot\mathbf{x}+g(t)-\hbar\omega t$, where $\xi(t)$ is the trajectory of a classical particle evolving in the potential $V(\mathbf{x}) = \frac{1}{2}m\omega^2\mathbf{x}^2$, with $\mathbf{x}_0$ and $\mathbf{v}_0$ as initial position and velocity and $g(t) = \int_0^t(-\frac{1}{2}m(\frac{d\xi(s)}{ds})^2 + \frac{1}{2}m\omega^2\xi(s)^2)ds$.

THEOREM 2. - *When $\hbar \to 0$, the density $\rho^{\hbar}(\mathbf{x}, t)$ and the action $S^{\hbar}(\mathbf{x}, t)$ converge to*

$$\rho(\mathbf{x}, t) = \delta(\mathbf{x} - \xi(t)) \quad and \quad S(\mathbf{x}, t) = m\frac{d\xi(t)}{dt} \cdot \mathbf{x} + g(t) \tag{9}$$

where $S(\mathbf{x}, t)$ and the trajectory $\xi(t)$ are solutions to the determinist Hamilton-Jacobi equations:

$$\frac{\partial S(\mathbf{x}, t)}{\partial t}\Big|_{\mathbf{x}=\xi(t)} + \frac{1}{2m}(\nabla S(\mathbf{x}, t))^2\Big|_{\mathbf{x}=\xi(t)} + V(\mathbf{x})\Big|_{\mathbf{x}=\xi(t)} = 0 \tag{10}$$

$$\frac{d\xi(t)}{dt} = \frac{\nabla S(\xi(t), t)}{m} \tag{11}$$

$$S(\mathbf{x}, 0) = m\mathbf{v}_0 \cdot \mathbf{x} \quad and \quad \xi(0) = \mathbf{x}_0. \tag{12}$$

Therefore, the kinematic of the wave packet converges to the single harmonic oscillator described by $\xi(t)$. Because this classical particle is completely defined by its initial conditions $\mathbf{x}_0$ and $\mathbf{v}_0$, it can be considered as *a discerned particle.* It is then possible to consider, unlike in the statistical semi-classical case, that the wave function can be viewed as a single quantum particle. The *determinist semi-classical case* is in line with the Copenhagen interpretation of the wave function which contains all the information on the particle. A natural interpretation is proposed by Schrödinger [5] in 1926 for the coherent states of the harmonic oscillator: the quantum particle is a spatially extended particle, represented by a wave packet whose center follows the classical trajectory.

3   Mean Field of Non-discerned Particles in Quantum Mechanics and Classical Mechanics

Let us consider N non-discerned identical particles ($N \gg 1$). We assume that an interaction exists between them and we can make the assumption of mean field, meaning that we consider that each particle is sensitive to a potential field $V(\mathbf{x}, \rho, t)$ depending on the particles' density.

In quantum mechanics, it is for instance the case of the single-particle wave function in a Bose-Einstein condensate (BEC). This single-particle wave function satisfies the Gross-Pitaevskiĭ equation in which one replaces the potential $V(\mathbf{x}, t)$ in the Schrödinger (1) and the Madelung equation (3) by

$$V(\mathbf{x}, \rho, t) = V_{ext}(\mathbf{x}, t) + Ng|\Psi(\mathbf{x}, t)|^2 \qquad (13)$$

with $\rho(\mathbf{x}, t) = N|\Psi(\mathbf{x}, t)|^2$ and $g = \frac{4\pi\hbar^2 a}{m}$ where a is the scattering length characterizing the interaction between two atoms at low-energy.

In classical mechanics, replacing $V(\mathbf{x}, t)$ by $V(\mathbf{x}, \rho, t)$, implies that the statistical Hamilton-Jacobi equations (6)(7)(8) become the Mean Field Hamilton-Jacobi equations:

$$\frac{\partial S(\mathbf{x}, t)}{\partial t} + \frac{1}{2m}(\nabla S(\mathbf{x}, t))^2 + V(\mathbf{x}, \rho, t) = 0 \qquad (14)$$

$$\frac{\partial \rho(\mathbf{x}, t)}{\partial t} + div\left(\rho(\mathbf{x}, t)\frac{\nabla S(\mathbf{x}, t)}{m}\right) = 0 \qquad \forall(\mathbf{x}, t) \qquad (15)$$

$$\rho(\mathbf{x}, 0) = \rho_0(\mathbf{x}) \quad and \quad S(\mathbf{x}, 0) = S_0(\mathbf{x}). \qquad (16)$$

Those are the equations of physics at a mesoscopic scale.

As we have just shown, the Mean Field Hamilton-Jacobi equations in classic mechanics exhibit some features of quantum mechanics: non-discerned particles and mean field. It is also possible to transpose these features to other fields of science is possible. This is the purpose of the next section.

Mean Field Hamilton-Jacobi equations are obtained in the semi-classical limit when the quantum potential $-\frac{\hbar^2}{2m}\frac{\triangle\sqrt{\rho^\hbar(\mathbf{x}, t)}}{\sqrt{\rho^\hbar(\mathbf{x}, t)}}$ converges to 0, when $\hbar \to 0$. The non locality deduced from the quantum potential is then lost: the interferences in the double-slit experiments and the non local correlations of EPR-B experiments. Therefore, one uses a nonlocality deduced from a potential dependent on the density $V(\mathbf{x}, \rho, t)$. In social systems, this potential is deduced from the information exchanged between agents.

4   Indiscernability of Agents and Mean Field in Economics

In the above sections, we saw the consequences of both non-discerned particles and mean field assumptions on equations in mechanics. In this section, we illustrate the role played by these two hypotheses in economics through a new branch of game theory: Mean Field Games. This former was defined recently in the seminal papers by J.-M. Lasry and P.-L. Lions [9,10,11] and is characterized by four assumptions:

1. Rational expectations
2. Continuum of agents
3. Anonymity of the agents
4. Social interactions of the mean field type

We present the usual assumption from the literature [12] and then, we will present a new possible reading of them.

"The first three assumptions are common in game theory. The first one - the rational expectation assumptions - was introduced around the 60's and is now well accepted among game theorists."

"The second one is often used to model games with a large number of players. It's a rather well accepted approximation that has been used for tractability purposes and here, for mean field games, the limit of a game with N players as N goes to infinity has been studied in [11] to support this assumption."

The first assumption has no counterpart in physics. The second one is not fundamental.

"The third one has always been implicit in game theory but is worth recalling. Basically, it says that agents are anonymous in the sense that any permutation of the agents does not change the outcome of the game."

The third assumption is central for the purpose of this article. The fact that any permutation of the agents does not change the outcome of the game is implicitly a way of considering non-discerned agents. In mechanics, the non-discerned particles hypothesis leads to statistical Hamilton-Jacobi equations and the mean field of non-discerned particle hypothesis leads to Mean Field Hamilton-Jacobi equations. The mean field of non-discerned particles exactly illustrates the specificity of Mean Field Games theory as it is explained below.

"The fourth assumption is specific to mean field games and is a hypothesis on interactions between players. The main idea is that a given agent cannot influence by himself (but marginally) the distribution of the population of players and therefore the strategies of others. By his behavior, however, a given agent contributes marginally to the statistics that are used by agents to decide upon their strategies. A consequence of this hypothesis is that changes either for characteristics or for strategies that concern any finite number of players do not change the outcome of the game."

Concerning the structure of the MFG equations (in the case of dynamic games), it is always a forward/backward structure that combines backward (Bellman) equations for the determination of individual strategies and forward (transport) equations to describe the global evolution of the game. It's indeed quite common to have such a structure. Since players find their optimal strategy using backward induction processes, the backward equation is natural and corresponds to a Bellman equation or a Hamilton-Jacobi-Bellman equation (HJB equation). Furthemore, to take into account the evolution of the game, a forward equation is needed and is often of the Kolmogorov-Fokker-Planck type.

These coupled forward/backward equations define Mean Field Games and can be applied to numerous economic problems: long-run oil production [13], labor market, growth theory [12] and also for population issues [14]. In the next section, we give more details about this last subject: population issues.

5   Application of Mean Field Games to Population Issues

This example does not directly deal with economics since it is an application of mean field games to individuals who want to form a community. It concerns individuals who want to be distributed as close as possible to each other but cannot form a Dirac distribution in presence of noise.

Mean Field Games are a natural framework to deal with population issues in which individuals optimize their position to satisfy their willingness to be with or without their peers in addition to being at a given location for instance. Many setups can be imagined going from people who all want to live near a given location but do not want to live near their peers to people who want just to live with their peers anywhere as long as they are gathered as a community.

Let us consider a continuum of individuals who have preferences about living with their peers. This type of problem is typically of the mean field game sort where individuals pay a price to move form one point to another and have a utility flow that is a function of the overall distribution of individuals in the population. It is possible to model it as follows.

Each agent lives in an n-dimensional space.

Each agent has a "utility" function than can be decomposed in two parts:

- Part 1: A pure preference part g (where g is increasing in the model to willingness to be together) that represents what it gets from being in a position $\mathbf{x}$ at time t. The function g depends on $\rho(\mathbf{x}, t)$ the distribution function of the population. In other words, g is a function of $\rho(\mathbf{x}, t)$.

- Part 2: A pure cost part h that corresponds to the price incurred to make a move to size α. In other words, h is a function of α.

The problem we have just presented can therefore be written as a control problem. The control problem consists in evaluating a Bellman function at each time t. The Bellman function u($\mathbf{x}$,t) is defined by the maximization under the control α of the mean of the integral over [t,T] of the discount "utility" function just defined above. The maximization is on the mean of the integral because each agent is moved by a Brownian motion in dimension n with the standard deviation σ. But this could be also done in a deterministic framework. We can therefore write the problem as a control one [14]:

$$u(\mathbf{x},t) = Max_{(\alpha-s)_{s>t},X_t=\mathbf{x}} \, \mathbf{E}[\int_t^T (g(\rho(X_s,s)) - h(|\alpha(X_s,s)|))e^{-\lambda(s-t)}ds] \quad (17)$$

with $dX_t = \alpha(X_t,t)dt + \sigma dW_t$.

As for any mean field game we use [9,10] to write the associated system of partial differential equations:

$$\frac{\partial u}{\partial t} + H(\nabla u) - \lambda u + g(\rho) + \frac{\sigma^2}{2}\Delta u = 0 \qquad (Hamilton - Jacobi) \qquad (18)$$

$$\frac{\partial \rho}{\partial t} + div(\rho H'(\nabla u)) - \frac{\sigma^2}{2}\Delta\rho = 0 \qquad (Kolmogorov) \qquad (19)$$

where $H(p) = max_\alpha(\alpha p - h(\alpha))$ and with the additional conditions

$$\rho(\mathbf{x},0) = \rho_0(\mathbf{x}) \quad and \quad u(\mathbf{x},T) = 0. \qquad (20)$$

H is the Hamiltonian. The quadratic cost framework is characterized by a simple Hamiltonian ($H(p) = 1/2p^2$) and therefore the system is simplified:

$$\frac{\partial u}{\partial t} + 1/2|\nabla u|^2 - \lambda u + g(\rho) + \frac{\sigma^2}{2}\Delta u = 0 \qquad (Hamilton - Jacobi) \qquad (21)$$

$$\frac{\partial \rho}{\partial t} + div(\rho\nabla u) - \frac{\sigma^2}{2}\Delta\rho = 0 \qquad (Kolmogorov) \qquad (22)$$

In the example, the Bellman function u plays the role of the action S in the Madelung equations.

Remark 1. *It is important to point out a difference between the Mean Field Hamilton-Jacobi equations in mechanics and the Mean Field Games equations in economics. The difference occurs in the initial conditions. Indeed, the Hamilton-Jacobi-Bellmann equation in the MFG theory is a backward equation because the initial conditions are on final time T. This due to the fact that it is an optimal control problem.*

6   Conclusion

Mean Field Hamilton-Jacobi equations (MFHJ)present two specific features: indiscernability and mean field.

The mean field limit is specific to macroscopic equations where the interaction between particles are non local as in Vlasov's equation of plasma. In social systems, the non local potential is deduced from the information exchanged between agents.

Indiscernability is often considered as specific to the quantum mechanics. We have shown that it is possible to extend it to classical mechanics without use of the Planck constant, with the Mean Field Hamilton-Jacobi equations (MFHJ).

In short, MFHJ equations can be seen as fluid equations in the mean field limit for non-discerned particles.

References

1. Greiner, W., Neise, L., Stöcker, H.: Thermodynamics and Statistical mechanics. Springer, New York (1995)
2. Madelung, E.: Zeit. Phys. 40, 322–326 (1926)
3. Gondran, M., Gondran, A.: Discerned and non-discerned particles in classical mechanics and convergence of quantum mechanics to classical mechanics. Annales de la Fondation Louis de Broglie 36, 117–135 (2011)
4. Gondran, M., Gondran, A.: The two limits of the Schrödinger equation in the semi-classical approximation: discerned and non-discerned particles in classical mechanics. In: Proceeding of AIP, Conference Foundations of Probability and Physics 6, Växjö, Sweden, vol. 1424 (June 2011)
5. Schrödinger, E.: Naturwissenschaften 14, 664–666 (1926)
6. de Broglie, L.: J. de Phys. 8, 225–241 (1927)
7. Bohm, D.: Phys. Rev. 85, 166–193 (1952)
8. Cohen-Tannoudji, C., Diu, B., Laloë, F.: Quantum Mechanics. Wiley, New York (1977)
9. Lasry, J.-M., Lions, P.L.: Jeux à champ moyen I:le cas stationnaire. C. R. Acad. Sci. Paris 343(9) (2006)
10. Lasry, J.-M., Lions, P.L.: Jeux à champ moyen II: horizon fini et contrôle optimal. C. R. Acad. Sci. Paris 343(10) (2006)
11. Lasry, J.-M., Lions, P.L.: Mean Field Games. Japanese Journal of Mathematics 2(1) (March 2007)
12. Guéant, O.: Mean Fields Games and Applications to Economics - Secondary topic: Discount rates and sustainable development, Ecole doctorale EDDIMO, Centre de Recherche CEREMADE, Université Paris Dauphine (June 30, 2009)
13. Fessler, D., Lautier, D., Lasry, J.-M.: The economics of sustainable development. Ed. Economica, 366 pages (2010) ISBN 978-2-7178-5851-8
14. Guéant, O.: A reference case for mean field games models. Cahier de la Chaire Finance et Développement Durable (10) (June 30, 2009)

Social-Psychological Harmonic Oscillators in the Self-regulation of Organizations and Systems

William F. Lawless[1] and Donald A. Sofge[2]

[1] Paine College, 1235 15th Street, Augusta, Georgia, USA
wlawless@paine.edu
[2] Naval Research Laboratory, 4555 Overlook Avenue SW, Washington, DC
donald.sofge@nrl.navy.mil

Abstract. We propose *ab initio* the existence of social-psychological harmonic oscillators (SPHO) acting computationally in the minds of an intelligent audience that a self-regulated collective exploits to solve problems, resolve complex issues, or entertain itself. Using computational intelligence, our ultimate goal is to self-regulate systems composed of humans, machines and robots. We conclude in an overview that self-regulation, characterized by our solution of the nonlinear tradeoffs between Fourier pairs of Gaussian distributions, affects decision-making differently for organizations and systems: When set inside of a democracy to solve well-defined problems, optimum performance requires command decision-making along with maximum cooperation among an organization's multitaskers (few challenges maximize oscillations); but, to solve ill-defined problems across a system requires maximum competition among participants and organizations (challenges minimize oscillations).

Keywords: Interdependence, incomplete information, conservation of information.

1   Introduction

We have previously established theoretically that computational intelligence can exist to control organizations, systems, and systems of systems [30]. Less well-established are the mathematical foundations to control the system [27]. We continue to develop self-regulation from a social physics perspective, mathematics to support our findings, and weaknesses where known.

Self-regulation is an important element of self-organization. Solving a control theory for self-regulation will not only increase our understanding of organizations and systems, but also the capability of organizations and systems to manage themselves with computational intelligence. The age of smart systems approaches;[1] e.g., during the last Iraqi war, four predator pilotless drones were aloft; in the war in

---

[1] *Wall Street Journal* (2012, 3/5), "The Car of the Future Will Drive You".

J.R. Busemeyer et al. (Eds.): QI 2012, LNCS 7620, pp. 227–238, 2012.
© Springer-Verlag Berlin Heidelberg 2012

Afghanistan today,[2] many tens are aloft at a time.[3] But even though partially autonomous, by lacking intelligent interactions among them, these systems are not computationally intelligent. Smart systems fit with the two goals of *Artificial Intelligence*: to build intelligent machines; and to understand intelligent behavior [45].

Our prior research [30] has established that cooperation is required for organizational effectiveness, especially as organizations grow in size in their need to reduce instability and gain market control. We also concluded that illusions drive social dynamics (oscillations). But in an attempt to reduce oscillations by encouraging members to adhere to a single worldview along with punishment for those who do not, increased cooperation reduces an organization's ability to innovate. Illusions like rumors occur in all forms of social structures [19], often at odds with an organization's single worldview. In command organizations, leaders use censorship for control [34], but rumors are difficult to stop with threats alone.[4,5] At one extreme, in a system isolated from competition [39], social well-being collapses and social evolution ceases (e.g., North Korea). In less extreme examples where government commands large swaths of the economy (e.g., China), forced cooperation increases corruption, reduces effectiveness in responding to national emergencies (e.g., financial collapses), and reduces social welfare.[6] And at the other extreme, in a highly competitive environment where organizations struggle to survive, Darwin [17] stressed that cooperation in a competitive environment becomes important to those in collectives who are "ready to warn each other of danger, to aid and defend each other" to survive.[7] In democracies, rumors are directly challenged and dampened [31].

If an organization or system is operated perfectly [14], the organization emits zero additional information [15], compared to a baseline composed of the individuals who comprise the organization, making a perfectly run organization appear to be "dark" to outsiders and itself [31], possibly accounting for the negligible associations found between managers and the performance of their firms [8]. Inversely, the turmoil in a competitive society produces more information than its absence, a paradox involving tradeoffs underlying the physics of the conservation of information (COI).

---

[2] The USAF alone now "flies at least 20 Predator drones—twice as many as one year ago—over vast stretches of hostile Afghan territory each day", *New York Times* (2010), "Drones are playing a growing role in Afghanistan", retrieved 3/14/2012 from nytimes.com.

[3] It is predicted that 30,000 drones will be in use domestically by 2020. (*The New York Times* (2012, 2/21), "A scary, and useful, technology", retrieved 3/14/12 from nytimes.com)

[4] *New York Times* (2012, 3/30), "Coup Rumors Spur China to Hem in Social Networking Sites"

[5] "Perhaps the new leadership that emerges after this fall's Party Congress will be forced to announce a new reform program to repair the regime's battered image. But as long as the decisions are made behind closed doors, the rumors will continue to fly." *Wall Street Journal* (2012, 4/11), "Murder and Bo Xilai. China's latest purge exposes the Communist Party's dirty laundry."

[6] China is one of the most polluted countries on the planet (fully 90% of its shallow groundwater is contaminated, in *Science* (2011, 11/11), "China to Spend Billions Cleaning Up Groundwater").

[7] Inadvertently exemplifying the importance of cooperation inside of organizations, Abigail Thernstrom became famous for saying that American universities are "islands of repressions in a sea of freedom." (Magee, 2002, p. 255)

Efficiency minimizes redundancy and waste. For classical computational models of quantum interactions, Feynman [21] called them inefficient. He claimed that only a quantum computer running quantum interactions would be efficient. We have made similar claims that the traditional models of dynamic states of interdependence, like game theory, would be inefficient [30]. Indeed, game theory is an unsatisfactory model of interdependence [42].

That interdependence produces incommensurable stories is not only the foundation of game theory, but also the first mathematical solution to the Prisoner's Dilemma Game, known today after Nash (1951), its author, as an example of Nash equilibria (NE). Game theory was one of the first methods to model interdependence rationally and to solve it with NE in the laboratory for two sets of non-cooperative opponents. NE are "toy" problem solutions which Luce and Raiffa [33] concluded produced unfair distributions of a game's resources. But Luce and Raiffa also warned that it was unlikely that "any sociology be derived from the single assumption of individual rationality" (p. 196). Axelrod [1] claimed that NE solutions are adverse to social welfare, asserting that for the evolution of cooperation, society should forcibly replace individual "self-interests" with cooperation. But from our perspective based on organizational and system tradeoffs, the problem with "rationality" is that only unopposed self-interests can be rationalized whereas the conflict associated with opposed self-interests precludes rational explanations [31]. Asked why he was against attempts by the present U.S. Congress to regulate stock market derivatives, Becker [6] stated that "competitive interest groups … [preclude] a systematic bias … [but that] Markets are hard to appreciate."

When two different groups are governed by self-interests, it means the existence of biases between them. For example, confirmation bias [16] makes it difficult for open discussions between "believers" in opposing camps. But, competing self-interests control biases and illusions, the foundation for juries, the practice of science, free speech, and free markets [30]. That is why dictatorships censor opposing viewpoints, inadvertently promoting rumors.[8]

In contrast to traditional and rational approaches to social science and bounded rationality, and based on models of interdependent uncertainty, we have concluded that Nash equilibria (NE) are invaluable to society just as entanglement is to quantum computation. Traditionally, an NE occurs when participants cannot improve their self-interests based on rational choices they and others make. We reinterpret an NE as a set of opposed positions motivated by self-interests of social groups. Those who occupy an NE drive their views into relatively stable oppositions with the ultimate goal of obtaining social, financial, or political support for their and their tribes' self-interests. From our perspective [30], however, with reality being not easy to access or capture, an NE plus feedback provides sufficient information and knowledge for a system to solve computationally difficult, intractable, or otherwise ill-posed problems.

Despite the evidence against conventional game theory, we consider our mathematical approach to be high-risk research. Deriving a theory of complementary uncertainty among conjugate variables as Bohr [9] advised was considered by Von Neumann & Morgenstern (p. 148 [44]) to be "inconceivable".

---

[8] China censored media accounts of its bullet train disaster; *Wall Street Journal* (2011, 10/3), "China Bullet Trains Trip on Technology".

2   Self-regulation: Two Field Studies

Case Study 1: The U.S. Department of Energy (DOE). We began our field studies with trying to understand the mismanagement of U.S. military nuclear wastes generated during the production of nuclear weapons. Lilienthal [32], the first chair of the U.S. Atomic Energy Commission (AEC), replaced by the Energy Research and Development Administration (ERDA) and now by DOE, recognized that AEC's policy of self-regulation, isolated from competitive challenges, would compromise the practices of its scientists. Hidden behind claims of national security, it was easy for military nuclear managers to assert that they were protecting the environment.

Until 1983, isolated from competition by national security, DOE maintained to the U.S. Congress that it was protecting the air, water and soil (p. I-1 [20]). But DOE alone determined that its environmental protections were equivalent to or exceeded Federal and State regulations for commercial facilities. However, after extraordinary environmental contamination across the entire DOE complex was exposed [29], the public and Congress forced DOE to comply with the US Environmental Protection Agency (EPA) and State regulations. The estimate today is about $200 billion alone just to cleanup Hanford, WA and Savannah River Site (SRS), SC, the two sites in DOE with the largest budgets. Self-regulation for a isolated system had failed.

The DOE cleanup after 1983 has become more competitive and successful. Today, DOE faces competitive threats to its interpretations and its oversight from multiple sources. The National Academy of Sciences, the Defense National Facilities Safety Board, and DOE's Citizen Advisory Boards (CABs) have joined with EPA and State regulators, and sometimes with the Nuclear Regulatory Commission, to check DOE's decisions. In this new environment, DOE has made significant strides in cleaning up its complex, especially at SRS [30].

Case Study 2: DOE and Citizen Advisory Boards (CABs). The second case study provides comparative data on CAB decisions. In agreement with Ostrom [37] that a resource commons can be better self-regulated by a wide association of users better than could the government, nine different DOE sites across its complex asked for help from citizen advisors across the DOE system. The results for these CABs are categorized by whether they were governed by either consensus or majority rules.

Comparing decisions by consensus rules with majority rules produced the first ever prediction for social physics [30]: DOE had collected the recommendations of its scientists to speed the shipment of its Transuranic wastes to its WIPP repository in NM. It presented these recommendations to its nine CABs. Three of four consensus-ruled CABs rejected that advice, compared to four of five majority ruled boards, supporting DOE's scientists.

DOE's Hanford site has a consensus ruled CAB; the SRS site has a majority ruled CAB. But by increasing cooperation among DOE's citizen advisors, consensus rules contributed to "gridlock" and conflicts at DOE Hanford site that sometimes were not resolved until adjudicated by U.S. Federal courts [30]. We attributed gridlock to the number of unchallenged risk perceptions (illusions). In contrast to the conflict from the consensus-ruled board at DOE Hanford, the competition from majority rules among citizen advisors, scientists and DOE not only challenged illusions, but also accelerated DOE's cleanup, especially at DOE-SRS. Majority rules relied on the best arguments available, including scientific facts.

The U.S. Federal Reserve Board, European Union, Roman Catholic Church, and commercial enterprises[9] are examples of self-regulated organizations. In these cases, self-regulation depends on "transparency" to meet public objectives. However, when the rules for self-regulation are determined solely by the organization or system and closed to the public, "transparency" is an illusion, unless driven by competition.

3   Mathematics Model

To develop interdependence theory, we adapted Cohen's [13] interpretation of the classical uncertainty principle for signal processing. With Rieffel [40], we linked quantum entanglement and social interdependence theory. Next, we initially assumed that interdependence could be simplified with bistable models. An example of bistability is in Figure 1.

Fig. 1A. On the left is an image of an Abrams M1A1 Main Battle Tank that generates a stable interpretation (e.g., www.army-technology.com/projects/abrams). All who view the tank reach the same interpretation. Fig. 1B. On the right is a bistable illusion of two-women that creates a bistable interpretation (an older woman looking downward and to the observer's left; or a younger women looking away over her right shoulder). For bistable illusions, observers cannot "see" both interpretations of its single data set at the same time [10].

Social-Psychological Harmonic Oscillators

Collecting information from well-defined networks or organizations for social network analysis (SNA) is relatively straightforward. But even when the information is readily available, the signals collected from social networks have not led to valid predictions about their actions or stability [36]. This failure with SNAs, game theory, and organizations in general [38] led to a request for new social theory to better understand the effects of interdependence in social networks and organizations [28].

An NE acts as a point of conflict that draws an audience and drives its attention back and forth as a conflict is driven across time by self-interests, generating a model of a social-psychological harmonic oscillator (SPHO). We have associated findings from the literature that link moderated conflict and competition to improved learning

---

[9] *Wall Street Journal* (2010, 4/28), "Documents Show BP Opposed New, Stricter Safety Rules". These new rules might have prevented BP's oil spill in the Gulf in 2010.

[18], political processes [30], decision-making in the courtroom [23], and environmental cleanup decisions [30]. SPHOs are integral to an audience's suspension of disbelief in entertainment [41]. In contrast, the repression of SPHO oscillators in a system characterizes consensus-driven minority rule such as a dictatorship (e.g., China), which significantly reduces social welfare.

Conservation of Information (COI). The key to building abstract representations necessary to construct an SPHO is to locate opposing clusters and a neutral audience in Hilbert space for the shared geospatial interpretations of concepts. A Hilbert space is an abstract space defined so that vector positions and angles permit distance, reflection, rotation and geospatial measurements, or subspaces with local convergences where measurements can occur.

We specify the state of bistable system with a state column vector $|\psi\rangle$. If an operator A_n maps another state vector n onto itself plus a coefficient x_n,

$$A_n |n\rangle = x_n |n\rangle, \tag{1}$$

then $|n\rangle$ is an eigenvector, its coefficient x_n is its eigenvalue, and n is the index number of the bistable state of a two-state social system (e.g., guilty-not guilty). When it exists, a complete set of eigenfunctions forms a basis for $|\psi\rangle = \sum_n a_n |n\rangle$, where $|a_n|^2$ is the probability that a measurement of A_n collapses it into $|n\rangle$ with observable x unless $|\psi\rangle$ is already one (e.g., a classical image of a military tank transforms into a tank, but the interpretation of states oscillating between $|\psi\rangle$ and $|\phi\rangle$ for a bistable state--e.g., a bistable illusion--is transformed into the other interpretation as attention shifts; [30]). a_n is the coefficient of an orthonormal basis, normalizing $|a_n|^2$.

Operators map state vectors into eigenfunctions; the outer product from two eigenvalues, $|n\rangle\langle n|$, is a projector, P_n. It maps a eigenvector into an observable,

$$P_n |\psi\rangle = |n\rangle\langle n||\psi\rangle = a_n |n\rangle, \tag{2}$$

where the expectation value of a projector is the likelihood that a measurement produced that state,

$$\langle\psi| P_n |\psi\rangle = |a_n|^2, \tag{3}$$

and where projectors for an operator form a spectral representation of its eigenvectors,

$$A_n = \sum_n x_n |n\rangle\langle n|. \tag{4}$$

We represent a function of an operator as

$$f(A_n) = \sum_n f(x_n) |n\rangle\langle n|. \tag{5}$$

The commutator of two operators A and B is:

$$[A,B] = AB - BA. \tag{6}$$

When the eigenvalues of the two operators are equal (Equation 6), as it should be in rational discourse under command authorities and in dictatorships, the commutator vanishes, i.e., $[A,B] = 0$. However, when the commutator exists, then

$[A,B] = AB - BA = iC \neq [B,A]$. In that case, the two eigenfunctions for community operators A and B are different, producing an "oscillator" when they form an orthonormal couple or SPHO with commutator C before an audience of neutrals.

The oscillation defines a social-psychological decision space embedded within an organization or system. It is called an "oscillator" because decision-making occurs during rapid-fire turn-taking sessions that "rotate" attention for the topic under discussion in the minds of listeners or deciders first in one valence direction (e.g., "endorsing" a proposition) followed by the opposite (e.g., "rejecting" a proposition) to produce a "rocking" or back and forth process for an SPHO, like the merger and acquisition (M&A) negotiations between a hostile predator organization and its prey target, as commonly witnessed by investors.[10] But oscillations likely do not occur in the minds of the agents who drive them [30].

This becomes at the atomic level the Heisenberg uncertainty principle $\Delta A \Delta B \geq 1/2 <C>$ (p. 256, [24]). It models the variance around the expectation value of two operators along with the expectation value of their commutator. But how to proceed at the social level?

We believe that with his checkerboard illusion, Adelson [2] established a floor effect (see Figure 2). Adelson found that a photometer, but not a human, could distinguish that the two cells in the illusion below were of the same darkness. Humans are biased by grouping processes and experiences to misjudge the illusion.

Fig. 2. The Checkerboard illusion [2]. The brain construes the shadowed area in checker square B to be lighter than the darkened square in A, but both are equally dark.

With signal detection theory (SDT; see [13]), the uncertainty principle in Equation [6] becomes a Fourier pair consisting of standard deviations that models tradeoffs for individuals, organizations and systems:

$$\sigma_A \sigma_B \geq \tfrac{1}{2}. \tag{7}$$

From Equation (7), as variance in factor A broadens, variance in factor B narrows. At the social level, to model social welfare across a system or between two organizations, we used Lotka-Volterra type equations with its limit cycles to capture the effects of NE [34]. Moreover, by letting Equation 6 represent an inner or simple dot product, where $cos\ 90\ deg = 0$, because a limit cycle produces 90 deg rotations

---

[10] Daines, R.M., Nair, V.B., & Drabkin, D. (2006), *Oracle's Hostile Takeover of PeopleSoft.* Harvard Business Review.

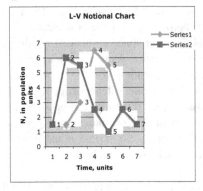
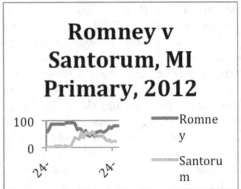

Fig. 3. Instead of as a limit cycle (N_1 versus N_2; in [34]), the data are displayed with N over time, t. *Left*: Arbitrary parameters produce "frictionless" oscillations. We interpret N_1 and N_2 to be in competition at time 1 (and $t = 3.5$, 6 and 7). The public acts at time 2 (and $t = 3$, 4 and 5) to produce social stability. *Right*. Despite the arbitrary nature of the data in the left graph, the 2012 Republican campaign for Presidential Nominee in Michigan captures the limit cycle on the left at about the middle of February 2012 (at the far left, Governor Romney is on top, falls and then raises above his Challenger Sen. Santorum by the end of the primary.

[7], the orthogonal beliefs of a NE and a limit cycle become synonymous, linking linear algebra to social macro effects.

Self-Reports ($\sigma_{Observation}$) and Action (σ_{Action}). Often, subjective reports disagree with action; e.g., self-esteem and academics [5]; management and firm performance [8]; or book knowledge and air-to-air combat [30]. We propose that context and responses to queries can be parallel or orthogonal; e.g., knowing that at a given time, t, conservatives (**A**) and liberals (**B**) viewing the same data agree implies that community states [**A,B**] are commutative (i.e., parallel, where $cos\ 0$ deg $= 1$),[11] but otherwise they are not (i.e., orthogonal, where $cos\ 90$ deg $= 0$).[12] With $\psi_{neutral}$ as the state of an individual neutral, and say |0> representing a neutral's view of reality and |1> reflecting its behavior, then for orthogonal action-observations or orthogonal beliefs held by a neutral individual forms a superposition: $\psi_{neutral} >= a|0> + b|1>$.

Self-reports cannot be relied upon [31].[13] The reasons are many; e.g., confirmation biases affect processing new information [16]. Even experts misjudge the causes of

---

[11] For an example of agreement between the *Journal* and *Times*, see: Emshwiller, J.R. & Fields, G. (2012, 3/27), "Prosecutors Are Rarely Punished Over Disclosure" *The Wall Street Journal*; and Savage, C. (2011, 11/21), "Court-Appointed Investigator Offers Scathing Report on Prosecution of Senator Stevens", *The New York Times*.

[12] For an example of disagreement in the *Wall Street Journal* alone over climate change, see the Op-Ed ""No Need to Panic About Global Warming" (2012, 1/27), followed by the first reply in Letters: The Anthropogenic Climate-Change Debate Continues (2012, 2/7).

[13] Despite the supposed adherence by the women who reported taking HIV prevention pills 95% of the time, the measure of effective drug levels in their blood near the time of infection was <26% (News, 2012, *Science*, 335: 1291).

their behavior [43]. It is possible as we have argued that self-reports of behaviors and actual behaviors are mutually exclusive [31]. And it is possible that the state of orthogonality has survival value; e.g., normative beliefs.

Further, neutrals do not belong to factions. Accepting this as correct, an interdependent state for a dyad of neutrals is non-factorable: $|\psi_{dyad}\rangle = 1/\sqrt{2}(a|00\rangle + b|11\rangle)$. Thus, measuring individual or groups of neutrals in a state of interdependence produces incomplete information.

4   Discussion

Per Bohr [9], complementarity between actors and observers and incommensurable cultures generate conjugate or bistable information couples that he and Heisenberg [26] suggested paralleled the uncertainty principle at the atomic level. Our model tests their speculation and extends it to society with NEs in the form of Fourier pairs (Equation 7; [30]). Unlike a repressed society (China, Cuba), free markets require random exploration and stochastic resonance (religion, science, business, politics, entertainment, philosophy, etc.). Our model indicates the existence of a measurement problem that cannot be erased, but it can be exploited. Measuring the participants of a pole at an NE leads to the expression of biases. However, neutrals, by definition, are unable to capture both sides of the argument they have heard (Equation 10).

Thus, the information available to humans, organizations, or systems is incomplete and uncertain, requiring debate for resolution. Carley (2002) concluded that humans became social to reduce uncertainty. But we have concluded that this uncertainty has a minimum irreducibility that promotes the existence of tradeoffs between any two factors in an interaction (e.g., uncertainty in worldviews, stories or business models, σ_{Plans}, and their execution, $\sigma_{Execution}$).

The lack of an SPHO identifies decisions made by minority (consensus) or authoritarian rules (e.g., decisions common to military, authoritarian government or CEO business decisions; cf. [30]). Unlike an organization's central command, a democratic space is defined for a system as a space where decisions characterized by SPHOs are made by majority rule (e.g., jury, political, or scientific debate). SHPOs generalize to entertainment; e.g., Hasson and his colleagues [25] found that a Clint Eastwood movie engages an audience's attention with this rocking process. This insight suggests that the reverse engineering of forcibly darkened (e.g., terrorists, Mafia) or highly skilled organizations is possible [30].

5   Summary and Future Directions

The operators A and B are community interaction matrices that locate social objects interdependent in social space (shared conceptual space) and are in turn anchored (embedded) geospatially. Interdependent states are non-separable and non-classical; but disturbances from measurement collapse interdependent states into classical information states. Two agents, Einstein and Bohr, meet in Copenhagen to discuss their interpretations of conjugate variables in quantum mechanics, each holding a skill set needed by science that permits the two to debate while both are aware of their different functions and social standing in science, generating bistable social perspectives that reflect separate social constituencies in opposing world views that profoundly disturbed science and society even in the theater today (e.g., [22]). Classical interpretations of quantum--and socially interdependent--realities inescapably produce endless debate that can degenerate into violence unless moderated by neutrals. Based on physics, this finding alone significantly advances our understanding of human systems and underscores how an audience or the larger society moderates conflict and exploits it to solve problems (NE).

Our theory of interdependence has made significant progress. However, we are only scratching the surface. Knowledge does not produce entropy [15]. But since power laws are prevalent [4], does self-regulation and interdependence convert Gaussians into fat-tailed distributions that, say, change the view of the stock market as a random walk into an interdependent random walk? And does it include emotion [30]? That is, with COI, can social emotion produce the contagion associated with stock market bubbles and panics?

Acknowledgements. 1. This material is based upon work supported by, or in part by, the U. S. Army Research Laboratory--U. S. Army Research Office under contract/grant number W911NF-10-1-0252. 2. The first author blew the whistle on DOE in 1983, charging DOE with covering-up widespread environmental contamination from mismanaging military nuclear wastes (Lawless, 1985).

References

1. Axelrod, R.: The evolution of cooperation. Basic, New York (1984)
2. Adelson, E.H.: Lightness perceptions and lightness illusions. In: Gazzaniga, M. (ed.) The New Cognitive Sciences, 2nd edn., MIT Press (2000)
3. Ambrose, S.H.: Paleolithic technology and human evolution. Science 291, 1748–1753 (2001)
4. Barabási, A.-L.: Scale-free networks: A decade and beyond. Science 325, 412–413 (2009)
5. Baumeister, R.F., Campbell, J.D., Krueger, J.I., Vohs, K.D.: Exploding the self- esteem myth. Sci. American (2005)
6. Becker, G.: Weekend interview. The Wall Street Journal A13 (March 27-28, 2010)
7. Beninċà, E., Jöhnk, K.D., Heerkloss, R., Huisman, J.: Coupled predator–prey oscillations in a chaotic food web. Ecology Letters 12(12), 1367–1378 (2009)
8. Bloom, N., Dorgan, S., Dowdy, J., Van Reenen, J.: Mgt practice and productivity. Qtrly J. Econ. 122(4), 1351–1408 (2007)
9. Bohr, N.: Science and the unity of knowledge. In: Leary, L. (ed.) The Unity of Knowledge, pp. 44–62. Doubleday, New York (1955)
10. Cacioppo, J.T., Berntson, G.G., Crites Jr., S.L.: Social neuroscience: Principles, psychophysiology, arousal and response. Social Psychology Handbook, Guilford (1996)
11. Carley, K.M.: Simulating society: The tension between transparency and veridicality. Social Agents: ecology, exchange, and evolution. University of Chicago, ANL (2002)
12. Carley, K.M.: Destabilization of covert networks. Computational & Mathematical Organizational Theory 12, 51–66 (2006)

13. Cohen, L.: Time-frequency analysis: theory and applications. Prentice-Hall (1995)
14. Conant, R.C., Ashby, W.R.: Every good regulator of a system must be a model of that system. Internationl Journal of Systems Science 1(2), 889–897 (1970)
15. Conant, R.C.: Laws of information which govern systems. IEEE Transaction on Systems, Man, and Cybernetics 6, 240–255 (1976)
16. Darley, J.M., Gross, P.H.: A hypothesis-confirming bias in labeling effects. Journal of Personality and Social Psychology 44, 20–33 (1983)
17. Darwin, C.: The descent of man, and selection in relation to sex. Appleton, New York (1871)
18. Dietz, T., Ostrom, E., Stern, P.C.: The struggle to govern the commons. Science 302, 1907 (2003)
19. Difonzo, N.: Rumor Psychology: Social and Organizational Approaches. APA (2006)
20. ERDA, Waste management operations, Savannah River Plant, Aiken, SC, Final EIS, Report ERDA-1537 (1977)
21. Feynman, R.: Feynman lectures on computation. Addison-Wesley, New York (1996)
22. Frayn, M.: Copenhagen (1998)
23. Freer, R.D., Purdue, W.C.: Civil procedure. Anderson, Cincinnati (1996)
24. Gershenfeld, N.: The physics of information technology, Cambridge (2000)
25. Hasson, U., Nir, Y., Levy, I., Fuhrmann, G., Malach, R.: Science 303, 1634–1640 (2004)
26. Heisenberg, W.: Physics and philosophy. The revolution in modern science, pp. 167–186. Prometheus Books (1958/1999)
27. Jamshidi, M.: Control of system of systems. In: Nanayakkara, T., Sahin, F., Jamshidi, M. (eds.) Intelligent Control Systems with an introduction to System of Systems. ch. 8, vol. 2. Taylor & Francis Publishers, London (2009)
28. Jasny, B.R., Zahn, L.M., Marshall, E.: Science 325, 405 (2009)
29. Lawless, W.F.: Problems with military nuclear wastes. Bulletin of the Atomic Scientists 41(10), 38–42 (1985)
30. Lawless, W.F., Rifkin, S., Sofge, D.A., Hobbs, S.H., Angjellari-Dajci., F., Chaudron, L., Wood, J.: Conservation of Information: Reverse engineering dark social systems. Structure and Dynamics 4(2) (2010); (escholarship.org/uc/item/38475290)
31. Lawless, W.F., Angjellari-Dajci, F., Sofge, D.A., Grayson, J., Sousa, J.L., Rychly, L.: A New Approach to Organizations: Stability and Transformation in Dark Social Networks. Journal of Enterprise Transformation 1(4), 290–322 (2011)
32. Lilienthal, D.: Change, hope, and the bomb. Princeton University Press, Princeton (1963)
33. Luce, R.D., Raiffa, H.: Games and decision. Wiley, Chichester (1967)
34. May, R.M.: Stability and complexity in model ecosystems. Princeton University Press, Princeton (1973/2001)
35. Nash Jr., J.F.: Non-cooperative games. Annals of Mathematics Journal 54, 296–301 (1951)
36. NRC, Applications of Social Network Analysis for building community disaster resilience. In: Magsino, S.L. (ed.) Rapporteur, NRC for DHS, Workshop, February 11-12. National Academy Press, Washington, DC (2009)
37. Ostrom, E.: A general framework for analyzing sustainability of social-ecological systems. Science 325, 419–422 (2009)
38. Pfeffer, J., Fong, C.T.: Building organization theory from first principles. Organization Science 16, 372–388 (2005)
39. Ridley, M.: From Phoenecia to Hayek to the 'Cloud'. Human progress has always depended on spontaneous collaboration to harness dispersed knowledge. The Wall Street Journal (2011) (retrieved 9/24/11 from wsj.com.)

40. Rieffel, E.G.: Certainty and uncertainty in quantum information processing. In: Quantum Interaction: AAAI Spring Symposium. AAAI Press, Stanford University (2007)
41. Sarris, A.: The American cinema: Directors and directions. De Capo Press (1968) (Reprinted 1996)
42. Schweitzer, F., Fagiolo, G., Sornette, D., Vega-Redondo, F., Vespignani, A., White, D.R.: Economic networks: The new challenges. Science 325, 422–425 (2009)
43. Shafir, E., LeBoeuf, R.A.: Rationality. Annual Review of Psychology 53, 491–517 (2002)
44. Von Neumann, J., Morgenstern, O.: Theory of games and economic behavior. Princeton Univ. Press (1953)
45. Ying, M.: Quantum computation, quantum theory and AI. Artificial Intelligence 174, 162–176 (2010)

Author Index